Shojo Beat

Kaze
HIKARU

15

Story & Art by
Taeko Watanabe

Contents

Story Thus Far

It is the end of the Bakufu era, the 3rd year of Bunkyu (1863) in Kyoto. The Shinsengumi is a band of warriors formed to protect the shogun.

Tominaga Sei, the daughter of a former Bakufu bushi, joined the Shinsengumi disguised as a boy by the name of Kamiya Seizaburo to avenge her father and brother. She has continued her training under the only person in the Shinsengumi who knows her true identity, Okita Soji, and she aspires to become a true *bushi*.

When Okita suggests Sei return to life as a girl, she challenges him to a fight with real katana—the outcome of which will determine whether she stays or goes. Her special moves that take advantage of her femininity fail, but her efforts demonstrate her maturity in both heart and skill as bushi, and Okita once again allows her to stay with the troop.

Meanwhile, the newly recruited Nakamura Goro instantly recognizes Sei to be a girl, and he begins to pursue her in earnest. The wavering emotions of Okita, though unintentional, cause Sei to hesitate. What fate will this summer bring for the two?

Characters

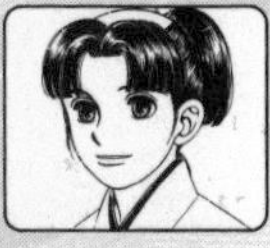

Tominaga Sei
She disguises herself as a boy to enter the Mibu-Roshi. She trains under Soji, aspiring to become a true *bushi*. But secretly, she is in love with Soji.

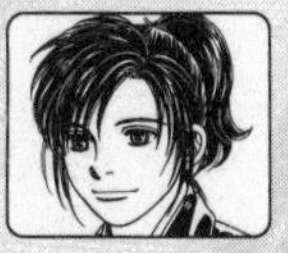

Okita Soji
Assistant vice captain of the Shinsengumi, and licensed master of the Ten'nen Rishin-Ryu. He supports the troop alongside Kondo and Hijikata and guides Seizaburo with a kind yet firm hand.

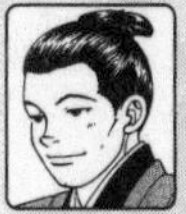

Kondo Isami
Captain of the Shinsengumi and fourth grandmaster of the Ten'nen Rishin-ryu. A passionate, warm and well-respected leader.

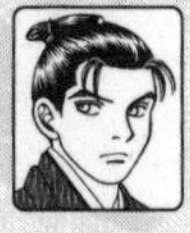

Hijikata Toshizo
Vice captain of the Shinsengumi. He commands both the group and himself with a rigid strictness. He is also known as the "Oni vice captain."

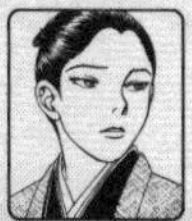

Ito Kashitaro
Councilor of the Shinsengumi. A skilled swordsman yet also an academic. A theorist with an inclination towards anti-Bakufu sentiments.

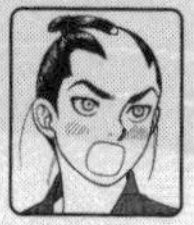

Nakamura Goro
A new recruit to the Shinsengumi. He is convinced Sei is a girl and is passionately pursuing her.

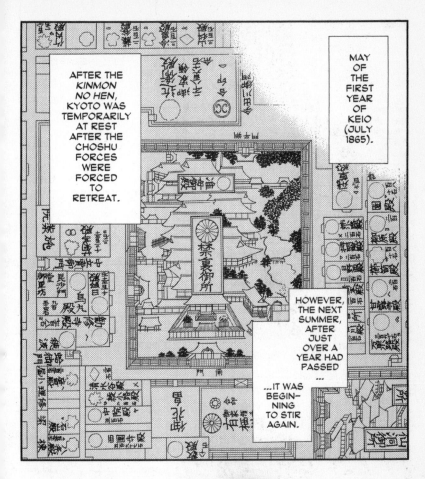

MAY OF THE FIRST YEAR OF KEIO (JULY 1865).
AFTER THE KINMON NO HEN, KYOTO WAS TEMPORARILY AT REST AFTER THE CHOSHU FORCES WERE FORCED TO RETREAT.
禁裏御所
HOWEVER, THE NEXT SUMMER, AFTER JUST OVER A YEAR HAD PASSED...
...IT WAS BEGINNING TO STIR AGAIN.

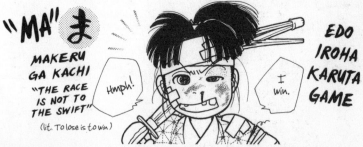

"MA" ま
MAKERU GA KACHI
"THE RACE IS NOT TO THE SWIFT"
(lit. To lose is to win)
I win.
Hmph!
EDO IROHA KARUTA GAME

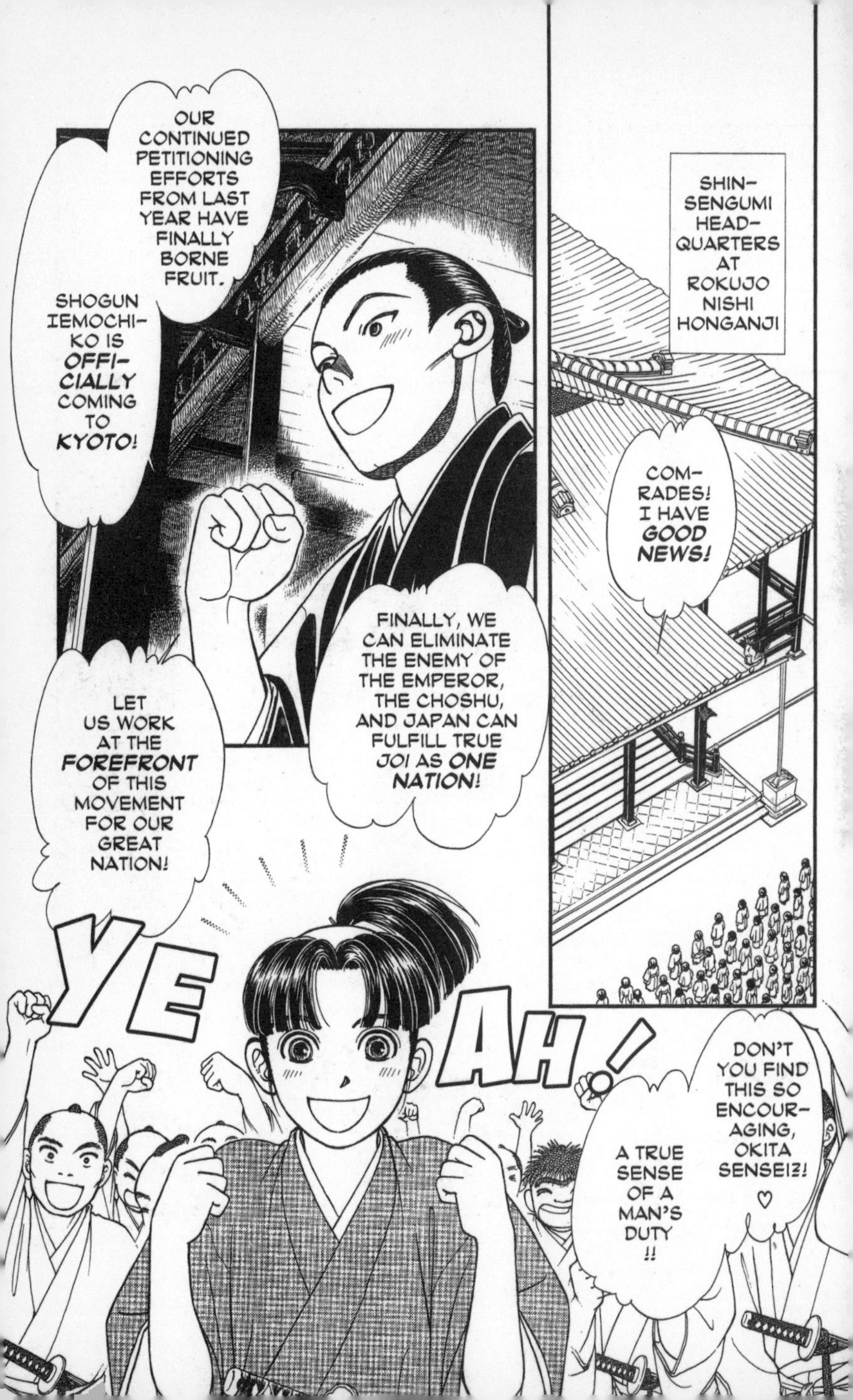

SHINSENGUMI HEADQUARTERS AT ROKUJO NISHI HONGANJI
COMRADES! I HAVE GOOD NEWS!
OUR CONTINUED PETITIONING EFFORTS FROM LAST YEAR HAVE FINALLY BORNE FRUIT.
SHOGUN IEMOCHIKO IS OFFICIALLY COMING TO KYOTO!
FINALLY, WE CAN ELIMINATE THE ENEMY OF THE EMPEROR, THE CHOSHU, AND JAPAN CAN FULFILL TRUE JOI AS ONE NATION!
LET US WORK AT THE FOREFRONT OF THIS MOVEMENT FOR OUR GREAT NATION!
YEAH!
DON'T YOU FIND THIS SO ENCOURAGING, OKITA SENSEI!? ♡
A TRUE SENSE OF A MAN'S DUTY!!

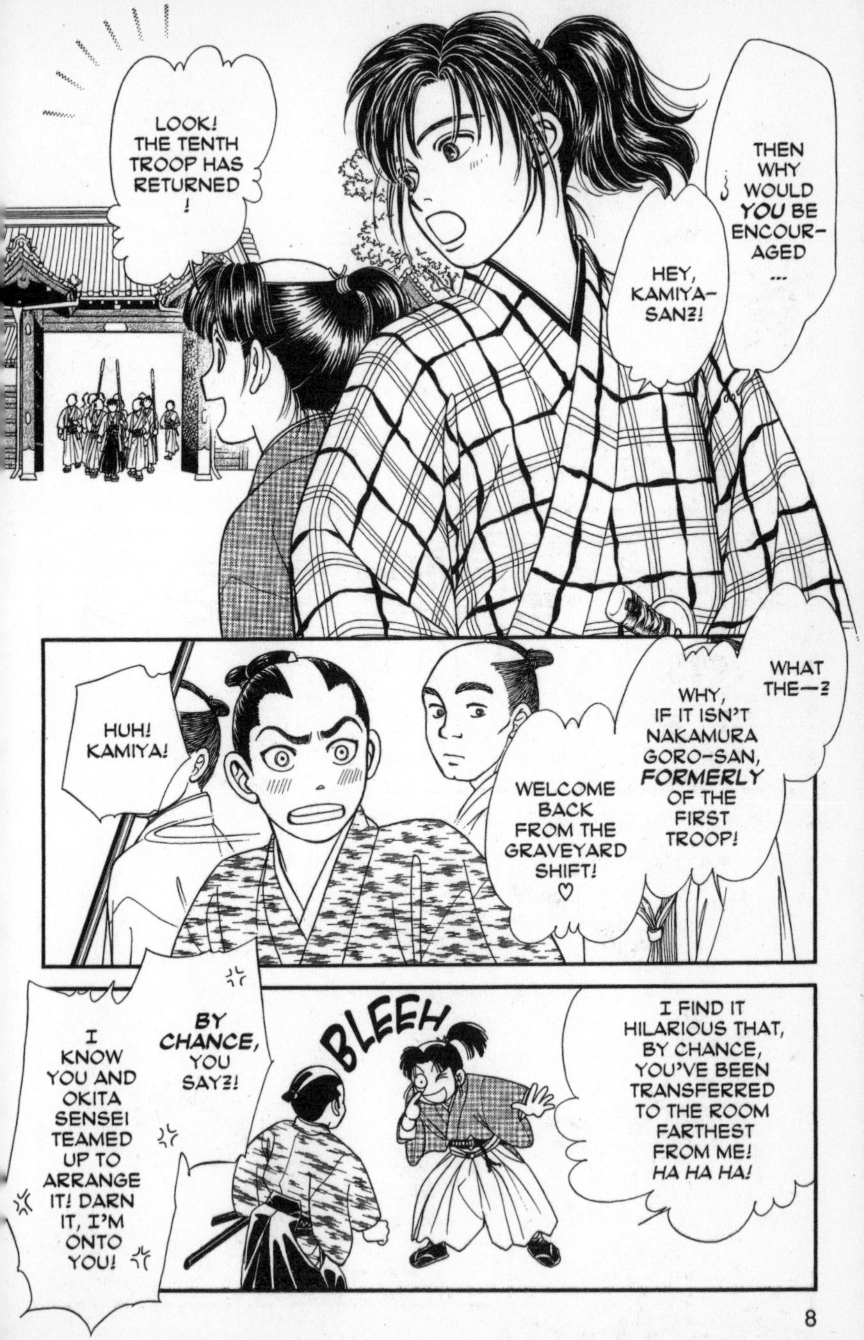
THEN WHY WOULD YOU BE ENCOURAGED...
HEY, KAMIYA-SAN?!
LOOK! THE TENTH TROOP HAS RETURNED!
WHAT THE—?
WHY, IF IT ISN'T NAKAMURA GORO-SAN, FORMERLY OF THE FIRST TROOP!
WELCOME BACK FROM THE GRAVEYARD SHIFT! ♡
HUH! KAMIYA!
I FIND IT HILARIOUS THAT, BY CHANCE, YOU'VE BEEN TRANSFERRED TO THE ROOM FARTHEST FROM ME! HA HA HA!
BLEEH
BY CHANCE, YOU SAY?!
I KNOW YOU AND OKITA SENSEI TEAMED UP TO ARRANGE IT! DARN IT, I'M ONTO YOU!

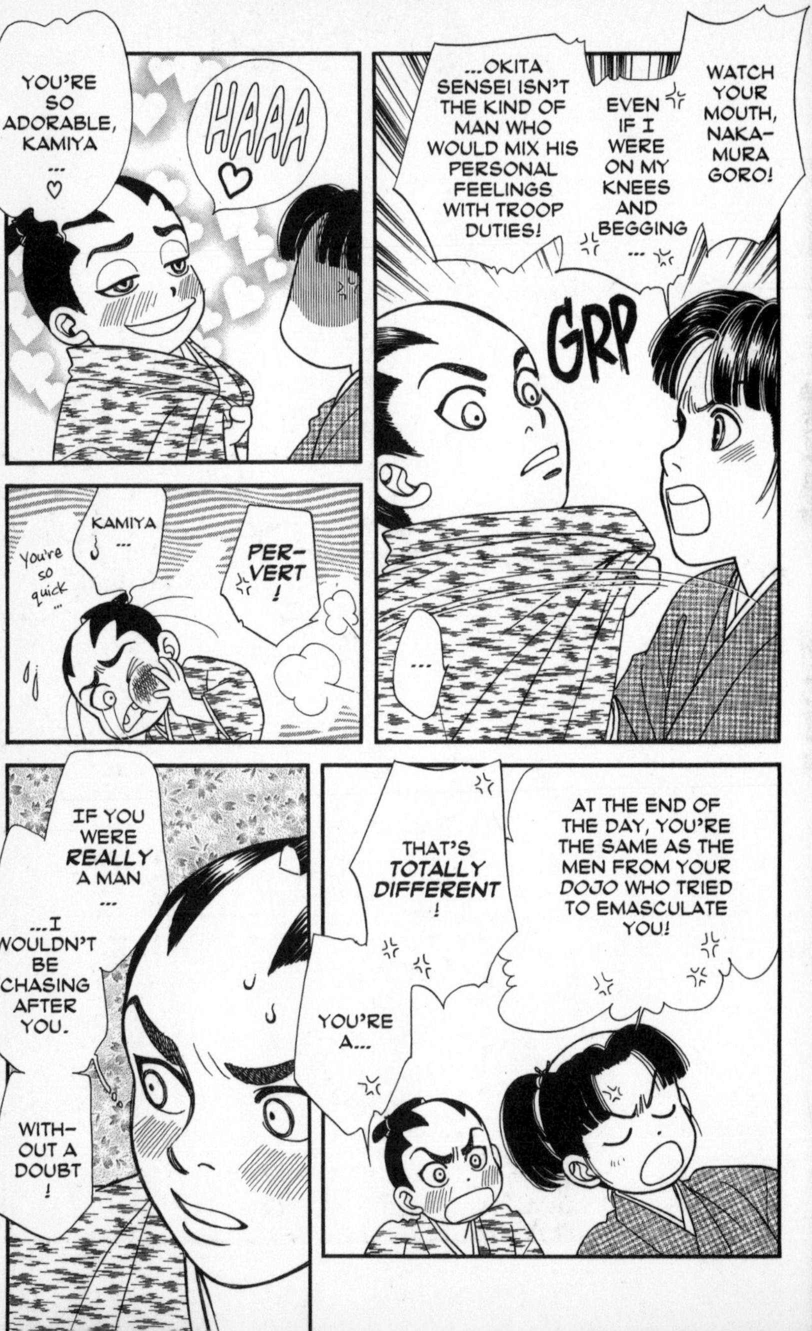
WATCH YOUR MOUTH, NAKAMURA GORO!
EVEN IF I WERE ON MY KNEES AND BEGGING ...
...OKITA SENSEI ISN'T THE KIND OF MAN WHO WOULD MIX HIS PERSONAL FEELINGS WITH TROOP DUTIES!
GRP
...
HAAA ♡
YOU'RE SO ADORABLE, KAMIYA ... ♡
PER-VERT!
KAMIYA ...
You're so quick ...
AT THE END OF THE DAY, YOU'RE THE SAME AS THE MEN FROM YOUR DOJO WHO TRIED TO EMASCULATE YOU!
THAT'S TOTALLY DIFFERENT!
YOU'RE A...
IF YOU WERE REALLY A MAN ...
...I WOULDN'T BE CHASING AFTER YOU.
WITHOUT A DOUBT!

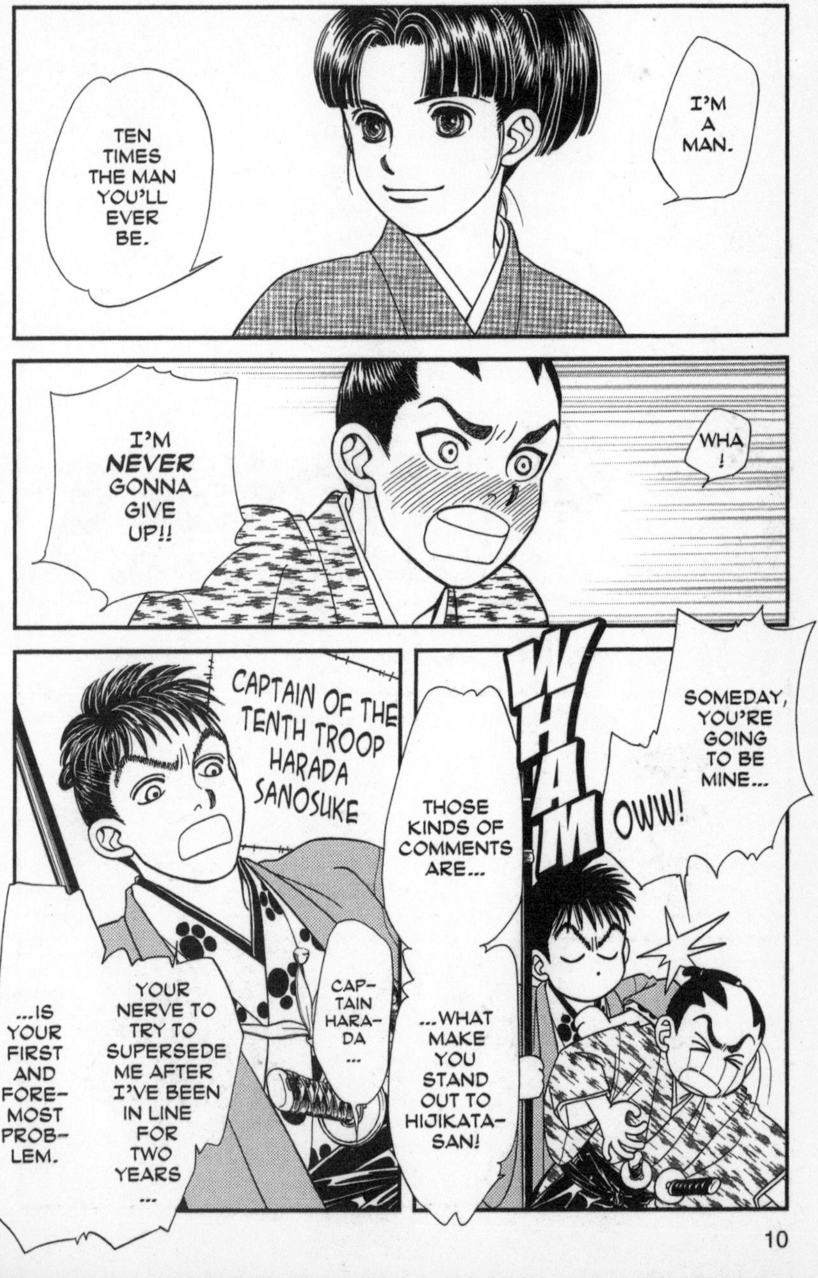
I'M A MAN.
TEN TIMES THE MAN YOU'LL EVER BE.
WHA !
I'M *NEVER* GONNA GIVE UP!!
SOMEDAY, YOU'RE GOING TO BE MINE...
WHAM
OWW!
THOSE KINDS OF COMMENTS ARE...
...WHAT MAKE YOU STAND OUT TO HIJIKATA-SAN!
CAPTAIN OF THE TENTH TROOP HARADA SANOSUKE
CAP-TAIN HARADA...
YOUR NERVE TO TRY TO SUPERSEDE ME AFTER I'VE BEEN IN LINE FOR TWO YEARS...
...IS YOUR FIRST AND FORE-MOST PROB-LEM.

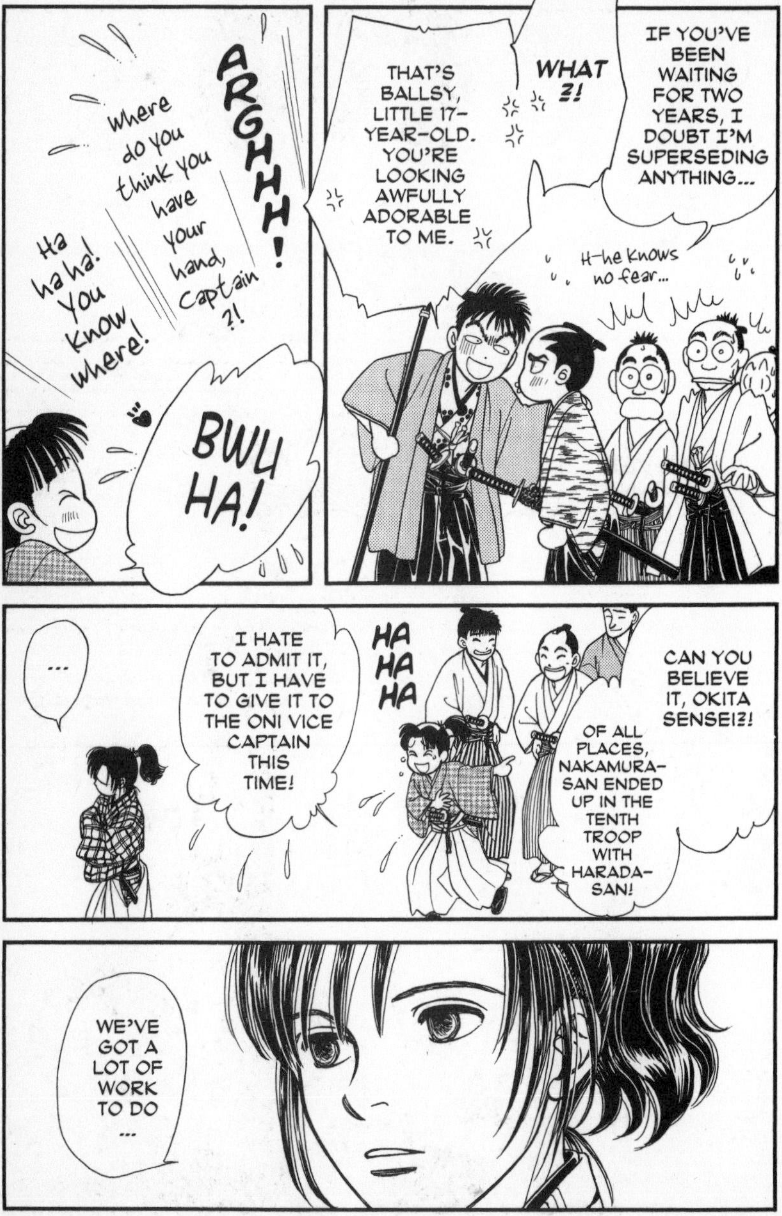

IF YOU'VE BEEN WAITING FOR TWO YEARS, I DOUBT I'M SUPERSEDING ANYTHING...
WHAT ?!
THAT'S BALLSY, LITTLE 17-YEAR-OLD. YOU'RE LOOKING AWFULLY ADORABLE TO ME.
H-he knows no fear...
ARGHHH!
Where do you think you have your hand, Captain ?!
Ha ha ha! You know where!
BWU HA!
CAN YOU BELIEVE IT, OKITA SENSEI?!
OF ALL PLACES, NAKAMURA-SAN ENDED UP IN THE TENTH TROOP WITH HARADA-SAN!
HA HA HA
I HATE TO ADMIT IT, BUT I HAVE TO GIVE IT TO THE ONI VICE CAPTAIN THIS TIME!
...
WE'VE GOT A LOT OF WORK TO DO ...

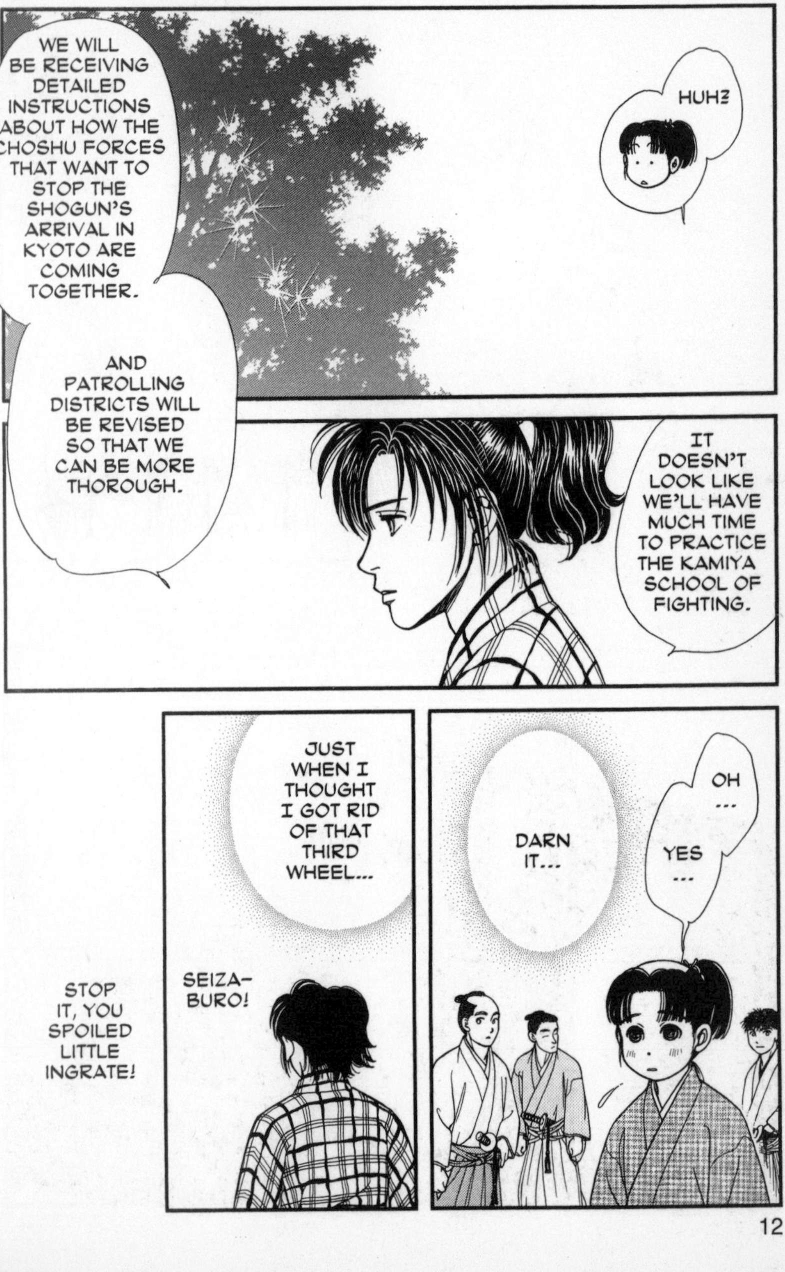
WE WILL BE RECEIVING DETAILED INSTRUCTIONS ABOUT HOW THE CHOSHU FORCES THAT WANT TO STOP THE SHOGUN'S ARRIVAL IN KYOTO ARE COMING TOGETHER.
HUH?
AND PATROLLING DISTRICTS WILL BE REVISED SO THAT WE CAN BE MORE THOROUGH.
IT DOESN'T LOOK LIKE WE'LL HAVE MUCH TIME TO PRACTICE THE KAMIYA SCHOOL OF FIGHTING.
OH ... YES ...
DARN IT...
JUST WHEN I THOUGHT I GOT RID OF THAT THIRD WHEEL...
SEIZA-BURO!
STOP IT, YOU SPOILED LITTLE INGRATE!

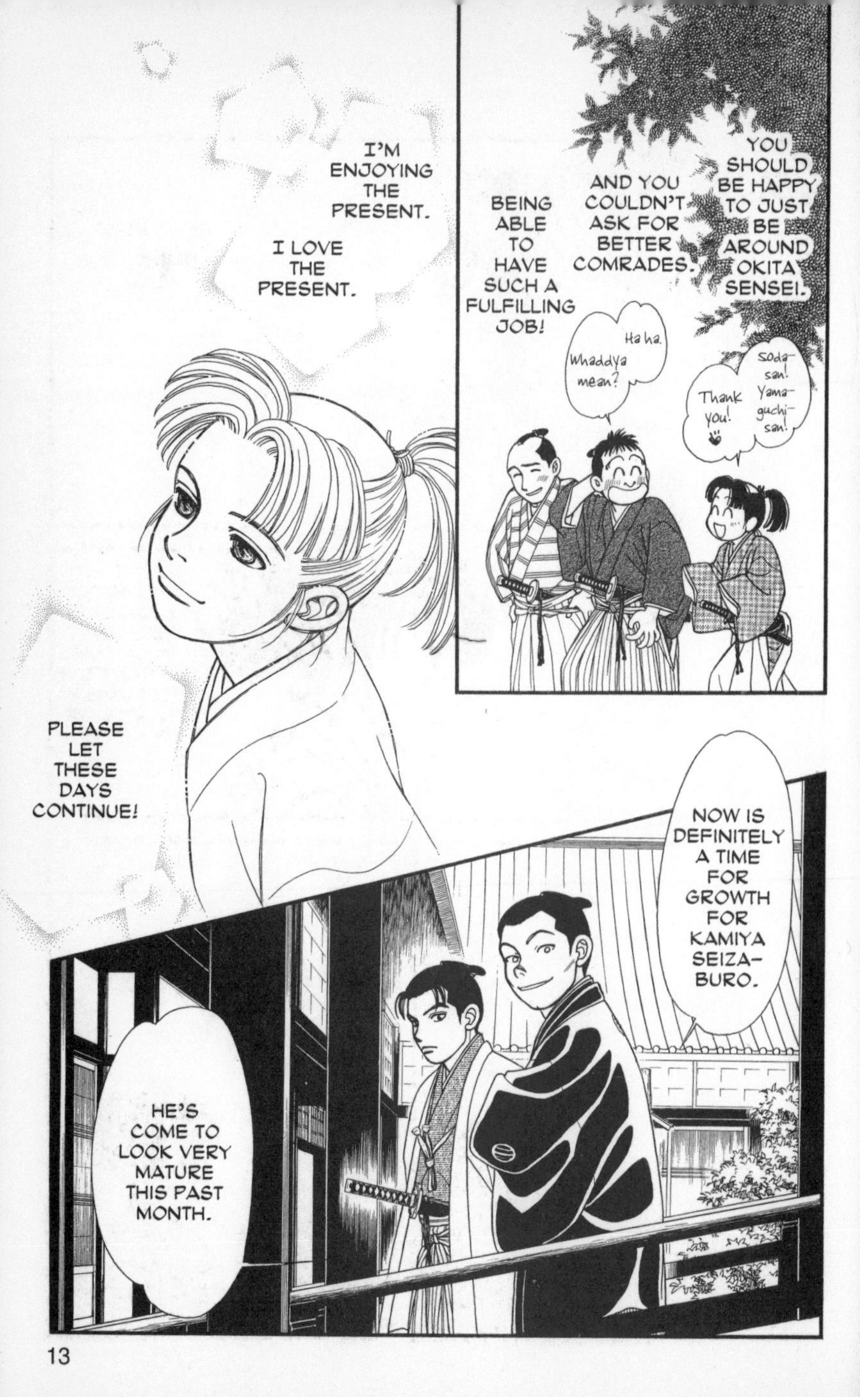
YOU SHOULD BE HAPPY TO JUST BE AROUND OKITA SENSEI.
AND YOU COULDN'T ASK FOR BETTER COMRADES.
BEING ABLE TO HAVE SUCH A FULFILLING JOB!
Soda-san! Yama-guchi-san! Thank you!
Ha ha. Whaddya mean?
I'M ENJOYING THE PRESENT.
I LOVE THE PRESENT.
PLEASE LET THESE DAYS CONTINUE!
NOW IS DEFINITELY A TIME FOR GROWTH FOR KAMIYA SEIZA-BURO.
HE'S COME TO LOOK VERY MATURE THIS PAST MONTH.

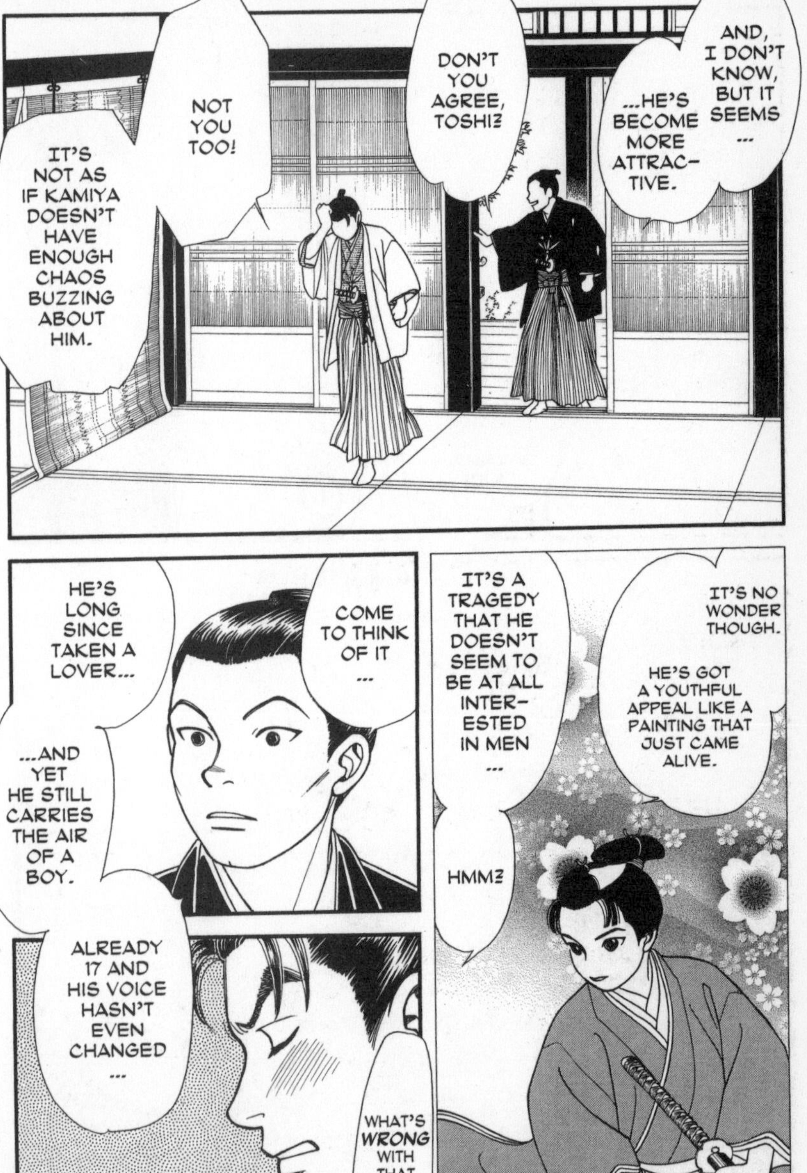
AND, I DON'T KNOW, BUT IT SEEMS ...
...HE'S BECOME MORE ATTRACTIVE.
DON'T YOU AGREE, TOSHI?
NOT YOU TOO!
IT'S NOT AS IF KAMIYA DOESN'T HAVE ENOUGH CHAOS BUZZING ABOUT HIM.
IT'S NO WONDER THOUGH.
HE'S GOT A YOUTHFUL APPEAL LIKE A PAINTING THAT JUST CAME ALIVE.
IT'S A TRAGEDY THAT HE DOESN'T SEEM TO BE AT ALL INTERESTED IN MEN ...
HMM?
COME TO THINK OF IT ...
HE'S LONG SINCE TAKEN A LOVER...
...AND YET HE STILL CARRIES THE AIR OF A BOY.
ALREADY 17 AND HIS VOICE HASN'T EVEN CHANGED ...
WHAT'S **WRONG** WITH THAT?!

A true *pre-genpuku* look is with the bangs pulled up and a long-sleeved kimono.

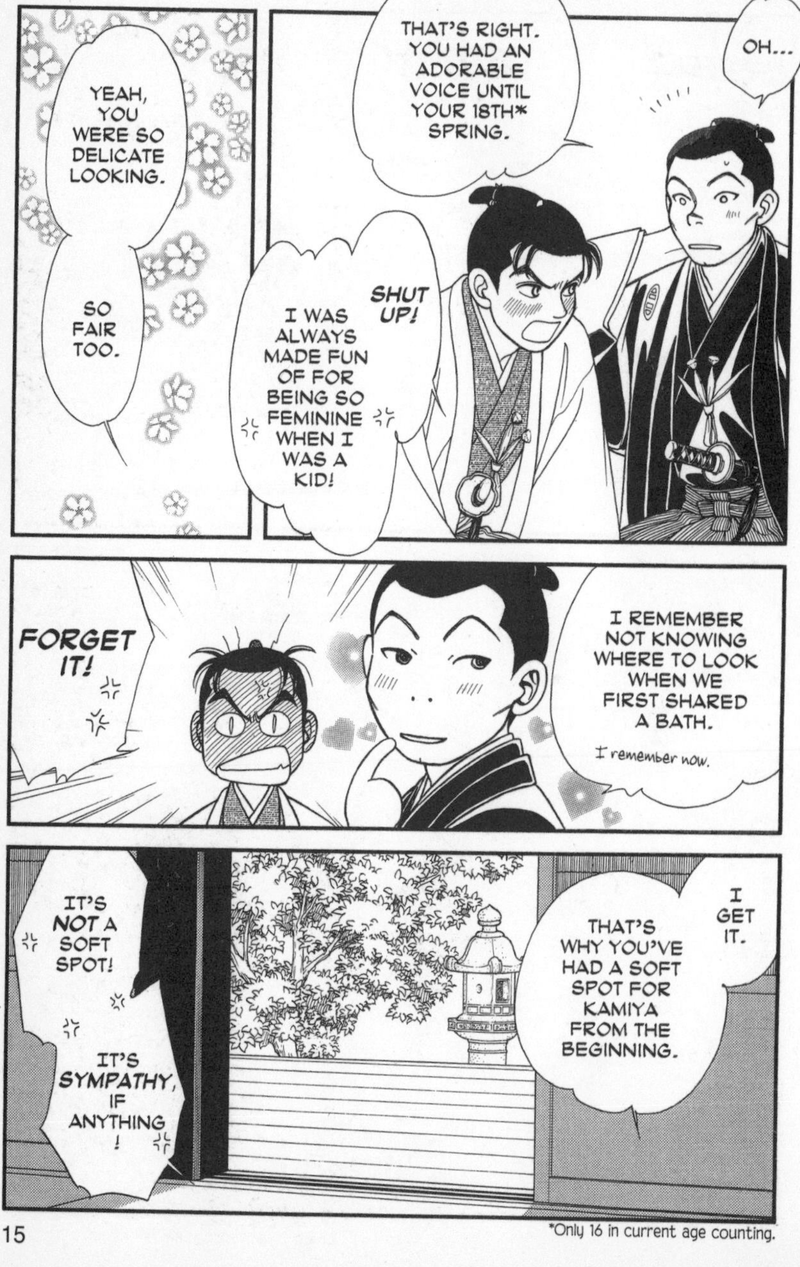
OH...
THAT'S RIGHT. YOU HAD AN ADORABLE VOICE UNTIL YOUR 18TH* SPRING.
SHUT UP!
I WAS ALWAYS MADE FUN OF FOR BEING SO FEMININE WHEN I WAS A KID!
YEAH, YOU WERE SO DELICATE LOOKING.
SO FAIR TOO.
I REMEMBER NOT KNOWING WHERE TO LOOK WHEN WE FIRST SHARED A BATH.
I remember now.
FORGET IT!
I GET IT.
THAT'S WHY YOU'VE HAD A SOFT SPOT FOR KAMIYA FROM THE BEGINNING.
IT'S NOT A SOFT SPOT!
IT'S SYMPATHY, IF ANYTHING!

*Only 16 in current age counting.

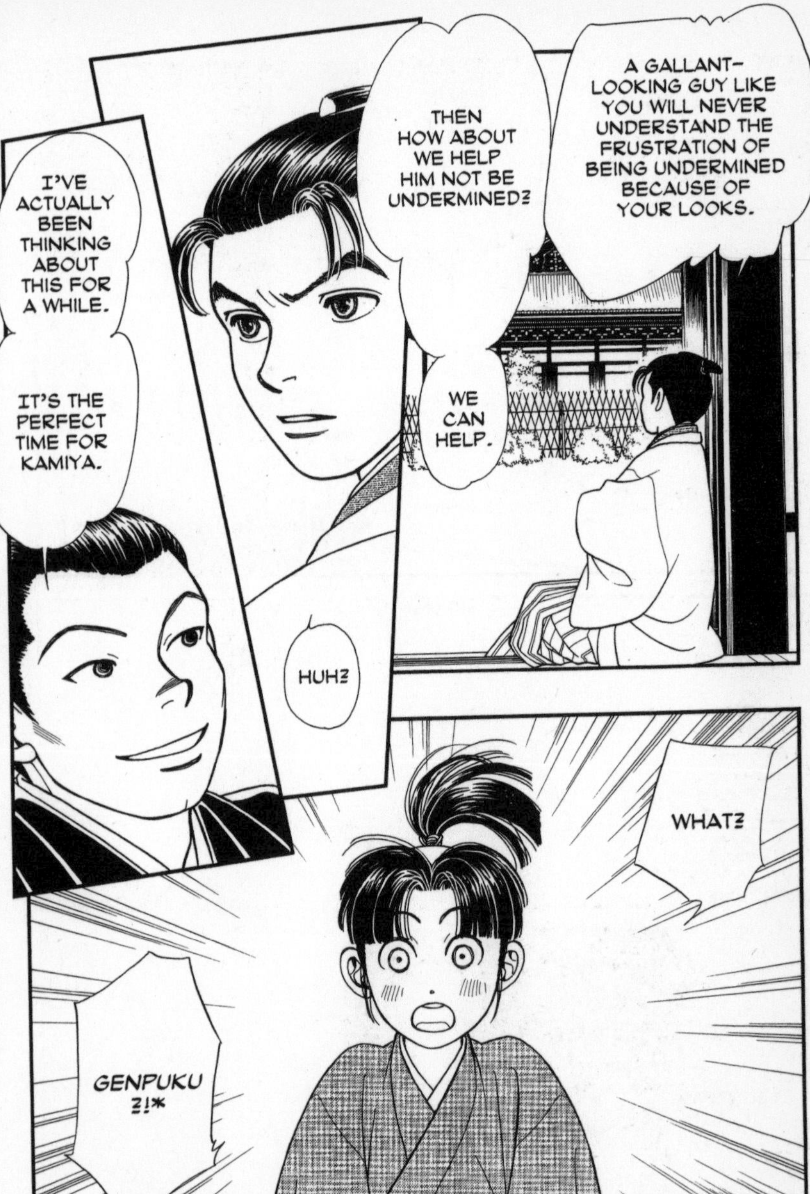
A GALLANT-LOOKING GUY LIKE YOU WILL NEVER UNDERSTAND THE FRUSTRATION OF BEING UNDERMINED BECAUSE OF YOUR LOOKS.
THEN HOW ABOUT WE HELP HIM NOT BE UNDERMINED?
WE CAN HELP.
HUH?
I'VE ACTUALLY BEEN THINKING ABOUT THIS FOR A WHILE.
IT'S THE PERFECT TIME FOR KAMIYA.
WHAT?
GENPUKU?!*

*A coming-of-age ceremony

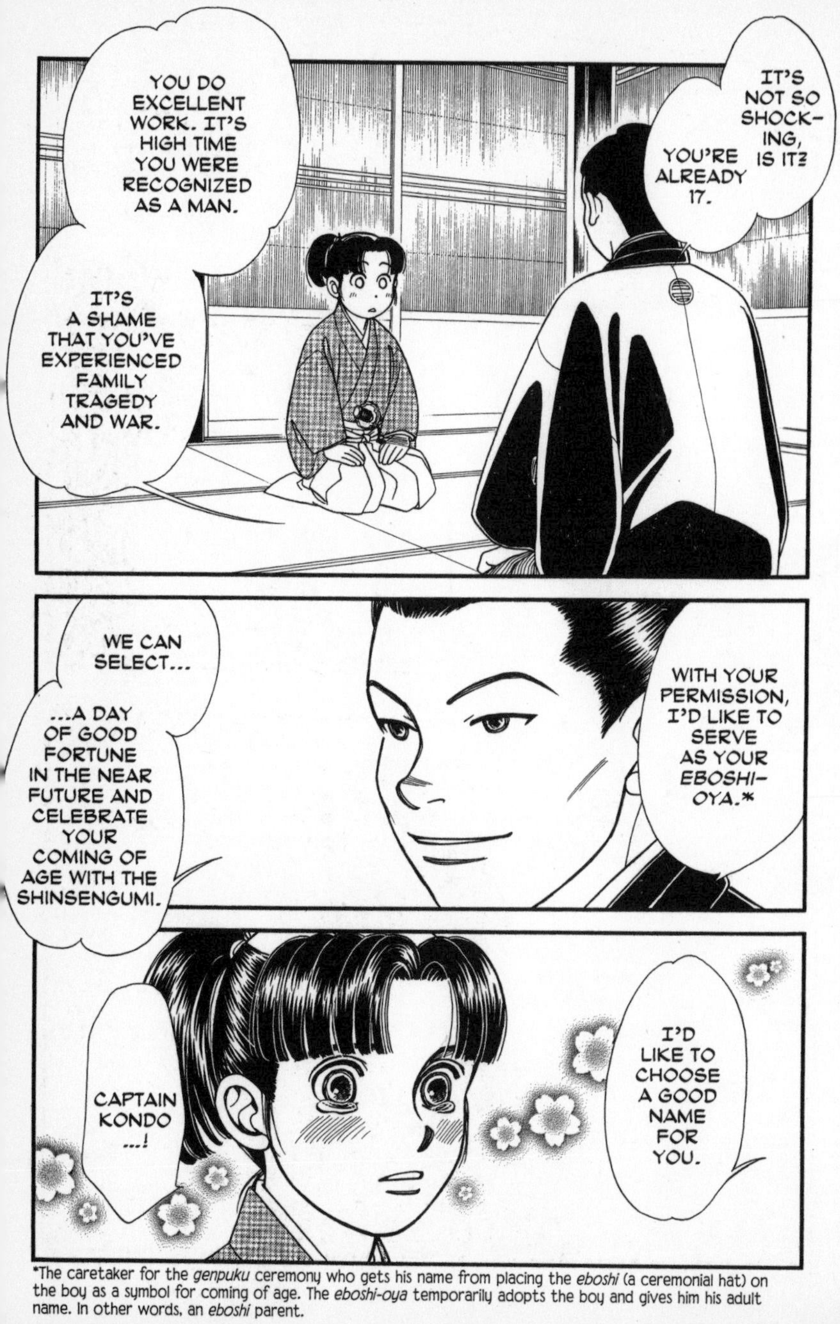
IT'S NOT SO SHOCKING, IS IT?
YOU'RE ALREADY 17.
YOU DO EXCELLENT WORK. IT'S HIGH TIME YOU WERE RECOGNIZED AS A MAN.
IT'S A SHAME THAT YOU'VE EXPERIENCED FAMILY TRAGEDY AND WAR.
WITH YOUR PERMISSION, I'D LIKE TO SERVE AS YOUR *EBOSHI-OYA*.*
WE CAN SELECT...
...A DAY OF GOOD FORTUNE IN THE NEAR FUTURE AND CELEBRATE YOUR COMING OF AGE WITH THE SHINSENGUMI.
I'D LIKE TO CHOOSE A GOOD NAME FOR YOU.
CAPTAIN KONDO ...!

*The caretaker for the *genpuku* ceremony who gets his name from placing the *eboshi* (a ceremonial hat) on the boy as a symbol for coming of age. The *eboshi-oya* temporarily adopts the boy and gives him his adult name. In other words, an *eboshi* parent.

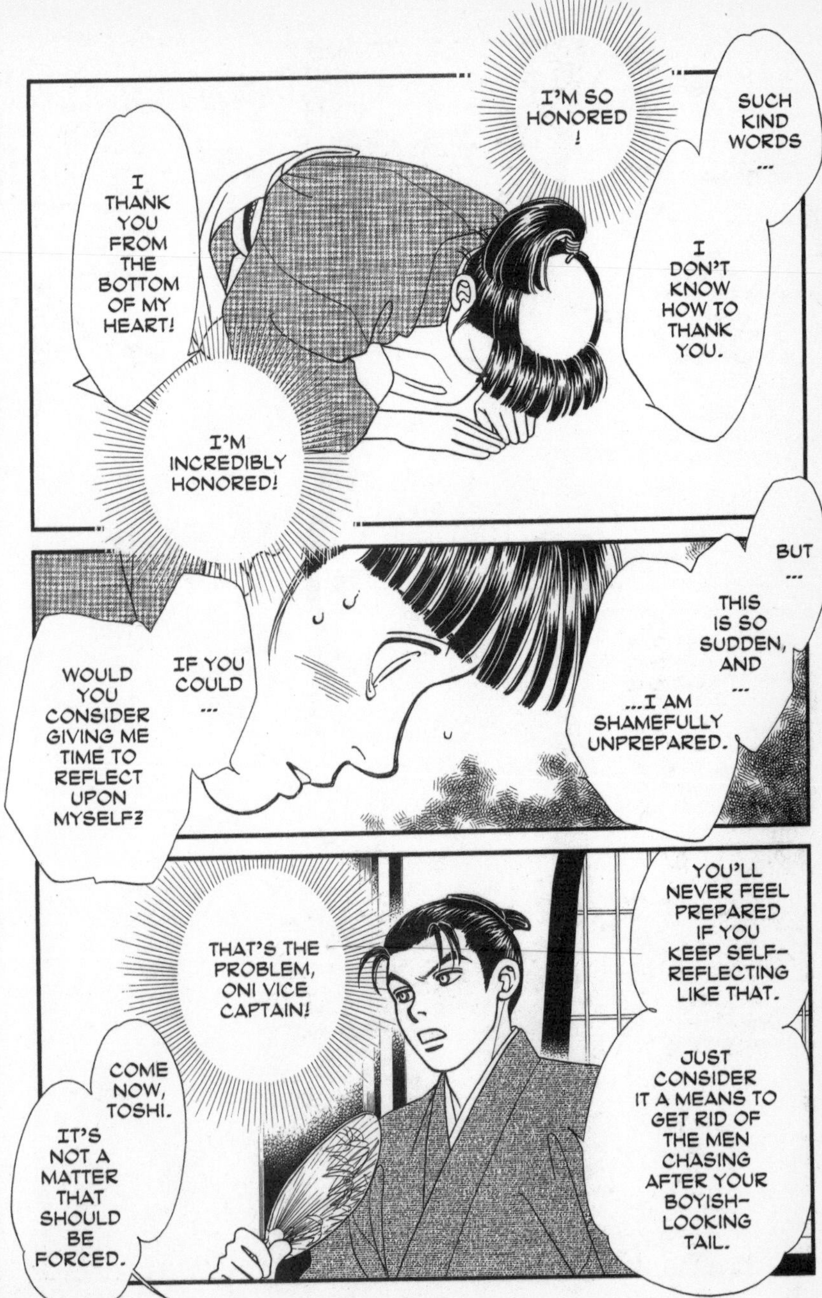
SUCH KIND WORDS...
I DON'T KNOW HOW TO THANK YOU.
I'M SO HONORED!
I THANK YOU FROM THE BOTTOM OF MY HEART!
I'M INCREDIBLY HONORED!
BUT...
THIS IS SO SUDDEN, AND...
...I AM SHAMEFULLY UNPREPARED.
IF YOU COULD...
WOULD YOU CONSIDER GIVING ME TIME TO REFLECT UPON MYSELF?
YOU'LL NEVER FEEL PREPARED IF YOU KEEP SELF-REFLECTING LIKE THAT.
JUST CONSIDER IT A MEANS TO GET RID OF THE MEN CHASING AFTER YOUR BOYISH-LOOKING TAIL.
THAT'S THE PROBLEM, ONI VICE CAPTAIN!
COME NOW, TOSHI.
IT'S NOT A MATTER THAT SHOULD BE FORCED.

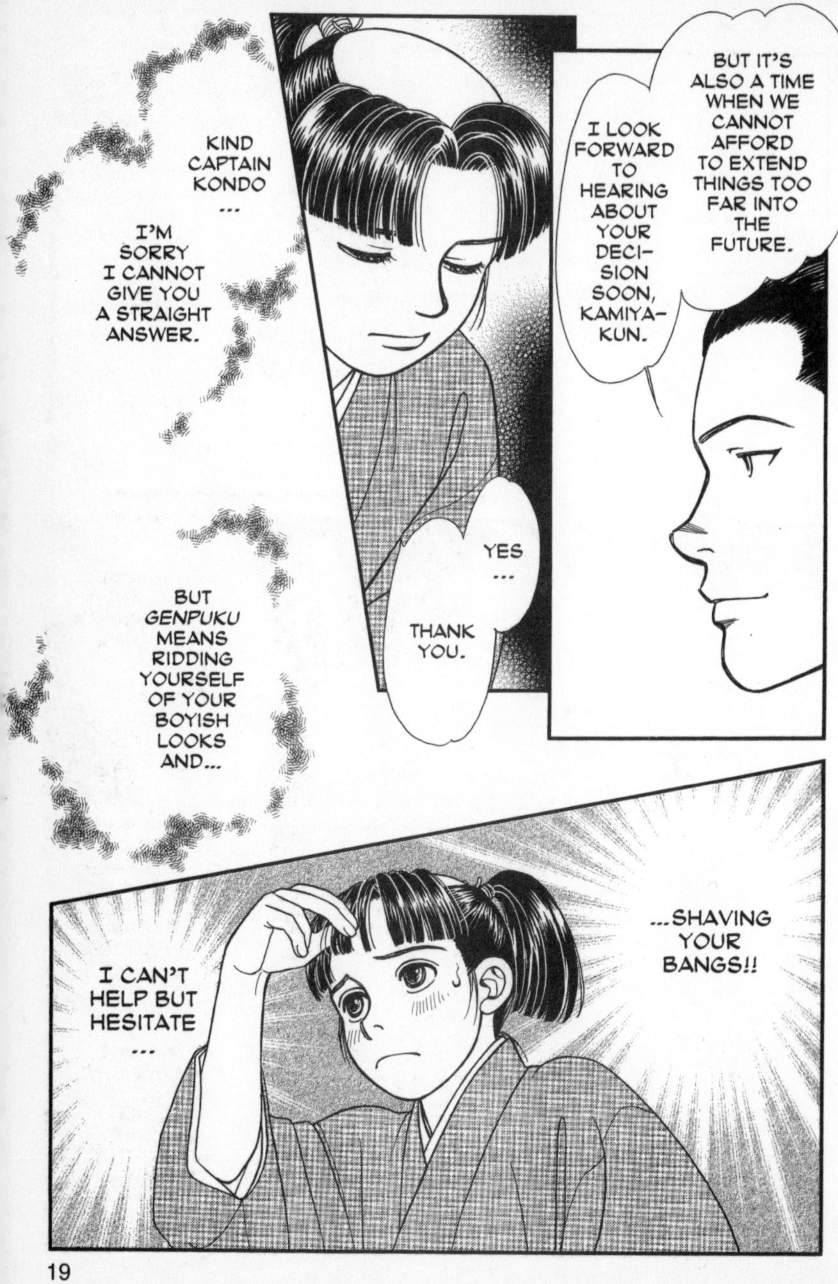
BUT IT'S ALSO A TIME WHEN WE CANNOT AFFORD TO EXTEND THINGS TOO FAR INTO THE FUTURE.
I LOOK FORWARD TO HEARING ABOUT YOUR DECI-SION SOON, KAMIYA-KUN.
YES ...
THANK YOU.
KIND CAPTAIN KONDO ...
I'M SORRY I CANNOT GIVE YOU A STRAIGHT ANSWER.
BUT *GENPUKU* MEANS RIDDING YOURSELF OF YOUR BOYISH LOOKS AND...
...SHAVING YOUR BANGS!!
I CAN'T HELP BUT HESITATE ...

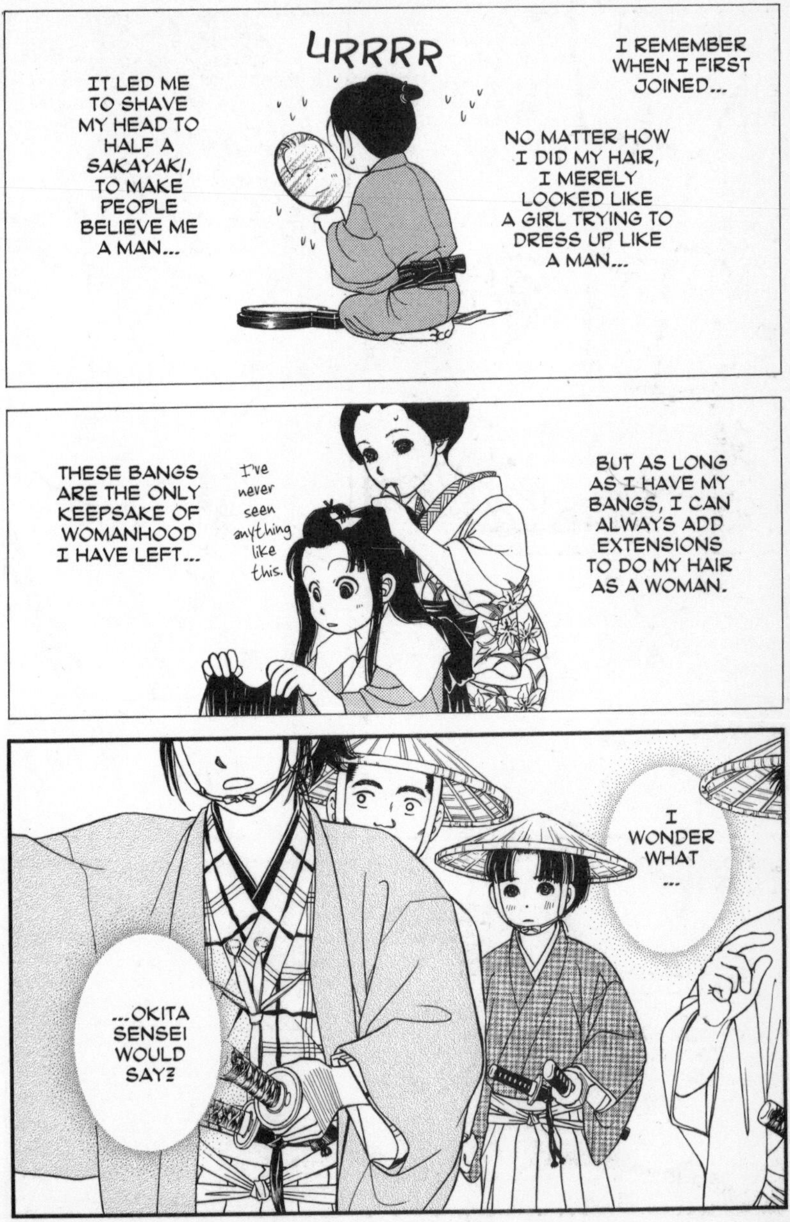
I REMEMBER WHEN I FIRST JOINED...
URRRR
NO MATTER HOW I DID MY HAIR, I MERELY LOOKED LIKE A GIRL TRYING TO DRESS UP LIKE A MAN...
IT LED ME TO SHAVE MY HEAD TO HALF A SAKAYAKI, TO MAKE PEOPLE BELIEVE ME A MAN...
BUT AS LONG AS I HAVE MY BANGS, I CAN ALWAYS ADD EXTENSIONS TO DO MY HAIR AS A WOMAN.
I've never seen anything like this.
THESE BANGS ARE THE ONLY KEEPSAKE OF WOMANHOOD I HAVE LEFT...
I WONDER WHAT...
...OKITA SENSEI WOULD SAY?

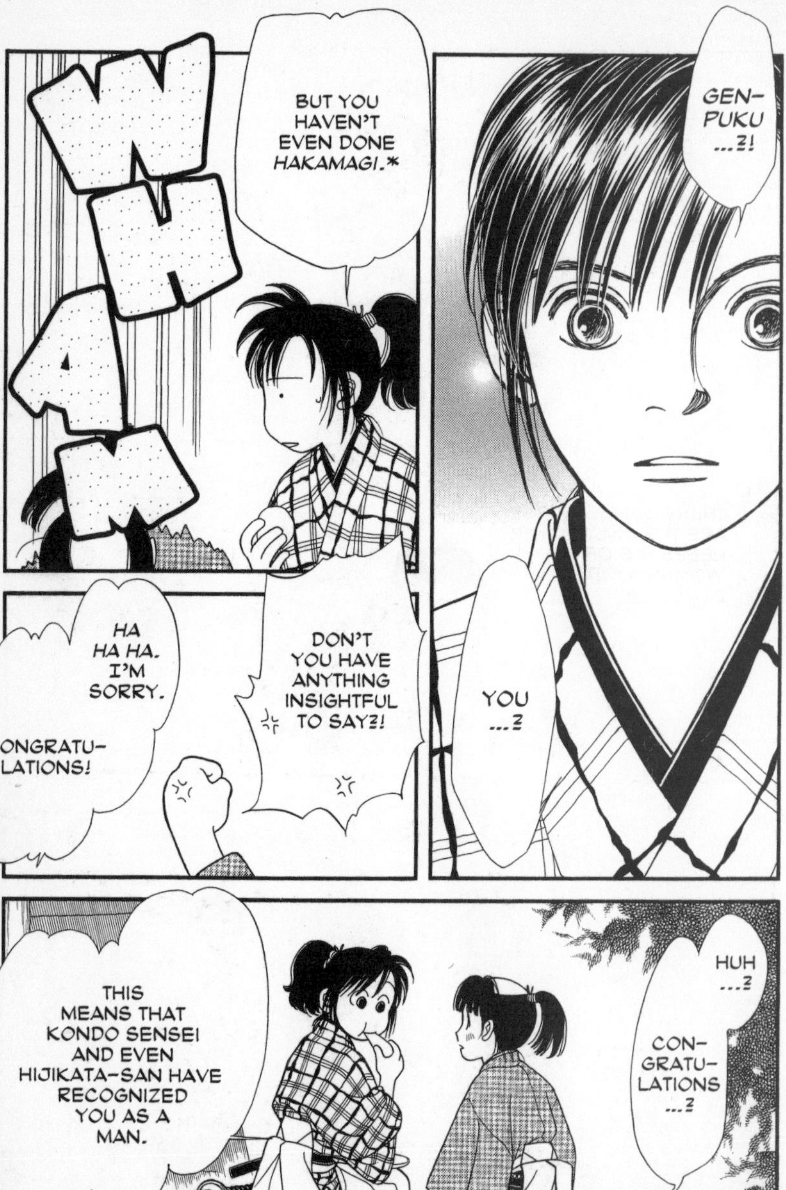
GEN-PUKU ...?!
YOU ...?
BUT YOU HAVEN'T EVEN DONE *HAKAMAGI*.*
WHAM
DON'T YOU HAVE ANYTHING INSIGHTFUL TO SAY?!
HA HA HA. I'M SORRY.
CONGRATULATIONS!
HUH ...?
CONGRATULATIONS ...?
THIS MEANS THAT KONDO SENSEI AND EVEN HIJIKATA-SAN HAVE RECOGNIZED YOU AS A MAN.

*The predecessor to the *Shichigosan* ceremony (a festival celebrating children) where 5-year-old boys wore a formal kimono.

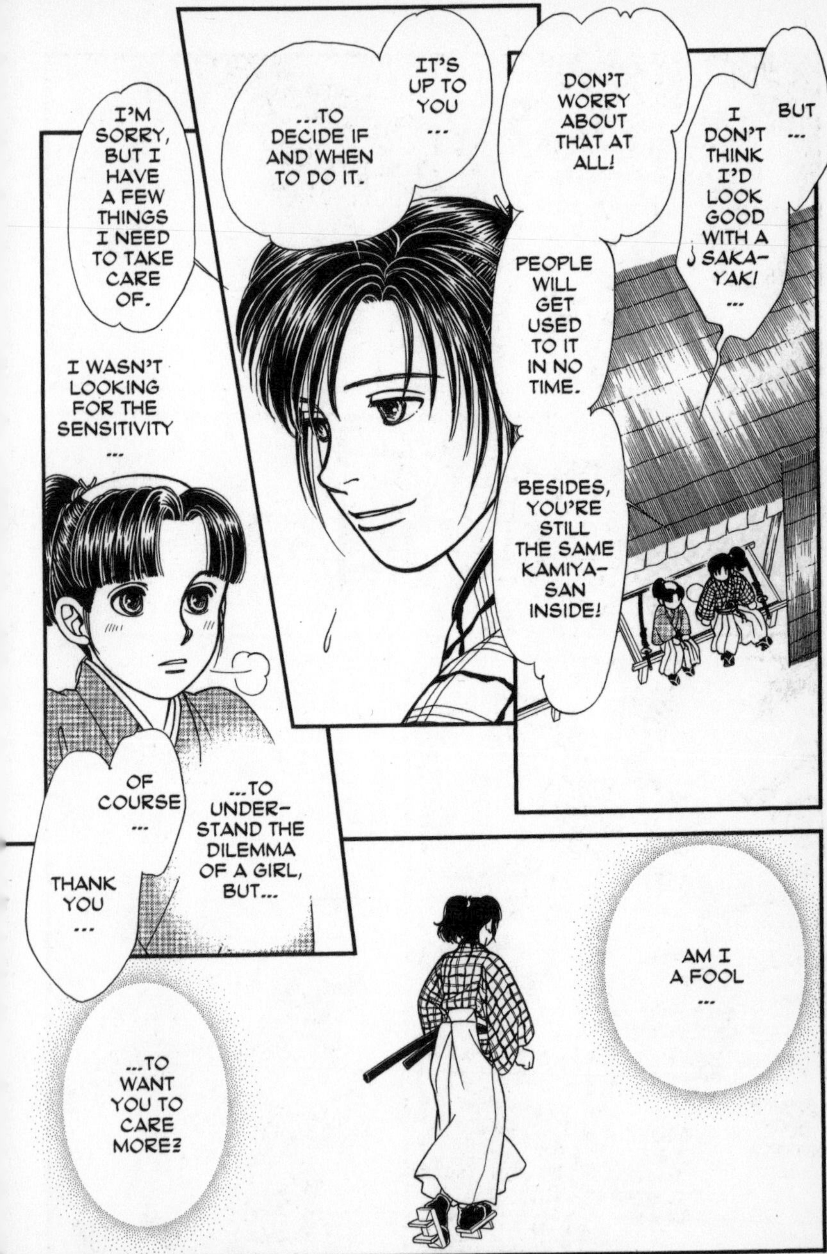
BUT ... I DON'T THINK I'D LOOK GOOD WITH A SAKAYAKI ...
DON'T WORRY ABOUT THAT AT ALL!
PEOPLE WILL GET USED TO IT IN NO TIME.
BESIDES, YOU'RE STILL THE SAME KAMIYA-SAN INSIDE!
IT'S UP TO YOU ...
...TO DECIDE IF AND WHEN TO DO IT.
I'M SORRY, BUT I HAVE A FEW THINGS I NEED TO TAKE CARE OF.
I WASN'T LOOKING FOR THE SENSITIVITY ...
...TO UNDERSTAND THE DILEMMA OF A GIRL, BUT...
OF COURSE ...
THANK YOU ...
AM I A FOOL ...
...TO WANT YOU TO CARE MORE?

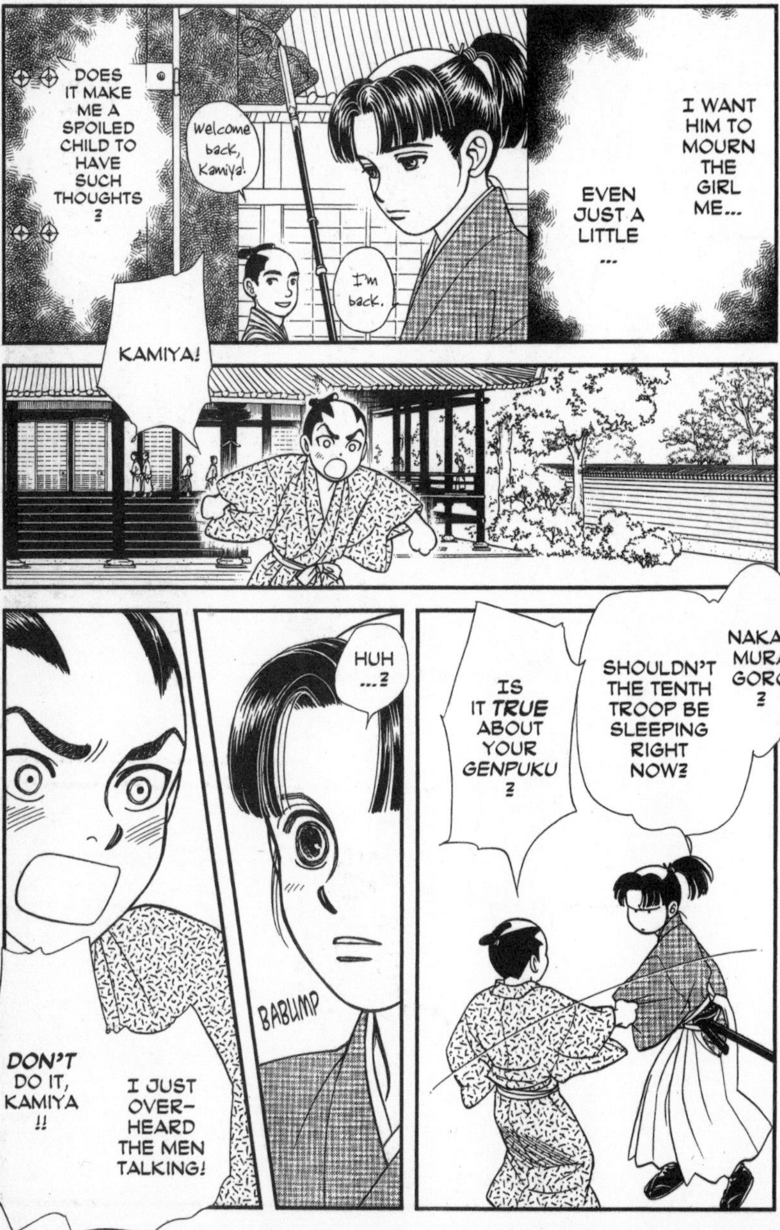
I WANT HIM TO MOURN THE GIRL ME...
EVEN JUST A LITTLE ...
Welcome back, Kamiya!
I'm back.
DOES IT MAKE ME A SPOILED CHILD TO HAVE SUCH THOUGHTS?
KAMIYA!
NAKA-MURA GORO?
SHOULDN'T THE TENTH TROOP BE SLEEPING RIGHT NOW?
IS IT TRUE ABOUT YOUR GENPUKU?
HUH ...?
BABUMP
I JUST OVER-HEARD THE MEN TALKING!
DON'T DO IT, KAMIYA !!

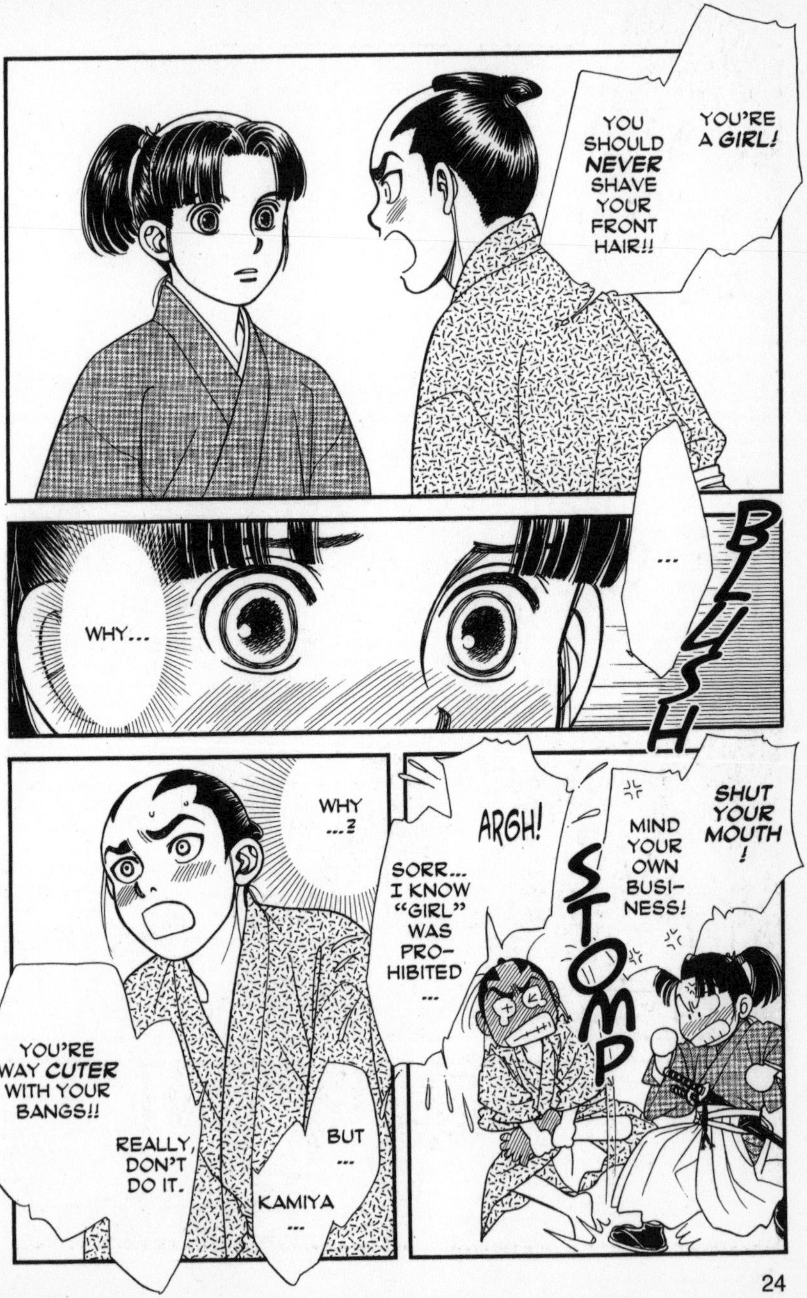
YOU'RE A *GIRL!*
YOU SHOULD **NEVER** SHAVE YOUR FRONT HAIR!!
BLUSH
...
WHY...
SHUT YOUR MOUTH!
MIND YOUR OWN BUSI-NESS!
STOMP
ARGH!
SORR... I KNOW "GIRL" WAS PRO-HIBITED ...
WHY ...?
BUT ...
KAMIYA ...
YOU'RE WAY **CUTER** WITH YOUR BANGS!!
REALLY, DON'T DO IT.

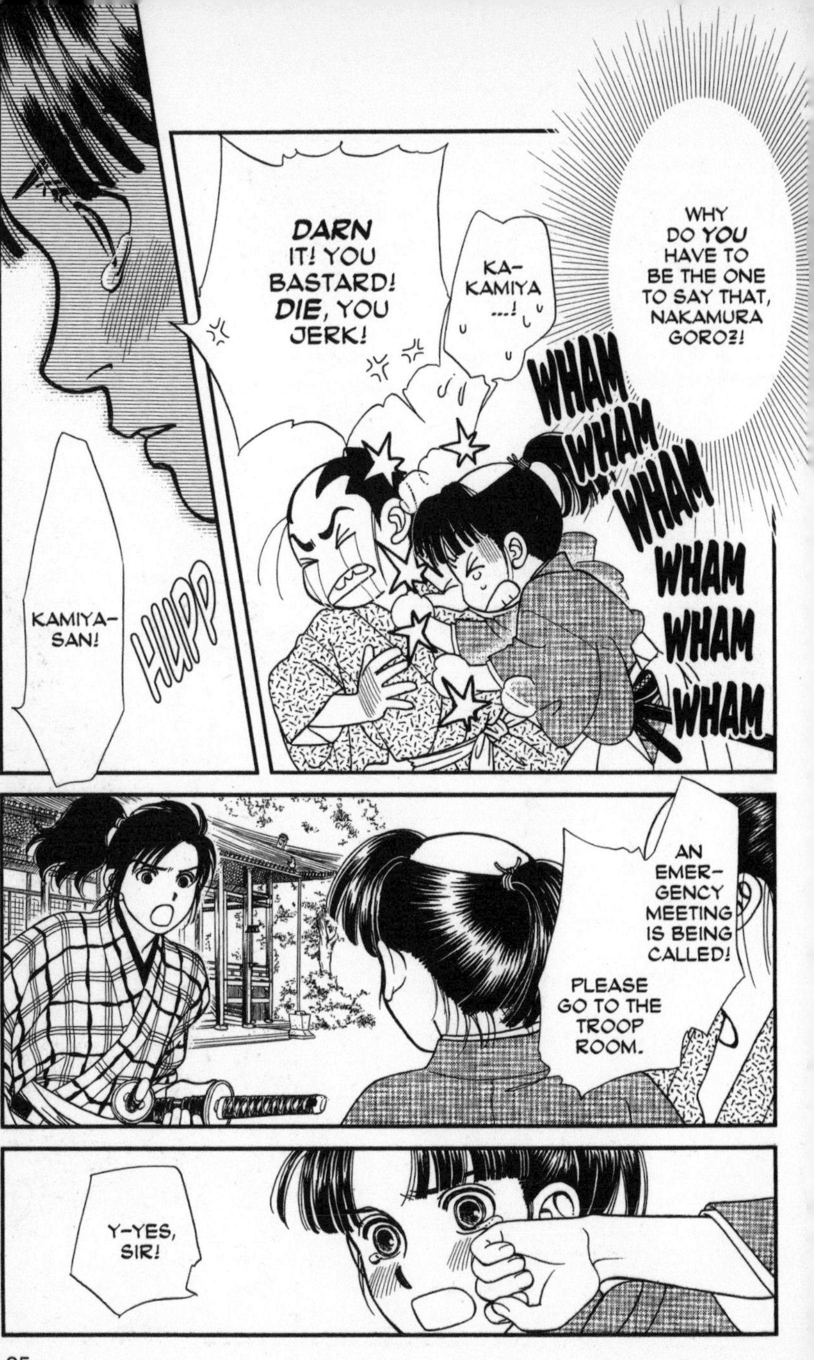
WHY DO YOU HAVE TO BE THE ONE TO SAY THAT, NAKAMURA GORO?!
WHAM WHAM WHAM WHAM WHAM WHAM
KA-KAMIYA...!
DARN IT! YOU BASTARD! DIE, YOU JERK!
HUPP
KAMIYA-SAN!
AN EMERGENCY MEETING IS BEING CALLED!
PLEASE GO TO THE TROOP ROOM.
Y-YES, SIR!

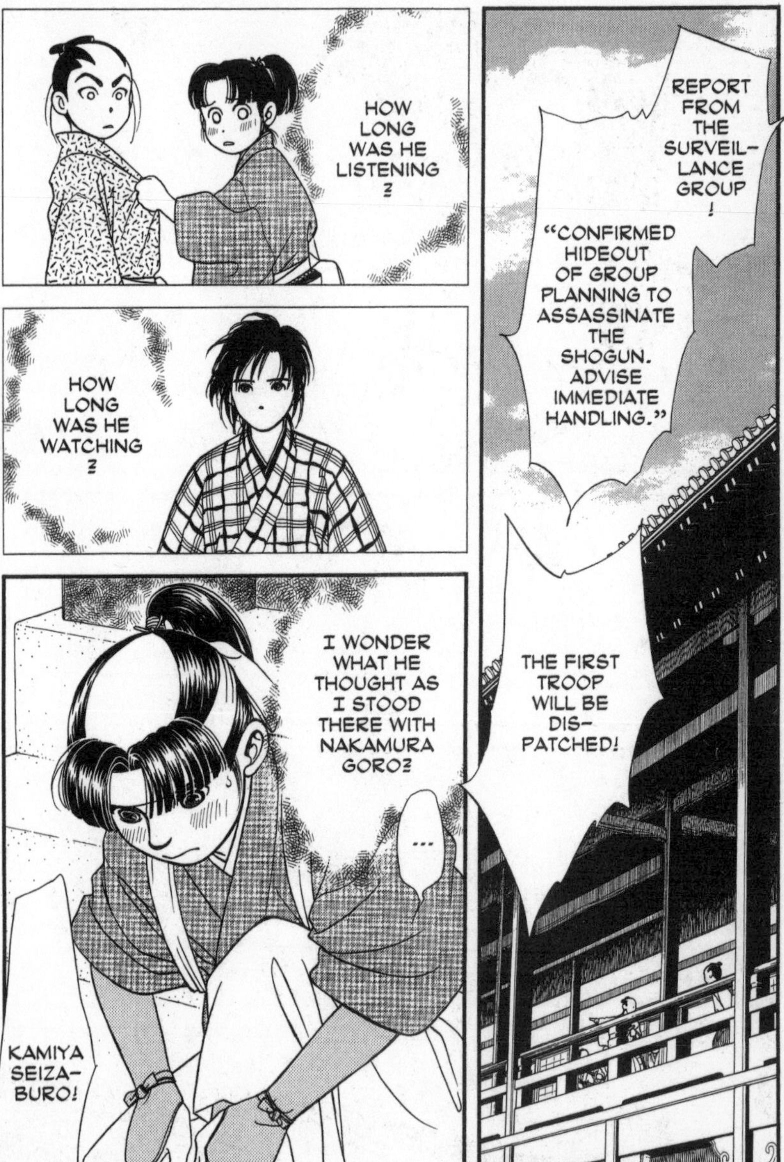
REPORT FROM THE SURVEIL-LANCE GROUP!
"CONFIRMED HIDEOUT OF GROUP PLANNING TO ASSASSINATE THE SHOGUN. ADVISE IMMEDIATE HANDLING."
THE FIRST TROOP WILL BE DIS-PATCHED!
HOW LONG WAS HE LISTENING?
HOW LONG WAS HE WATCHING?
I WONDER WHAT HE THOUGHT AS I STOOD THERE WITH NAKAMURA GORO?
...
KAMIYA SEIZA-BURO!

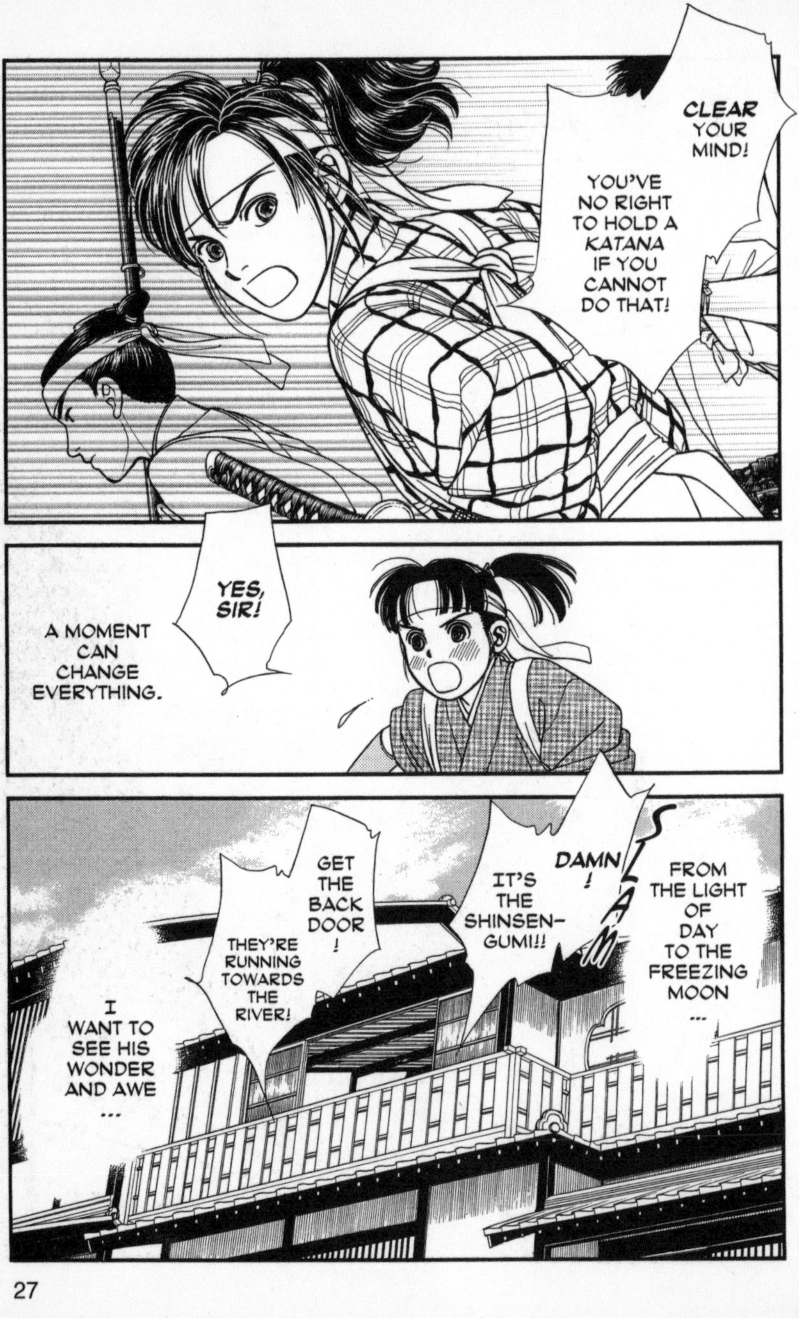
CLEAR YOUR MIND!
YOU'VE NO RIGHT TO HOLD A KATANA IF YOU CANNOT DO THAT!
YES, SIR!
A MOMENT CAN CHANGE EVERYTHING.
FROM THE LIGHT OF DAY TO THE FREEZING MOON ...
SLAM
DAMN!
IT'S THE SHINSEN-GUMI!!
GET THE BACK DOOR!
THEY'RE RUNNING TOWARDS THE RIVER!
I WANT TO SEE HIS WONDER AND AWE ...

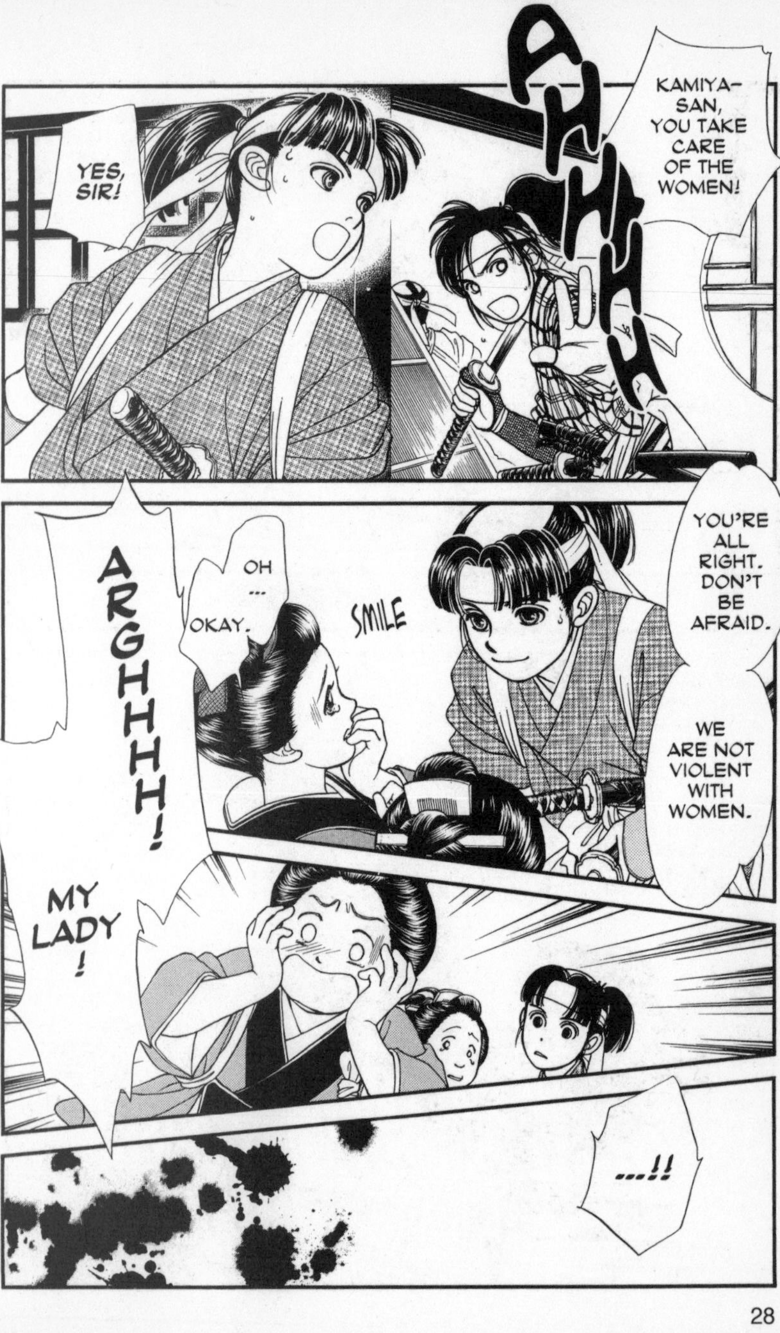
AHHHH
KAMIYA-SAN, YOU TAKE CARE OF THE WOMEN!
YES, SIR!
YOU'RE ALL RIGHT. DON'T BE AFRAID.
WE ARE NOT VIOLENT WITH WOMEN.
SMILE
OH ... OKAY.
ARGHHHH!
MY LADY!
...!!

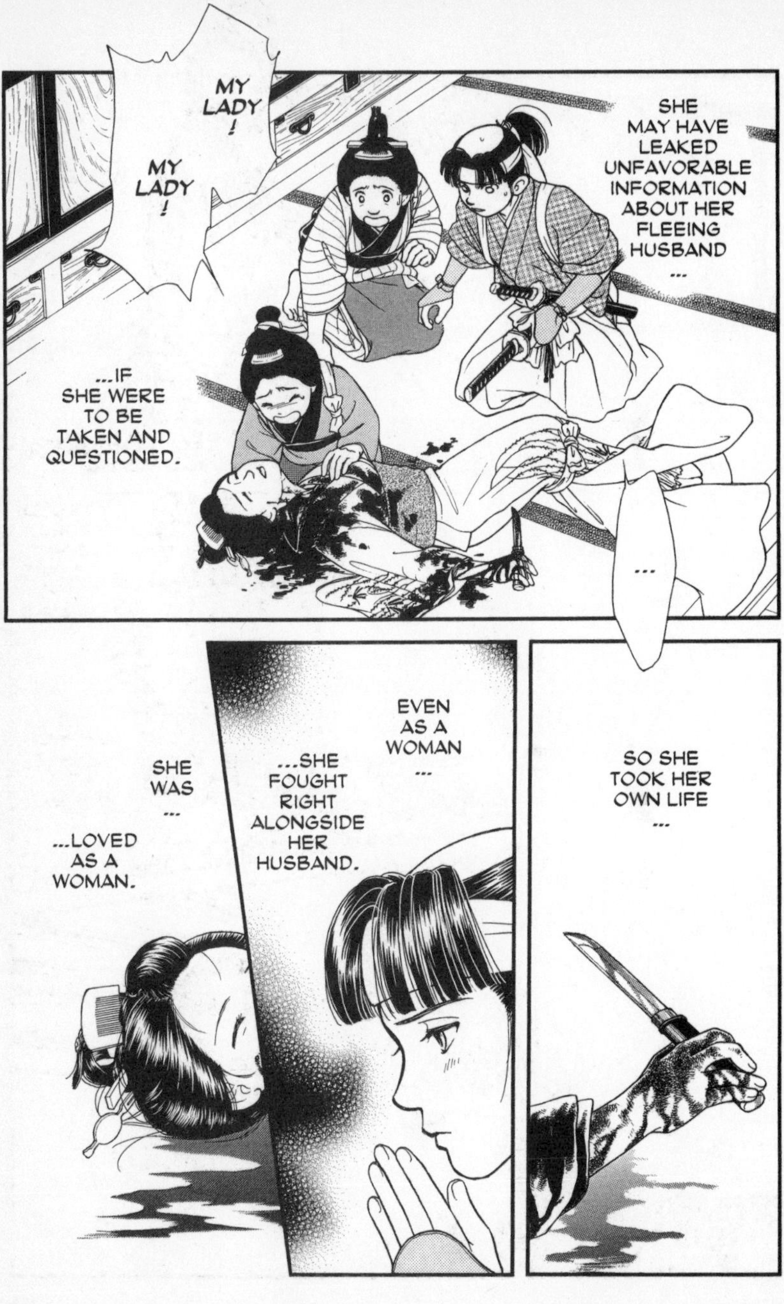
SHE MAY HAVE LEAKED UNFAVORABLE INFORMATION ABOUT HER FLEEING HUSBAND ...
MY LADY!
MY LADY!
...IF SHE WERE TO BE TAKEN AND QUESTIONED.
...
SO SHE TOOK HER OWN LIFE ...
EVEN AS A WOMAN ...
...SHE FOUGHT RIGHT ALONGSIDE HER HUSBAND.
SHE WAS ...
...LOVED AS A WOMAN.

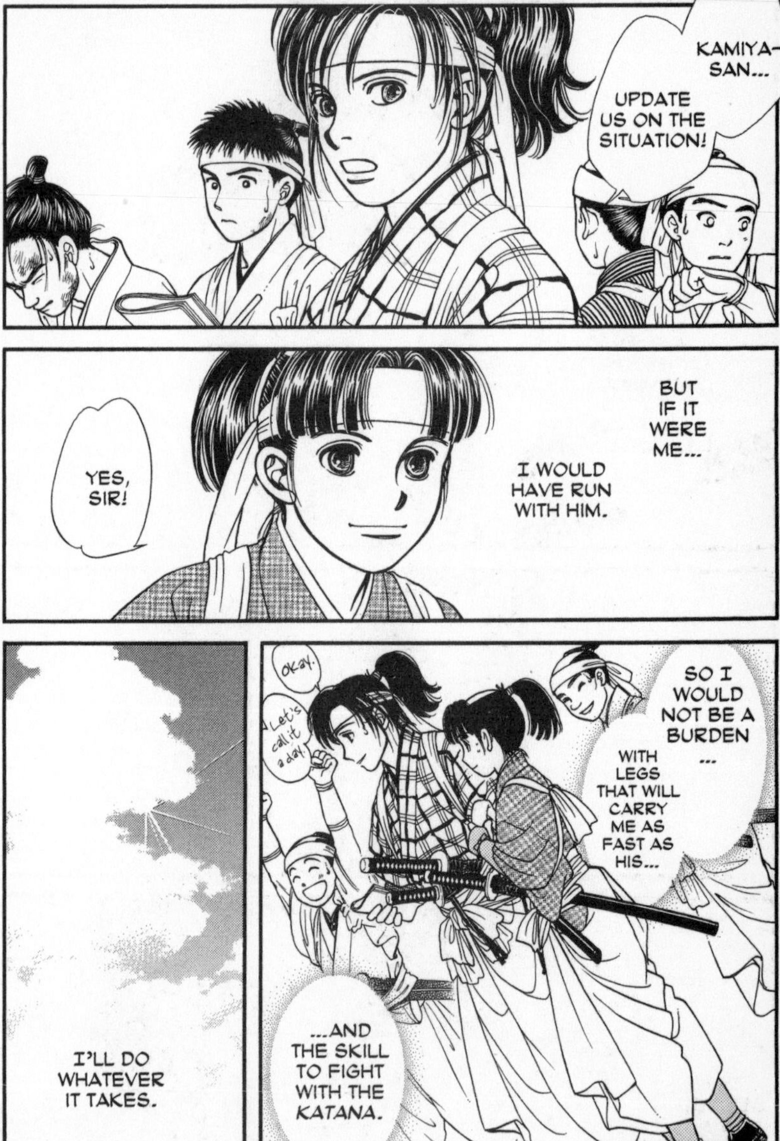
KAMIYA-SAN...
UPDATE US ON THE SITUATION!
BUT IF IT WERE ME...
I WOULD HAVE RUN WITH HIM.
YES, SIR!
SO I WOULD NOT BE A BURDEN ...
WITH LEGS THAT WILL CARRY ME AS FAST AS HIS...
okay.
Let's call it a day!
...AND THE SKILL TO FIGHT WITH THE KATANA.
I'LL DO WHATEVER IT TAKES.

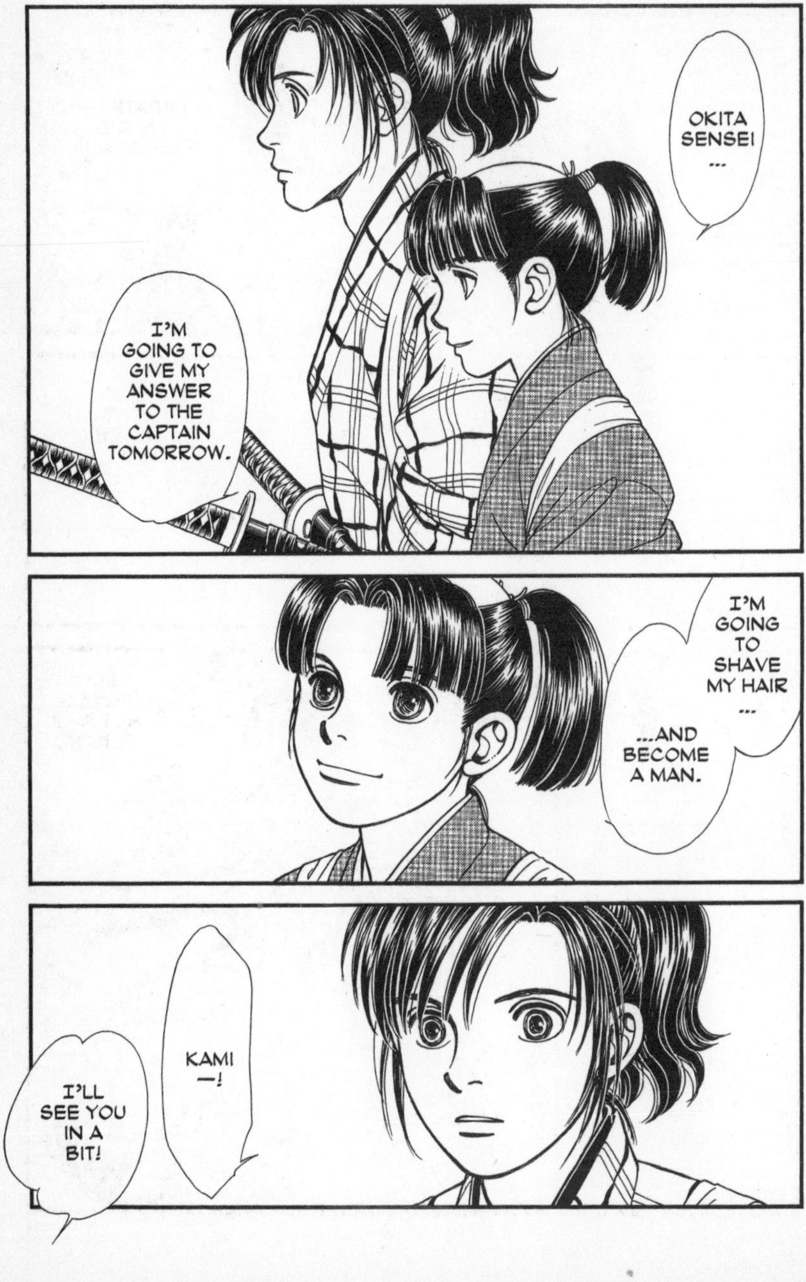
OKITA SENSEI ...
I'M GOING TO GIVE MY ANSWER TO THE CAPTAIN TOMORROW.
I'M GOING TO SHAVE MY HAIR ...
...AND BECOME A MAN.
KAMI —!
I'LL SEE YOU IN A BIT!

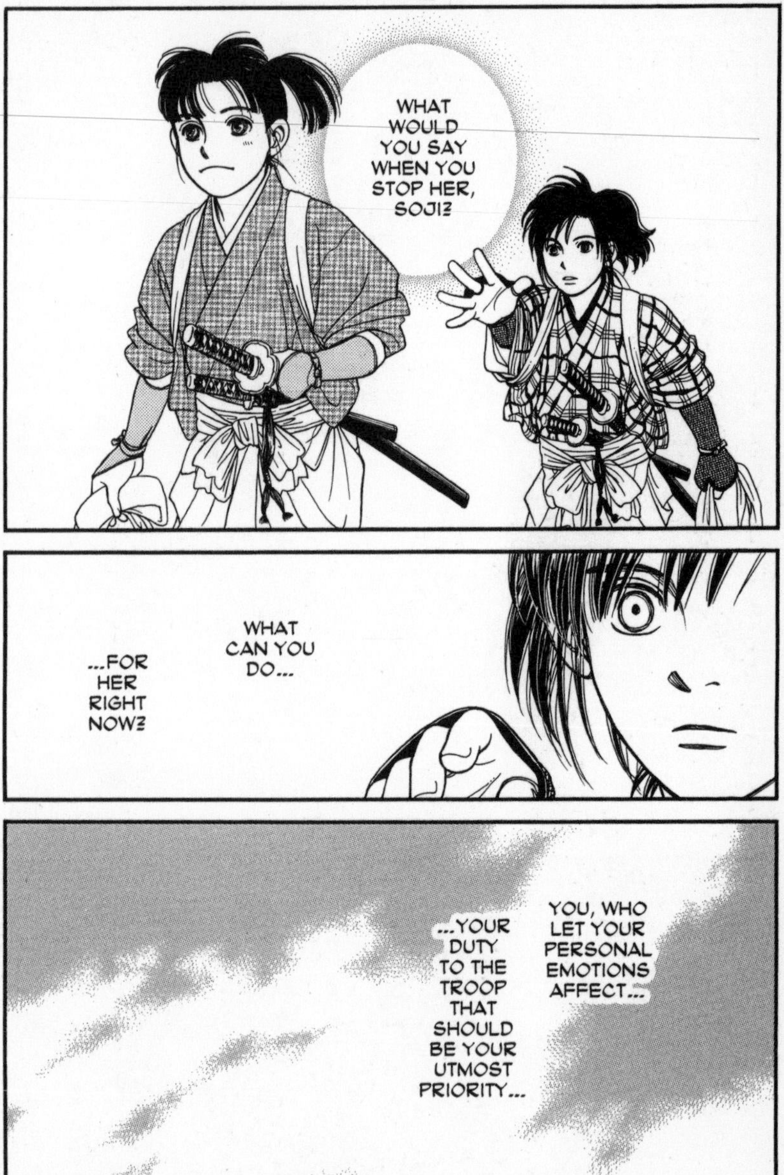
WHAT WOULD YOU SAY WHEN YOU STOP HER, SOJI?
WHAT CAN YOU DO...
...FOR HER RIGHT NOW?
YOU, WHO LET YOUR PERSONAL EMOTIONS AFFECT...
...YOUR DUTY TO THE TROOP THAT SHOULD BE YOUR UTMOST PRIORITY...

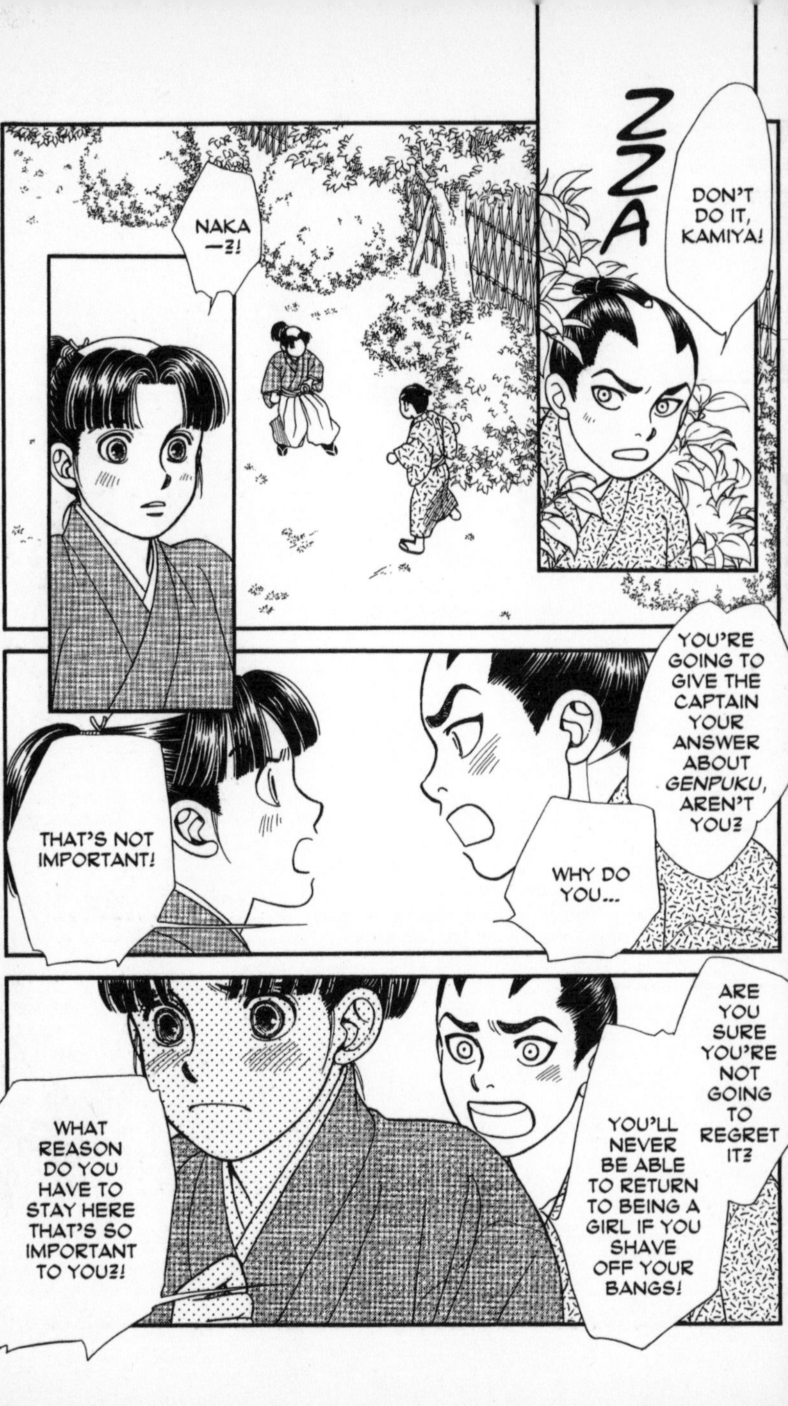
ZZA
DON'T DO IT, KAMIYA!
NAKA—?!
YOU'RE GOING TO GIVE THE CAPTAIN YOUR ANSWER ABOUT *GENPUKU*, AREN'T YOU?
WHY DO YOU...
THAT'S NOT IMPORTANT!
ARE YOU SURE YOU'RE NOT GOING TO REGRET IT?
YOU'LL NEVER BE ABLE TO RETURN TO BEING A GIRL IF YOU SHAVE OFF YOUR BANGS!
WHAT REASON DO YOU HAVE TO STAY HERE THAT'S SO IMPORTANT TO YOU?!

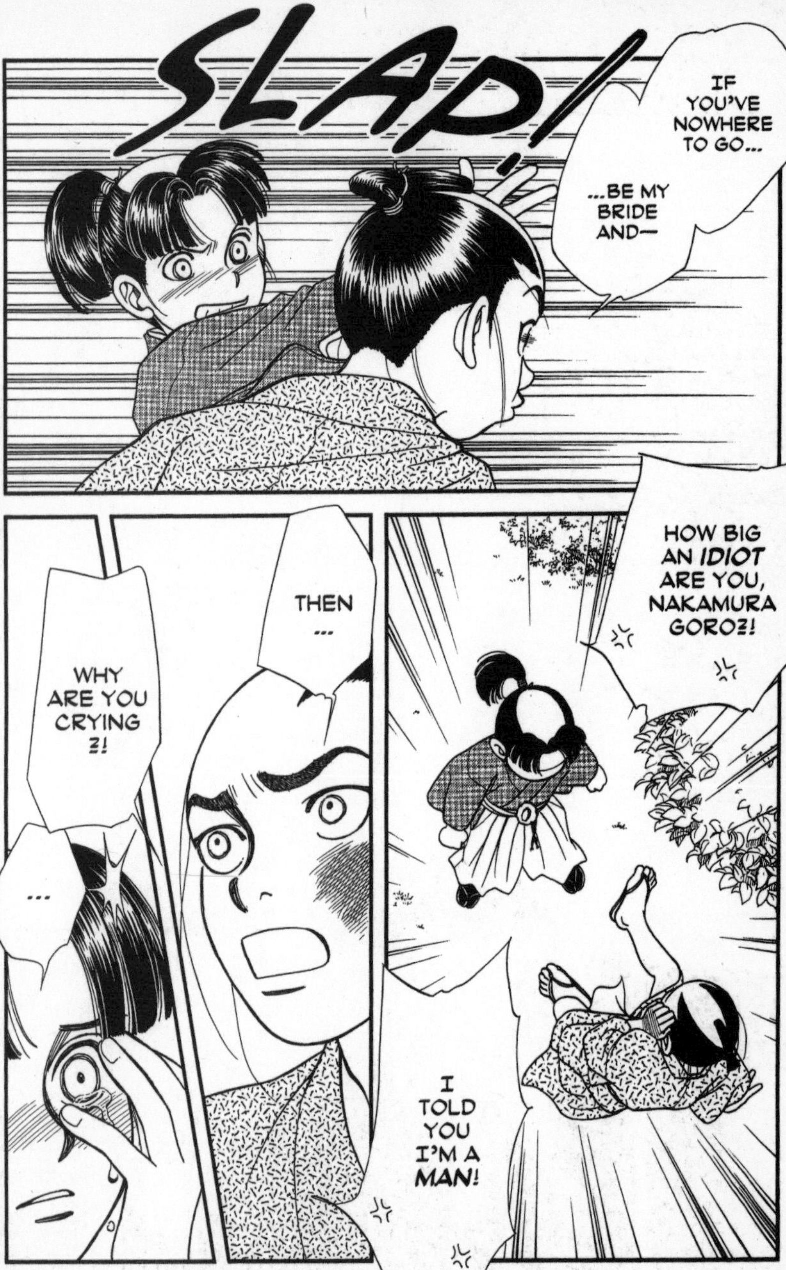
IF YOU'VE NOWHERE TO GO...
...BE MY BRIDE AND—
SLAP!
HOW BIG AN IDIOT ARE YOU, NAKAMURA GORO?!
I TOLD YOU I'M A MAN!
THEN...
WHY ARE YOU CRYING?!
...

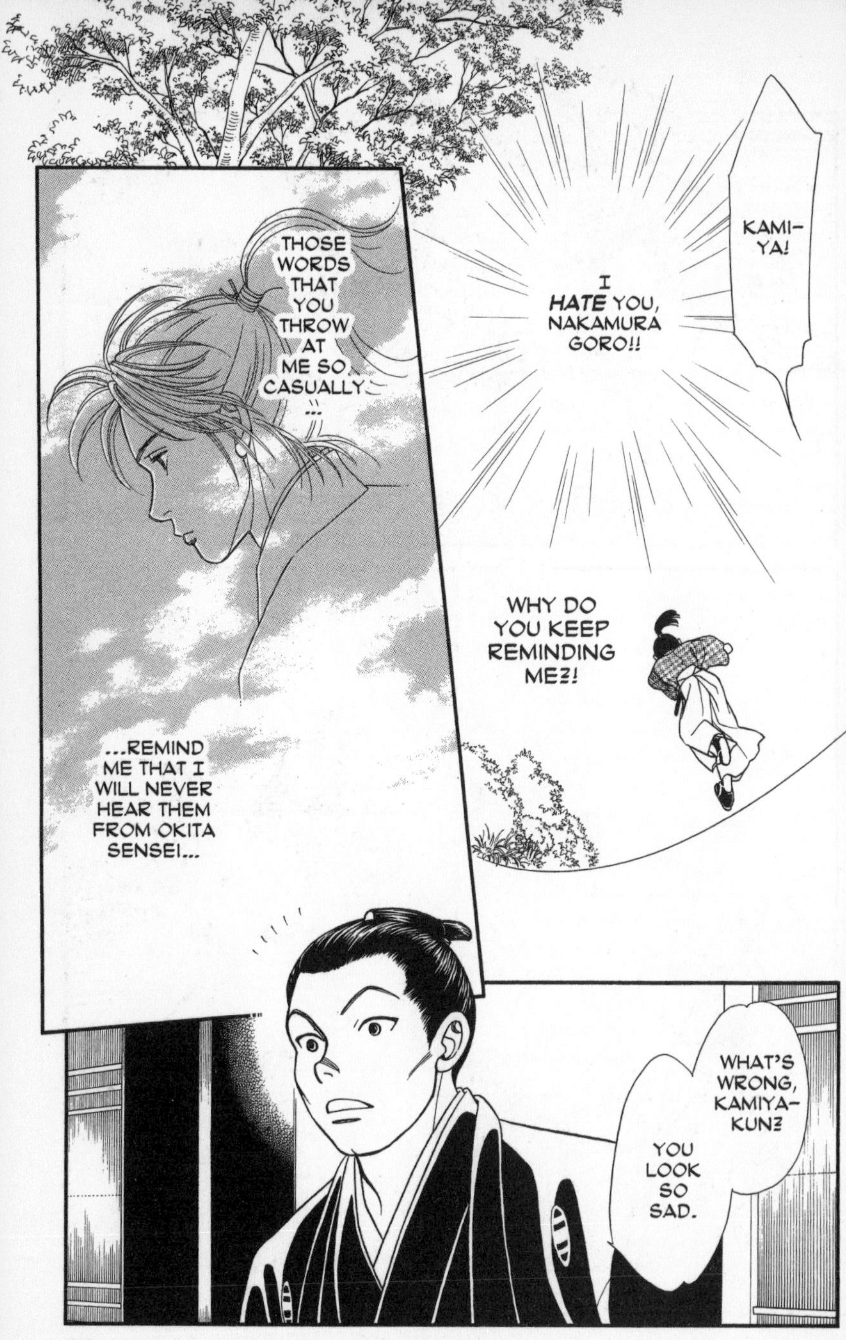
KAMI-YA!
I *HATE* YOU, NAKAMURA GORO!!
WHY DO YOU KEEP REMINDING ME?!
THOSE WORDS THAT YOU THROW AT ME SO CASUALLY...
...REMIND ME THAT I WILL NEVER HEAR THEM FROM OKITA SENSEI...
WHAT'S WRONG, KAMIYA-KUN?
YOU LOOK SO SAD.

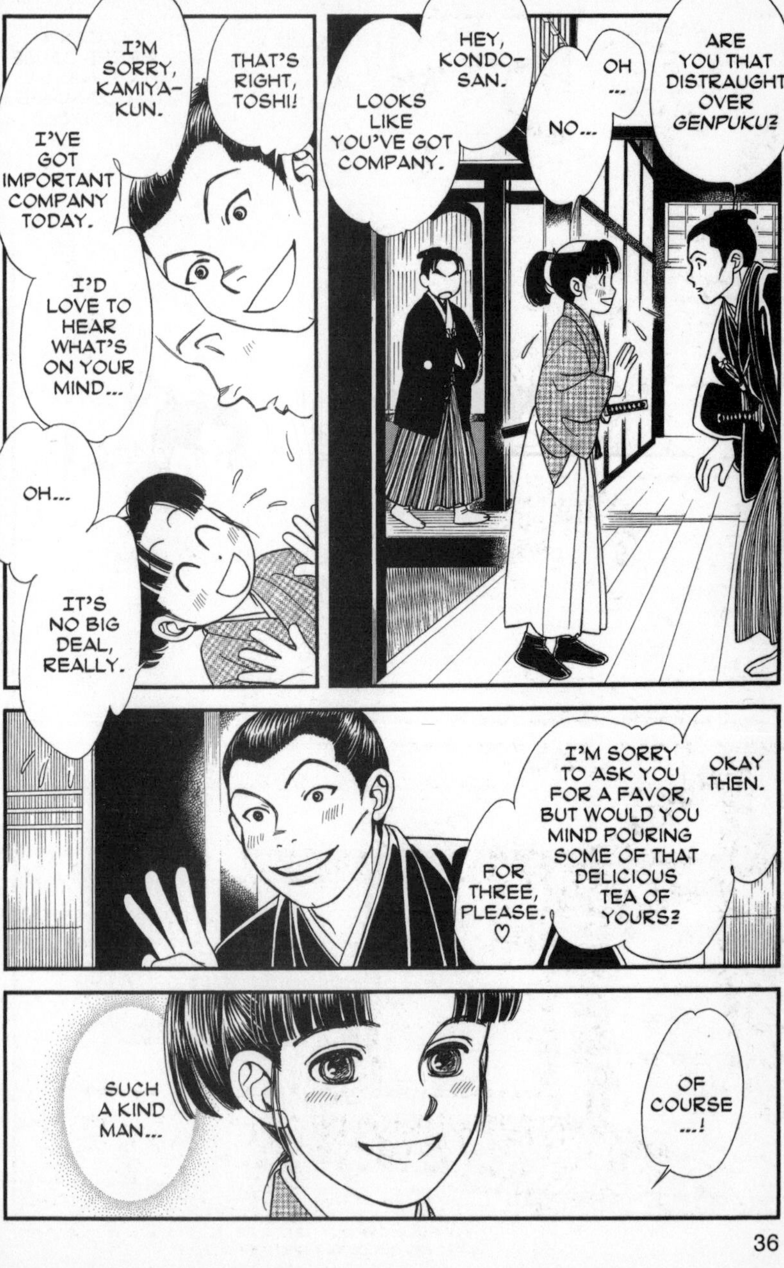
ARE YOU THAT DISTRAUGHT OVER GENPUKU?
OH ... NO...
HEY, KONDO-SAN.
LOOKS LIKE YOU'VE GOT COMPANY.
THAT'S RIGHT, TOSHI!
I'M SORRY, KAMIYA-KUN.
I'VE GOT IMPORTANT COMPANY TODAY.
I'D LOVE TO HEAR WHAT'S ON YOUR MIND...
OH...
IT'S NO BIG DEAL, REALLY.
OKAY THEN.
I'M SORRY TO ASK YOU FOR A FAVOR, BUT WOULD YOU MIND POURING SOME OF THAT DELICIOUS TEA OF YOURS?
FOR THREE, PLEASE. ♡
OF COURSE ...!
SUCH A KIND MAN...

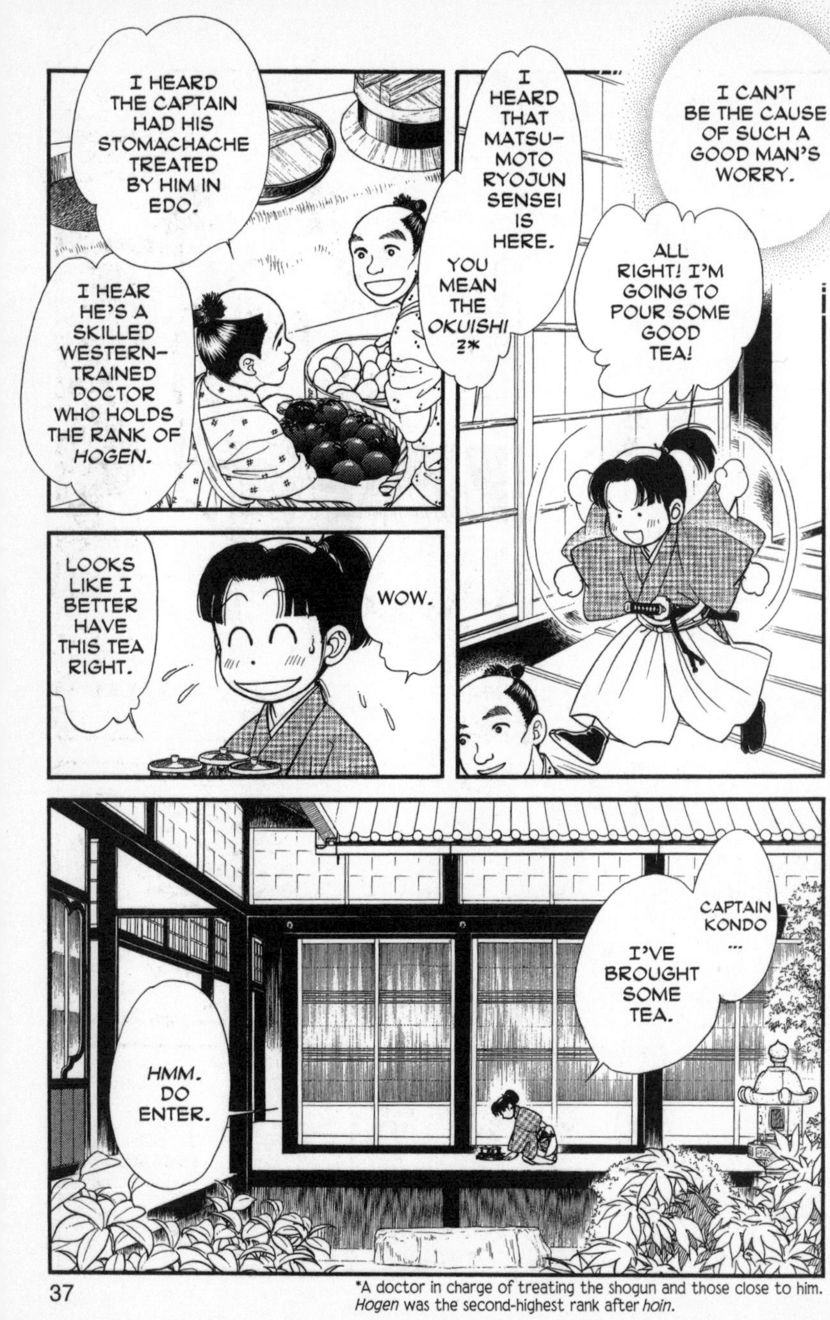

I CAN'T BE THE CAUSE OF SUCH A GOOD MAN'S WORRY.
I HEARD THAT MATSU-MOTO RYOJUN SENSEI IS HERE.
YOU MEAN THE *OKUISHI*?*
ALL RIGHT! I'M GOING TO POUR SOME GOOD TEA!
I HEARD THE CAPTAIN HAD HIS STOMACHACHE TREATED BY HIM IN EDO.
I HEAR HE'S A SKILLED WESTERN-TRAINED DOCTOR WHO HOLDS THE RANK OF *HOGEN*.
WOW.
LOOKS LIKE I BETTER HAVE THIS TEA RIGHT.
CAPTAIN KONDO...
I'VE BROUGHT SOME TEA.
HMM. DO ENTER.

*A doctor in charge of treating the shogun and those close to him. *Hogen* was the second-highest rank after *hoin*.

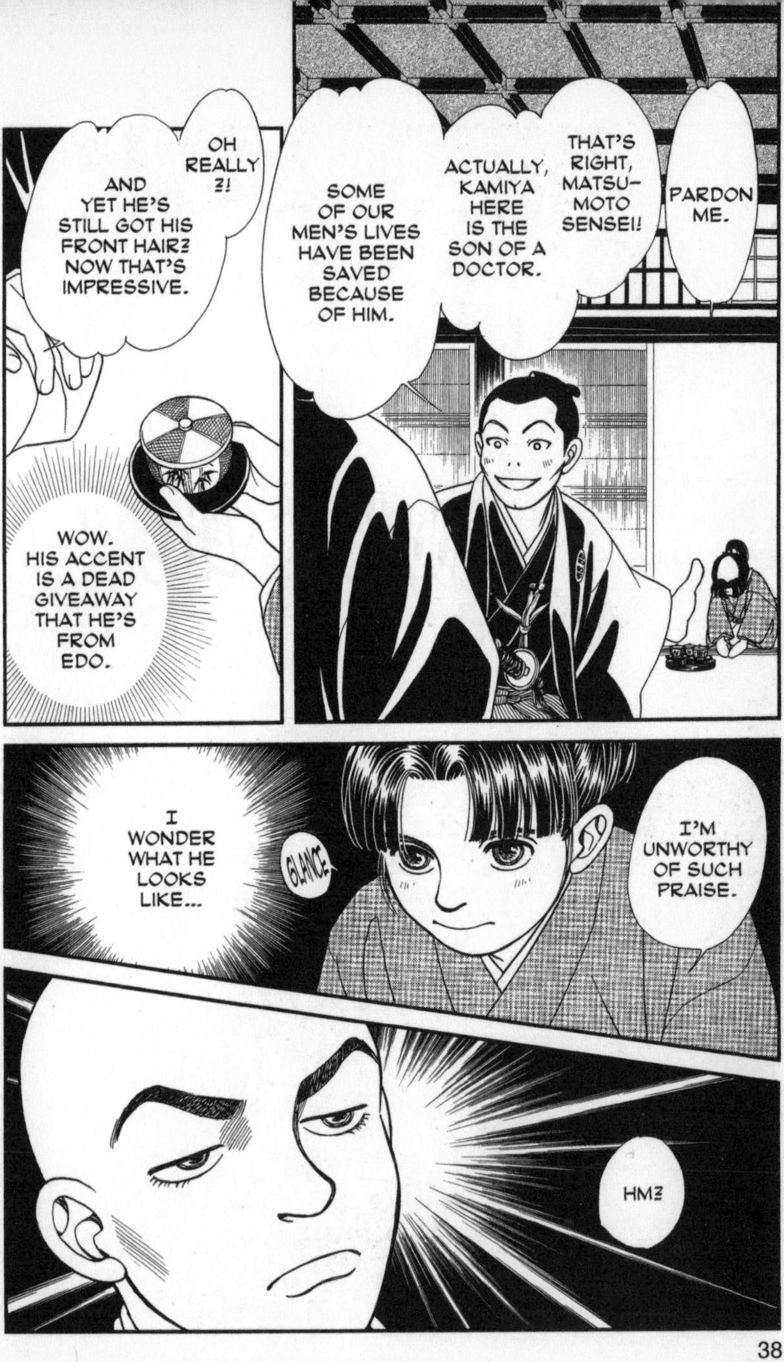
PARDON ME.
THAT'S RIGHT, MATSU-MOTO SENSEI!
ACTUALLY, KAMIYA HERE IS THE SON OF A DOCTOR.
SOME OF OUR MEN'S LIVES HAVE BEEN SAVED BECAUSE OF HIM.
OH REALLY?!
AND YET HE'S STILL GOT HIS FRONT HAIR? NOW THAT'S IMPRESSIVE.
WOW. HIS ACCENT IS A DEAD GIVEAWAY THAT HE'S FROM EDO.
I'M UNWORTHY OF SUCH PRAISE.
GLANCE
I WONDER WHAT HE LOOKS LIKE...
HM?

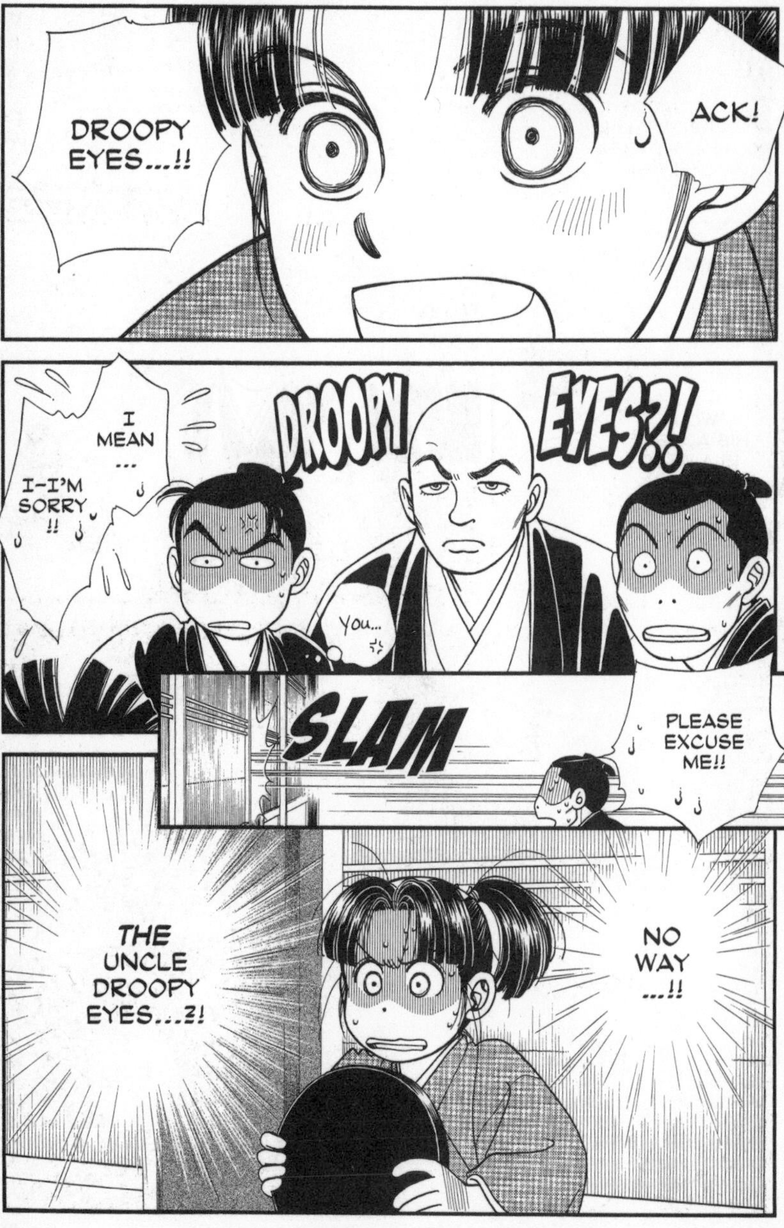
ACK!
DROOPY EYES...!!
DROOPY EYES?!
I MEAN ...
I-I'M SORRY !!
You...
PLEASE EXCUSE ME!!
SLAM
NO WAY ...!!
THE UNCLE DROOPY EYES...?!

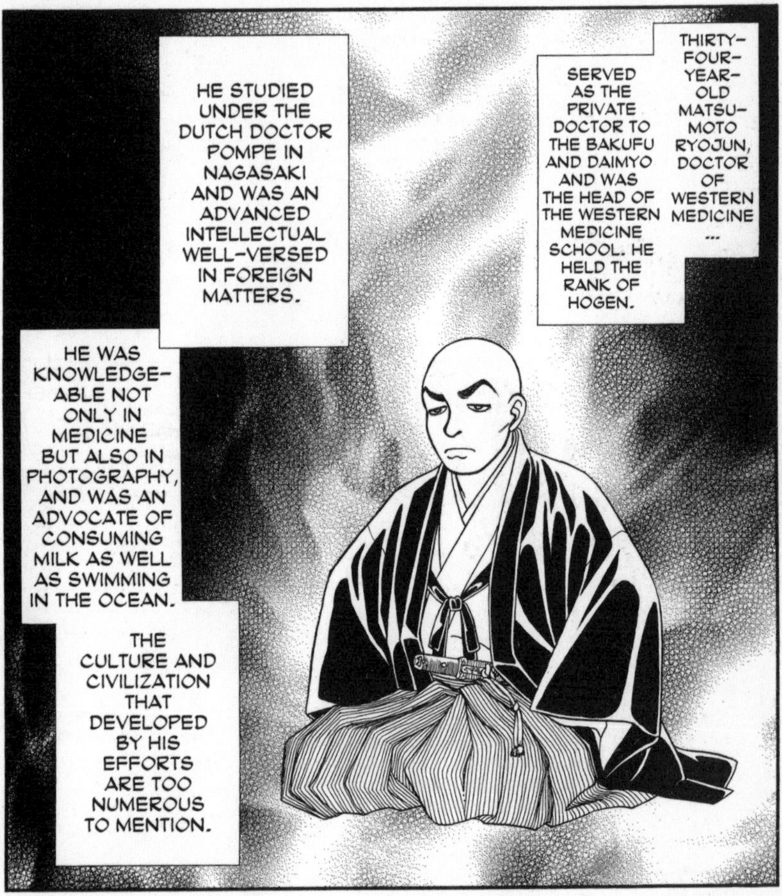
THIRTY-FOUR-YEAR-OLD MATSUMOTO RYOJUN, DOCTOR OF WESTERN MEDICINE ...
SERVED AS THE PRIVATE DOCTOR TO THE BAKUFU AND DAIMYO AND WAS THE HEAD OF THE WESTERN MEDICINE SCHOOL. HE HELD THE RANK OF HOGEN.
HE STUDIED UNDER THE DUTCH DOCTOR POMPE IN NAGASAKI AND WAS AN ADVANCED INTELLECTUAL WELL-VERSED IN FOREIGN MATTERS.
HE WAS KNOWLEDGEABLE NOT ONLY IN MEDICINE BUT ALSO IN PHOTOGRAPHY, AND WAS AN ADVOCATE OF CONSUMING MILK AS WELL AS SWIMMING IN THE OCEAN.
THE CULTURE AND CIVILIZATION THAT DEVELOPED BY HIS EFFORTS ARE TOO NUMEROUS TO MENTION.

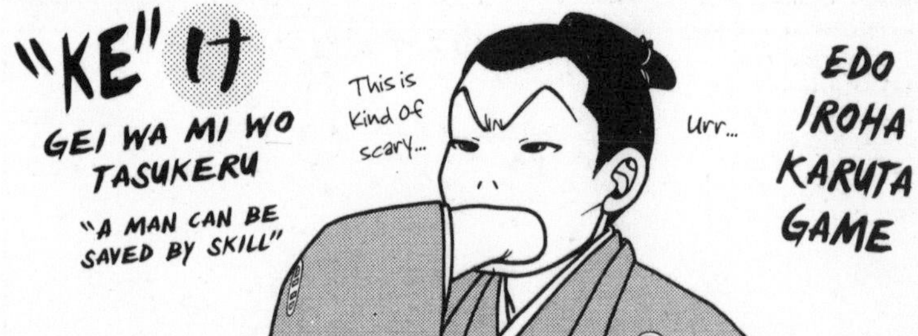
EDO IROHA KARUTA GAME
Urr...
This is kind of scary...
"KE" け
GEI WA MI WO TASUKERU
"A MAN CAN BE SAVED BY SKILL"

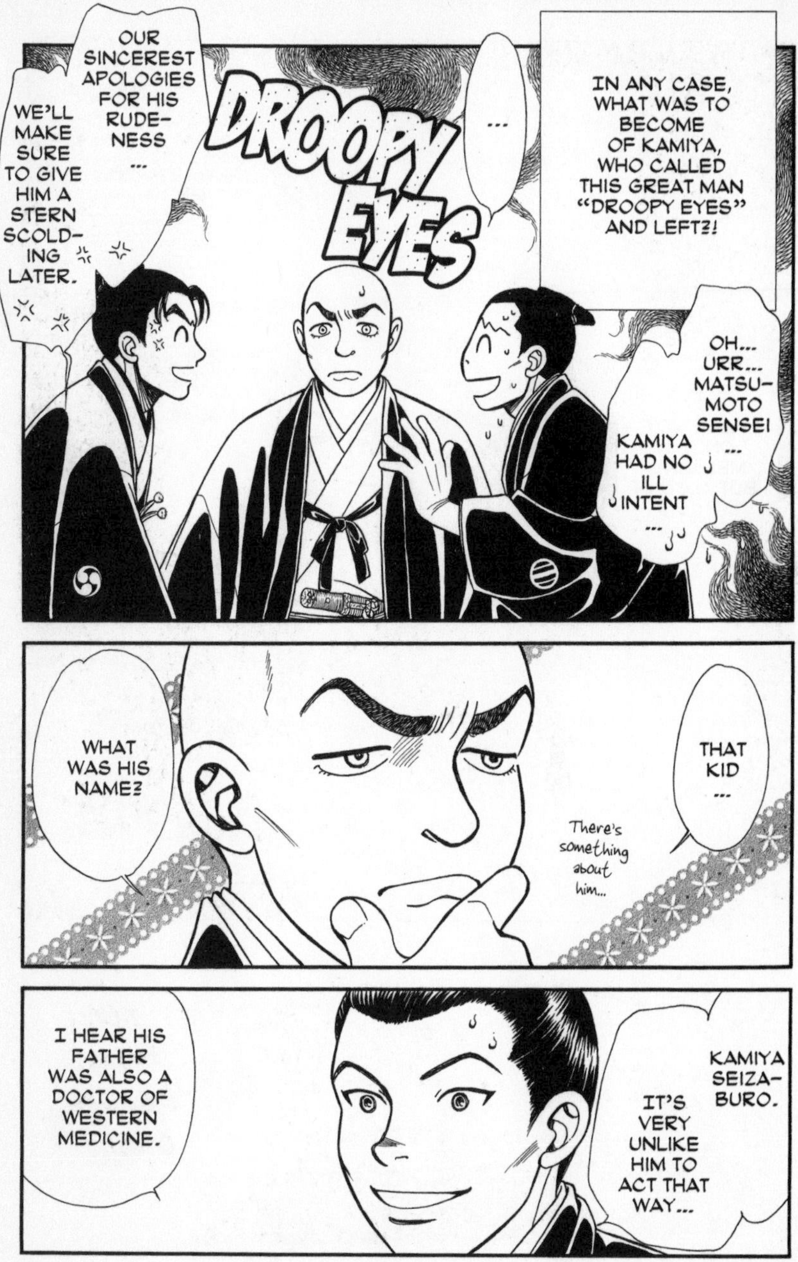
IN ANY CASE, WHAT WAS TO BECOME OF KAMIYA, WHO CALLED THIS GREAT MAN "DROOPY EYES" AND LEFT?!
...
DROOPY EYES
OUR SINCEREST APOLOGIES FOR HIS RUDENESS ...
WE'LL MAKE SURE TO GIVE HIM A STERN SCOLDING LATER.
OH... URR... MATSUMOTO SENSEI ...
KAMIYA HAD NO ILL INTENT ...
THAT KID ...
There's something about him...
WHAT WAS HIS NAME?
KAMIYA SEIZABURO.
IT'S VERY UNLIKE HIM TO ACT THAT WAY...
I HEAR HIS FATHER WAS ALSO A DOCTOR OF WESTERN MEDICINE.

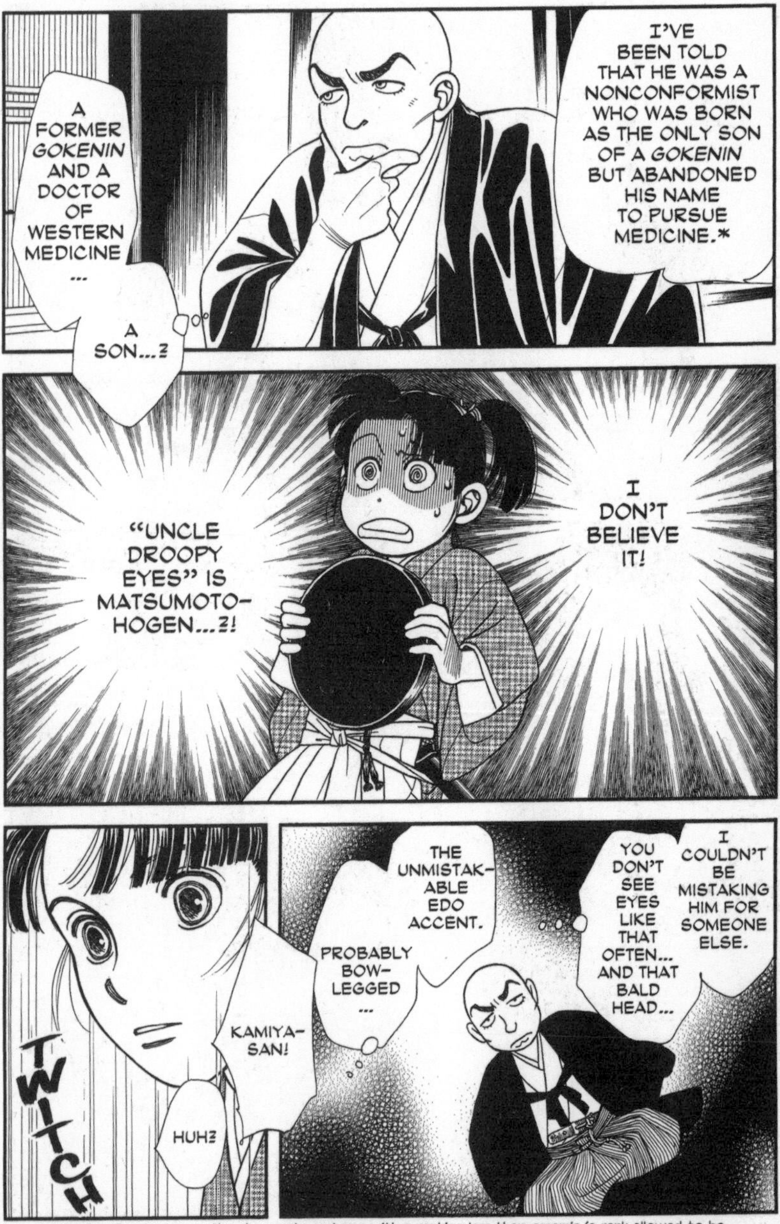
I'VE BEEN TOLD THAT HE WAS A NONCONFORMIST WHO WAS BORN AS THE ONLY SON OF A *GOKENIN* BUT ABANDONED HIS NAME TO PURSUE MEDICINE.*
A FORMER *GOKENIN* AND A DOCTOR OF WESTERN MEDICINE...
A SON...?
I DON'T BELIEVE IT!
"UNCLE DROOPY EYES" IS MATSUMOTO-HOGEN...?!
I COULDN'T BE MISTAKING HIM FOR SOMEONE ELSE.
YOU DON'T SEE EYES LIKE THAT OFTEN... AND THAT BALD HEAD...
THE UNMISTAKABLE EDO ACCENT.
PROBABLY BOW-LEGGED...
KAMIYA-SAN!
HUH?
TWITCH

*A samurai who directly serves the shogunate and one with a ranking less than *omemie* (a rank allowed to be received by the shogun). Although considered a lowly *bushi*, that rank was still seen in envy by Kondo and company.

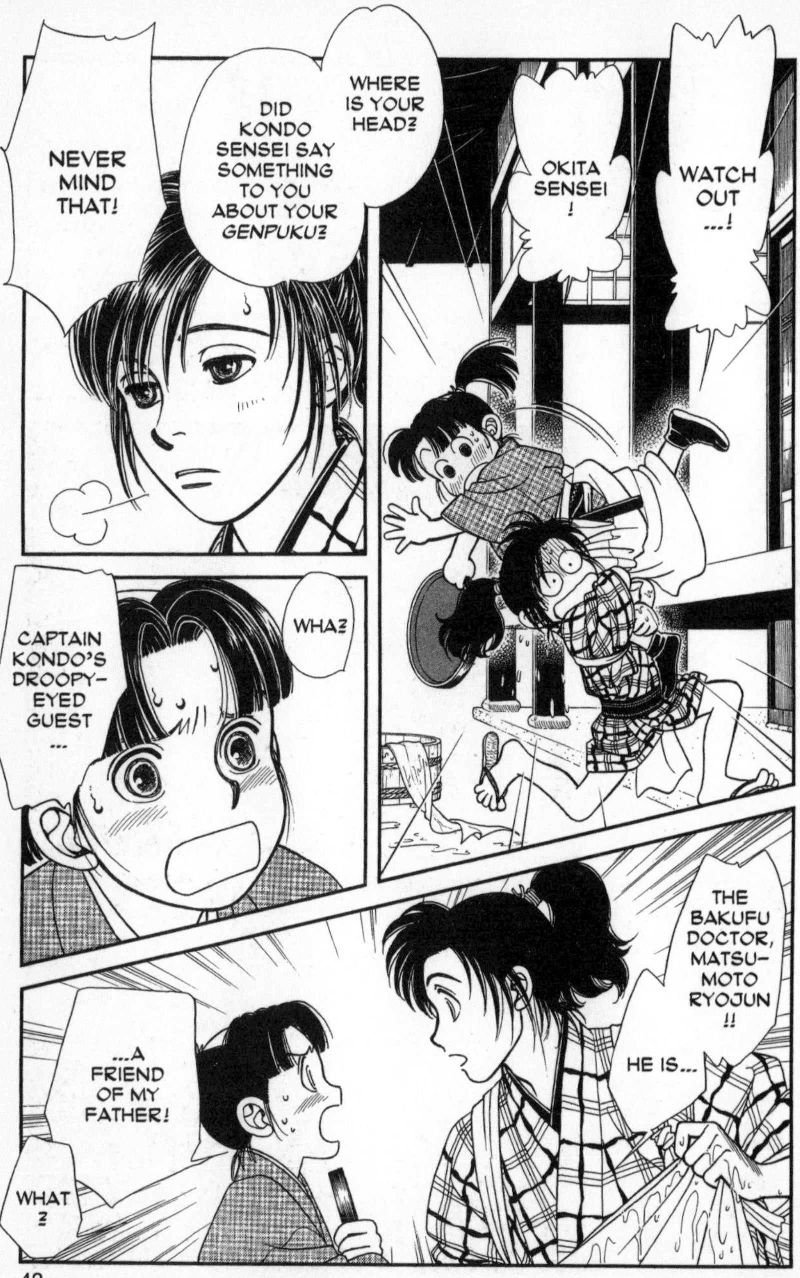
WATCH OUT ...!
OKITA SENSEI !
WHERE IS YOUR HEAD?
DID KONDO SENSEI SAY SOMETHING TO YOU ABOUT YOUR *GENPUKU*?
NEVER MIND THAT!
WHA?
CAPTAIN KONDO'S DROOPY-EYED GUEST ...
THE BAKUFU DOCTOR, MATSU-MOTO RYOJUN !!
HE IS...
...A FRIEND OF MY FATHER!
WHAT ?

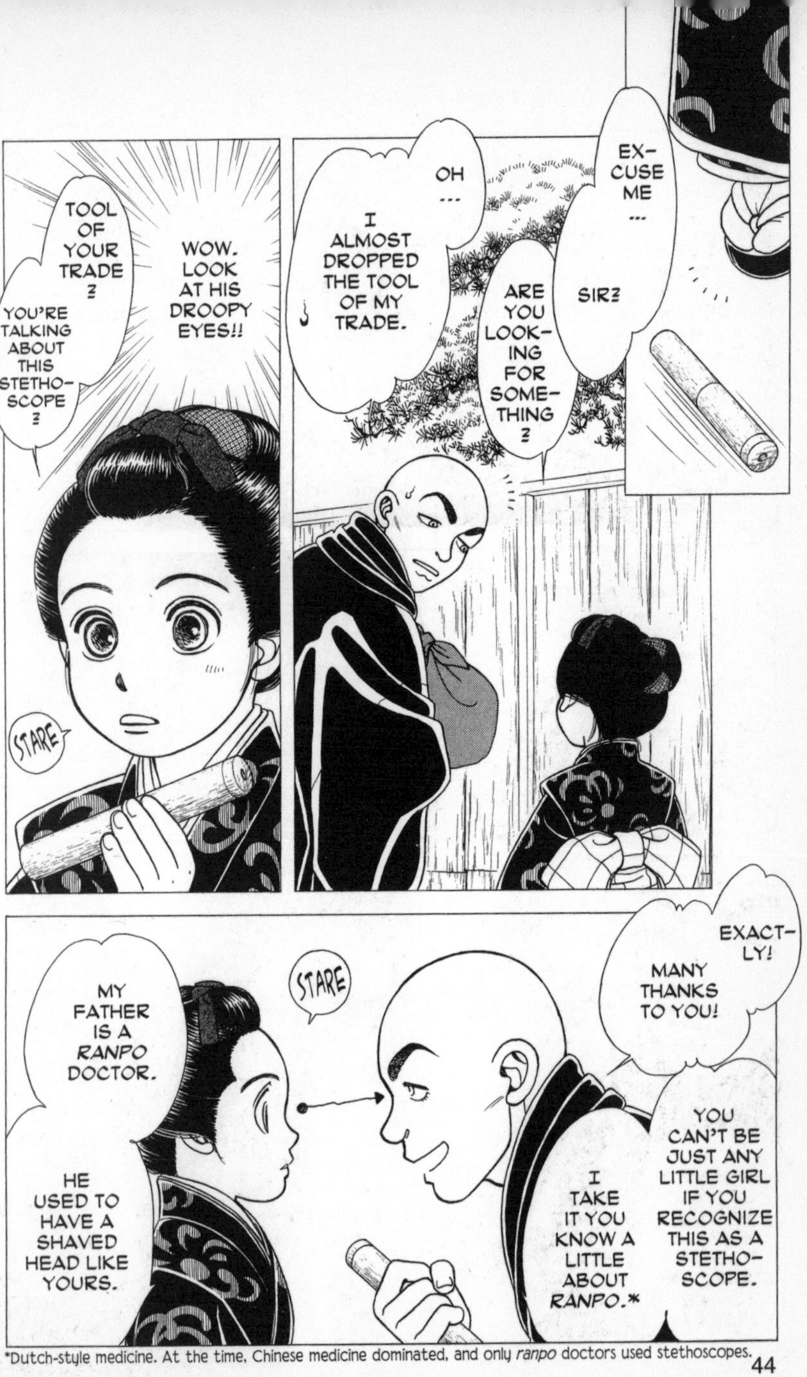
EXCUSE ME ...
SIR?
ARE YOU LOOKING FOR SOMETHING?
OH ...
I ALMOST DROPPED THE TOOL OF MY TRADE.
WOW. LOOK AT HIS DROOPY EYES!!
TOOL OF YOUR TRADE?
YOU'RE TALKING ABOUT THIS STETHOSCOPE?
STARE
EXACTLY!
MANY THANKS TO YOU!
YOU CAN'T BE JUST ANY LITTLE GIRL IF YOU RECOGNIZE THIS AS A STETHOSCOPE.
I TAKE IT YOU KNOW A LITTLE ABOUT *RANPO*.*
STARE
MY FATHER IS A *RANPO* DOCTOR.
HE USED TO HAVE A SHAVED HEAD LIKE YOURS.

*Dutch-style medicine. At the time, Chinese medicine dominated, and only *ranpo* doctors used stethoscopes.

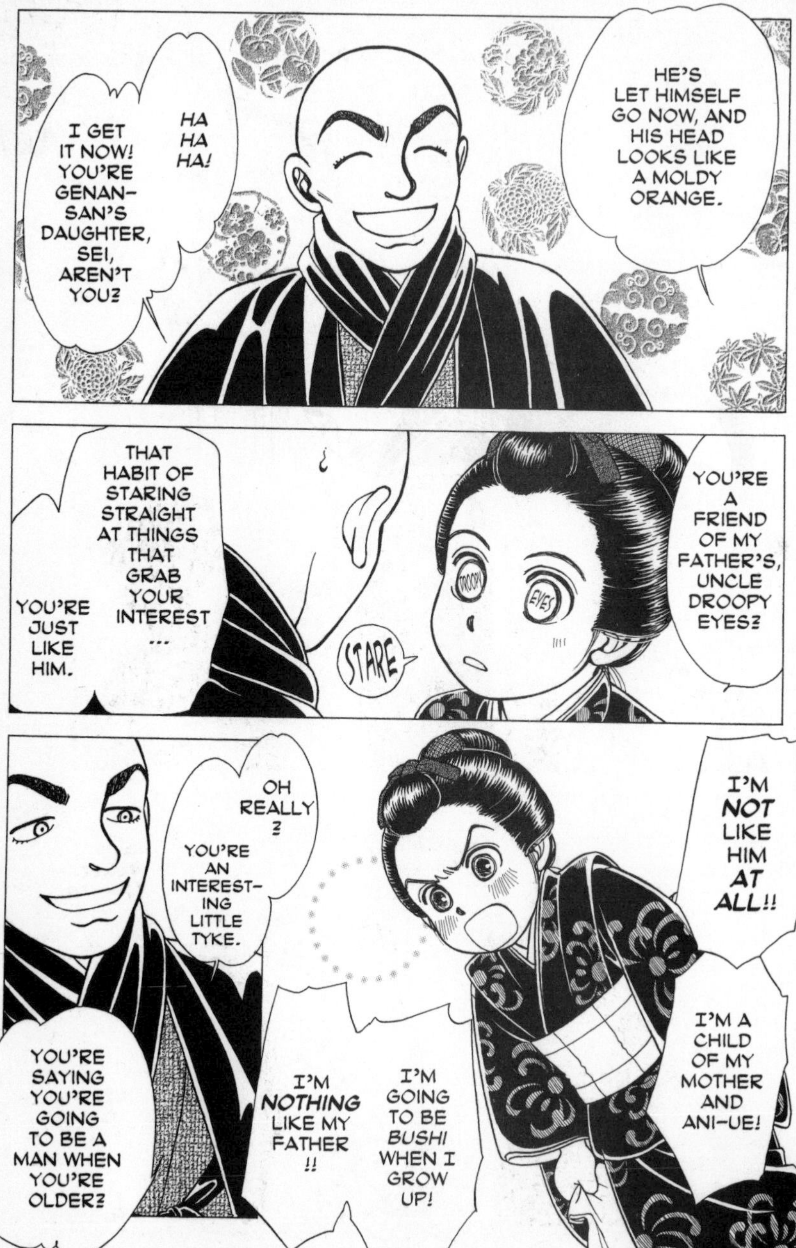
HE'S LET HIMSELF GO NOW, AND HIS HEAD LOOKS LIKE A MOLDY ORANGE.
HA HA HA!
I GET IT NOW! YOU'RE GENAN-SAN'S DAUGHTER, SEI, AREN'T YOU?
YOU'RE A FRIEND OF MY FATHER'S, UNCLE DROOPY EYES?
DROOPY
EYES
STARE
THAT HABIT OF STARING STRAIGHT AT THINGS THAT GRAB YOUR INTEREST...
YOU'RE JUST LIKE HIM.
I'M **NOT** LIKE HIM **AT ALL**!!
OH REALLY?
YOU'RE AN INTERESTING LITTLE TYKE.
I'M A CHILD OF MY MOTHER AND ANI-UE!
I'M GOING TO BE *BUSHI* WHEN I GROW UP!
I'M ***NOTHING*** LIKE MY FATHER!!
YOU'RE SAYING YOU'RE GOING TO BE A MAN WHEN YOU'RE OLDER?

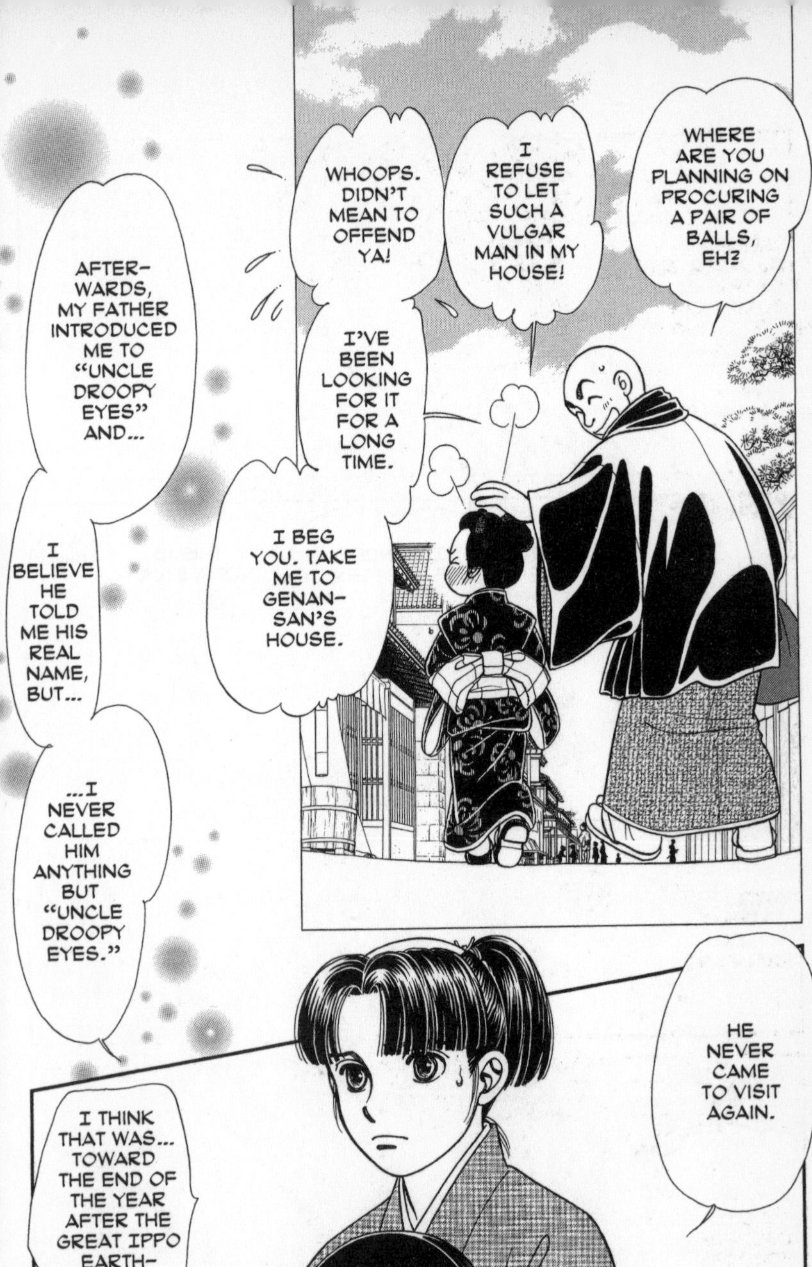
WHERE ARE YOU PLANNING ON PROCURING A PAIR OF BALLS, EH?
I REFUSE TO LET SUCH A VULGAR MAN IN MY HOUSE!
WHOOPS. DIDN'T MEAN TO OFFEND YA!
I'VE BEEN LOOKING FOR IT FOR A LONG TIME.
I BEG YOU. TAKE ME TO GENAN-SAN'S HOUSE.
AFTER-WARDS, MY FATHER INTRODUCED ME TO "UNCLE DROOPY EYES" AND...
I BELIEVE HE TOLD ME HIS REAL NAME, BUT...
...I NEVER CALLED HIM ANYTHING BUT "UNCLE DROOPY EYES."
HE NEVER CAME TO VISIT AGAIN.
I THINK THAT WAS... TOWARD THE END OF THE YEAR AFTER THE GREAT IPPO EARTH-QUAKE.*

*Otherwise known as the Great Ansei Earthquake of the second year of Ansei (1855).

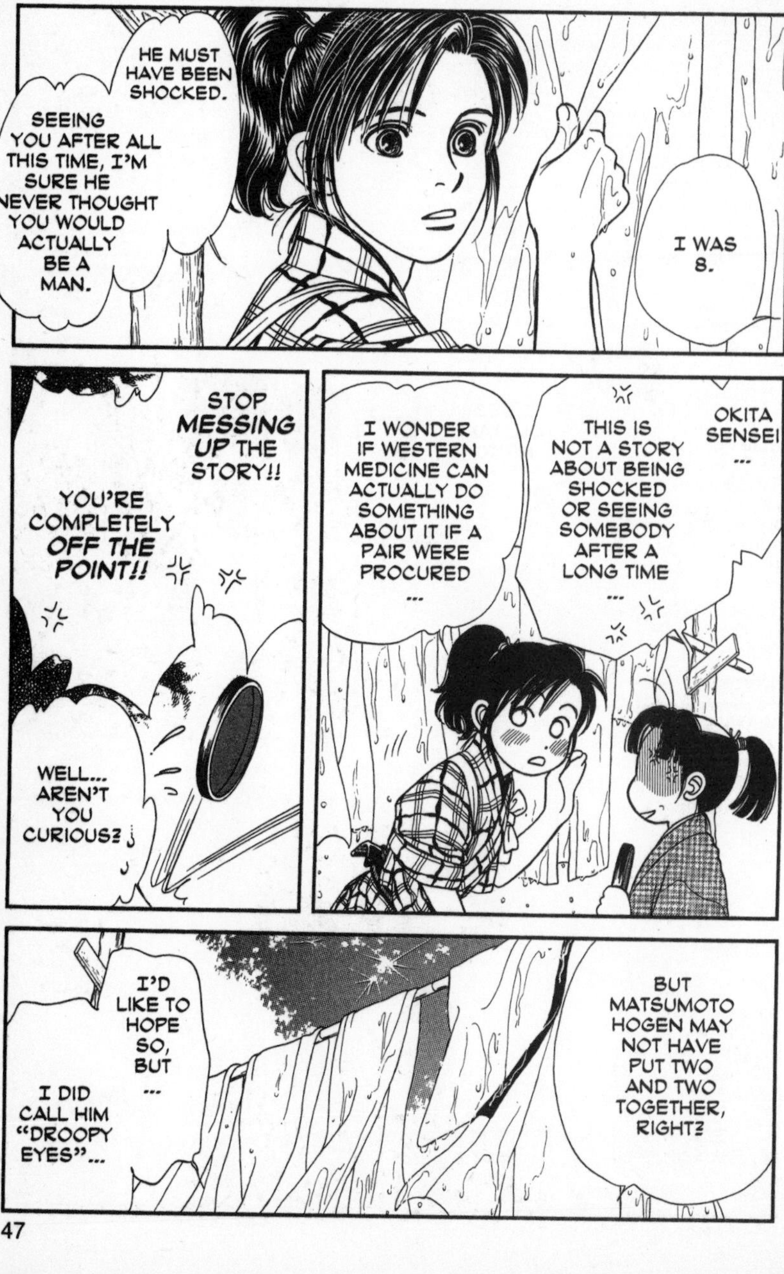
HE MUST HAVE BEEN SHOCKED.
SEEING YOU AFTER ALL THIS TIME, I'M SURE HE NEVER THOUGHT YOU WOULD ACTUALLY BE A MAN.
I WAS 8.
OKITA SENSEI...
THIS IS NOT A STORY ABOUT BEING SHOCKED OR SEEING SOMEBODY AFTER A LONG TIME...
I WONDER IF WESTERN MEDICINE CAN ACTUALLY DO SOMETHING ABOUT IT IF A PAIR WERE PROCURED...
STOP MESSING UP THE STORY!!
YOU'RE COMPLETELY OFF THE POINT!!
WELL... AREN'T YOU CURIOUS?
BUT MATSUMOTO HOGEN MAY NOT HAVE PUT TWO AND TWO TOGETHER, RIGHT?
I'D LIKE TO HOPE SO, BUT...
I DID CALL HIM "DROOPY EYES"...

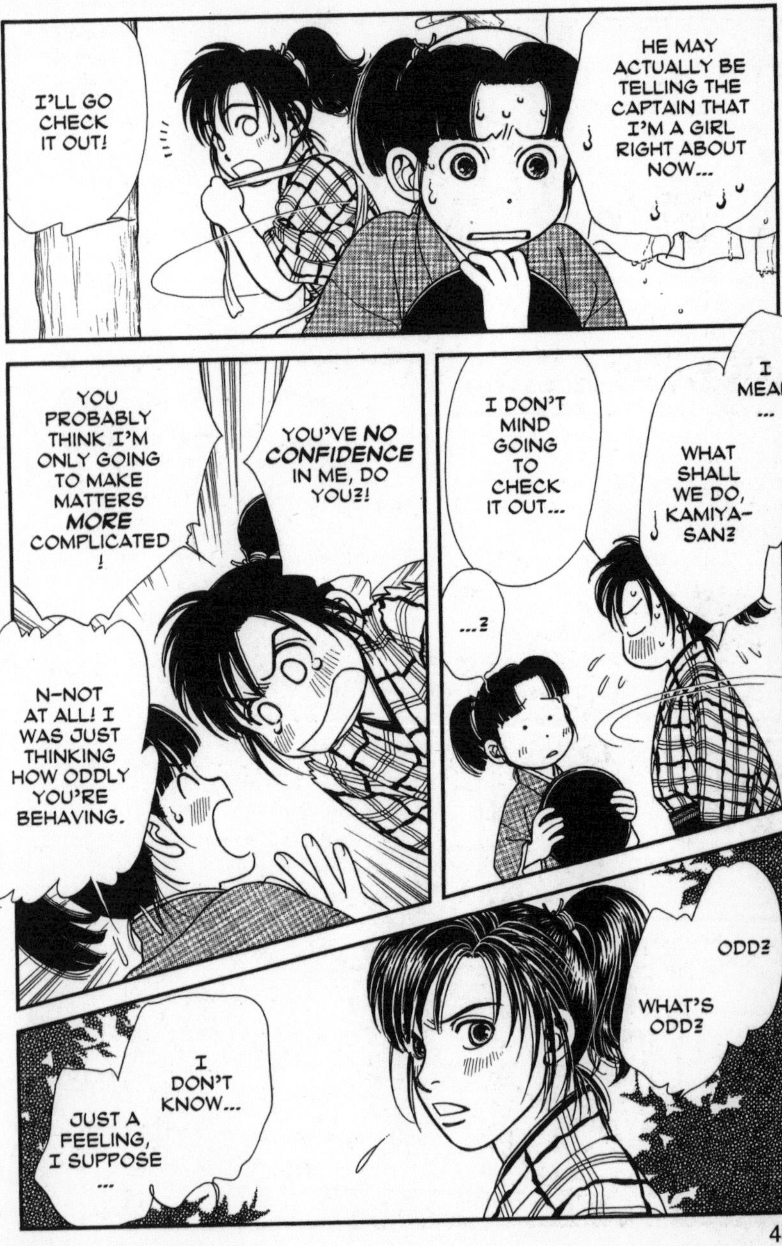
HE MAY ACTUALLY BE TELLING THE CAPTAIN THAT I'M A GIRL RIGHT ABOUT NOW...
I'LL GO CHECK IT OUT!
I MEAN...
WHAT SHALL WE DO, KAMIYA-SAN?
I DON'T MIND GOING TO CHECK IT OUT...
...?
YOU'VE NO CONFIDENCE IN ME, DO YOU?!
YOU PROBABLY THINK I'M ONLY GOING TO MAKE MATTERS MORE COMPLICATED!
N-NOT AT ALL! I WAS JUST THINKING HOW ODDLY YOU'RE BEHAVING.
ODD?
WHAT'S ODD?
I DON'T KNOW...
JUST A FEELING, I SUPPOSE...

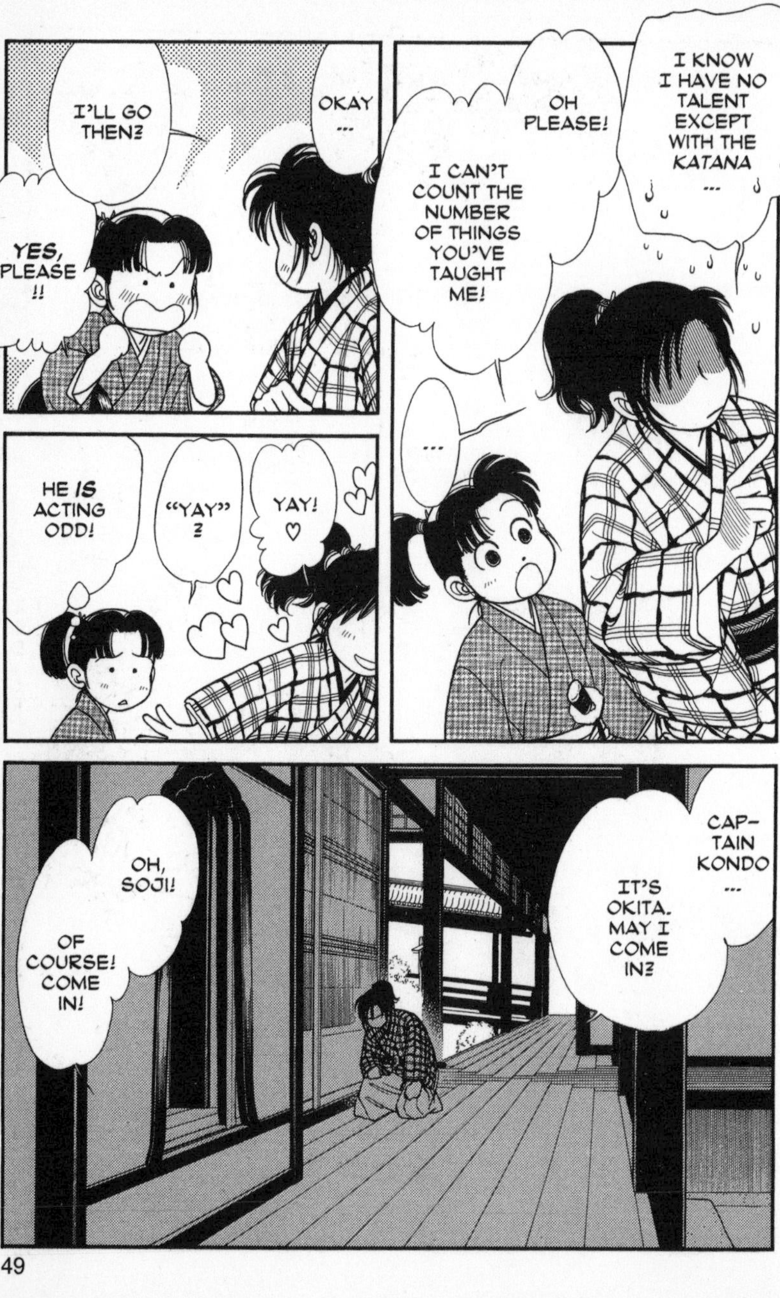
I KNOW I HAVE NO TALENT EXCEPT WITH THE *KATANA* ...
OH PLEASE!
I CAN'T COUNT THE NUMBER OF THINGS YOU'VE TAUGHT ME!
...
OKAY ...
I'LL GO THEN?
YES, PLEASE !!
YAY! ♥
"YAY" ?
HE *IS* ACTING ODD!
CAP-TAIN KONDO ...
IT'S OKITA. MAY I COME IN?
OH, SOJI!
OF COURSE! COME IN!

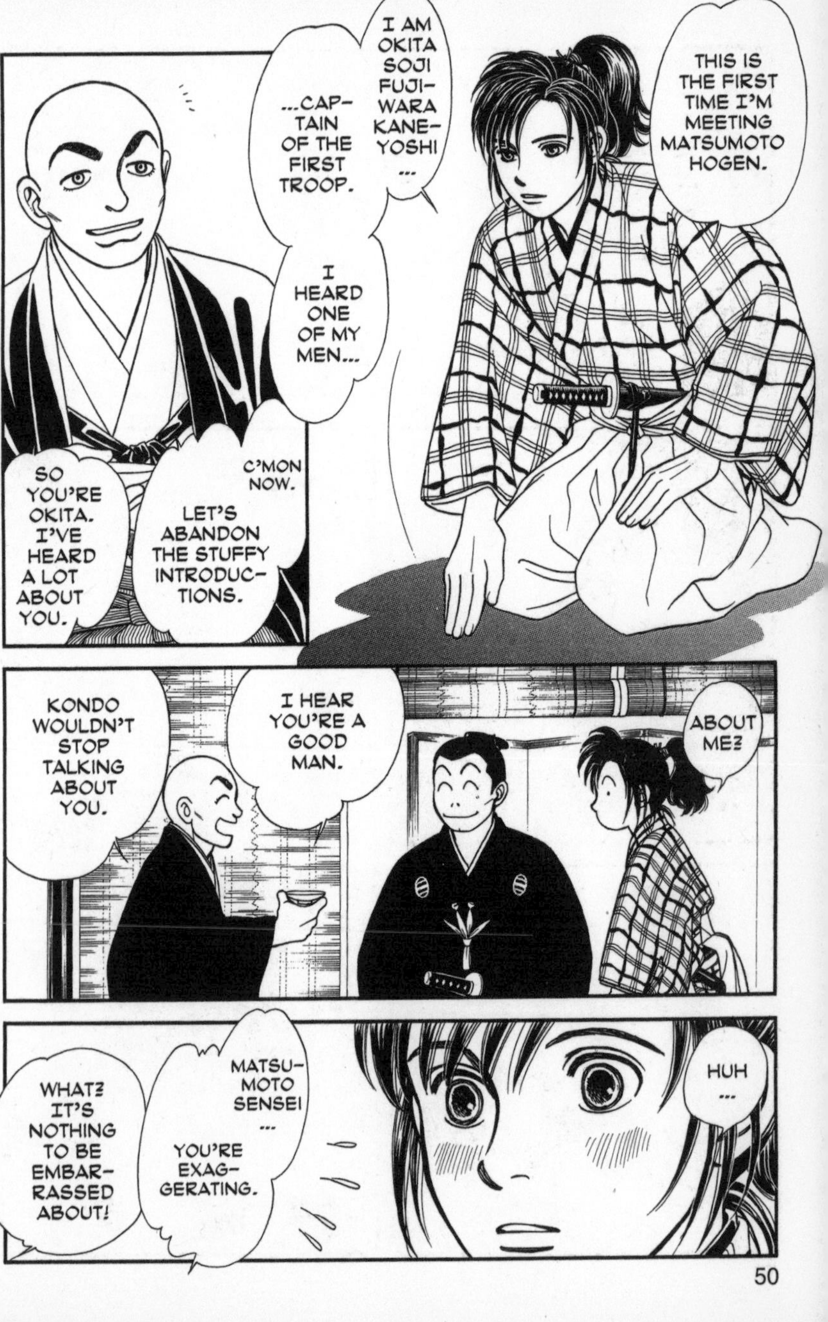
THIS IS THE FIRST TIME I'M MEETING MATSUMOTO HOGEN.
I AM OKITA SOJI FUJIWARA KANEYOSHI...
...CAPTAIN OF THE FIRST TROOP.
I HEARD ONE OF MY MEN...
C'MON NOW.
LET'S ABANDON THE STUFFY INTRODUCTIONS.
SO YOU'RE OKITA. I'VE HEARD A LOT ABOUT YOU.
ABOUT ME?
I HEAR YOU'RE A GOOD MAN.
KONDO WOULDN'T STOP TALKING ABOUT YOU.
HUH...
MATSUMOTO SENSEI...
YOU'RE EXAGGERATING.
WHAT? IT'S NOTHING TO BE EMBARRASSED ABOUT!

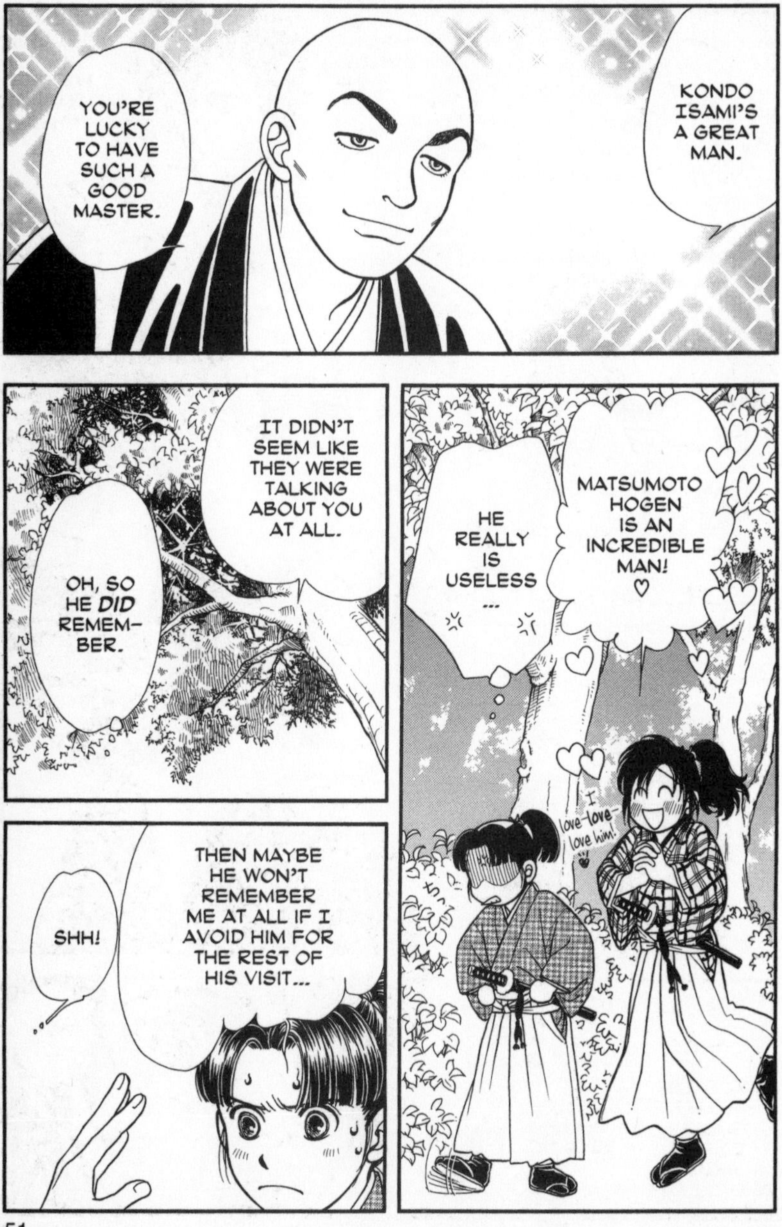
KONDO ISAMI'S A GREAT MAN.
YOU'RE LUCKY TO HAVE SUCH A GOOD MASTER.
MATSUMOTO HOGEN IS AN INCREDIBLE MAN! ♡
HE REALLY IS USELESS ...
I love-love-love him!
IT DIDN'T SEEM LIKE THEY WERE TALKING ABOUT YOU AT ALL.
OH, SO HE *DID* REMEMBER.
THEN MAYBE HE WON'T REMEMBER ME AT ALL IF I AVOID HIM FOR THE REST OF HIS VISIT...
SHH!

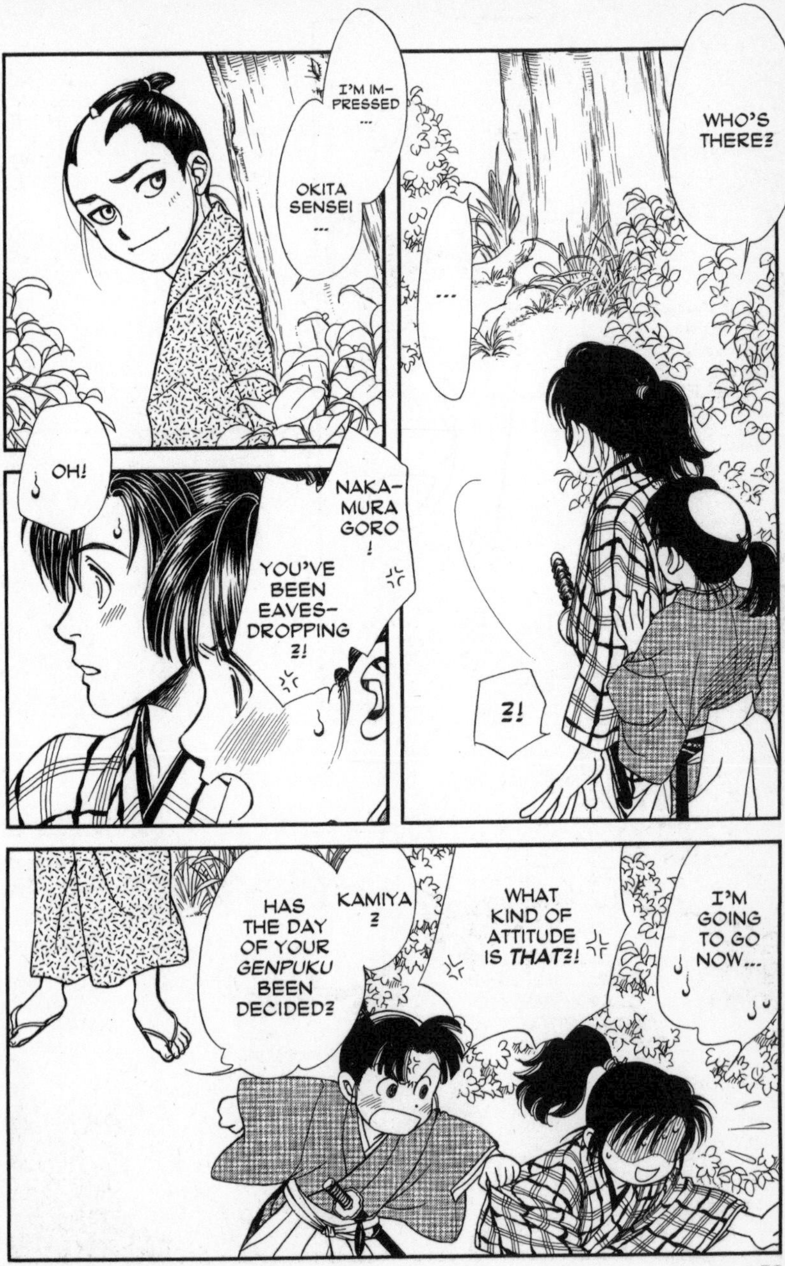
WHO'S THERE?
...
?!
I'M IM-PRESSED ...
OKITA SENSEI ...
NAKA-MURA GORO!
YOU'VE BEEN EAVES-DROPPING?!
OH!
I'M GOING TO GO NOW...
WHAT KIND OF ATTITUDE IS *THAT*?!
KAMIYA?
HAS THE DAY OF YOUR *GENPUKU* BEEN DECIDED?

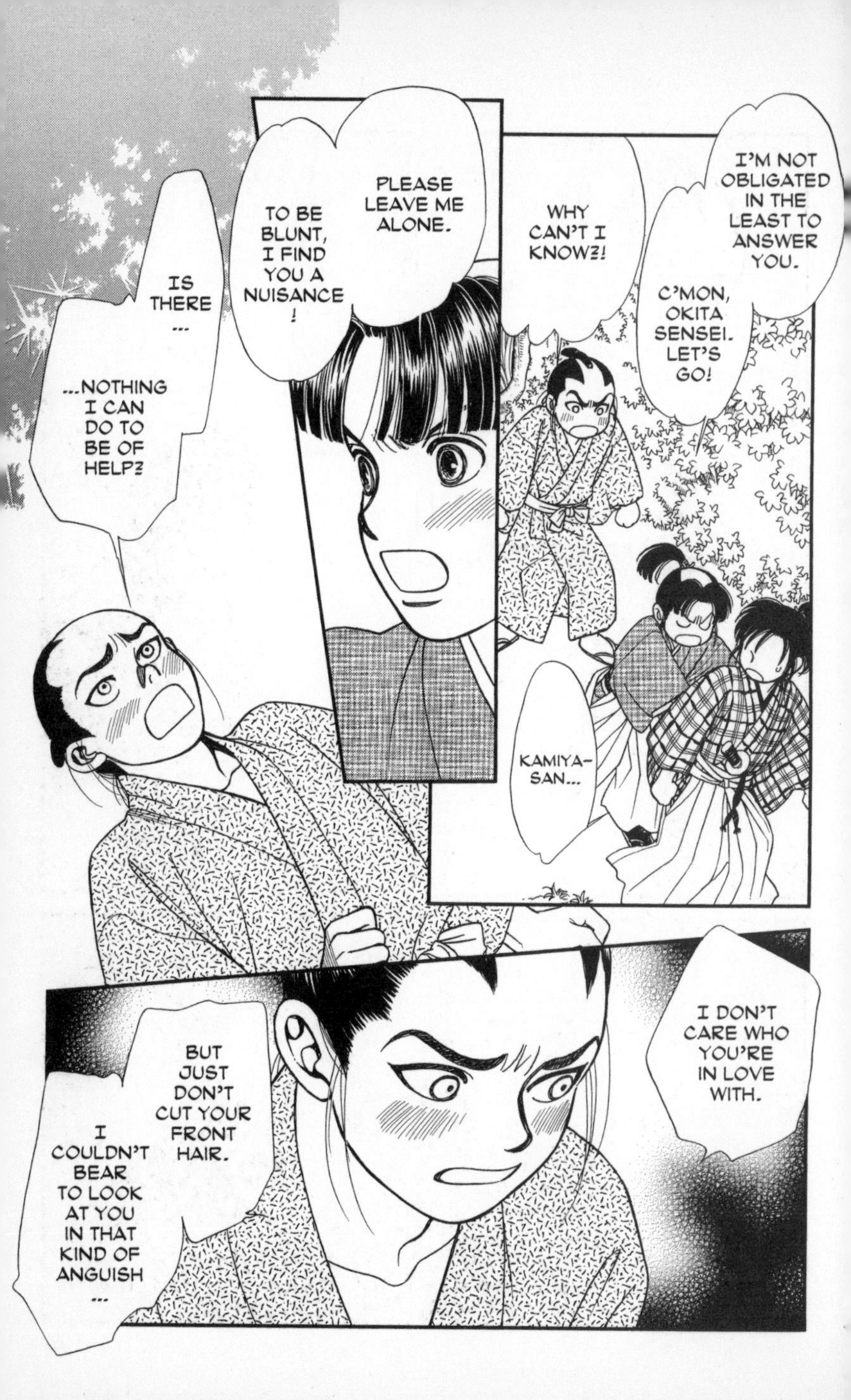
I'M NOT OBLIGATED IN THE LEAST TO ANSWER YOU.
WHY CAN'T I KNOW?!
C'MON, OKITA SENSEI. LET'S GO!
KAMIYA-SAN...
PLEASE LEAVE ME ALONE.
TO BE BLUNT, I FIND YOU A NUISANCE!
IS THERE...
...NOTHING I CAN DO TO BE OF HELP?
I DON'T CARE WHO YOU'RE IN LOVE WITH.
BUT JUST DON'T CUT YOUR FRONT HAIR.
I COULDN'T BEAR TO LOOK AT YOU IN THAT KIND OF ANGUISH...

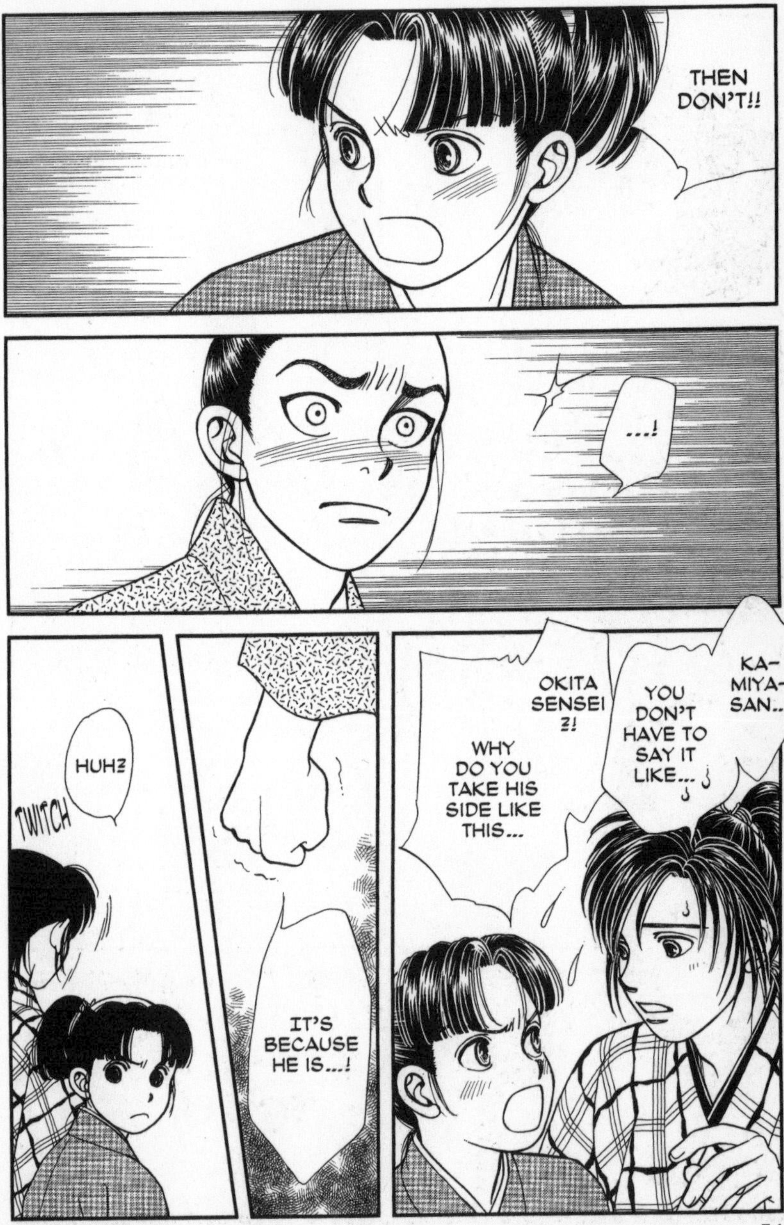
THEN DON'T!!
...!
KA-MIYA-SAN...
YOU DON'T HAVE TO SAY IT LIKE...
OKITA SENSEI ?!
WHY DO YOU TAKE HIS SIDE LIKE THIS...
IT'S BECAUSE HE IS...!
HUH?
TWITCH

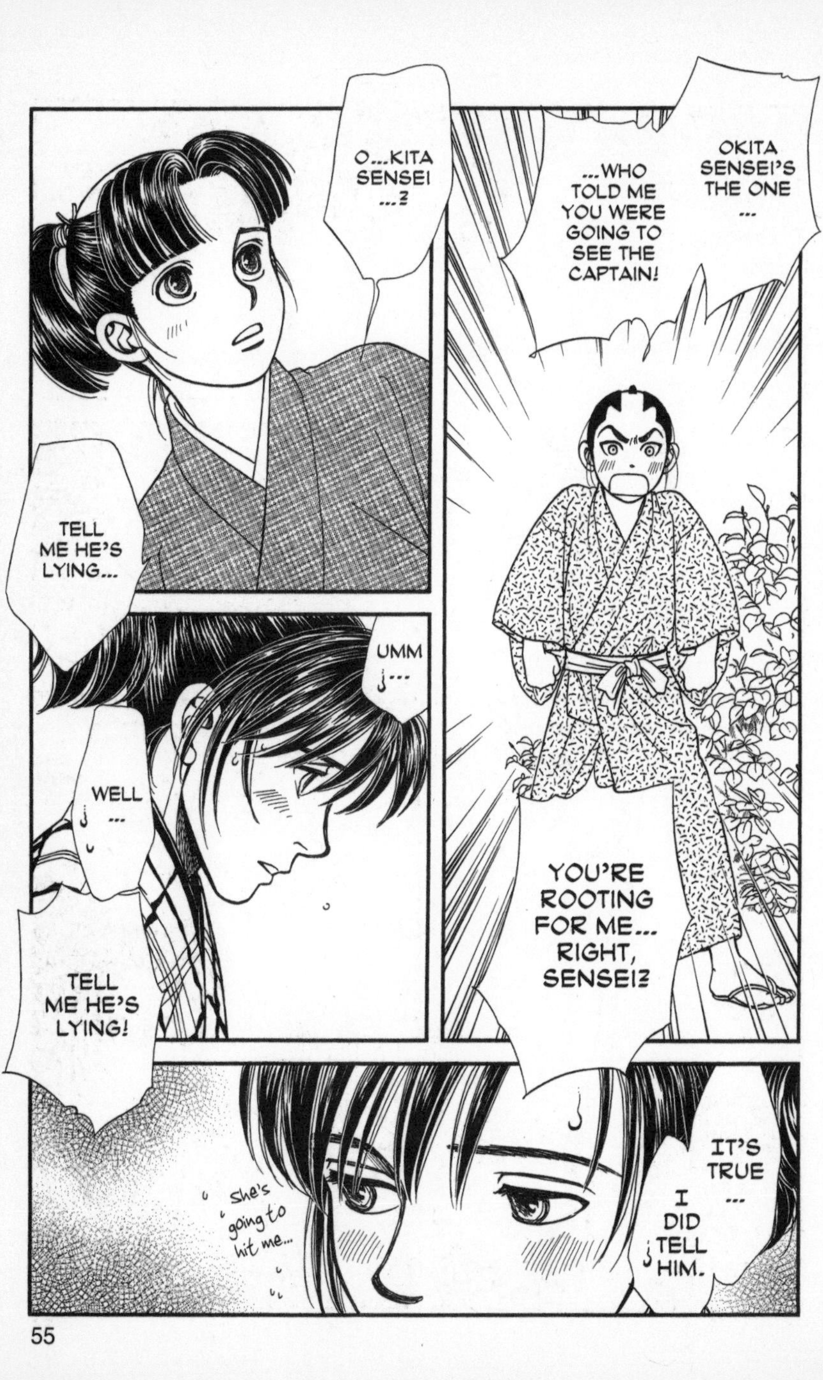
OKITA SENSEI'S THE ONE...
...WHO TOLD ME YOU WERE GOING TO SEE THE CAPTAIN!
YOU'RE ROOTING FOR ME... RIGHT, SENSEI?
O...KITA SENSEI...?
TELL ME HE'S LYING...
UMM...
WELL...
TELL ME HE'S LYING!
IT'S TRUE... I DID TELL HIM.
She's going to hit me...

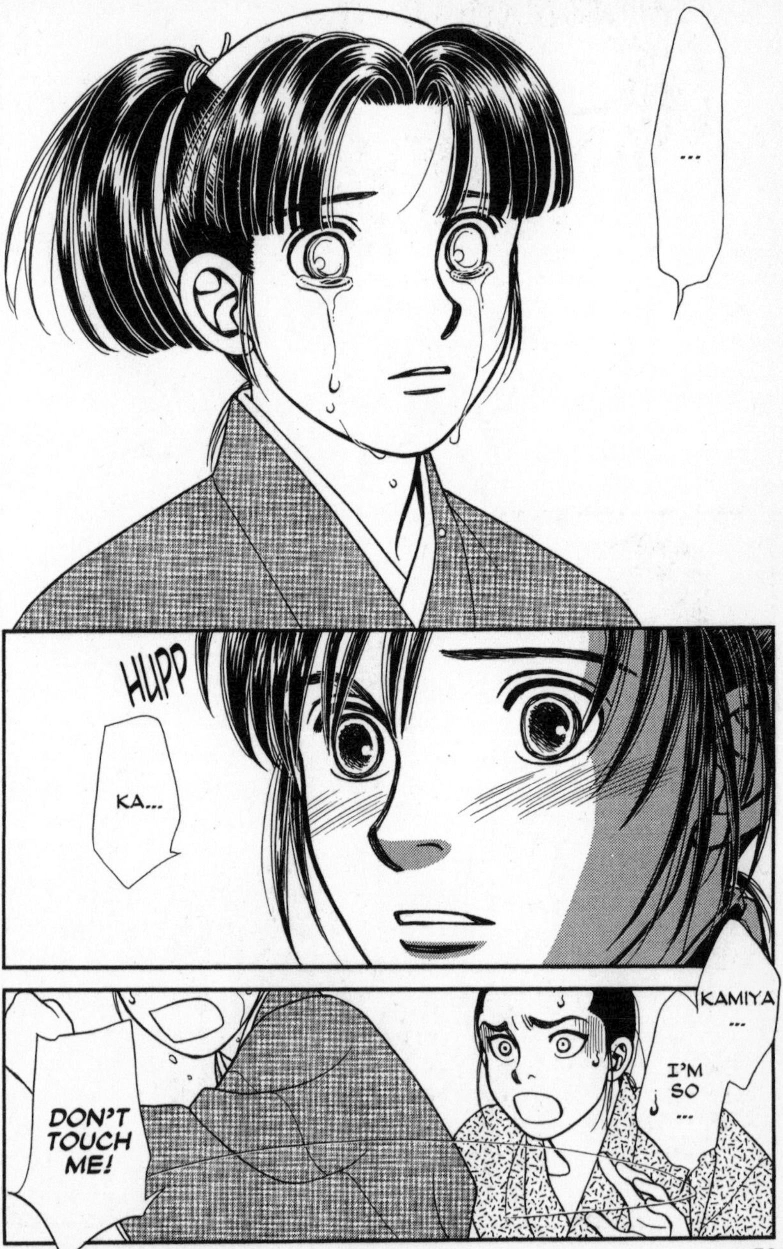
...
HUPP
KA...
KAMIYA ...
I'M SO ...
DON'T TOUCH ME!

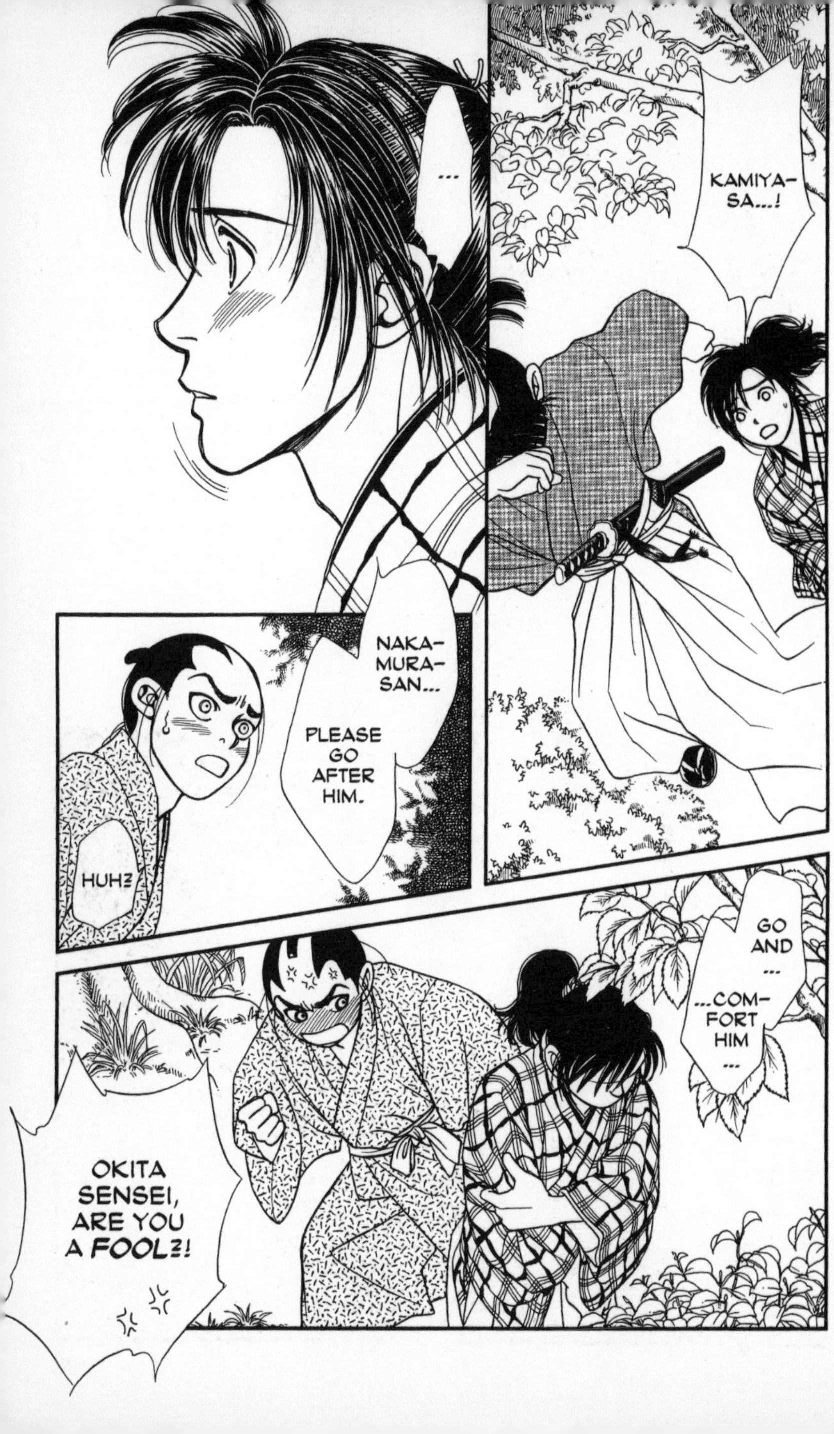
KAMIYA-SA...!
...
NAKA-MURA-SAN...
PLEASE GO AFTER HIM.
HUH?
GO AND ...
...COM-FORT HIM ...
OKITA SENSEI, ARE YOU A *FOOL*?!

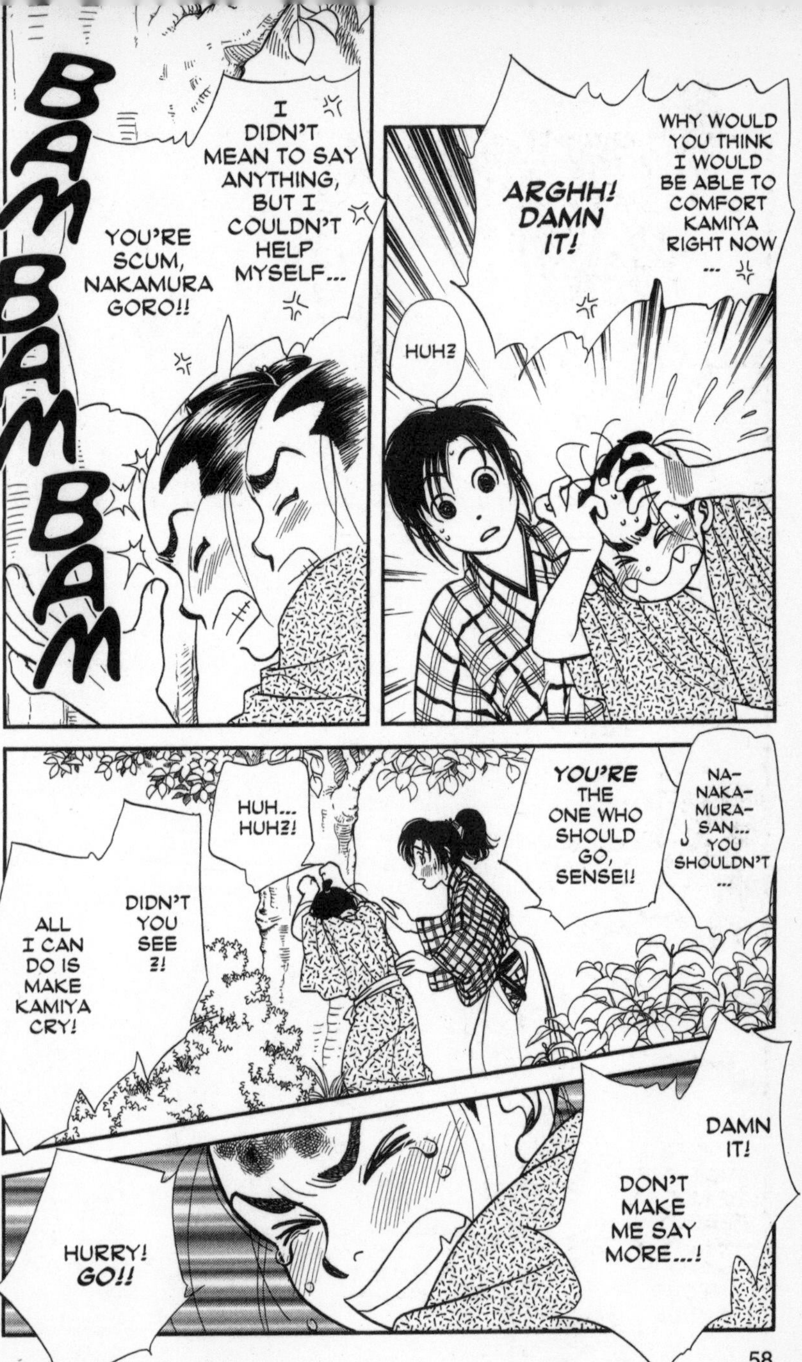
WHY WOULD YOU THINK I WOULD BE ABLE TO COMFORT KAMIYA RIGHT NOW ...
ARGHH! DAMN IT!
HUH?
I DIDN'T MEAN TO SAY ANYTHING, BUT I COULDN'T HELP MYSELF...
YOU'RE SCUM, NAKAMURA GORO!!
BAM BAM BAM BAM
NA-NAKAMURA-SAN... YOU SHOULDN'T ...
YOU'RE THE ONE WHO SHOULD GO, SENSEI!
HUH... HUH?!
DIDN'T YOU SEE?!
ALL I CAN DO IS MAKE KAMIYA CRY!
DAMN IT!
DON'T MAKE ME SAY MORE...!
HURRY! GO!!

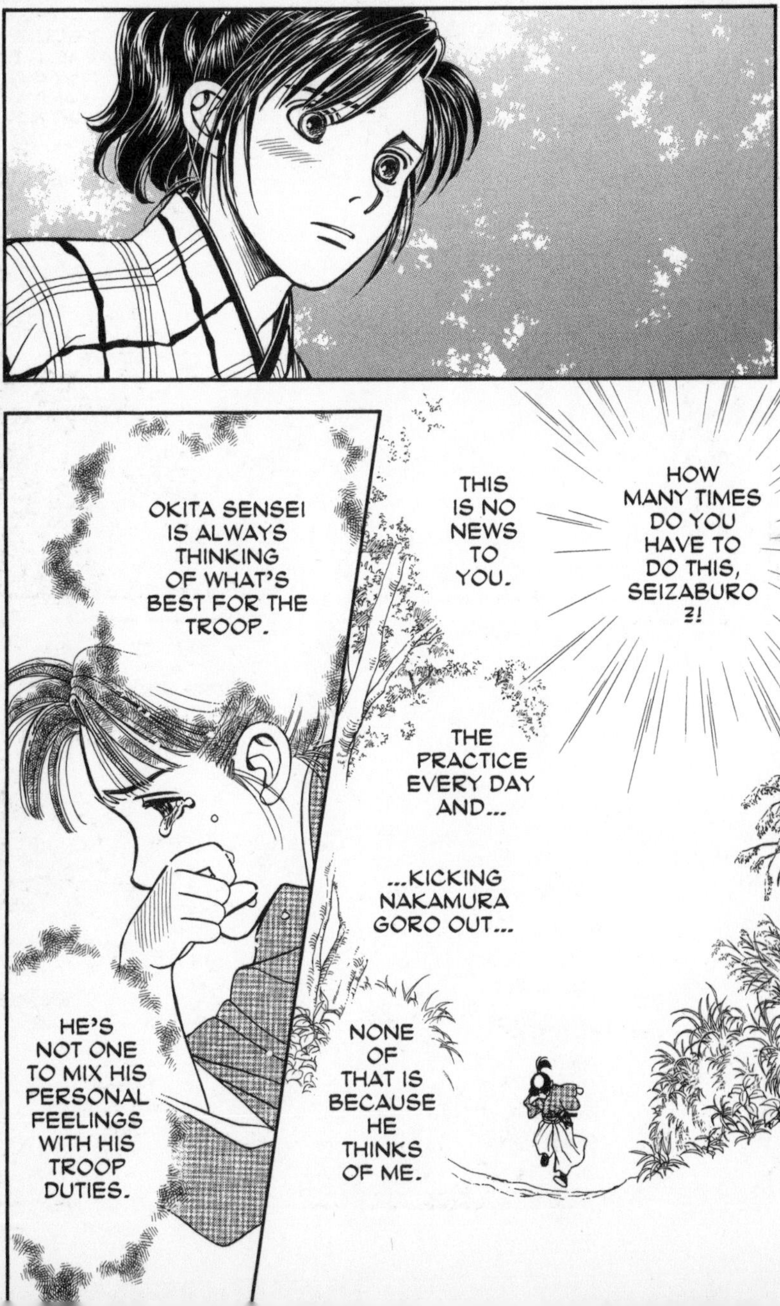
HOW MANY TIMES DO YOU HAVE TO DO THIS, SEIZABURO?!
THIS IS NO NEWS TO YOU.
OKITA SENSEI IS ALWAYS THINKING OF WHAT'S BEST FOR THE TROOP.
THE PRACTICE EVERY DAY AND...
...KICKING NAKAMURA GORO OUT...
NONE OF THAT IS BECAUSE HE THINKS OF ME.
HE'S NOT ONE TO MIX HIS PERSONAL FEELINGS WITH HIS TROOP DUTIES.

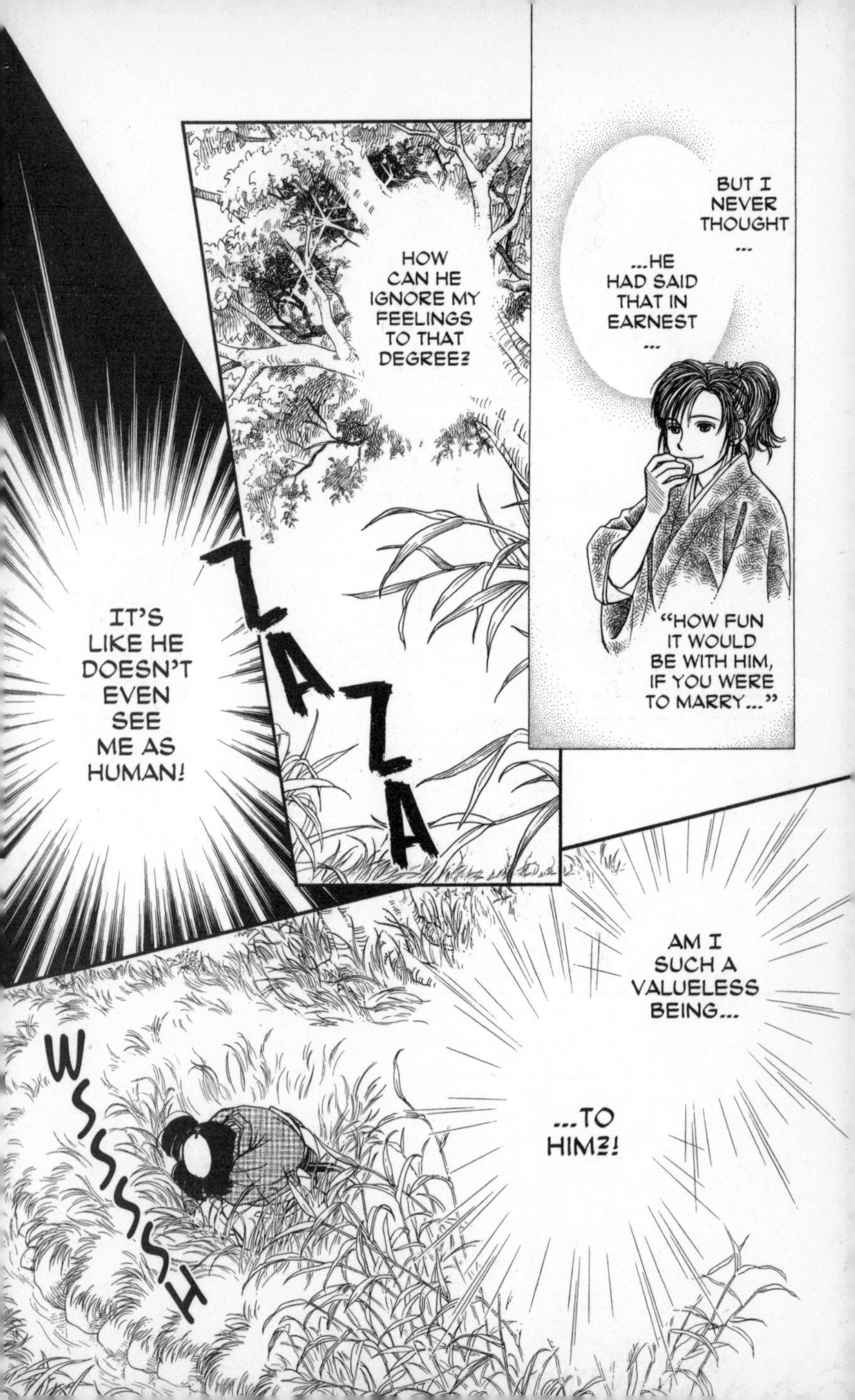
BUT I NEVER THOUGHT...
...HE HAD SAID THAT IN EARNEST...
"HOW FUN IT WOULD BE WITH HIM, IF YOU WERE TO MARRY..."
HOW CAN HE IGNORE MY FEELINGS TO THAT DEGREE?
ZAZA
IT'S LIKE HE DOESN'T EVEN SEE ME AS HUMAN!
AM I SUCH A VALUELESS BEING...
...TO HIM?!
WSSSSH

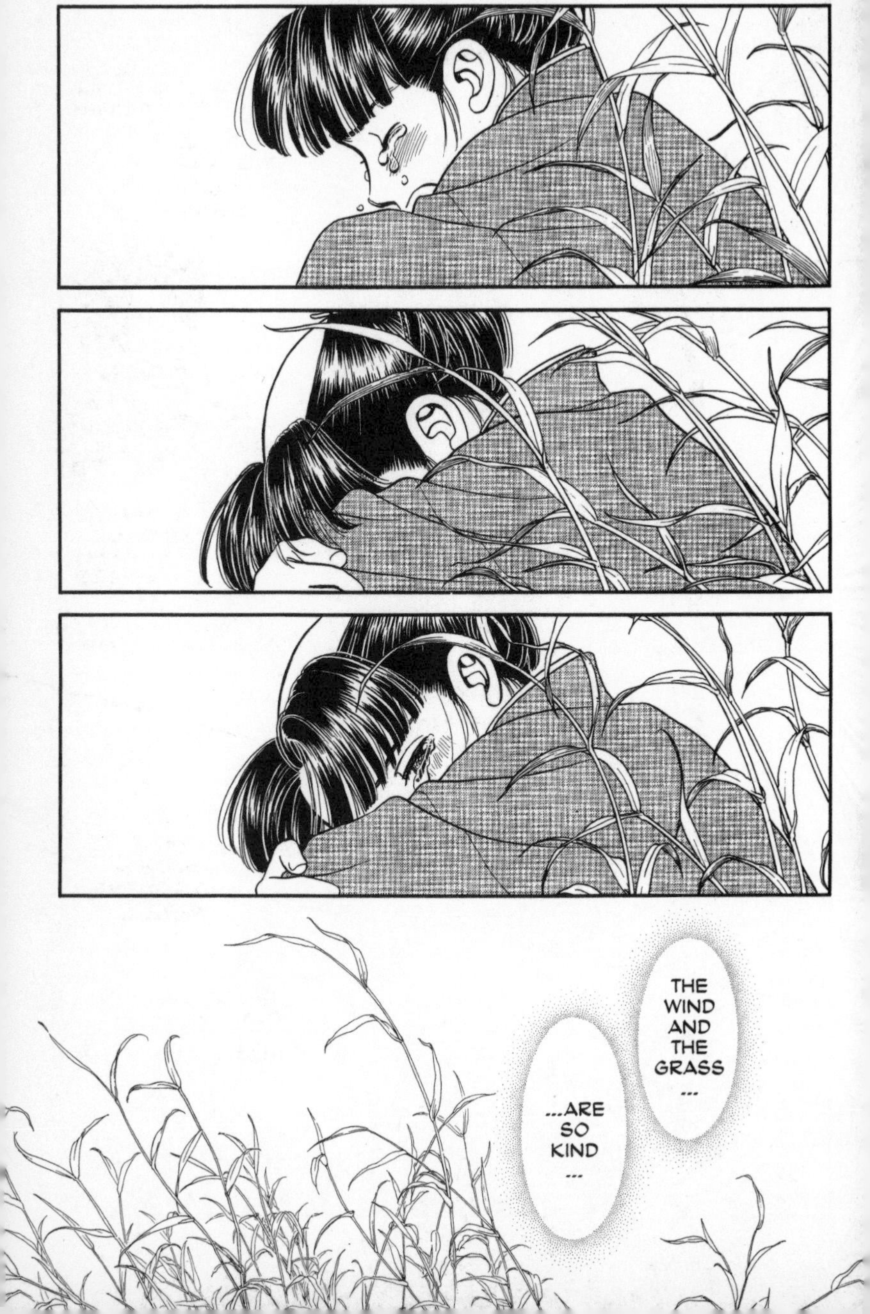
THE WIND AND THE GRASS...
...ARE SO KIND...

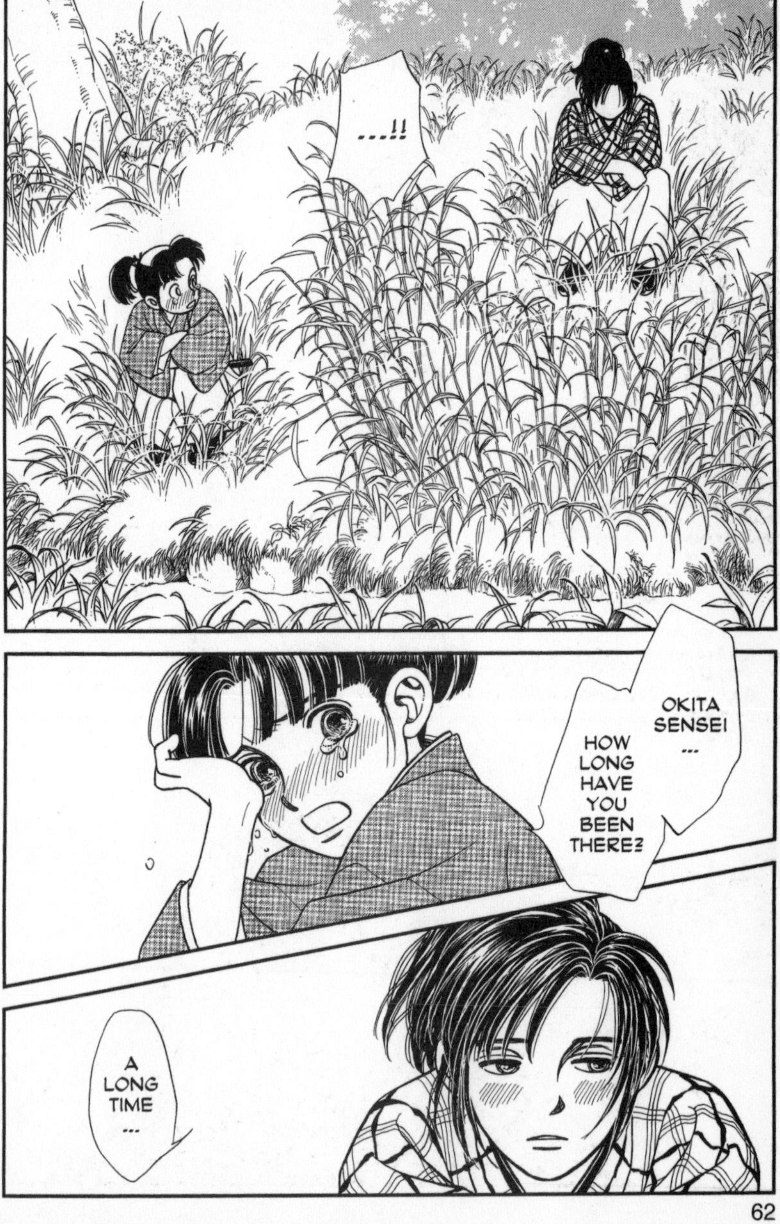
...!!
OKITA SENSEI ...
HOW LONG HAVE YOU BEEN THERE?
A LONG TIME ...

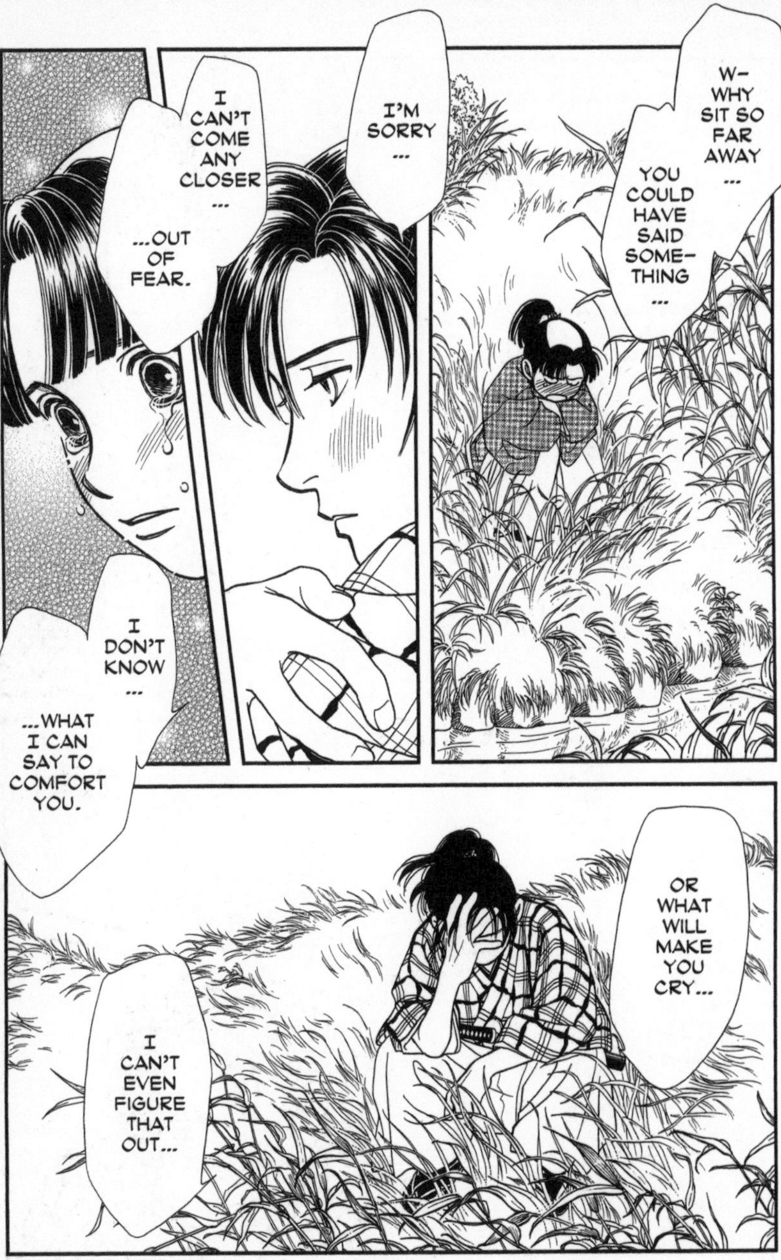
W- WHY SIT SO FAR AWAY ...
YOU COULD HAVE SAID SOME- THING ...
I'M SORRY ...
I CAN'T COME ANY CLOSER ...
...OUT OF FEAR.
I DON'T KNOW ...
...WHAT I CAN SAY TO COMFORT YOU.
OR WHAT WILL MAKE YOU CRY...
I CAN'T EVEN FIGURE THAT OUT...

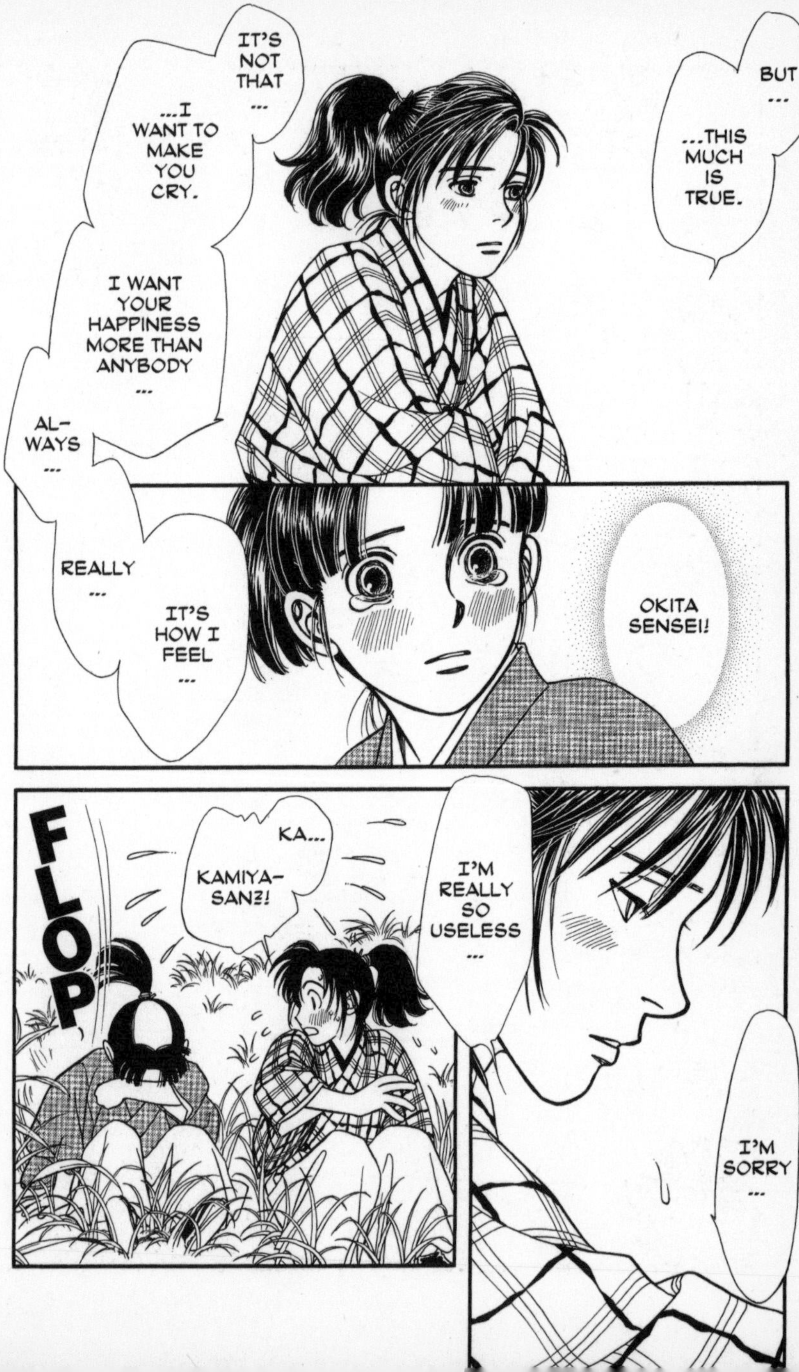
IT'S NOT THAT ...
...I WANT TO MAKE YOU CRY.
BUT ...
...THIS MUCH IS TRUE.
I WANT YOUR HAPPINESS MORE THAN ANYBODY ...
AL- WAYS ...
REALLY ...
IT'S HOW I FEEL ...
OKITA SENSEI!
I'M REALLY SO USELESS ...
I'M SORRY ...
KA...
KAMIYA-SAN?!
FLOP

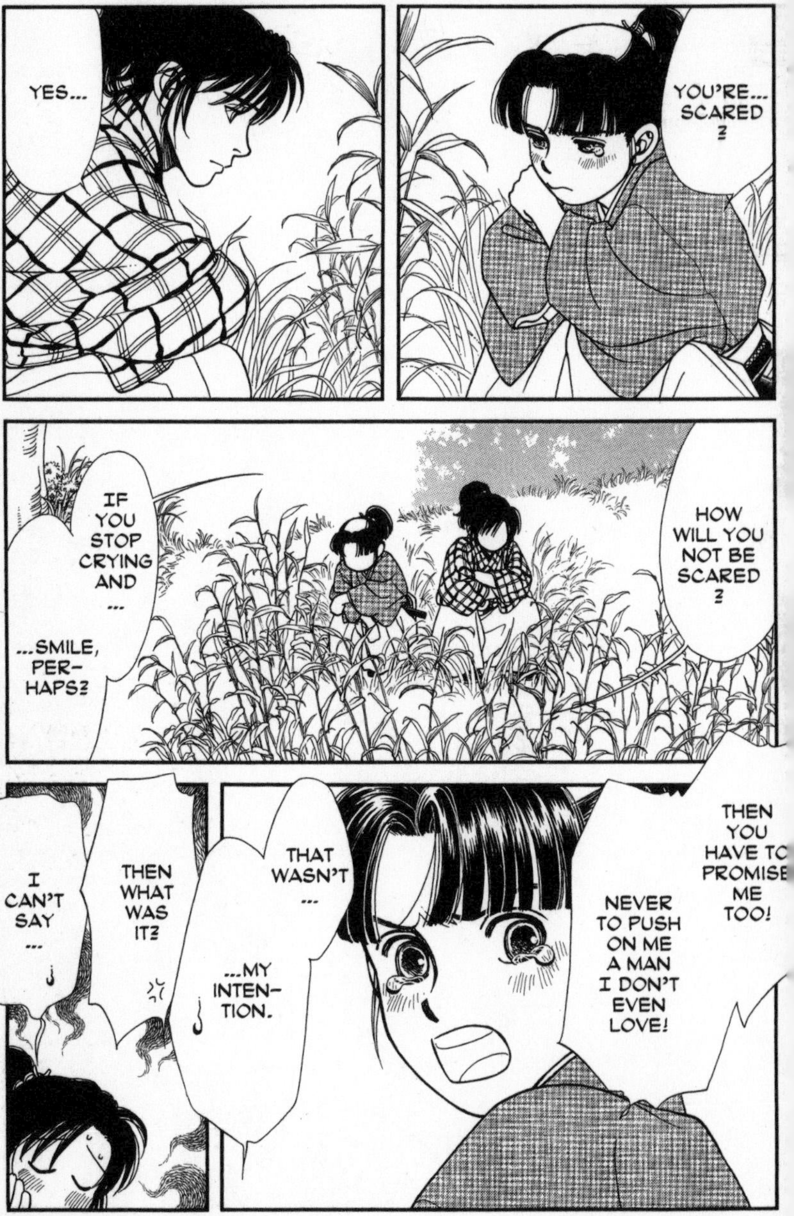

YOU'RE... SCARED?
YES...
HOW WILL YOU NOT BE SCARED?
IF YOU STOP CRYING AND...
...SMILE, PERHAPS?
THEN YOU HAVE TO PROMISE ME TOO!
NEVER TO PUSH ON ME A MAN I DON'T EVEN LOVE!
THAT WASN'T...
...MY INTENTION.
THEN WHAT WAS IT?
I CAN'T SAY...

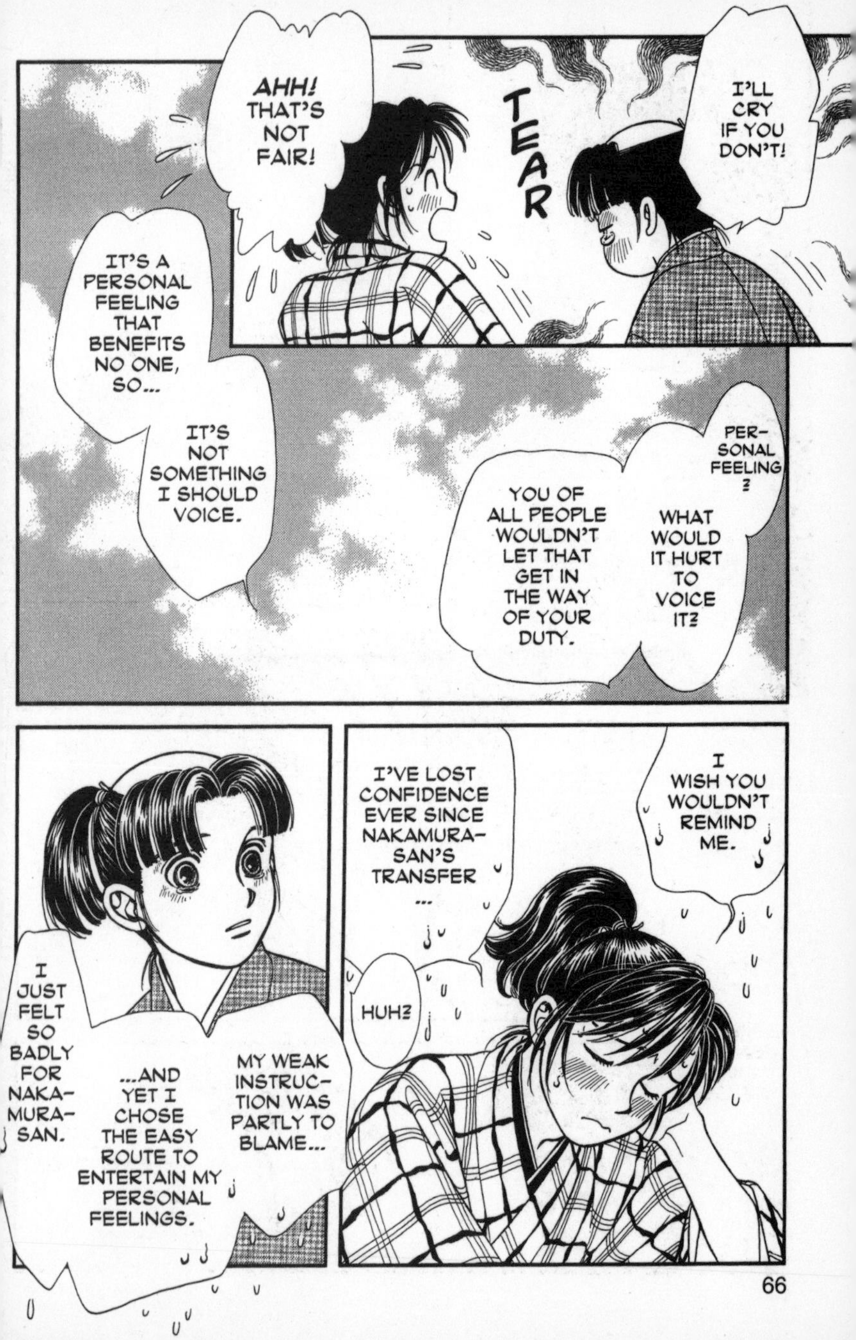
I'LL CRY IF YOU DON'T!
TEAR
AHH! THAT'S NOT FAIR!
PER-SONAL FEELING?
WHAT WOULD IT HURT TO VOICE IT?
YOU OF ALL PEOPLE WOULDN'T LET THAT GET IN THE WAY OF YOUR DUTY.
IT'S A PERSONAL FEELING THAT BENEFITS NO ONE, SO...
IT'S NOT SOMETHING I SHOULD VOICE.
I WISH YOU WOULDN'T REMIND ME.
I'VE LOST CONFIDENCE EVER SINCE NAKAMURA-SAN'S TRANSFER ...
HUH?
MY WEAK INSTRUCTION WAS PARTLY TO BLAME...
...AND YET I CHOSE THE EASY ROUTE TO ENTERTAIN MY PERSONAL FEELINGS.
I JUST FELT SO BADLY FOR NAKA-MURA-SAN.

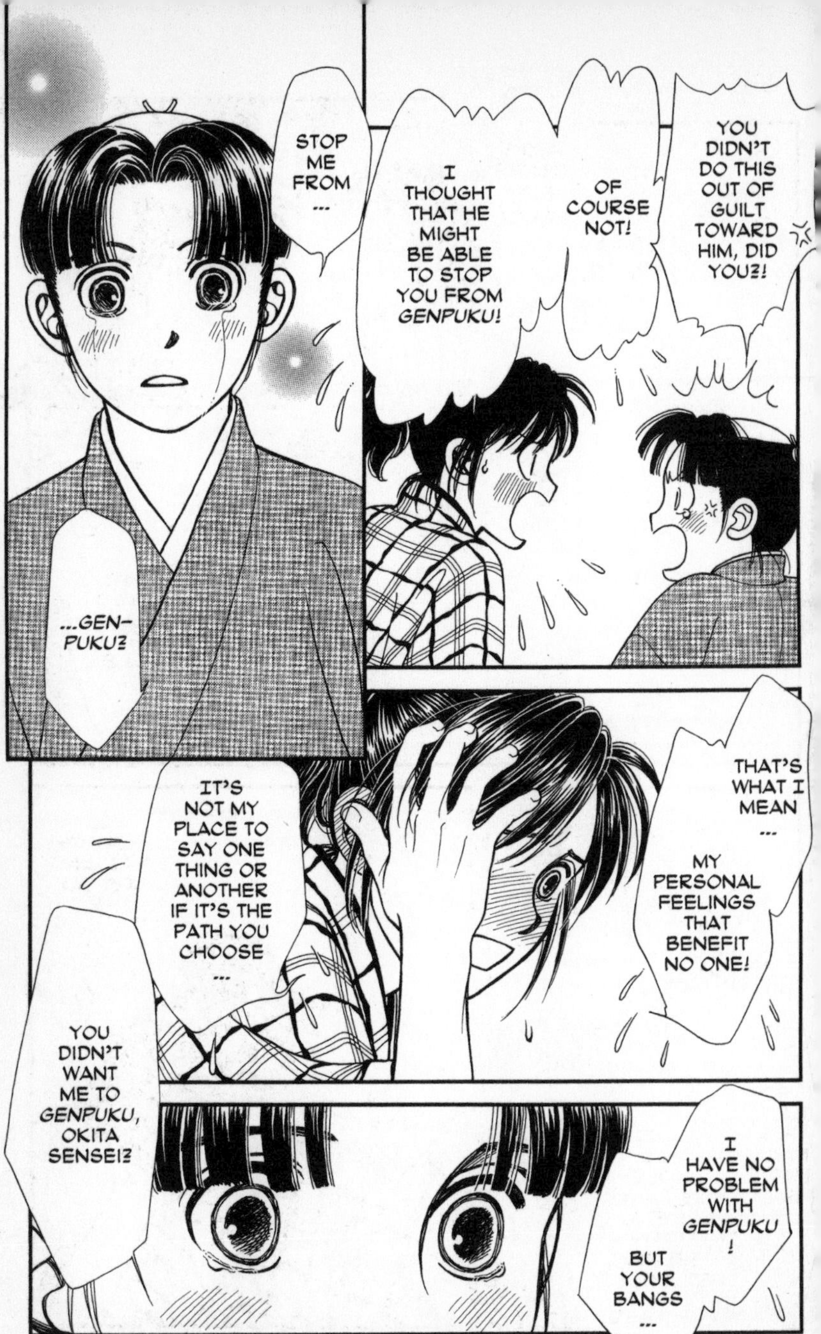
YOU DIDN'T DO THIS OUT OF GUILT TOWARD HIM, DID YOU?!
OF COURSE NOT!
I THOUGHT THAT HE MIGHT BE ABLE TO STOP YOU FROM *GENPUKU*!
STOP ME FROM ...
...GEN-PUKU?
THAT'S WHAT I MEAN ...
MY PERSONAL FEELINGS THAT BENEFIT NO ONE!
IT'S NOT MY PLACE TO SAY ONE THING OR ANOTHER IF IT'S THE PATH YOU CHOOSE ...
I HAVE NO PROBLEM WITH *GENPUKU* !
BUT YOUR BANGS ...
YOU DIDN'T WANT ME TO *GENPUKU*, OKITA SENSEI?

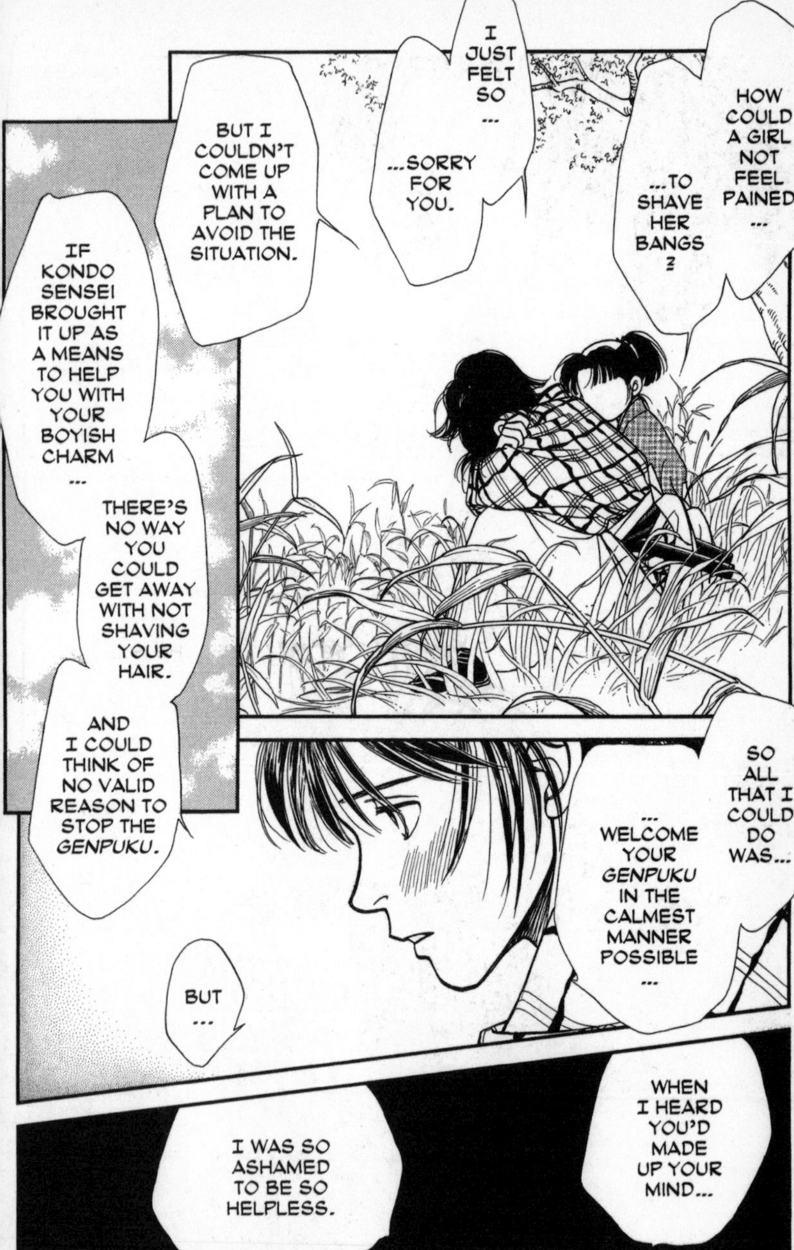
HOW COULD A GIRL NOT FEEL PAINED ...
...TO SHAVE HER BANGS?
I JUST FELT SO ...
...SORRY FOR YOU.
BUT I COULDN'T COME UP WITH A PLAN TO AVOID THE SITUATION.
IF KONDO SENSEI BROUGHT IT UP AS A MEANS TO HELP YOU WITH YOUR BOYISH CHARM ...
THERE'S NO WAY YOU COULD GET AWAY WITH NOT SHAVING YOUR HAIR.
AND I COULD THINK OF NO VALID REASON TO STOP THE *GENPUKU*.
SO ALL THAT I COULD DO WAS...
... WELCOME YOUR *GENPUKU* IN THE CALMEST MANNER POSSIBLE ...
BUT ...
WHEN I HEARD YOU'D MADE UP YOUR MIND...
I WAS SO ASHAMED TO BE SO HELPLESS.

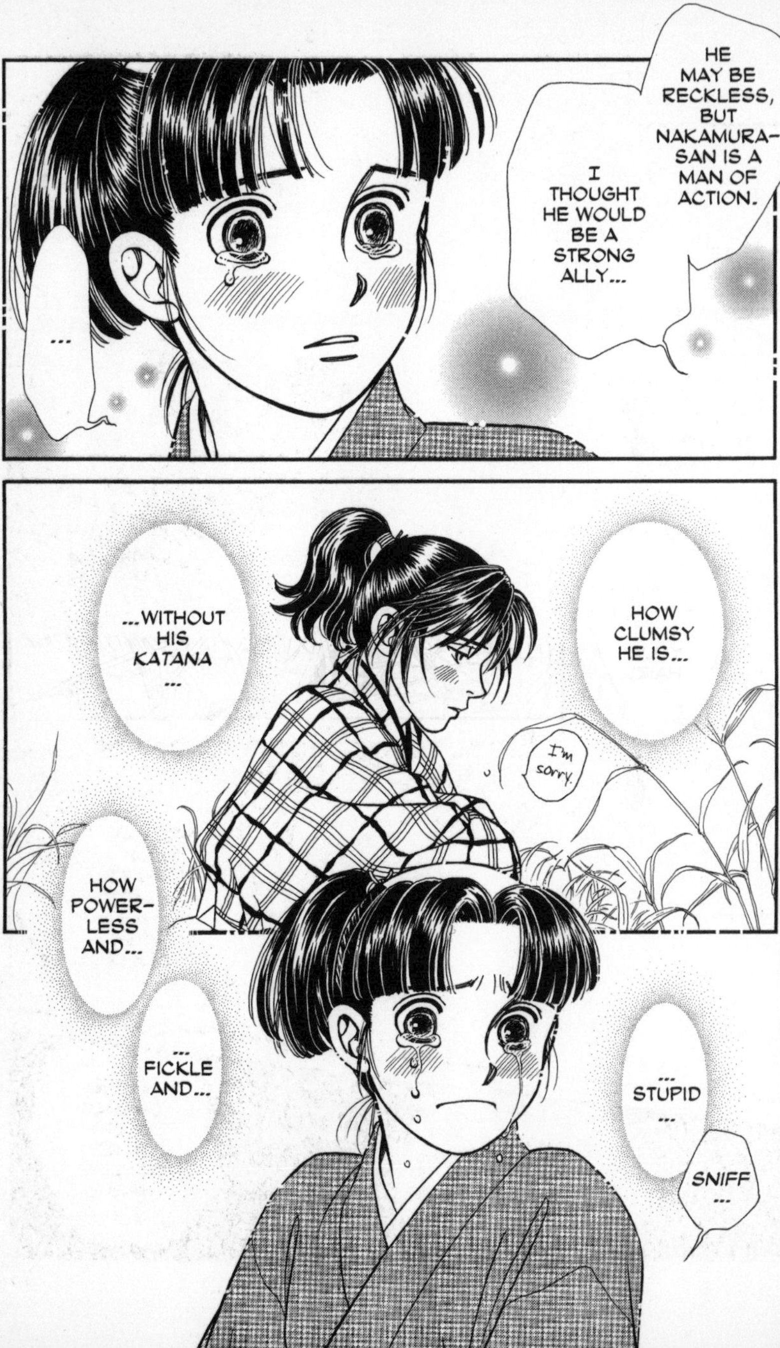

HE MAY BE RECKLESS, BUT NAKAMURA-SAN IS A MAN OF ACTION.
I THOUGHT HE WOULD BE A STRONG ALLY...
...
HOW CLUMSY HE IS...
I'm sorry.
...WITHOUT HIS KATANA ...
HOW POWER-LESS AND...
... FICKLE AND...
... STUPID ...
SNIFF ...

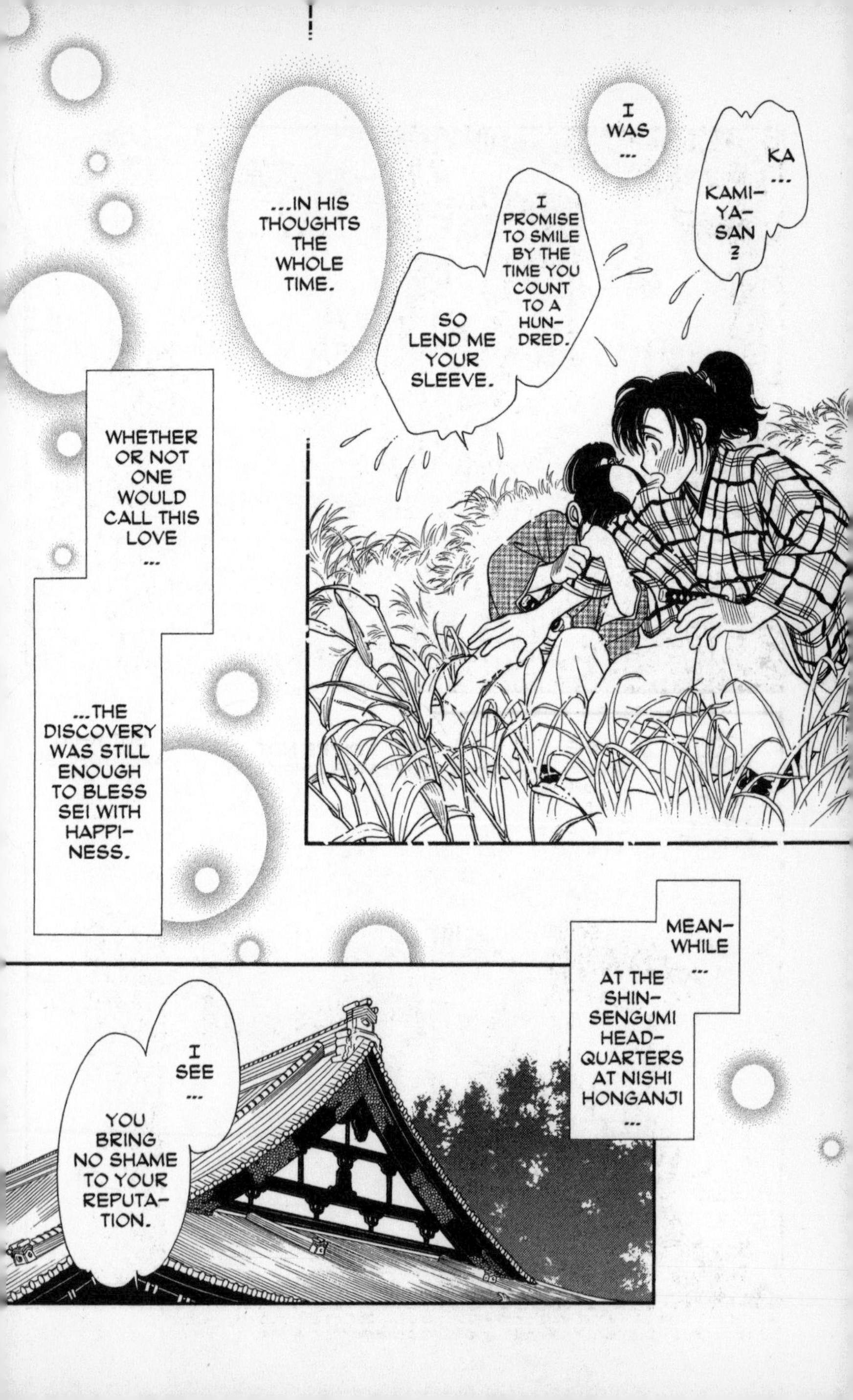
!
KA... KAMIYA-SAN?
I WAS...
I PROMISE TO SMILE BY THE TIME YOU COUNT TO A HUNDRED.
SO LEND ME YOUR SLEEVE.
...IN HIS THOUGHTS THE WHOLE TIME.
WHETHER OR NOT ONE WOULD CALL THIS LOVE...
...THE DISCOVERY WAS STILL ENOUGH TO BLESS SEI WITH HAPPINESS.
MEANWHILE... AT THE SHINSENGUMI HEADQUARTERS AT NISHI HONGANJI...
I SEE... YOU BRING NO SHAME TO YOUR REPUTATION.

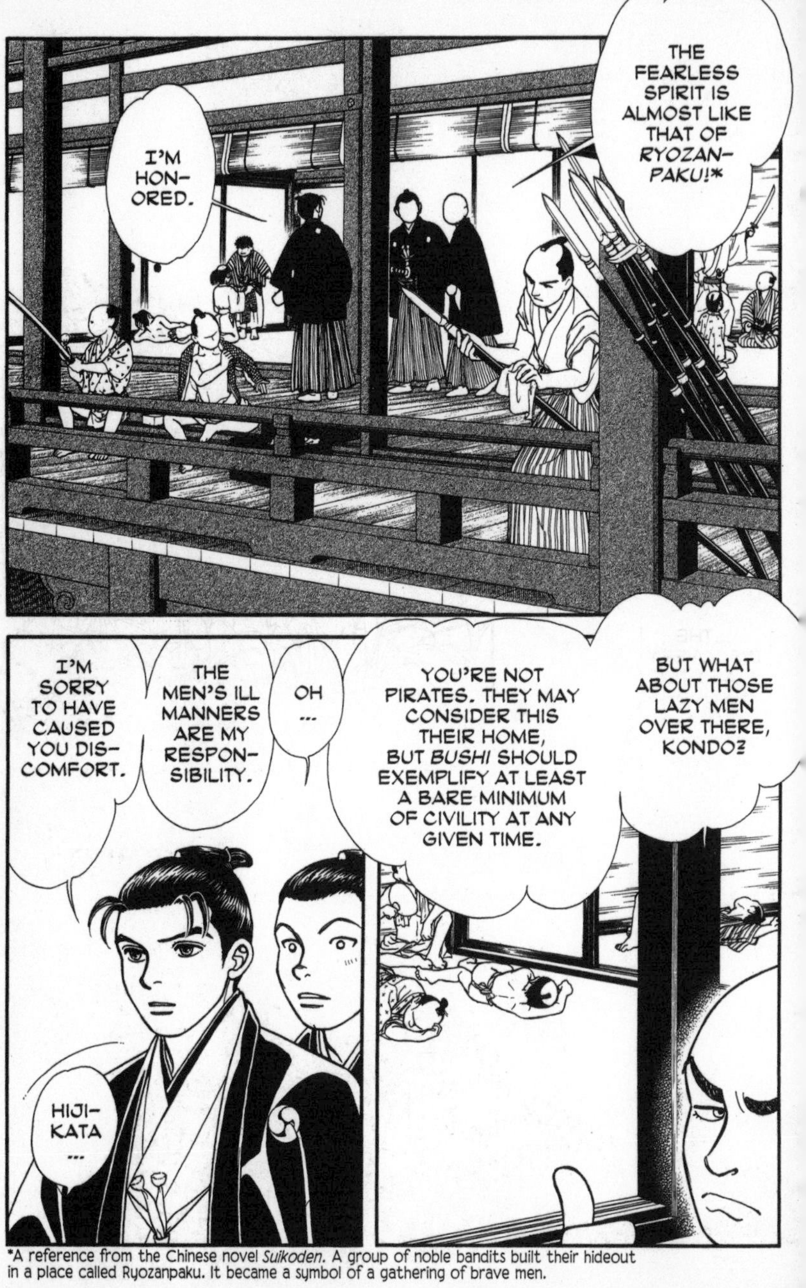
THE FEARLESS SPIRIT IS ALMOST LIKE THAT OF *RYOZAN-PAKU!**
I'M HON-ORED.
BUT WHAT ABOUT THOSE LAZY MEN OVER THERE, KONDO?
YOU'RE NOT PIRATES. THEY MAY CONSIDER THIS THEIR HOME, BUT *BUSHI* SHOULD EXEMPLIFY AT LEAST A BARE MINIMUM OF CIVILITY AT ANY GIVEN TIME.
OH ...
THE MEN'S ILL MANNERS ARE MY RESPON-SIBILITY.
I'M SORRY TO HAVE CAUSED YOU DIS-COMFORT.
HIJI-KATA ...

*A reference from the Chinese novel *Suikoden*. A group of noble bandits built their hideout in a place called Ryozanpaku. It became a symbol of a gathering of brave men.

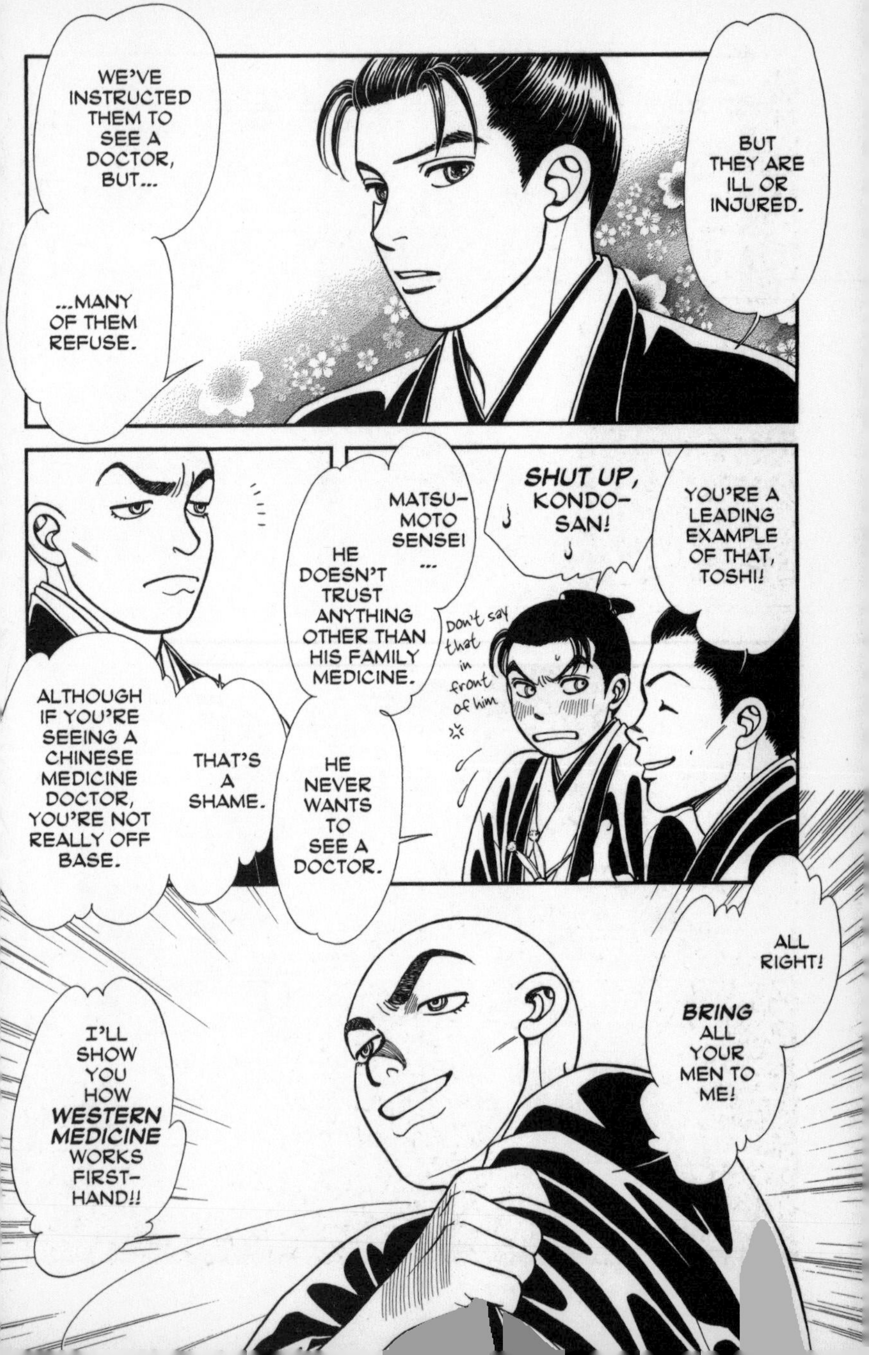
BUT THEY ARE ILL OR INJURED.
WE'VE INSTRUCTED THEM TO SEE A DOCTOR, BUT...
...MANY OF THEM REFUSE.
YOU'RE A LEADING EXAMPLE OF THAT, TOSHI!
SHUT UP, KONDO-SAN!
Don't say that in front of him
MATSU-MOTO SENSEI...
HE DOESN'T TRUST ANYTHING OTHER THAN HIS FAMILY MEDICINE.
HE NEVER WANTS TO SEE A DOCTOR.
THAT'S A SHAME.
ALTHOUGH IF YOU'RE SEEING A CHINESE MEDICINE DOCTOR, YOU'RE NOT REALLY OFF BASE.
ALL RIGHT!
BRING ALL YOUR MEN TO ME!
I'LL SHOW YOU HOW WESTERN MEDICINE WORKS FIRST-HAND!!

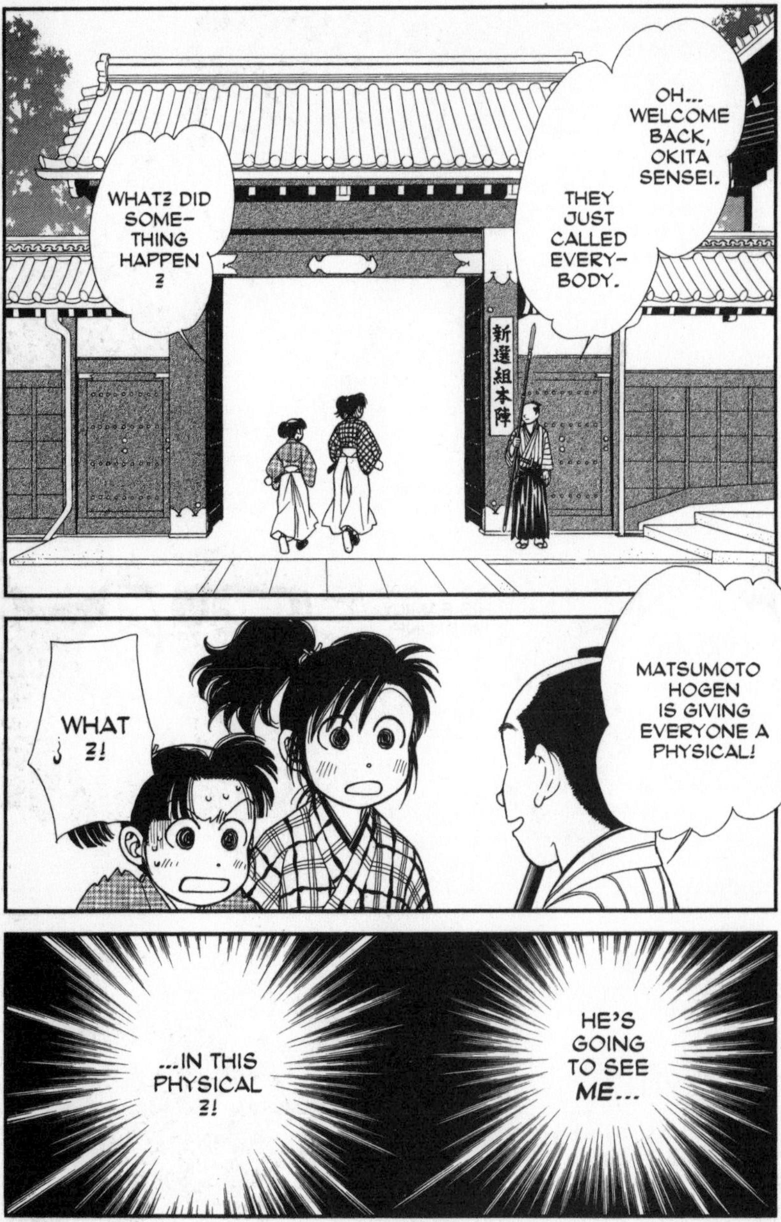
OH... WELCOME BACK, OKITA SENSEI.
THEY JUST CALLED EVERYBODY.
WHAT? DID SOMETHING HAPPEN?
新選組本陣
MATSUMOTO HOGEN IS GIVING EVERYONE A PHYSICAL!
WHAT?!
HE'S GOING TO SEE *ME*...
...IN THIS PHYSICAL?!

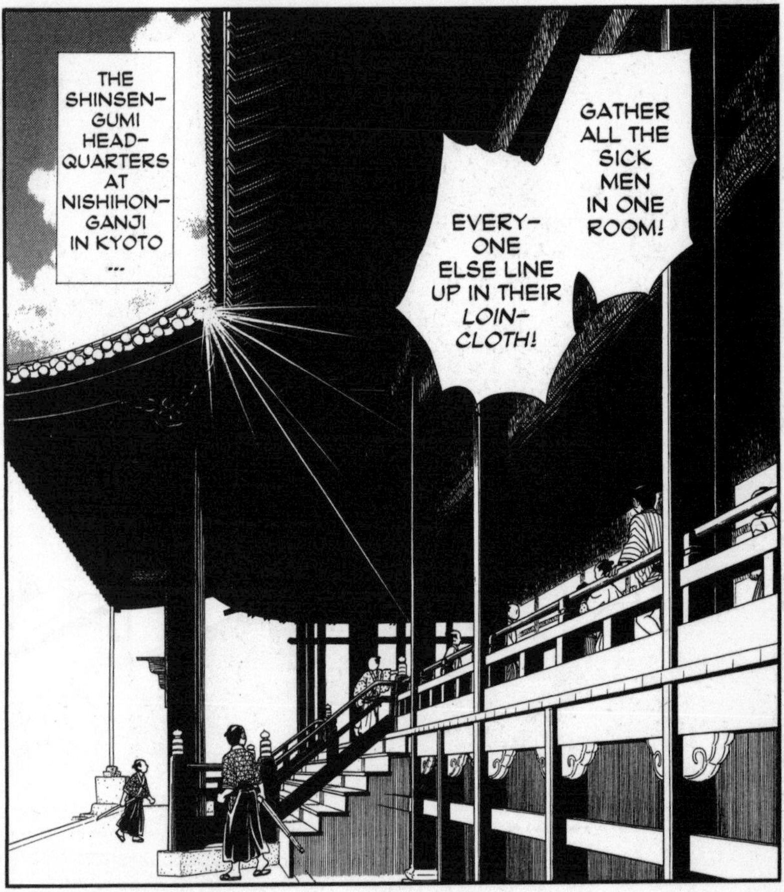
GATHER ALL THE SICK MEN IN ONE ROOM!
EVERYONE ELSE LINE UP IN THEIR LOINCLOTH!
THE SHINSENGUMI HEADQUARTERS AT NISHIHONGANJI IN KYOTO ...

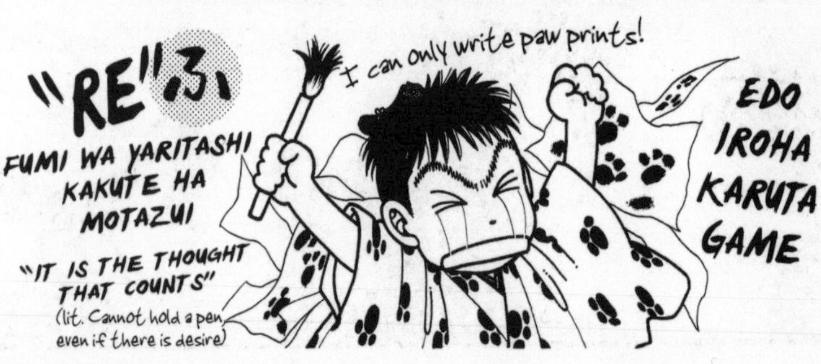
"RE" 3
EDO IROHA KARUTA GAME
I can only write paw prints!
FUMI WA YARITASHI KAKUTE HA MOTAZUI
"IT IS THE THOUGHT THAT COUNTS"
(lit. Cannot hold a pen even if there is desire)

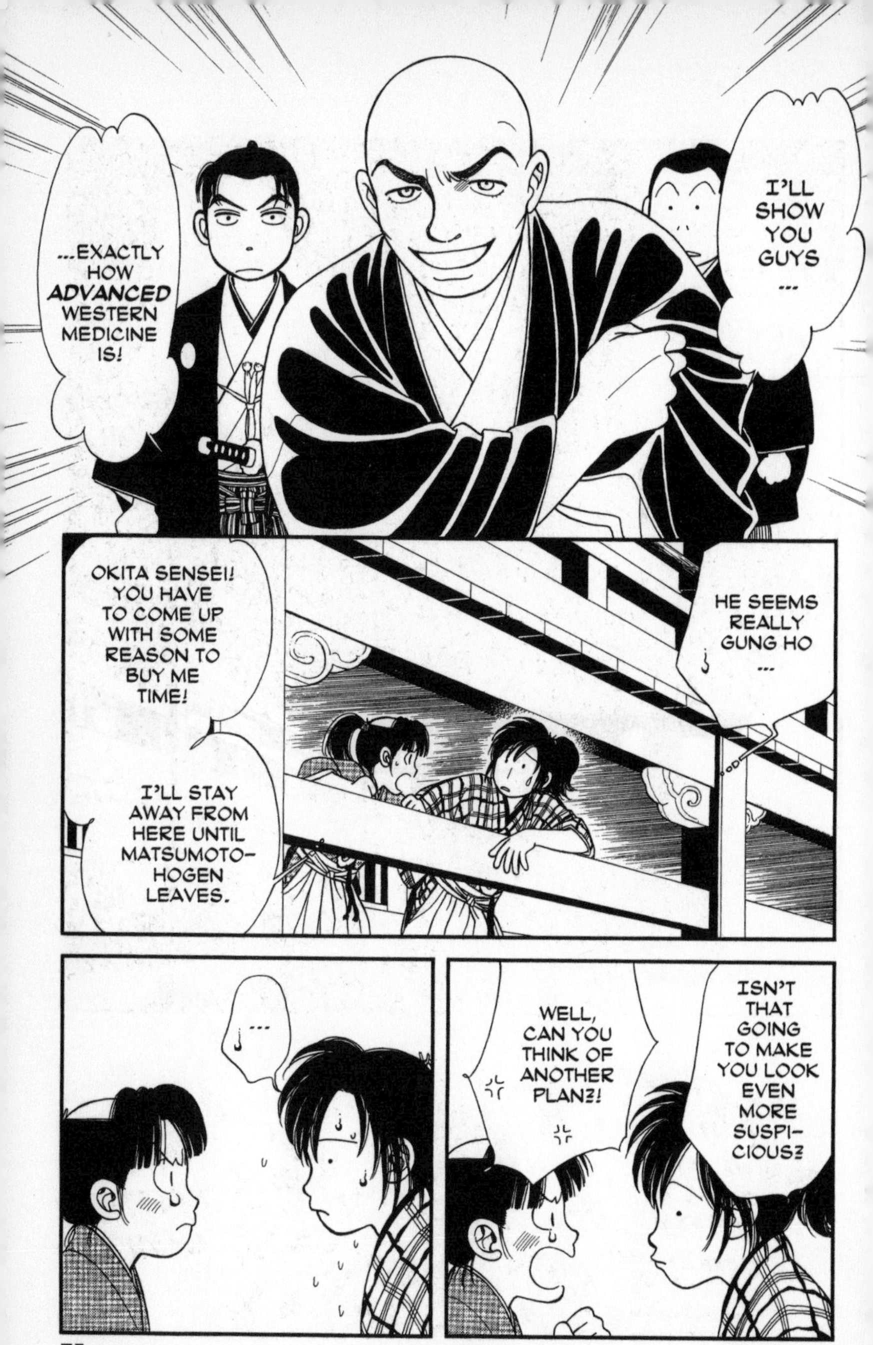
I'LL SHOW YOU GUYS ...
...EXACTLY HOW ADVANCED WESTERN MEDICINE IS!
HE SEEMS REALLY GUNG HO ...
OKITA SENSEI! YOU HAVE TO COME UP WITH SOME REASON TO BUY ME TIME!
I'LL STAY AWAY FROM HERE UNTIL MATSUMOTO-HOGEN LEAVES.
ISN'T THAT GOING TO MAKE YOU LOOK EVEN MORE SUSPICIOUS?
WELL, CAN YOU THINK OF ANOTHER PLAN?!
...

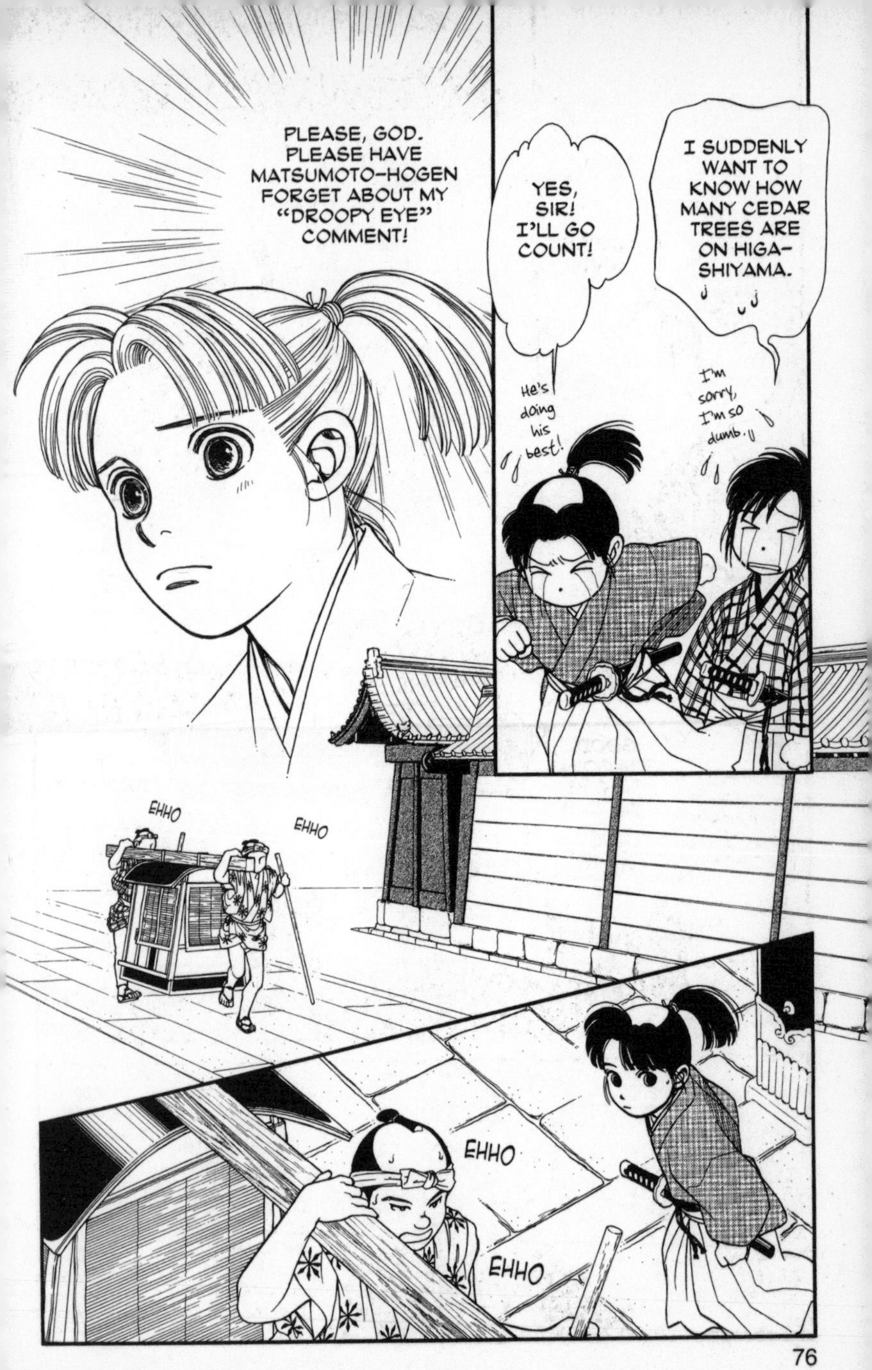
I SUDDENLY WANT TO KNOW HOW MANY CEDAR TREES ARE ON HIGA-SHIYAMA.
YES, SIR! I'LL GO COUNT!
I'm sorry, I'm so dumb.
He's doing his best!
PLEASE, GOD. PLEASE HAVE MATSUMOTO-HOGEN FORGET ABOUT MY "DROOPY EYE" COMMENT!
EHHO
EHHO
EHHO
EHHO

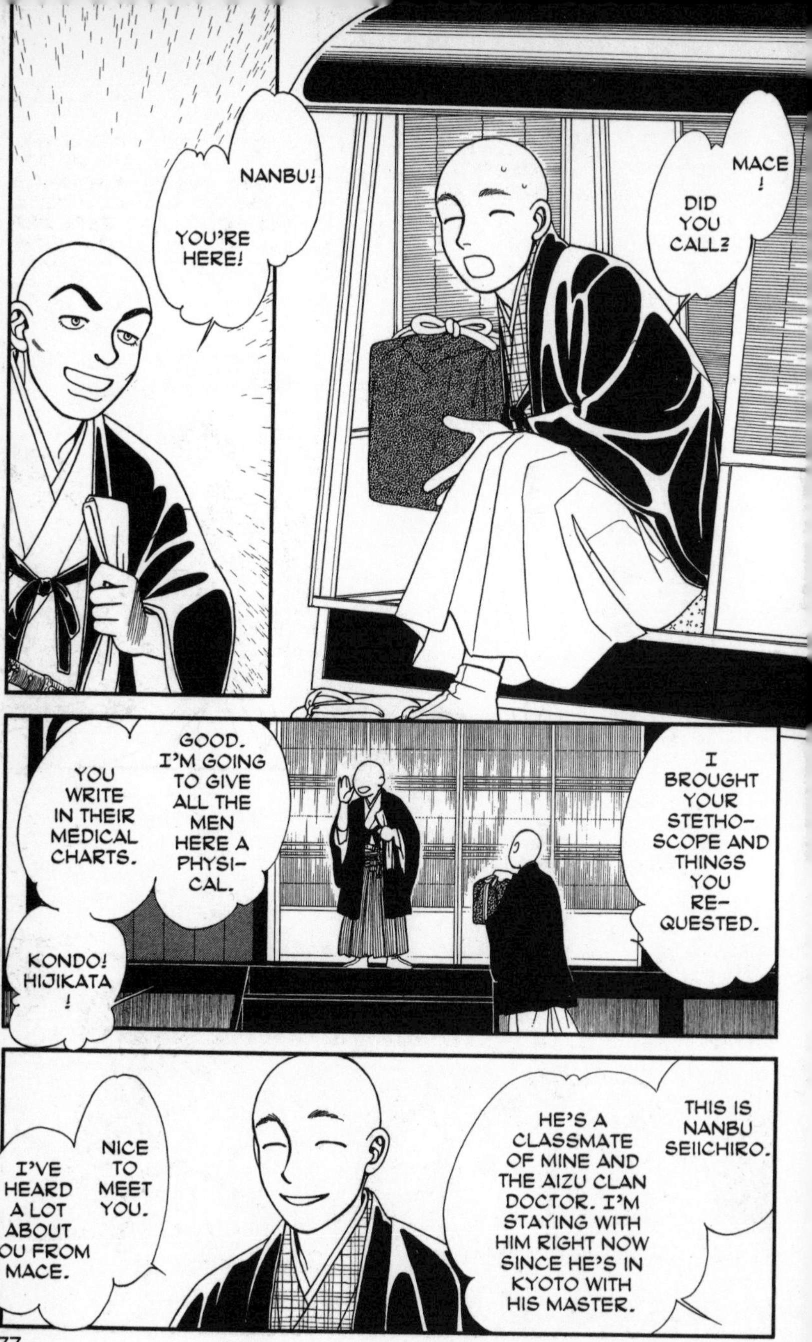
MACE! DID YOU CALL?
NANBU! YOU'RE HERE!
I BROUGHT YOUR STETHOSCOPE AND THINGS YOU REQUESTED.
GOOD. I'M GOING TO GIVE ALL THE MEN HERE A PHYSICAL.
YOU WRITE IN THEIR MEDICAL CHARTS.
KONDO! HIJIKATA!
THIS IS NANBU SEIICHIRO.
HE'S A CLASSMATE OF MINE AND THE AIZU CLAN DOCTOR. I'M STAYING WITH HIM RIGHT NOW SINCE HE'S IN KYOTO WITH HIS MASTER.
NICE TO MEET YOU.
I'VE HEARD A LOT ABOUT YOU FROM MACE.

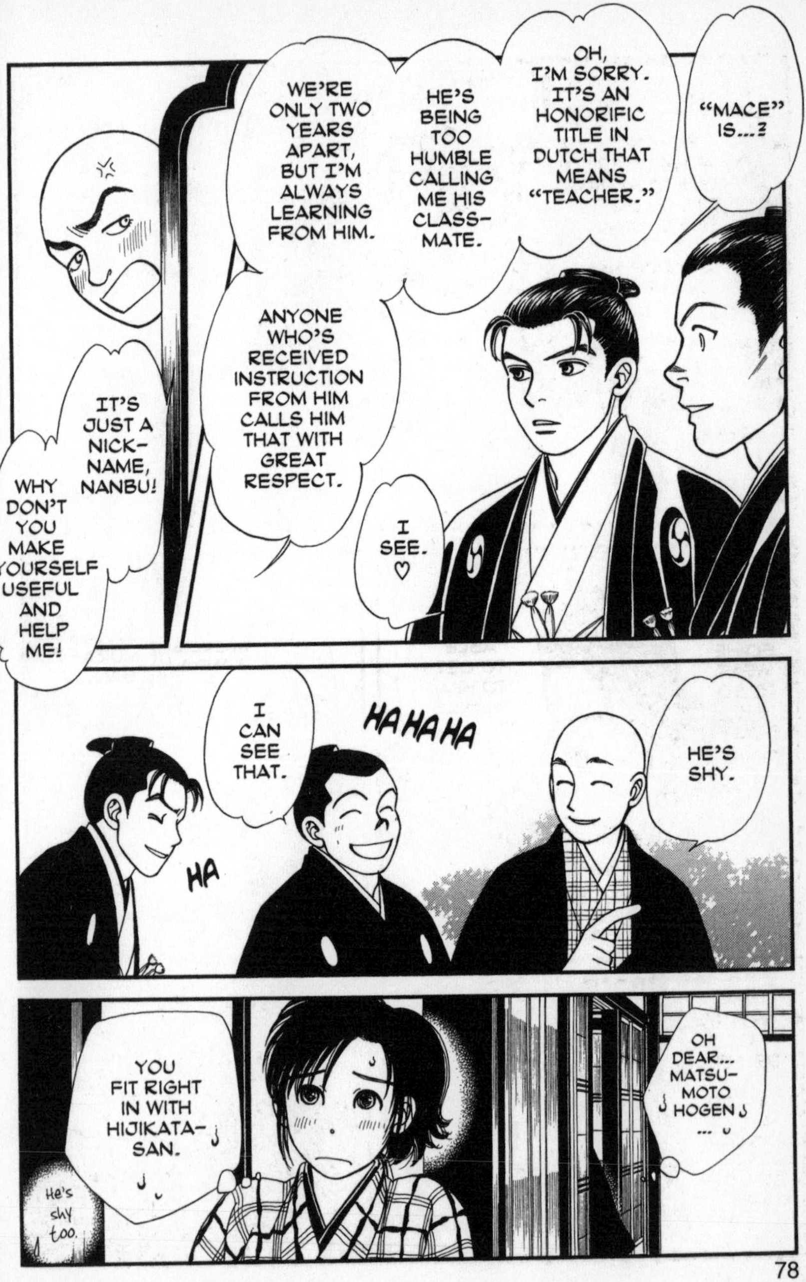
"MACE" IS...?
OH, I'M SORRY. IT'S AN HONORIFIC TITLE IN DUTCH THAT MEANS "TEACHER."
HE'S BEING TOO HUMBLE CALLING ME HIS CLASSMATE.
WE'RE ONLY TWO YEARS APART, BUT I'M ALWAYS LEARNING FROM HIM.
ANYONE WHO'S RECEIVED INSTRUCTION FROM HIM CALLS HIM THAT WITH GREAT RESPECT.
I SEE. ♡
IT'S JUST A NICKNAME, NANBU!
WHY DON'T YOU MAKE YOURSELF USEFUL AND HELP ME!
HE'S SHY.
HAHAHA
I CAN SEE THAT.
HA
OH DEAR... MATSUMOTO HOGEN...
YOU FIT RIGHT IN WITH HIJIKATA-SAN.
He's shy too.

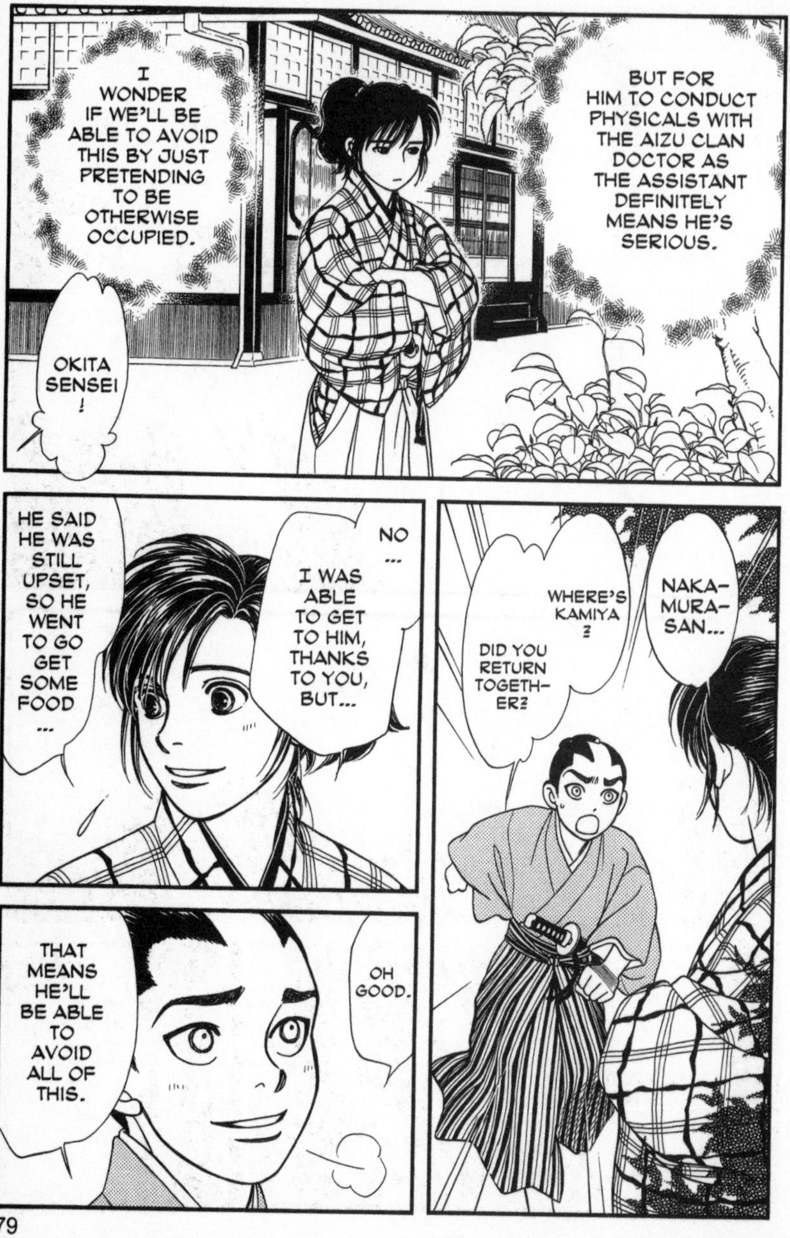
BUT FOR HIM TO CONDUCT PHYSICALS WITH THE AIZU CLAN DOCTOR AS THE ASSISTANT DEFINITELY MEANS HE'S SERIOUS.
I WONDER IF WE'LL BE ABLE TO AVOID THIS BY JUST PRETENDING TO BE OTHERWISE OCCUPIED.
OKITA SENSEI!
NAKAMURA-SAN...
WHERE'S KAMIYA?
DID YOU RETURN TOGETHER?
NO...
I WAS ABLE TO GET TO HIM, THANKS TO YOU, BUT...
HE SAID HE WAS STILL UPSET, SO HE WENT TO GO GET SOME FOOD...
OH GOOD.
THAT MEANS HE'LL BE ABLE TO AVOID ALL OF THIS.

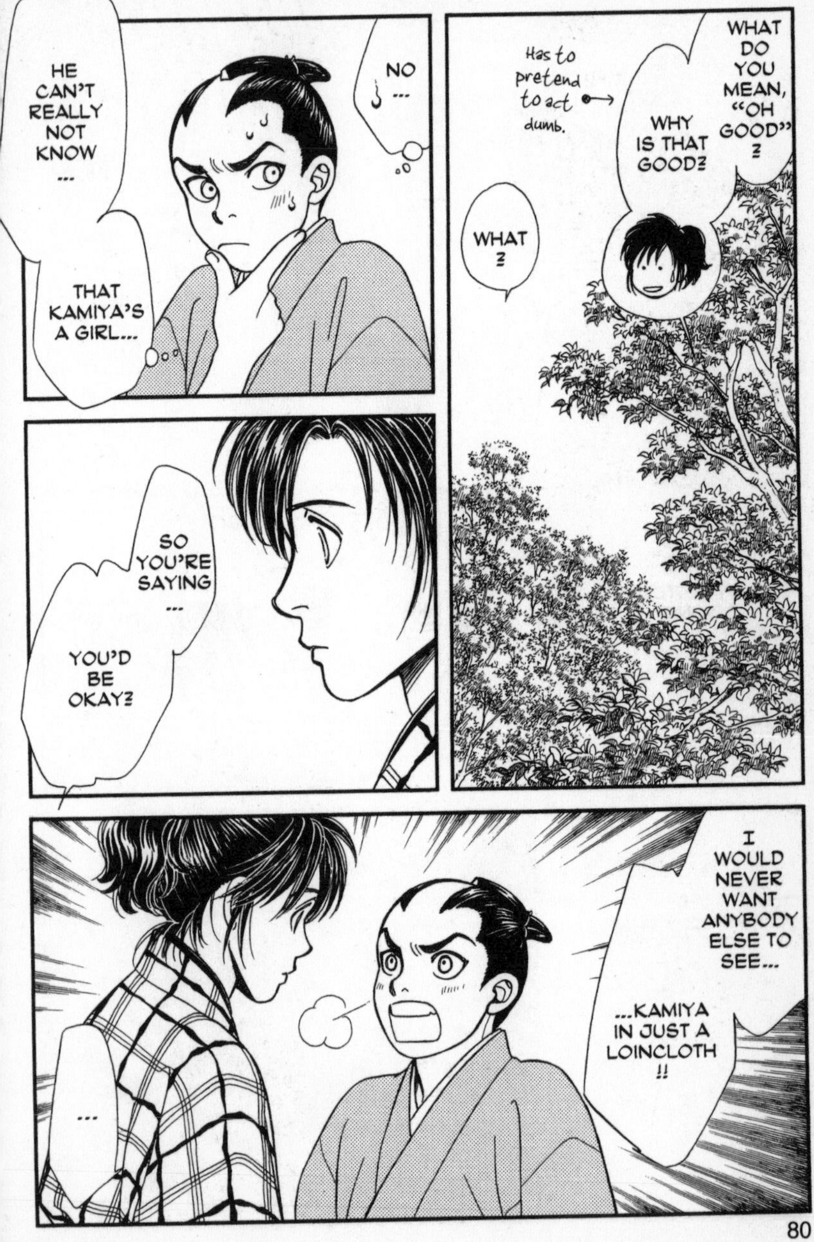
WHAT DO YOU MEAN, "OH GOOD"?
WHY IS THAT GOOD?
Has to pretend to act dumb.
WHAT?
NO ...
HE CAN'T REALLY NOT KNOW ...
THAT KAMIYA'S A GIRL...
SO YOU'RE SAYING ...
YOU'D BE OKAY?
I WOULD NEVER WANT ANYBODY ELSE TO SEE...
...KAMIYA IN JUST A LOINCLOTH !!
...

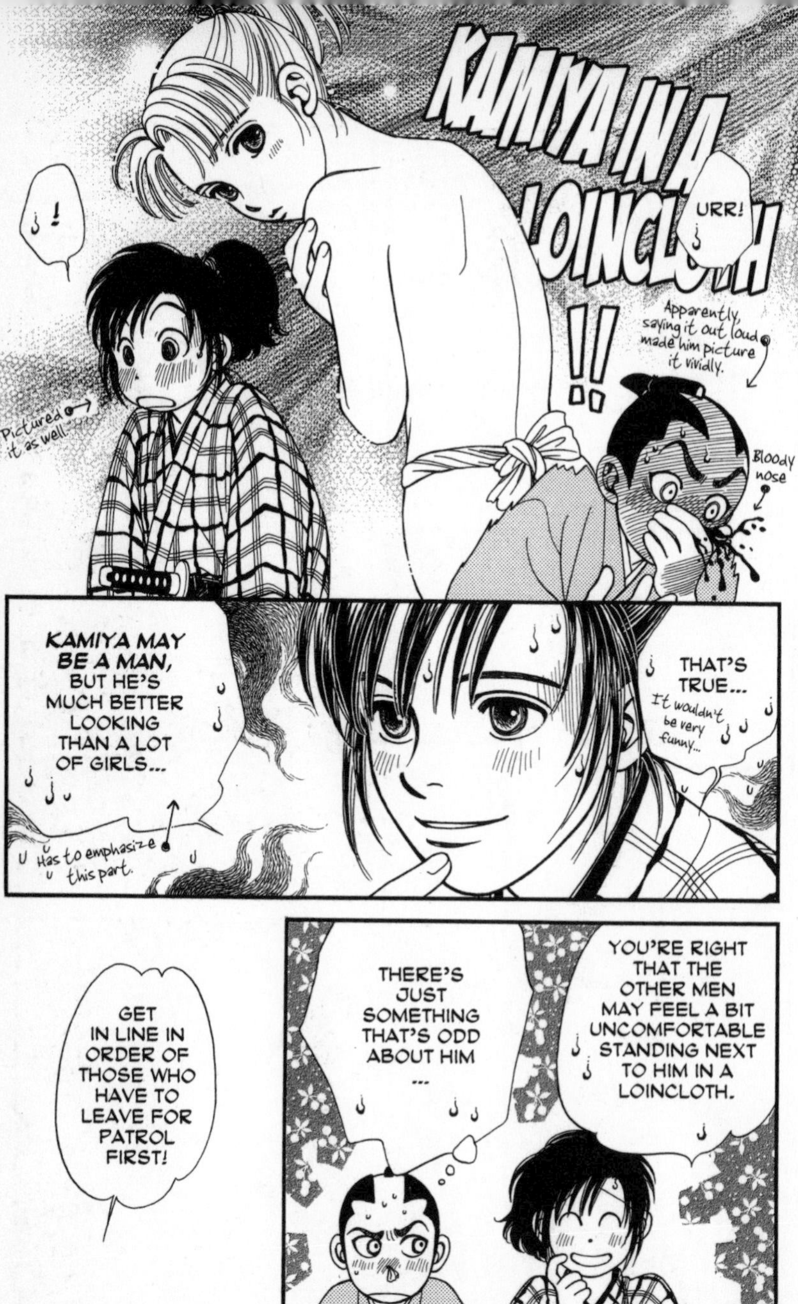
KAMIYA IN A LOINCLOTH!!
URR!
Apparently, saying it out loud made him picture it vividly.
Bloody nose
!
Pictured it as well.
THAT'S TRUE... It wouldn't be very funny...
KAMIYA MAY BE A MAN, BUT HE'S MUCH BETTER LOOKING THAN A LOT OF GIRLS...
Has to emphasize this part.
YOU'RE RIGHT THAT THE OTHER MEN MAY FEEL A BIT UNCOMFORTABLE STANDING NEXT TO HIM IN A LOINCLOTH.
THERE'S JUST SOMETHING THAT'S ODD ABOUT HIM ...
GET IN LINE IN ORDER OF THOSE WHO HAVE TO LEAVE FOR PATROL FIRST!

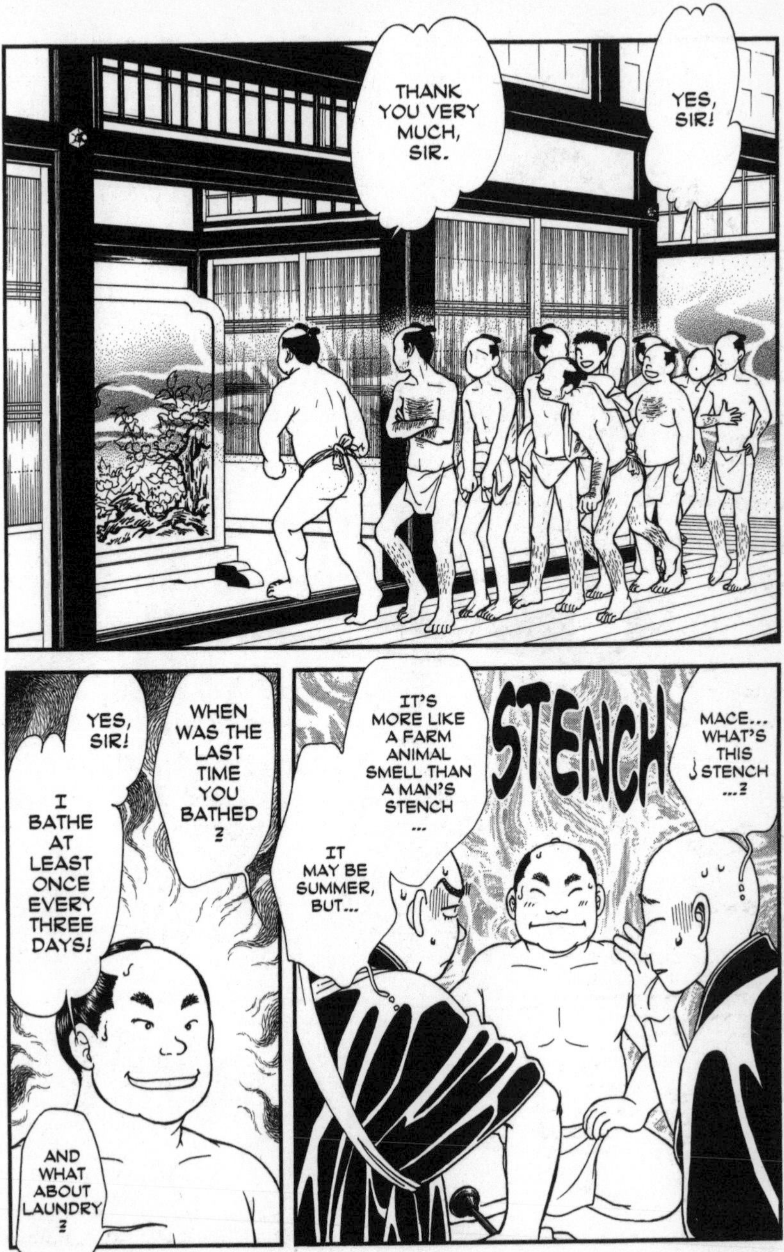
YES, SIR!
THANK YOU VERY MUCH, SIR.
MACE... WHAT'S THIS STENCH...?
STENCH
IT'S MORE LIKE A FARM ANIMAL SMELL THAN A MAN'S STENCH...
IT MAY BE SUMMER, BUT...
WHEN WAS THE LAST TIME YOU BATHED?
YES, SIR!
I BATHE AT LEAST ONCE EVERY THREE DAYS!
AND WHAT ABOUT LAUNDRY?

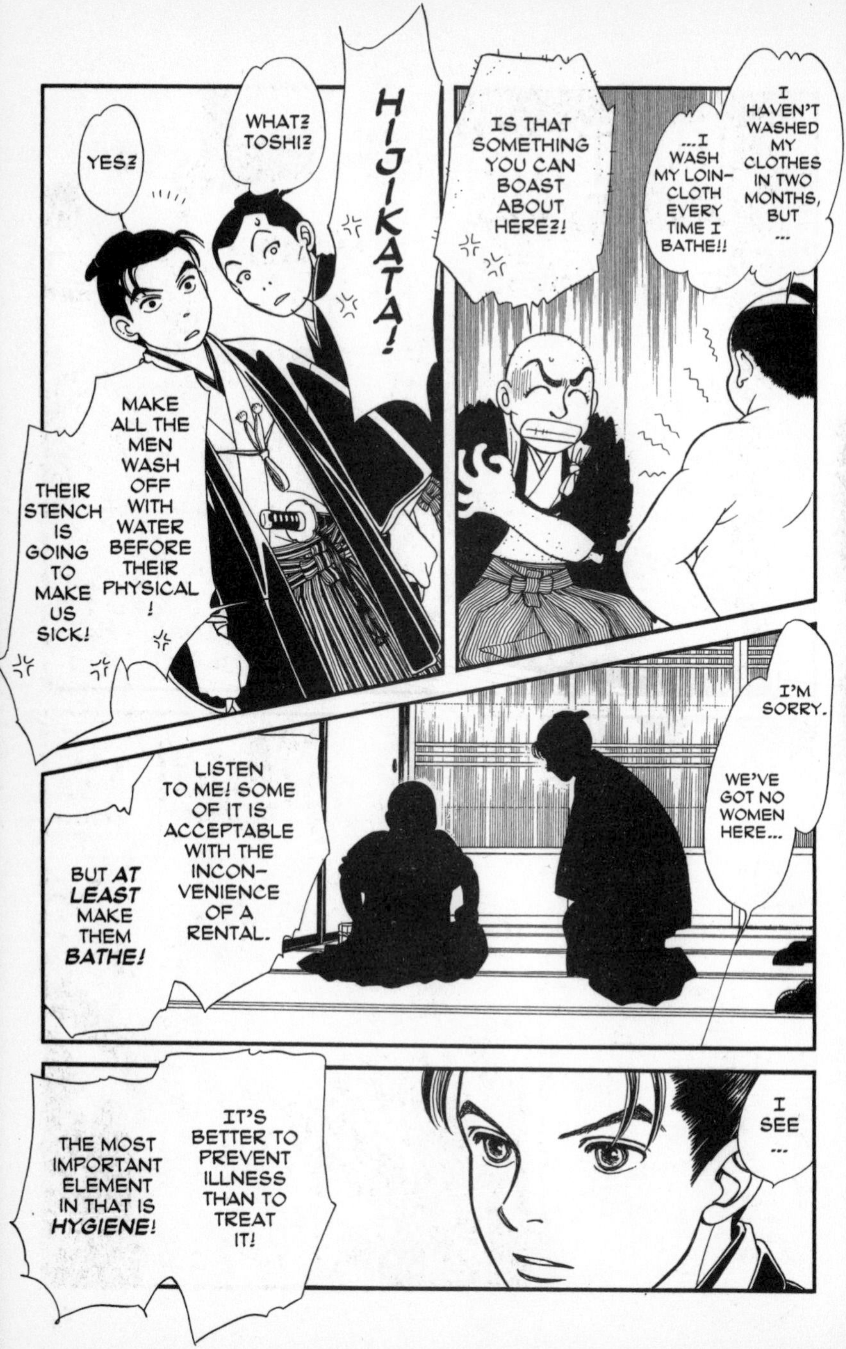
I HAVEN'T WASHED MY CLOTHES IN TWO MONTHS, BUT ...
...I WASH MY LOIN-CLOTH EVERY TIME I BATHE!!
IS THAT SOMETHING YOU CAN BOAST ABOUT HERE?!
HIJIKATA!
WHAT? TOSHI?
YES?
MAKE ALL THE MEN WASH OFF WITH WATER BEFORE THEIR PHYSICAL!
THEIR STENCH IS GOING TO MAKE US SICK!
I'M SORRY.
WE'VE GOT NO WOMEN HERE...
LISTEN TO ME! SOME OF IT IS ACCEPTABLE WITH THE INCON-VENIENCE OF A RENTAL.
BUT AT LEAST MAKE THEM BATHE!
I SEE ...
IT'S BETTER TO PREVENT ILLNESS THAN TO TREAT IT!
THE MOST IMPORTANT ELEMENT IN THAT IS HYGIENE!

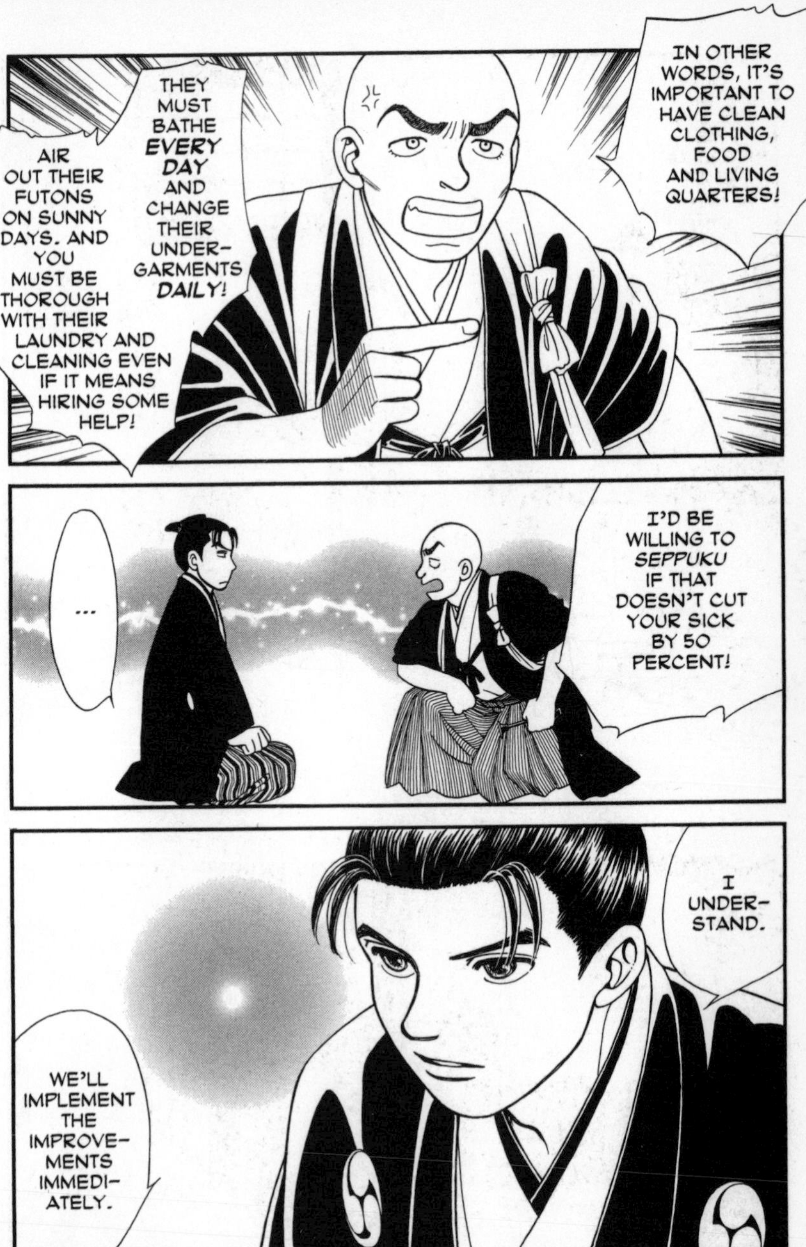
IN OTHER WORDS, IT'S IMPORTANT TO HAVE CLEAN CLOTHING, FOOD AND LIVING QUARTERS!
THEY MUST BATHE *EVERY DAY* AND CHANGE THEIR UNDER-GARMENTS *DAILY*!
AIR OUT THEIR FUTONS ON SUNNY DAYS. AND YOU MUST BE THOROUGH WITH THEIR LAUNDRY AND CLEANING EVEN IF IT MEANS HIRING SOME HELP!
I'D BE WILLING TO *SEPPUKU* IF THAT DOESN'T CUT YOUR SICK BY 50 PERCENT!
...
I UNDER-STAND.
WE'LL IMPLEMENT THE IMPROVE-MENTS IMMEDI-ATELY.

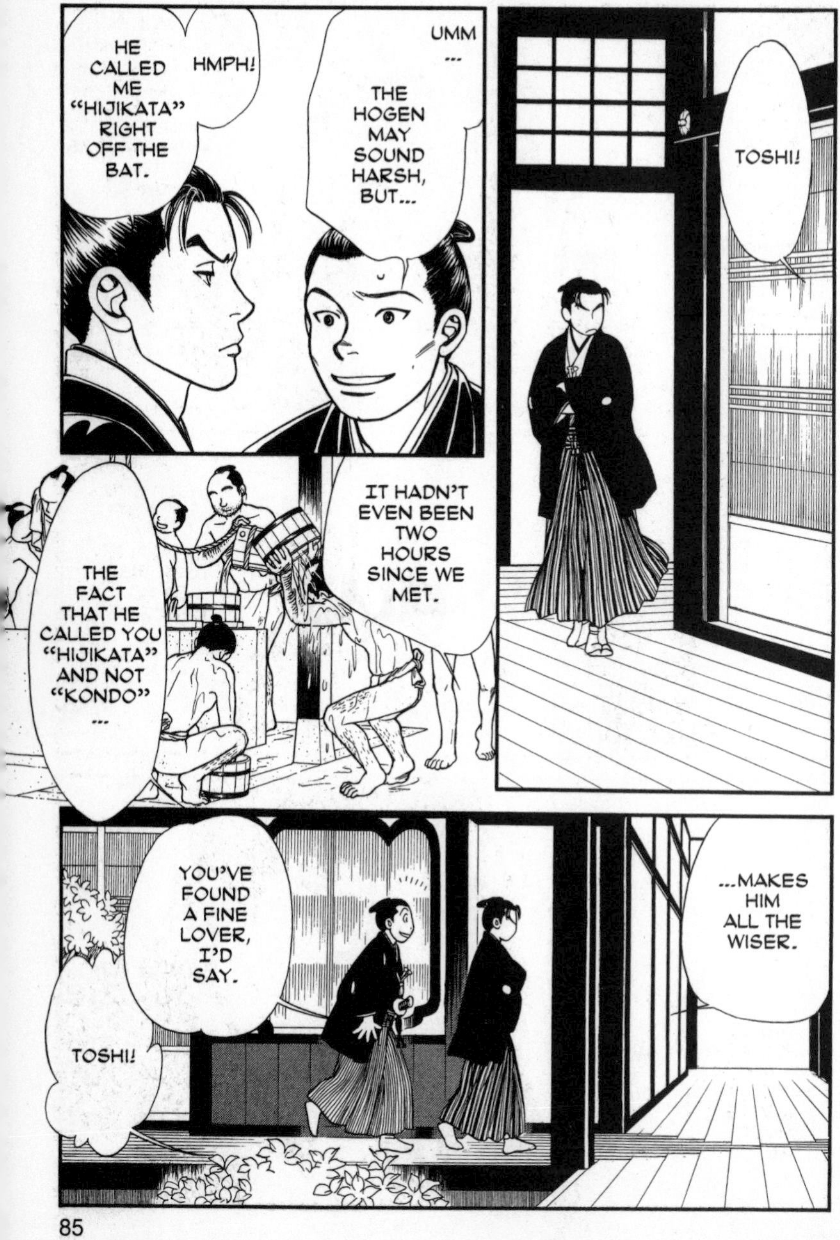
TOSHI!
UMM... THE HOGEN MAY SOUND HARSH, BUT...
HMPH!
HE CALLED ME "HIJIKATA" RIGHT OFF THE BAT.
IT HADN'T EVEN BEEN TWO HOURS SINCE WE MET.
THE FACT THAT HE CALLED YOU "HIJIKATA" AND NOT "KONDO"...
...MAKES HIM ALL THE WISER.
YOU'VE FOUND A FINE LOVER, I'D SAY.
TOSHI!

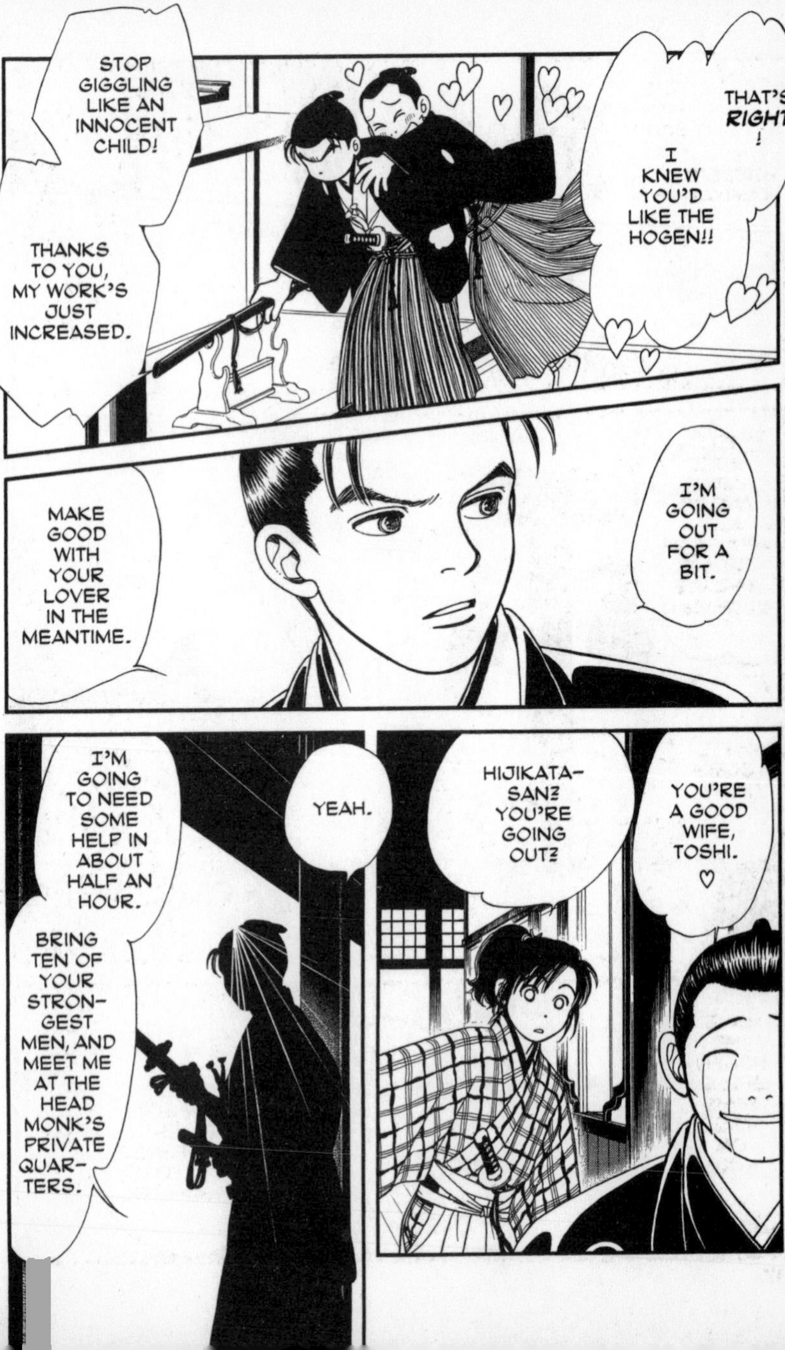
THAT'S RIGHT!
I KNEW YOU'D LIKE THE HOGEN!!
STOP GIGGLING LIKE AN INNOCENT CHILD!
THANKS TO YOU, MY WORK'S JUST INCREASED.
I'M GOING OUT FOR A BIT.
MAKE GOOD WITH YOUR LOVER IN THE MEANTIME.
YOU'RE A GOOD WIFE, TOSHI. ♡
HIJIKATA-SAN? YOU'RE GOING OUT?
YEAH.
I'M GOING TO NEED SOME HELP IN ABOUT HALF AN HOUR.
BRING TEN OF YOUR STRONGEST MEN, AND MEET ME AT THE HEAD MONK'S PRIVATE QUARTERS.

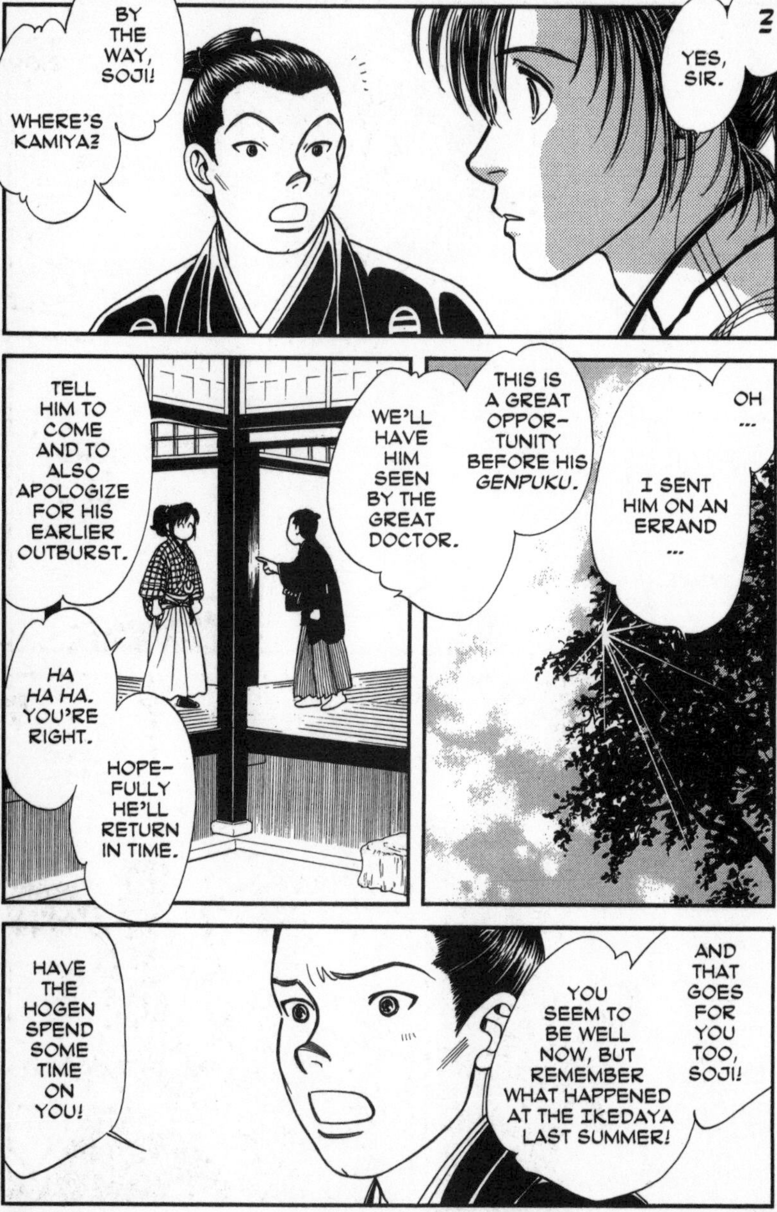
YES, SIR.
BY THE WAY, SOJI!
WHERE'S KAMIYA?
OH ...
I SENT HIM ON AN ERRAND ...
THIS IS A GREAT OPPORTUNITY BEFORE HIS *GENPUKU*.
WE'LL HAVE HIM SEEN BY THE GREAT DOCTOR.
TELL HIM TO COME AND TO ALSO APOLOGIZE FOR HIS EARLIER OUTBURST.
HOPEFULLY HE'LL RETURN IN TIME.
HA HA HA. YOU'RE RIGHT.
AND THAT GOES FOR YOU TOO, SOJI!
YOU SEEM TO BE WELL NOW, BUT REMEMBER WHAT HAPPENED AT THE IKEDAYA LAST SUMMER!
HAVE THE HOGEN SPEND SOME TIME ON YOU!

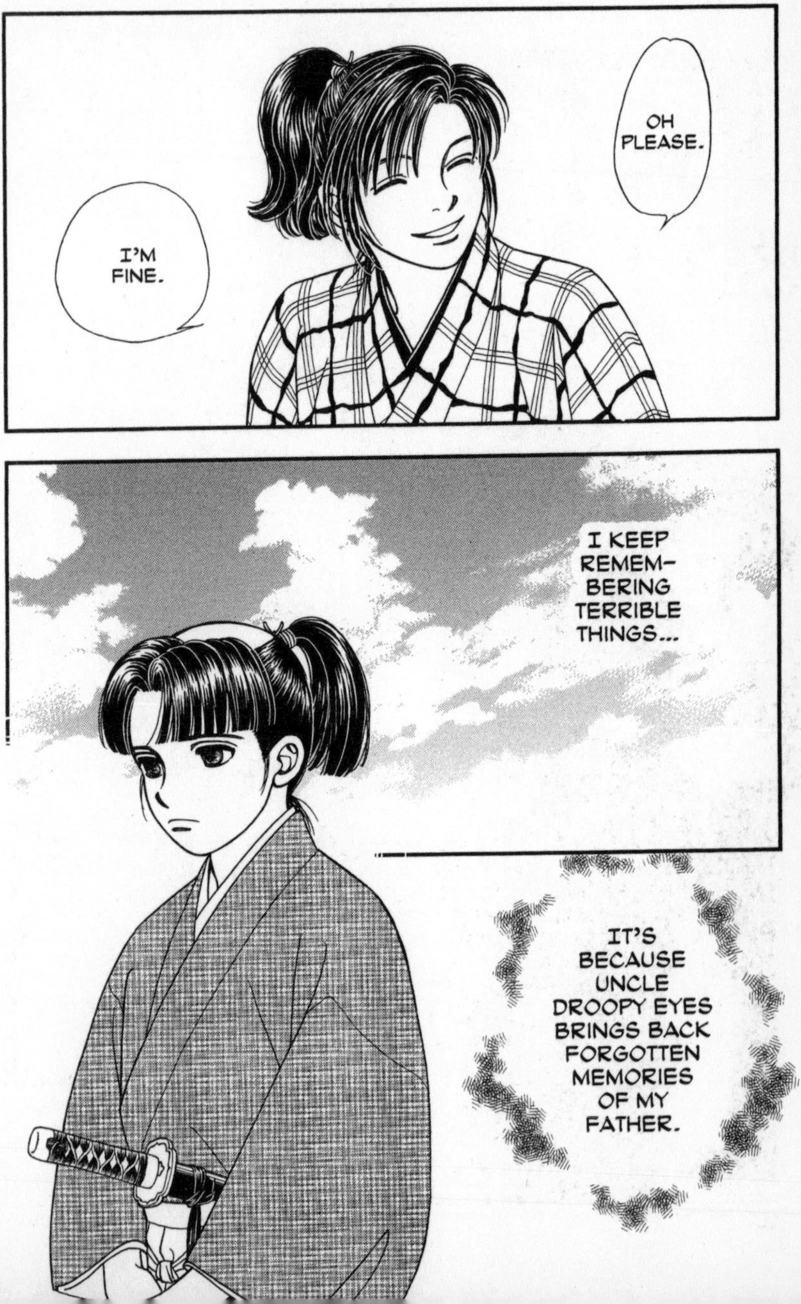
OH PLEASE.
I'M FINE.
I KEEP REMEMBERING TERRIBLE THINGS...
IT'S BECAUSE UNCLE DROOPY EYES BRINGS BACK FORGOTTEN MEMORIES OF MY FATHER.

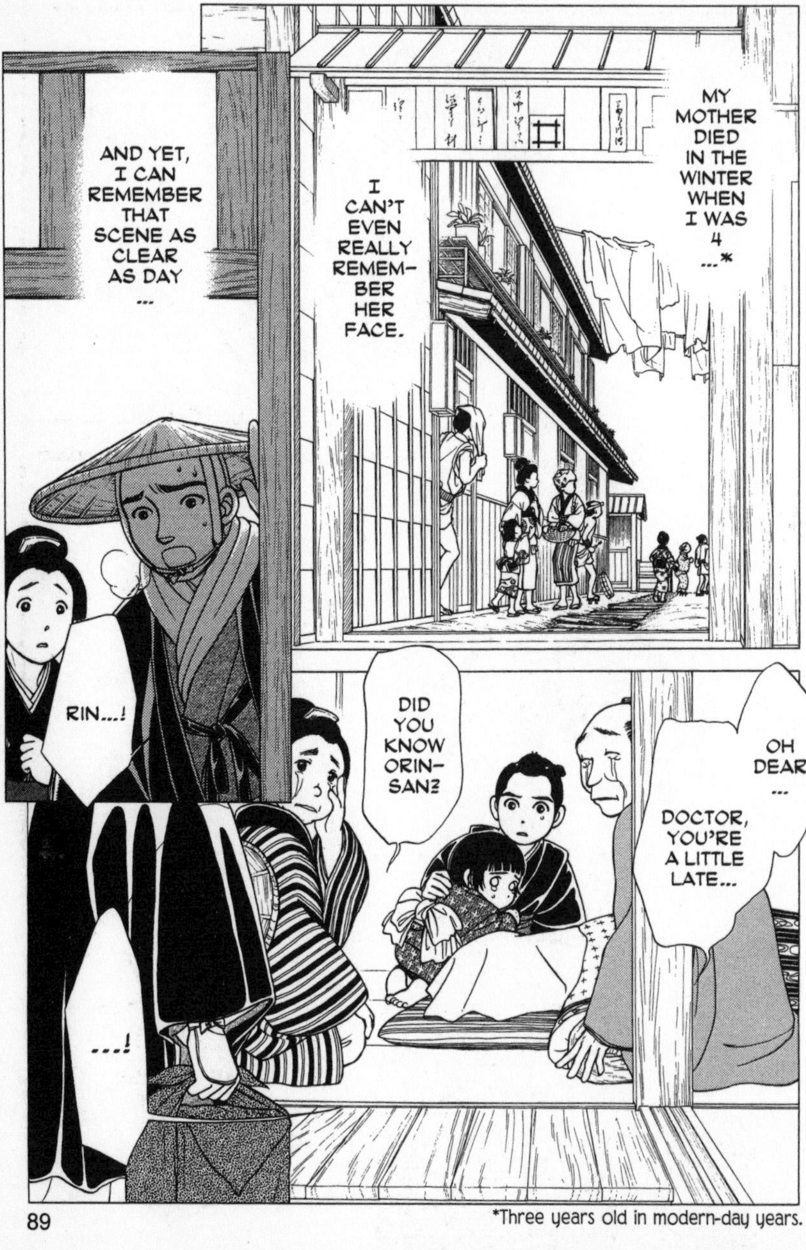
MY MOTHER DIED IN THE WINTER WHEN I WAS 4 ...*
I CAN'T EVEN REALLY REMEMBER HER FACE.
OH DEAR ...
DOCTOR, YOU'RE A LITTLE LATE...
DID YOU KNOW ORIN-SAN?
AND YET, I CAN REMEMBER THAT SCENE AS CLEAR AS DAY ...
RIN...!
...!

*Three years old in modern-day years.

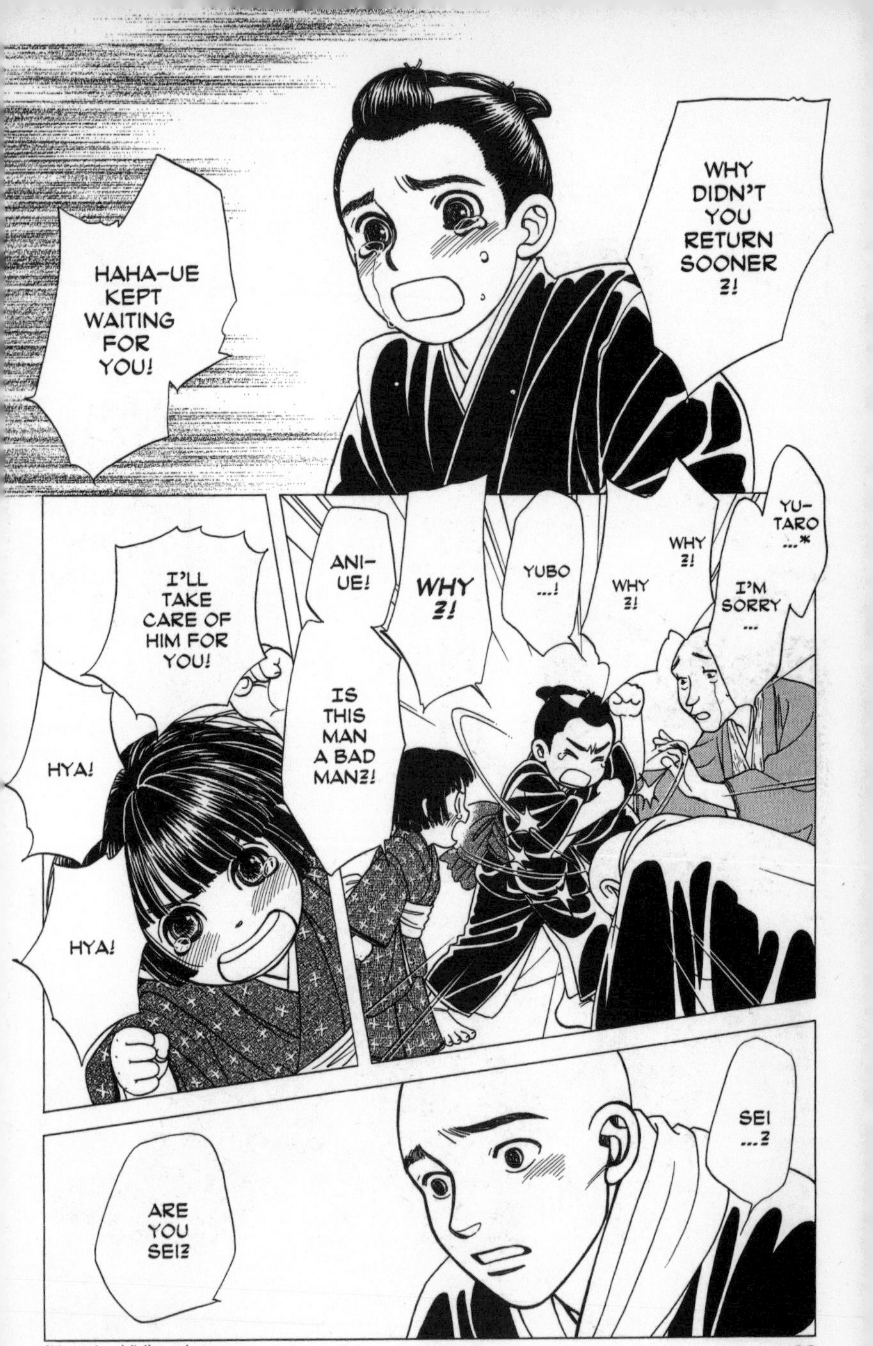
WHY DIDN'T YOU RETURN SOONER?!
HAHA-UE KEPT WAITING FOR YOU!
YU-TARO ...*
I'M SORRY ...
WHY?!
WHY?!
YUBO ...!
WHY?!
ANI-UE!
IS THIS MAN A BAD MAN?!
I'LL TAKE CARE OF HIM FOR YOU!
HYA!
HYA!
SEI ...?
ARE YOU SEI?

*Yuma's childhood name

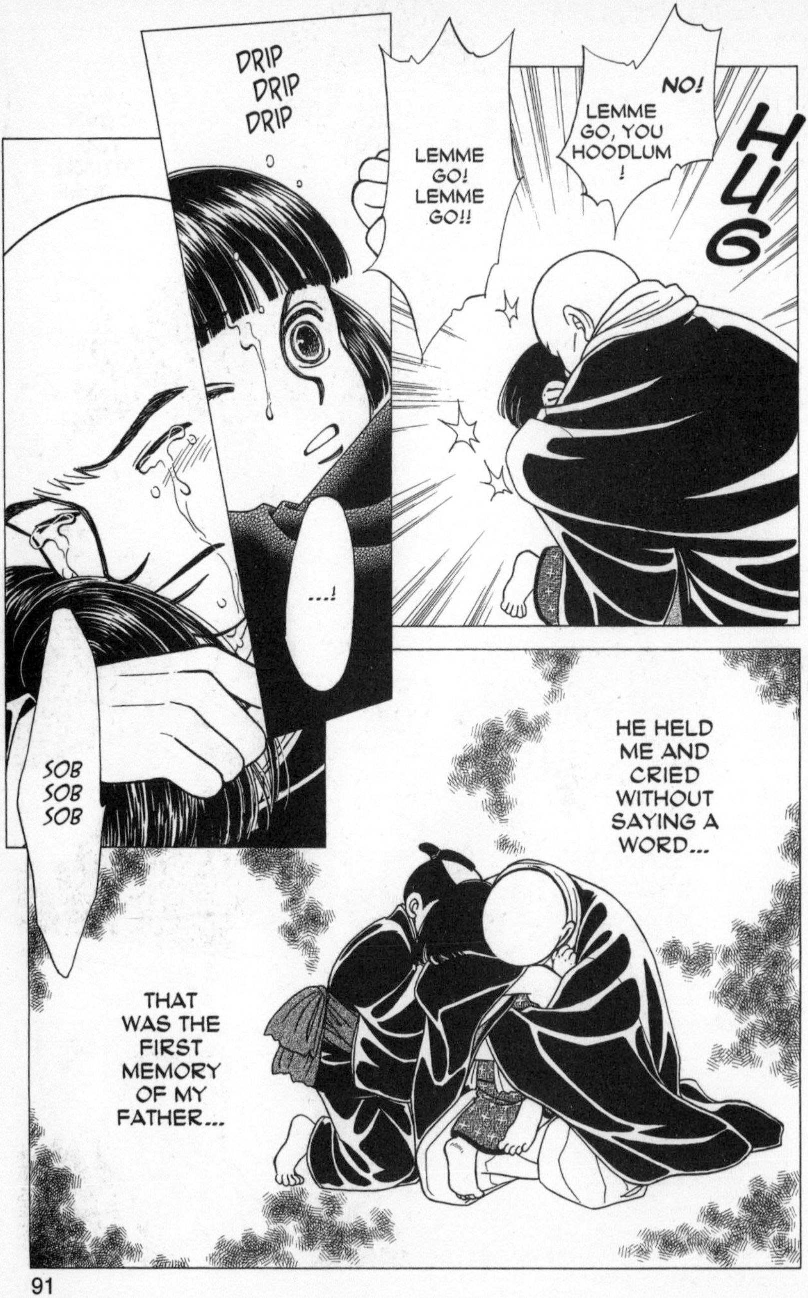
HUG
NO!
LEMME GO, YOU HOODLUM!
LEMME GO! LEMME GO!!
DRIP DRIP DRIP
...!
SOB SOB SOB
HE HELD ME AND CRIED WITHOUT SAYING A WORD...
THAT WAS THE FIRST MEMORY OF MY FATHER...

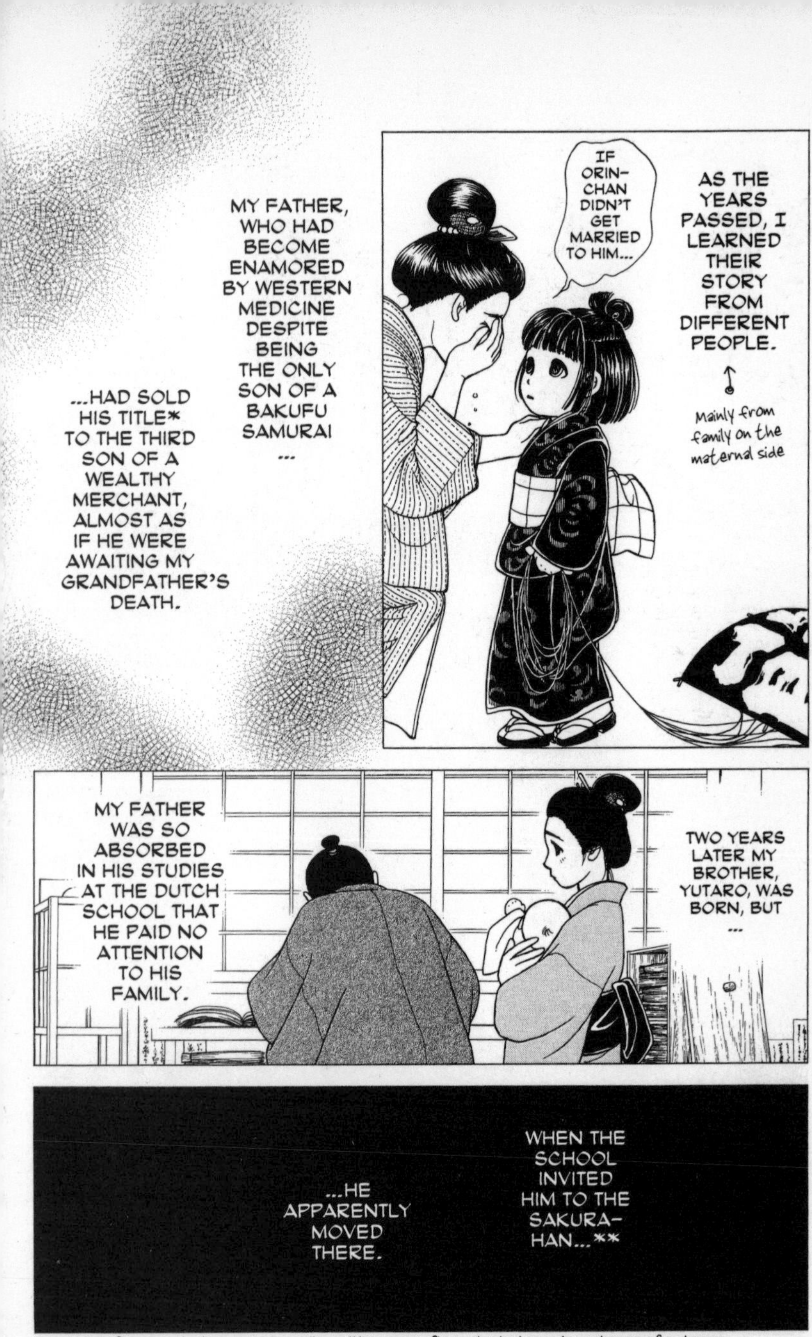
AS THE YEARS PASSED, I LEARNED THEIR STORY FROM DIFFERENT PEOPLE.
IF ORIN-CHAN DIDN'T GET MARRIED TO HIM...
Mainly from family on the maternal side
MY FATHER, WHO HAD BECOME ENAMORED BY WESTERN MEDICINE DESPITE BEING THE ONLY SON OF A BAKUFU SAMURAI...
...HAD SOLD HIS TITLE* TO THE THIRD SON OF A WEALTHY MERCHANT, ALMOST AS IF HE WERE AWAITING MY GRANDFATHER'S DEATH.
TWO YEARS LATER MY BROTHER, YUTARO, WAS BORN, BUT...
MY FATHER WAS SO ABSORBED IN HIS STUDIES AT THE DUTCH SCHOOL THAT HE PAID NO ATTENTION TO HIS FAMILY.
WHEN THE SCHOOL INVITED HIM TO THE SAKURA-HAN...**
...HE APPARENTLY MOVED THERE.

*Lowly Bakufu samurai who were struggling with money often adopted sons in exchange of a dowry.
**Present-day Sakura City in the Chiba Prefecture.

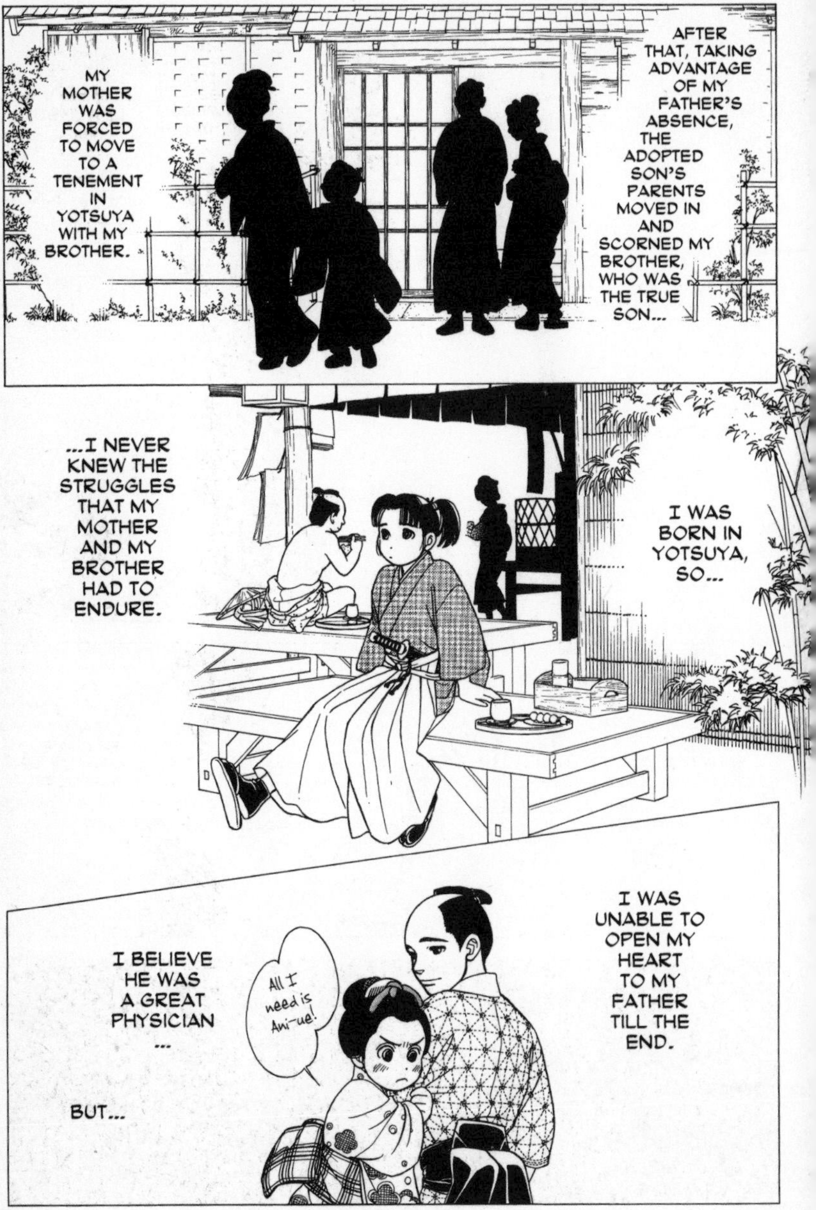
AFTER THAT, TAKING ADVANTAGE OF MY FATHER'S ABSENCE, THE ADOPTED SON'S PARENTS MOVED IN AND SCORNED MY BROTHER, WHO WAS THE TRUE SON...
MY MOTHER WAS FORCED TO MOVE TO A TENEMENT IN YOTSUYA WITH MY BROTHER.
I WAS BORN IN YOTSUYA, SO...
...I NEVER KNEW THE STRUGGLES THAT MY MOTHER AND MY BROTHER HAD TO ENDURE.
I WAS UNABLE TO OPEN MY HEART TO MY FATHER TILL THE END.
All I need is Ani-ue!
I BELIEVE HE WAS A GREAT PHYSICIAN ...
BUT...

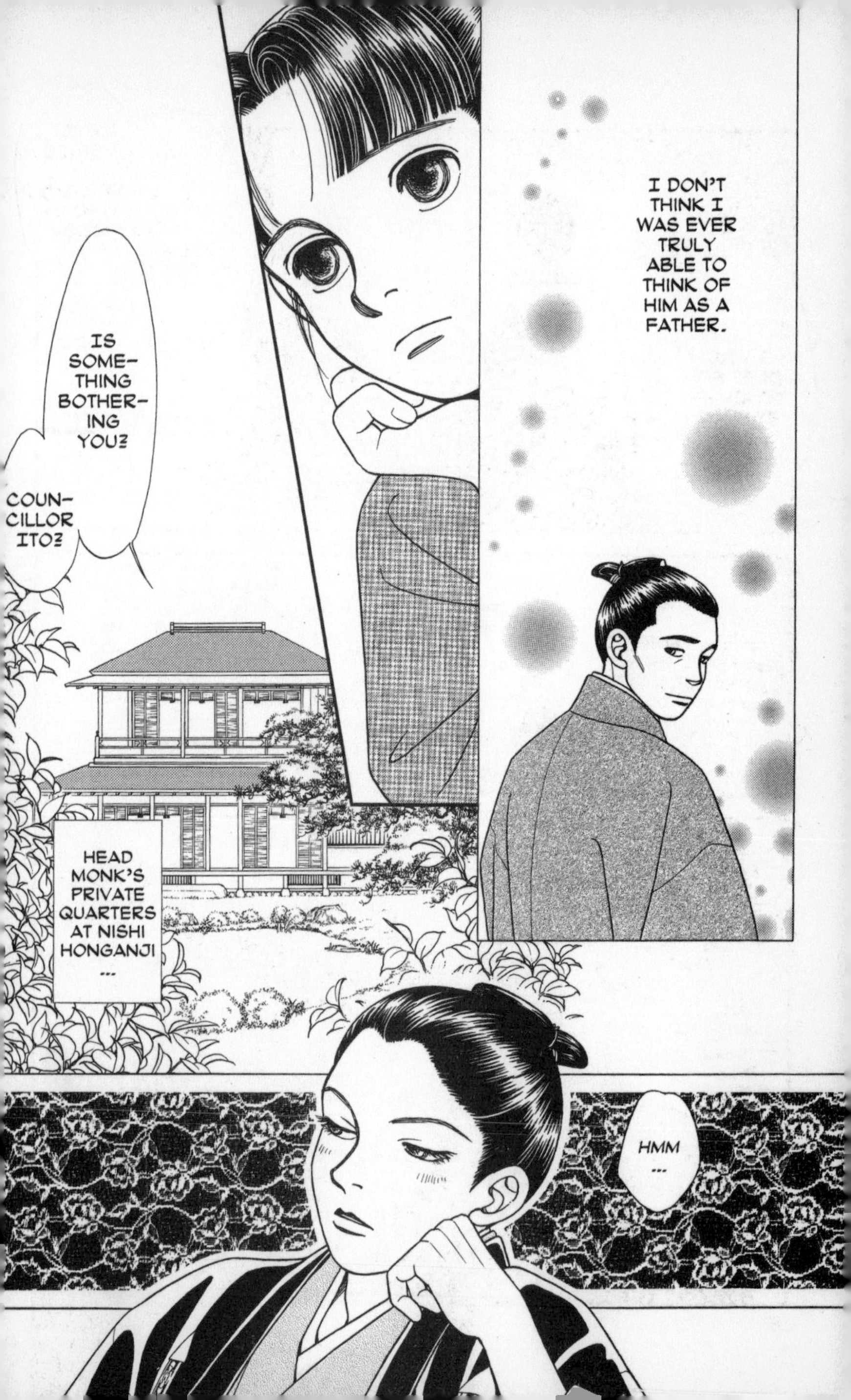
I DON'T THINK I WAS EVER TRULY ABLE TO THINK OF HIM AS A FATHER.
IS SOMETHING BOTHERING YOU?
COUNCILLOR ITO?
HEAD MONK'S PRIVATE QUARTERS AT NISHI HONGANJI ...
HMM ...

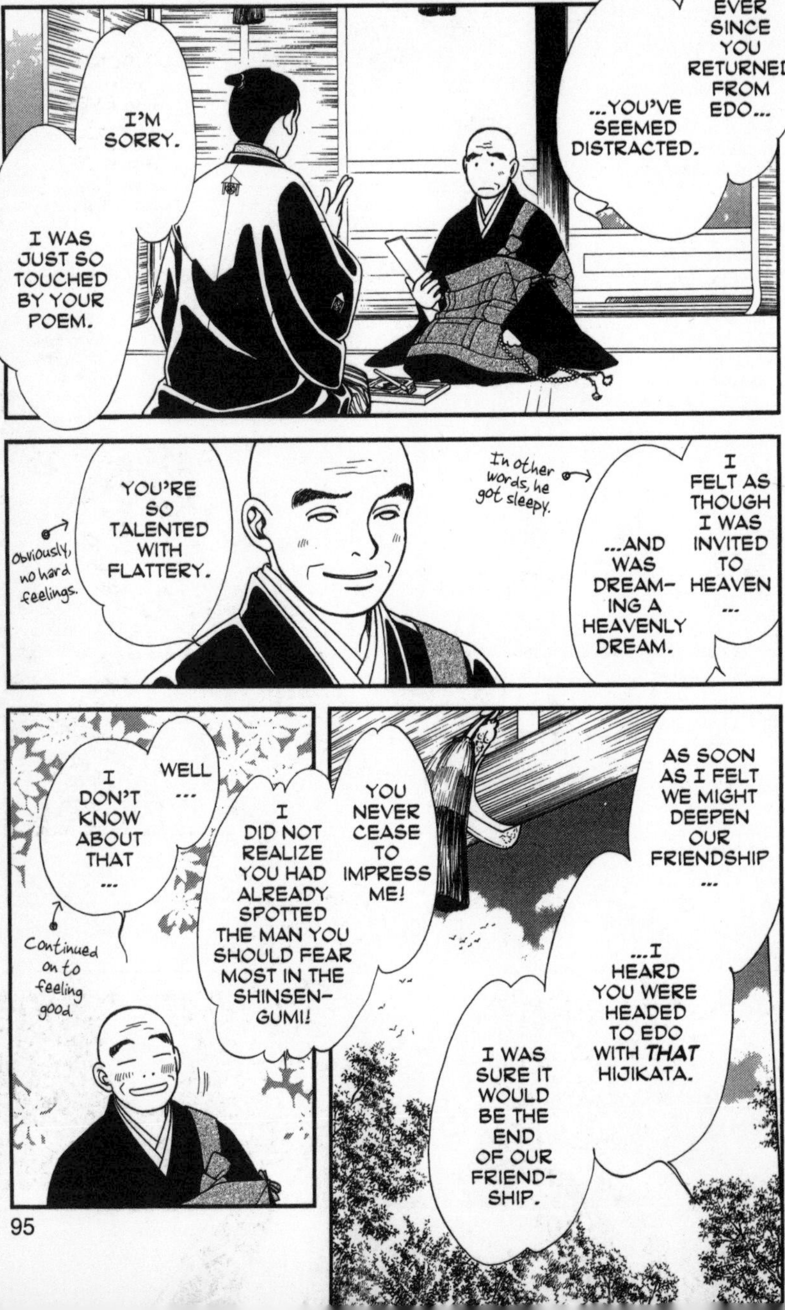
EVER SINCE YOU RETURNED FROM EDO...
...YOU'VE SEEMED DISTRACTED.
I'M SORRY.
I WAS JUST SO TOUCHED BY YOUR POEM.
I FELT AS THOUGH I WAS INVITED TO HEAVEN...
...AND WAS DREAMING A HEAVENLY DREAM.
In other words, he got sleepy.
YOU'RE SO TALENTED WITH FLATTERY.
Obviously, no hard feelings.
AS SOON AS I FELT WE MIGHT DEEPEN OUR FRIENDSHIP...
...I HEARD YOU WERE HEADED TO EDO WITH *THAT* HIJIKATA.
I WAS SURE IT WOULD BE THE END OF OUR FRIENDSHIP.
YOU NEVER CEASE TO IMPRESS ME!
I DID NOT REALIZE YOU HAD ALREADY SPOTTED THE MAN YOU SHOULD FEAR MOST IN THE SHINSENGUMI!
WELL...
I DON'T KNOW ABOUT THAT...
Continued on to feeling good.

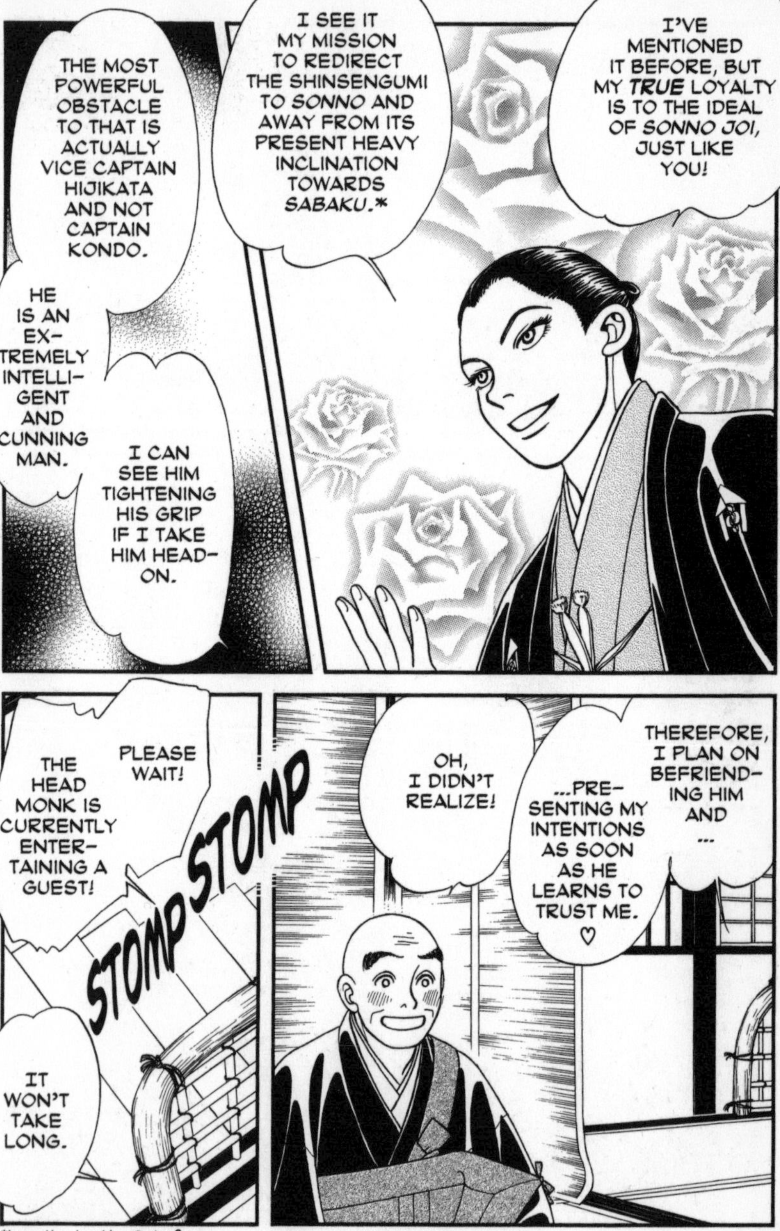
I'VE MENTIONED IT BEFORE, BUT MY TRUE LOYALTY IS TO THE IDEAL OF SONNO JOI, JUST LIKE YOU!
I SEE IT MY MISSION TO REDIRECT THE SHINSENGUMI TO SONNO AND AWAY FROM ITS PRESENT HEAVY INCLINATION TOWARDS SABAKU.*
THE MOST POWERFUL OBSTACLE TO THAT IS ACTUALLY VICE CAPTAIN HIJIKATA AND NOT CAPTAIN KONDO.
HE IS AN EXTREMELY INTELLIGENT AND CUNNING MAN.
I CAN SEE HIM TIGHTENING HIS GRIP IF I TAKE HIM HEAD-ON.
THEREFORE, I PLAN ON BEFRIENDING HIM AND ...
...PRESENTING MY INTENTIONS AS SOON AS HE LEARNS TO TRUST ME. ♡
OH, I DIDN'T REALIZE!
PLEASE WAIT!
THE HEAD MONK IS CURRENTLY ENTERTAINING A GUEST!
STOMP STOMP
IT WON'T TAKE LONG.

*Loyalty to the Bakufu

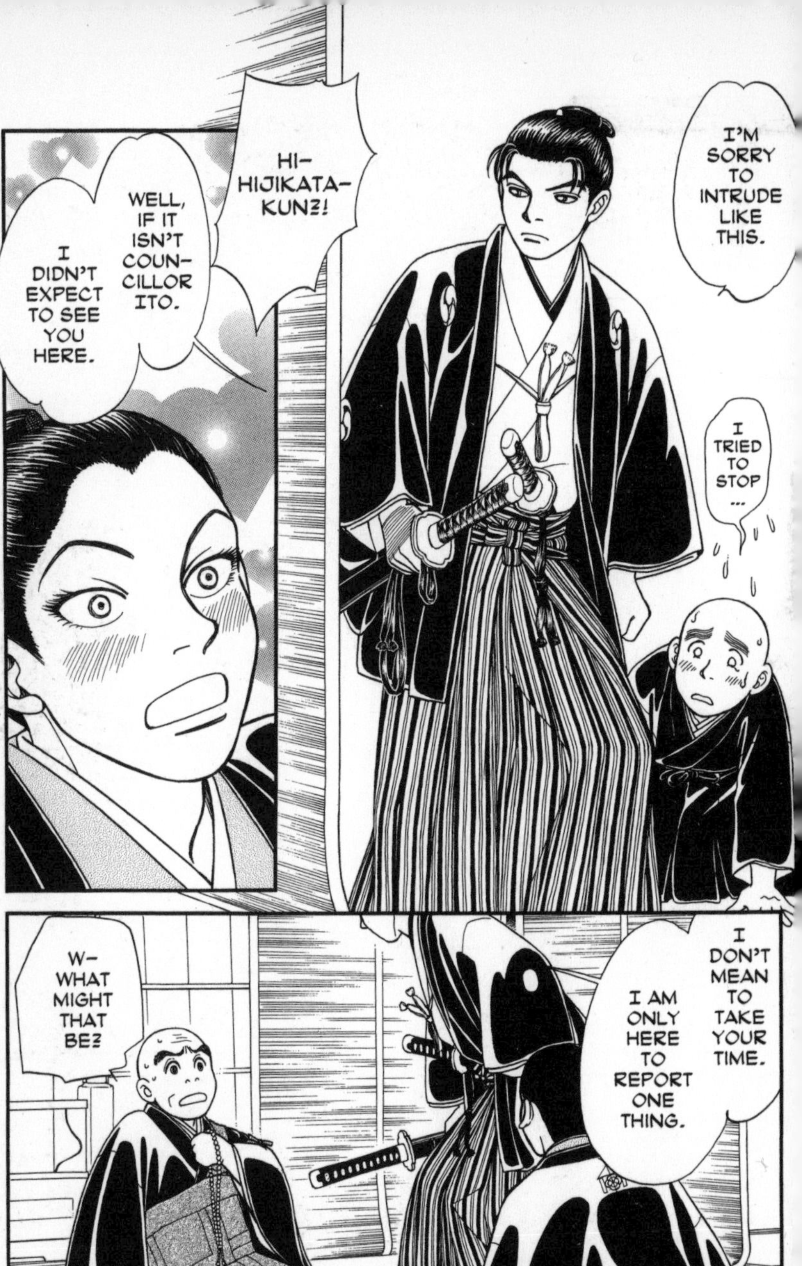
I'M SORRY TO INTRUDE LIKE THIS.
I TRIED TO STOP ...
HI-HIJIKATA-KUN?!
WELL, IF IT ISN'T COUNCILLOR ITO.
I DIDN'T EXPECT TO SEE YOU HERE.
I DON'T MEAN TO TAKE YOUR TIME.
I AM ONLY HERE TO REPORT ONE THING.
W-WHAT MIGHT THAT BE?

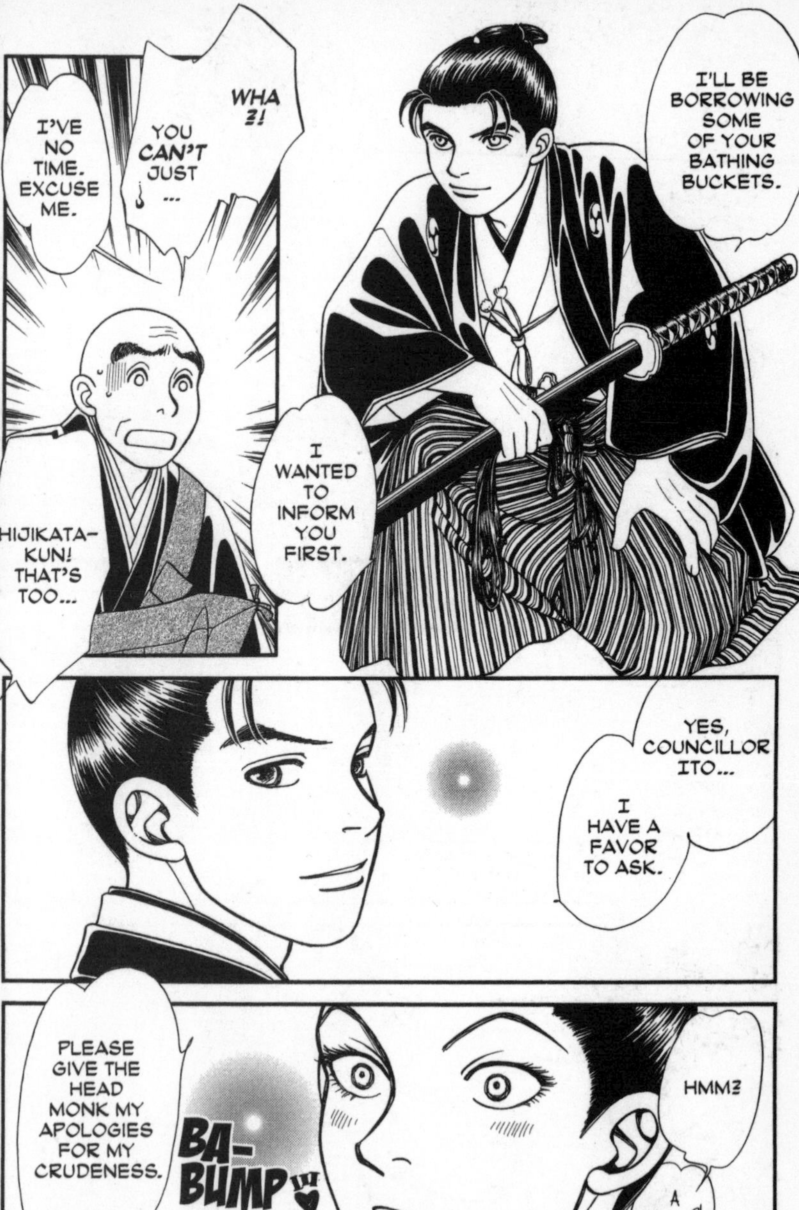
I'LL BE BORROWING SOME OF YOUR BATHING BUCKETS.
I WANTED TO INFORM YOU FIRST.
WHA?!
YOU CAN'T JUST ...
I'VE NO TIME. EXCUSE ME.
HIJIKATA-KUN! THAT'S TOO...
YES, COUNCILLOR ITO...
I HAVE A FAVOR TO ASK.
HMM?
A favor?!
BA-BUMP
PLEASE GIVE THE HEAD MONK MY APOLOGIES FOR MY CRUDENESS.

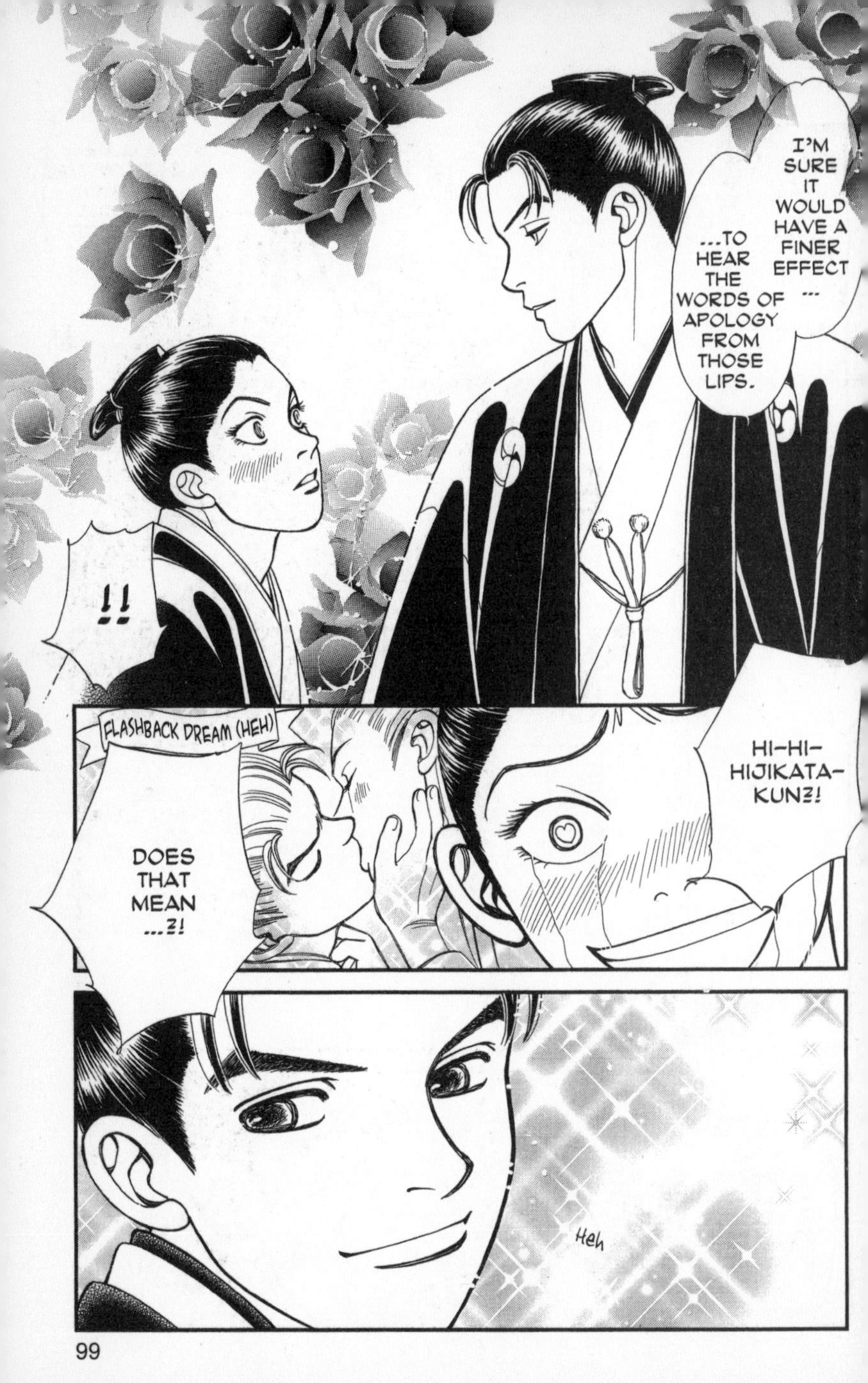
I'M SURE IT WOULD HAVE A FINER EFFECT ...
...TO HEAR THE WORDS OF APOLOGY FROM THOSE LIPS.
!!
HI-HI-HIJIKATA-KUN?!
FLASHBACK DREAM (HEH)
DOES THAT MEAN ...?!
Heh

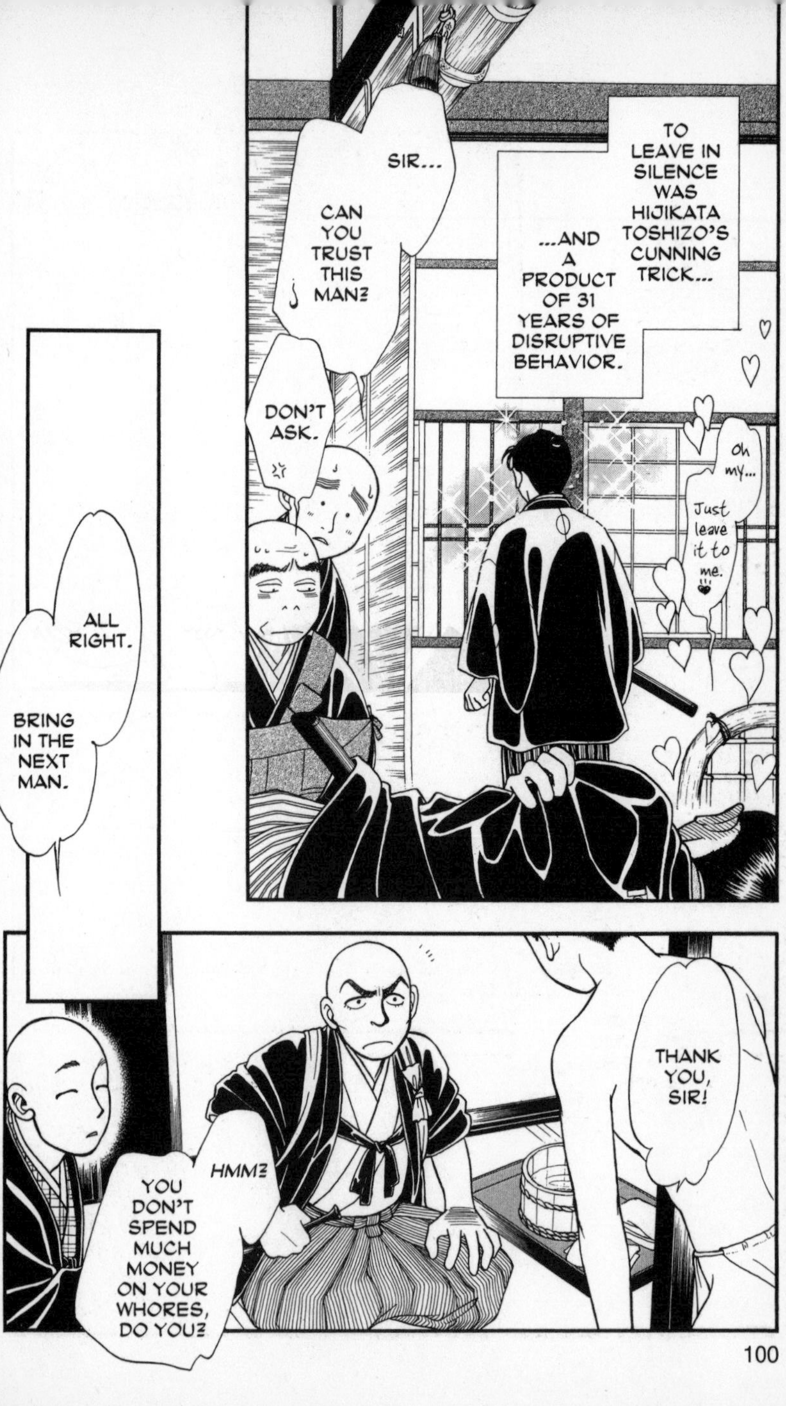
TO LEAVE IN SILENCE WAS HIJIKATA TOSHIZO'S CUNNING TRICK...
...AND A PRODUCT OF 31 YEARS OF DISRUPTIVE BEHAVIOR.
Oh my... Just leave it to me.
SIR... CAN YOU TRUST THIS MAN?
DON'T ASK.
ALL RIGHT. BRING IN THE NEXT MAN.
THANK YOU, SIR!
HMM? YOU DON'T SPEND MUCH MONEY ON YOUR WHORES, DO YOU?

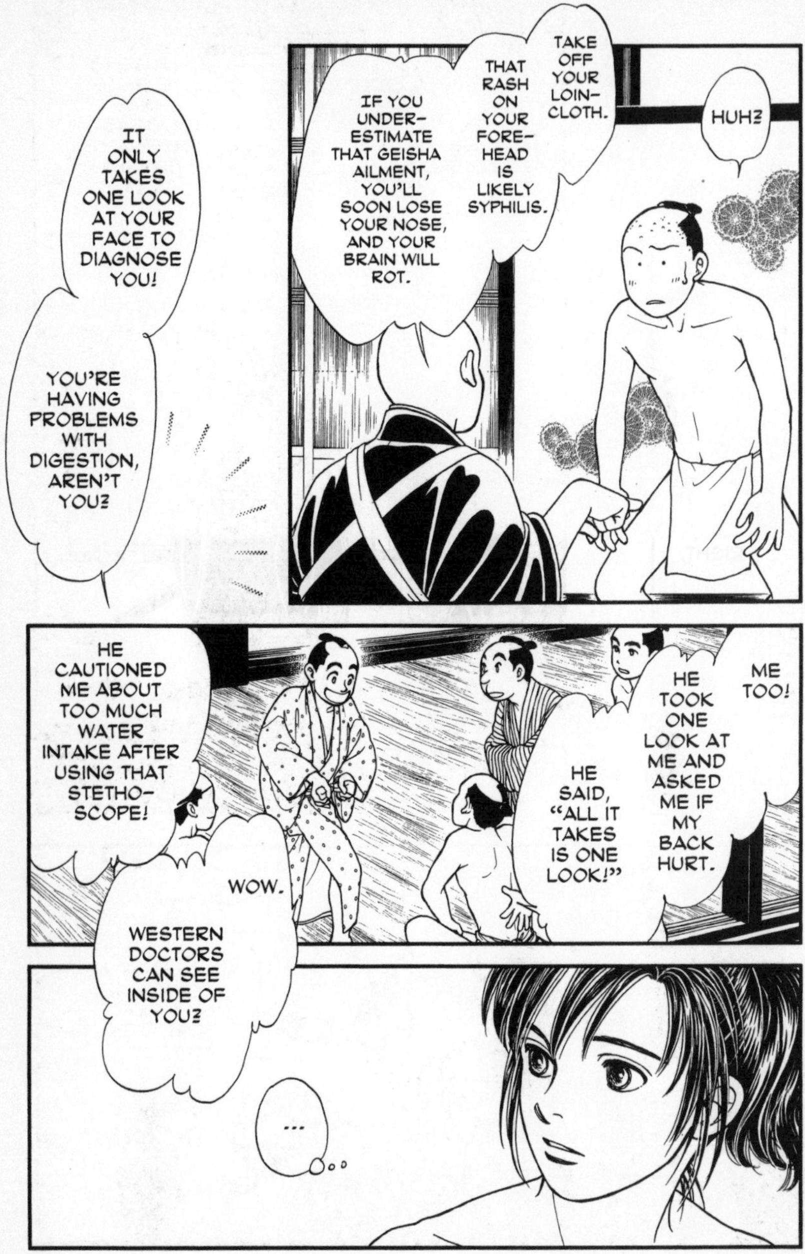
HUH?
TAKE OFF YOUR LOIN-CLOTH.
THAT RASH ON YOUR FORE-HEAD IS LIKELY SYPHILIS.
IF YOU UNDER-ESTIMATE THAT GEISHA AILMENT, YOU'LL SOON LOSE YOUR NOSE, AND YOUR BRAIN WILL ROT.
IT ONLY TAKES ONE LOOK AT YOUR FACE TO DIAGNOSE YOU!
YOU'RE HAVING PROBLEMS WITH DIGESTION, AREN'T YOU?
ME TOO!
HE TOOK ONE LOOK AT ME AND ASKED ME IF MY BACK HURT.
HE SAID, "ALL IT TAKES IS ONE LOOK!"
HE CAUTIONED ME ABOUT TOO MUCH WATER INTAKE AFTER USING THAT STETHO-SCOPE!
WOW.
WESTERN DOCTORS CAN SEE INSIDE OF YOU?
...

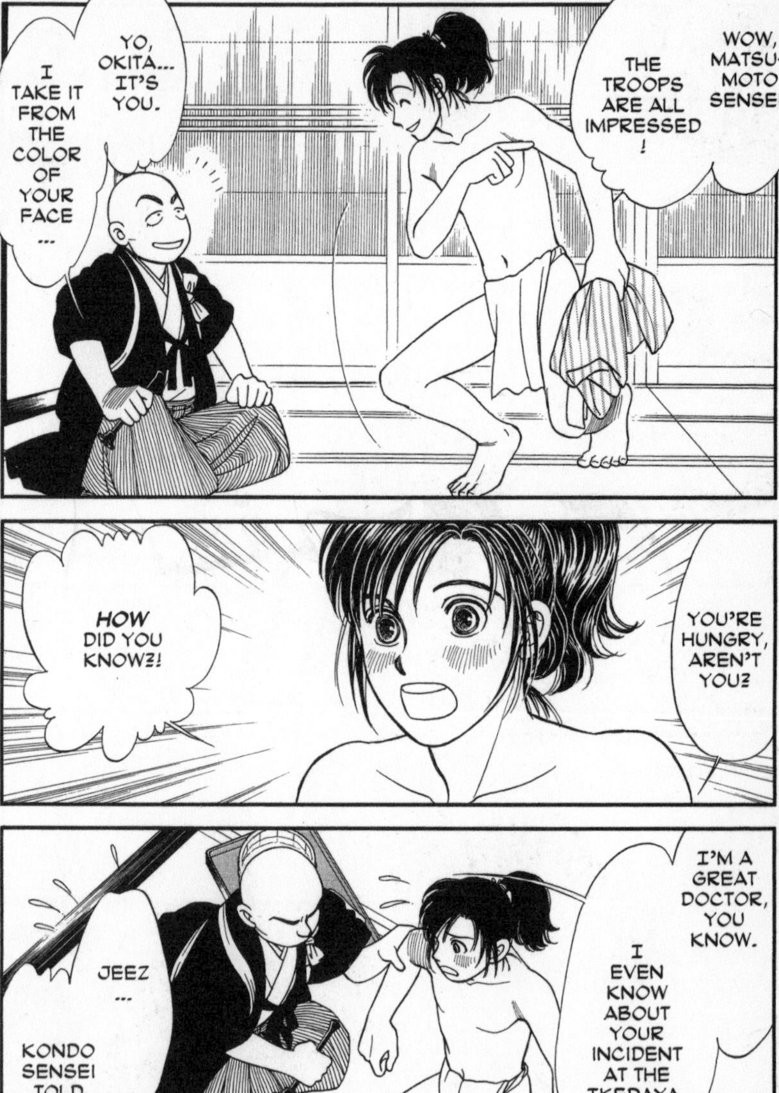
WOW, MATSU-MOTO SENSEI.
THE TROOPS ARE ALL IMPRESSED!
YO, OKITA... IT'S YOU.
I TAKE IT FROM THE COLOR OF YOUR FACE...
YOU'RE HUNGRY, AREN'T YOU?
HOW DID YOU KNOW?!
I'M A GREAT DOCTOR, YOU KNOW.
I EVEN KNOW ABOUT YOUR INCIDENT AT THE IKEDAYA.
JEEZ...
KONDO SENSEI TOLD YOU ALL THAT?

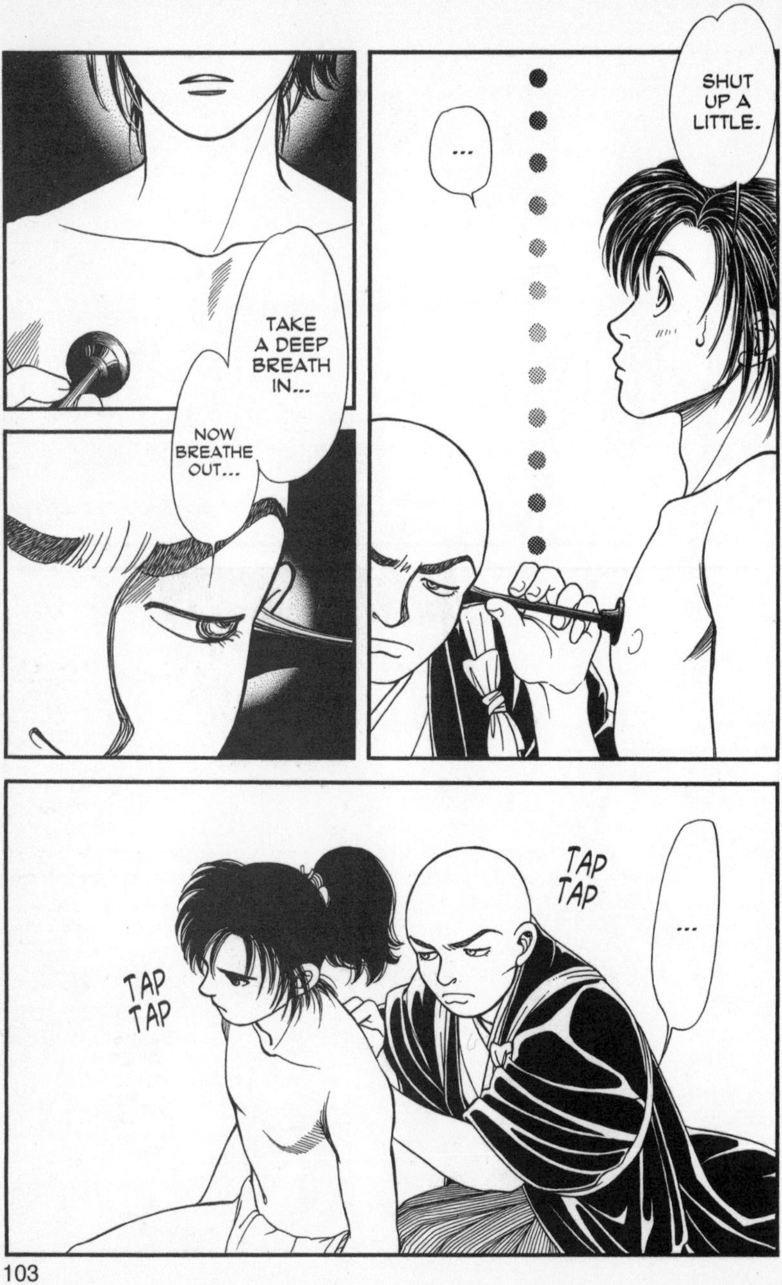
SHUT UP A LITTLE.
...
TAKE A DEEP BREATH IN...
NOW BREATHE OUT...
...
TAP TAP
TAP TAP

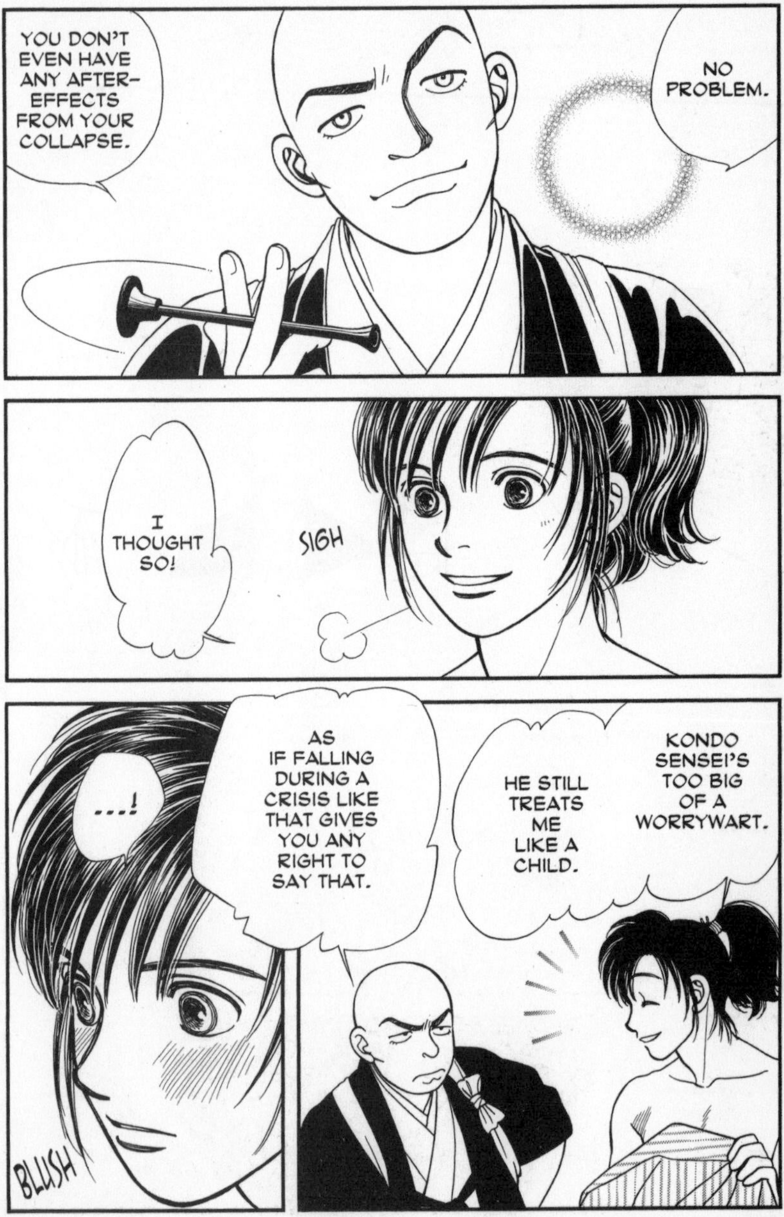
NO PROBLEM.
YOU DON'T EVEN HAVE ANY AFTER-EFFECTS FROM YOUR COLLAPSE.
SIGH
I THOUGHT SO!
KONDO SENSEI'S TOO BIG OF A WORRYWART.
HE STILL TREATS ME LIKE A CHILD.
AS IF FALLING DURING A CRISIS LIKE THAT GIVES YOU ANY RIGHT TO SAY THAT.
...!
BLUSH

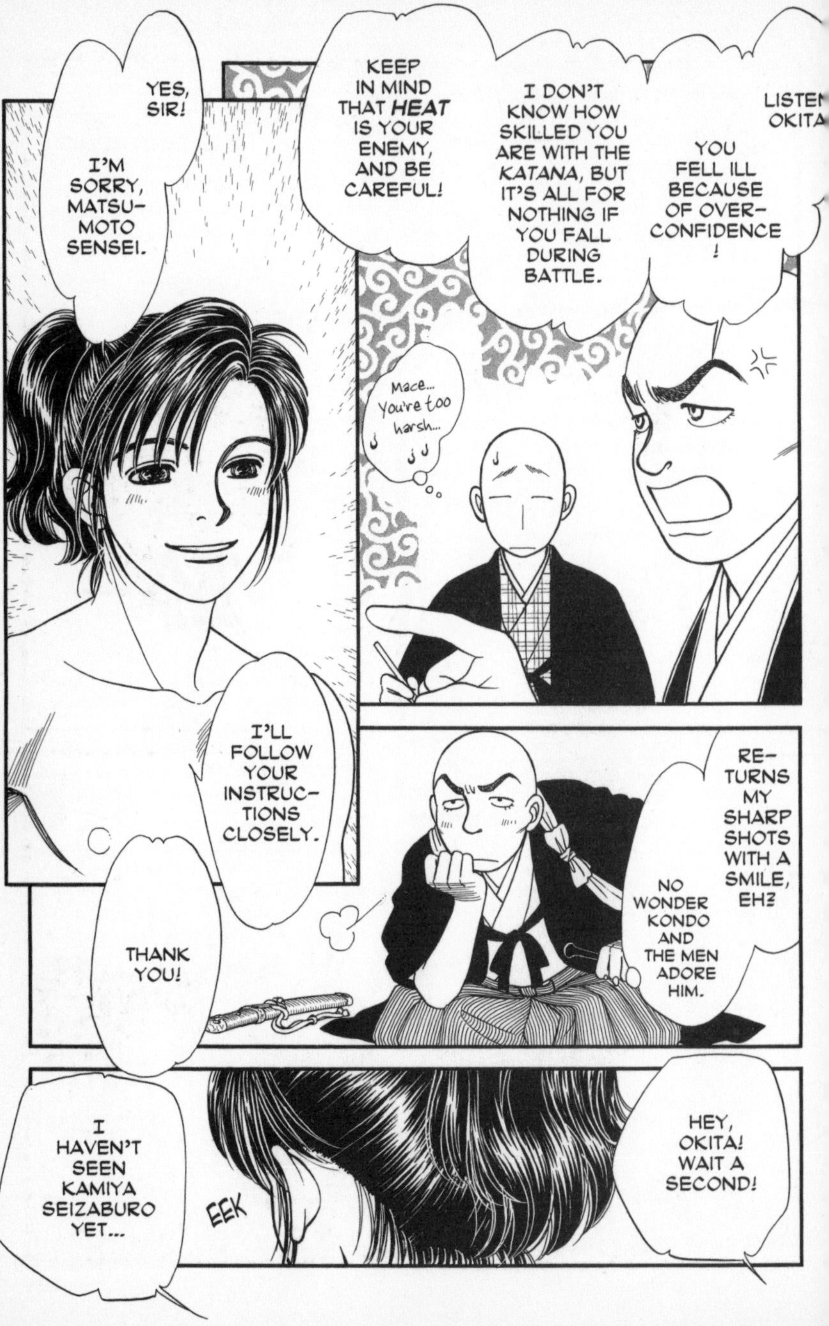
LISTEN OKITA
YOU FELL ILL BECAUSE OF OVER-CONFIDENCE!
I DON'T KNOW HOW SKILLED YOU ARE WITH THE *KATANA*, BUT IT'S ALL FOR NOTHING IF YOU FALL DURING BATTLE.
KEEP IN MIND THAT ***HEAT*** IS YOUR ENEMY, AND BE CAREFUL!
Mace... You're too harsh...
YES, SIR!
I'M SORRY, MATSU-MOTO SENSEI.
I'LL FOLLOW YOUR INSTRUC-TIONS CLOSELY.
THANK YOU!
RE-TURNS MY SHARP SHOTS WITH A SMILE, EH?
NO WONDER KONDO AND THE MEN ADORE HIM.
HEY, OKITA! WAIT A SECOND!
EEK
I HAVEN'T SEEN KAMIYA SEIZABURO YET...

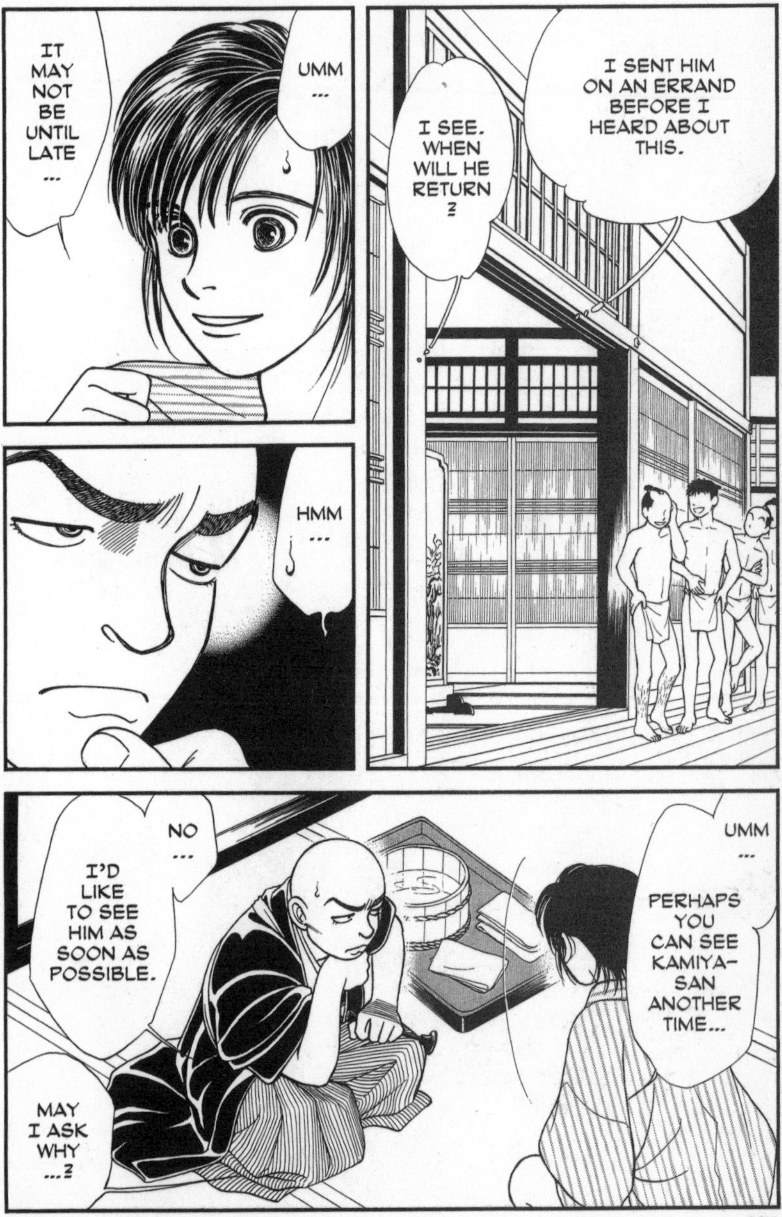
I SENT HIM ON AN ERRAND BEFORE I HEARD ABOUT THIS.
I SEE. WHEN WILL HE RETURN?
UMM...
IT MAY NOT BE UNTIL LATE...
HMM...
UMM...
PERHAPS YOU CAN SEE KAMIYA-SAN ANOTHER TIME...
NO...
I'D LIKE TO SEE HIM AS SOON AS POSSIBLE.
MAY I ASK WHY...?

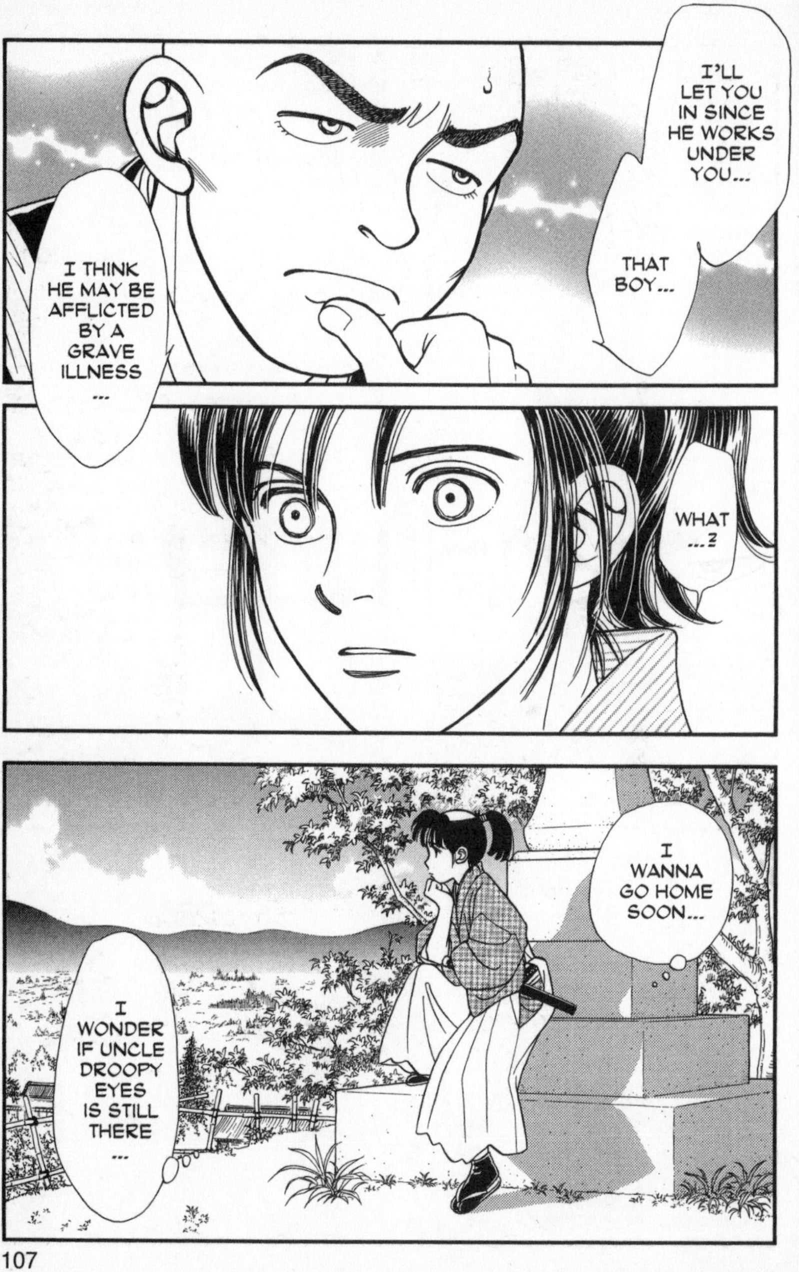
I'LL LET YOU IN SINCE HE WORKS UNDER YOU...
THAT BOY...
I THINK HE MAY BE AFFLICTED BY A GRAVE ILLNESS ...
WHAT ...?
I WANNA GO HOME SOON...
I WONDER IF UNCLE DROOPY EYES IS STILL THERE ...

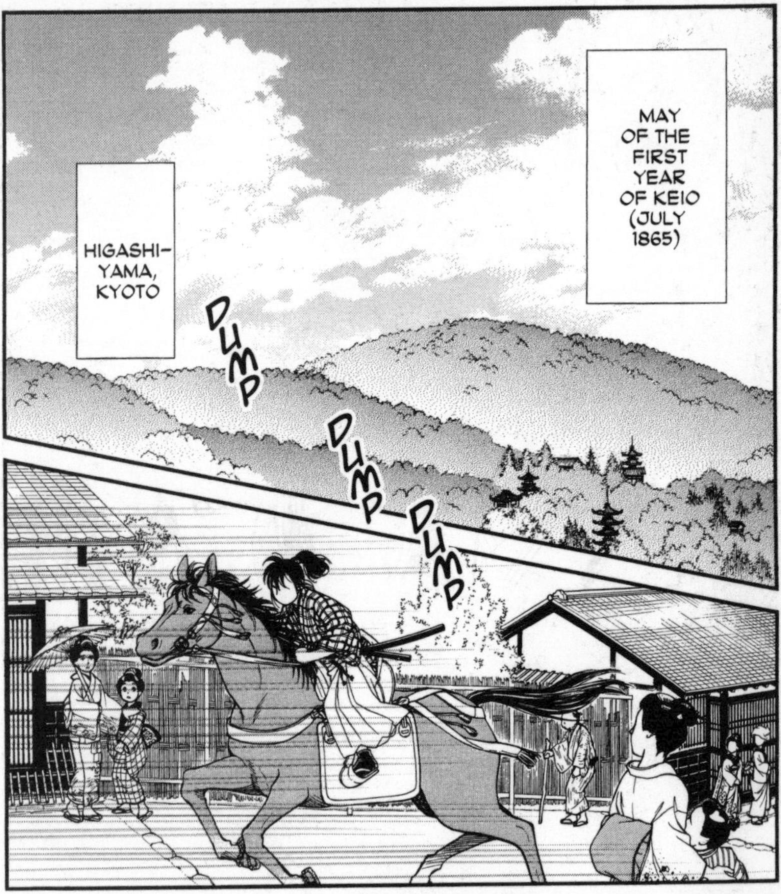
MAY OF THE FIRST YEAR OF KEIO (JULY 1865)
HIGASHI-YAMA, KYOTO
DUMP
DUMP
DUMP
DUMP

"KO" こ

KO WA SANGAI NO KUBIKAZE
"CHILDREN SUCK THE MOTHER WHEN THEY ARE YOUNG AND THE FATHER WHEN THEY ARE OLD"
(lit. Children are bound to us all through our three incarnations)

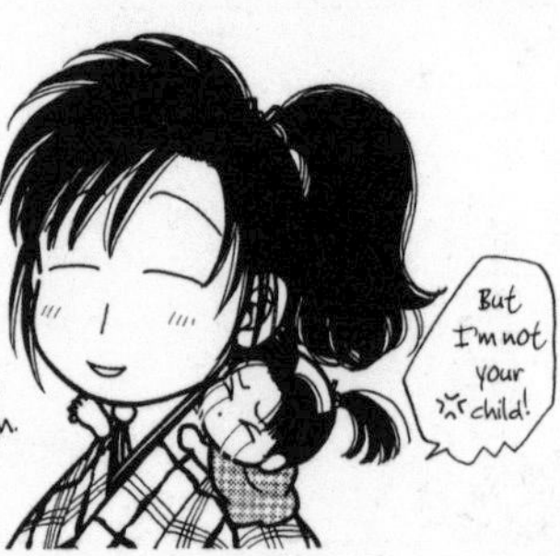
But I'm not your child!
I'm still happy though.

EDO IROHA KARUTA GAME

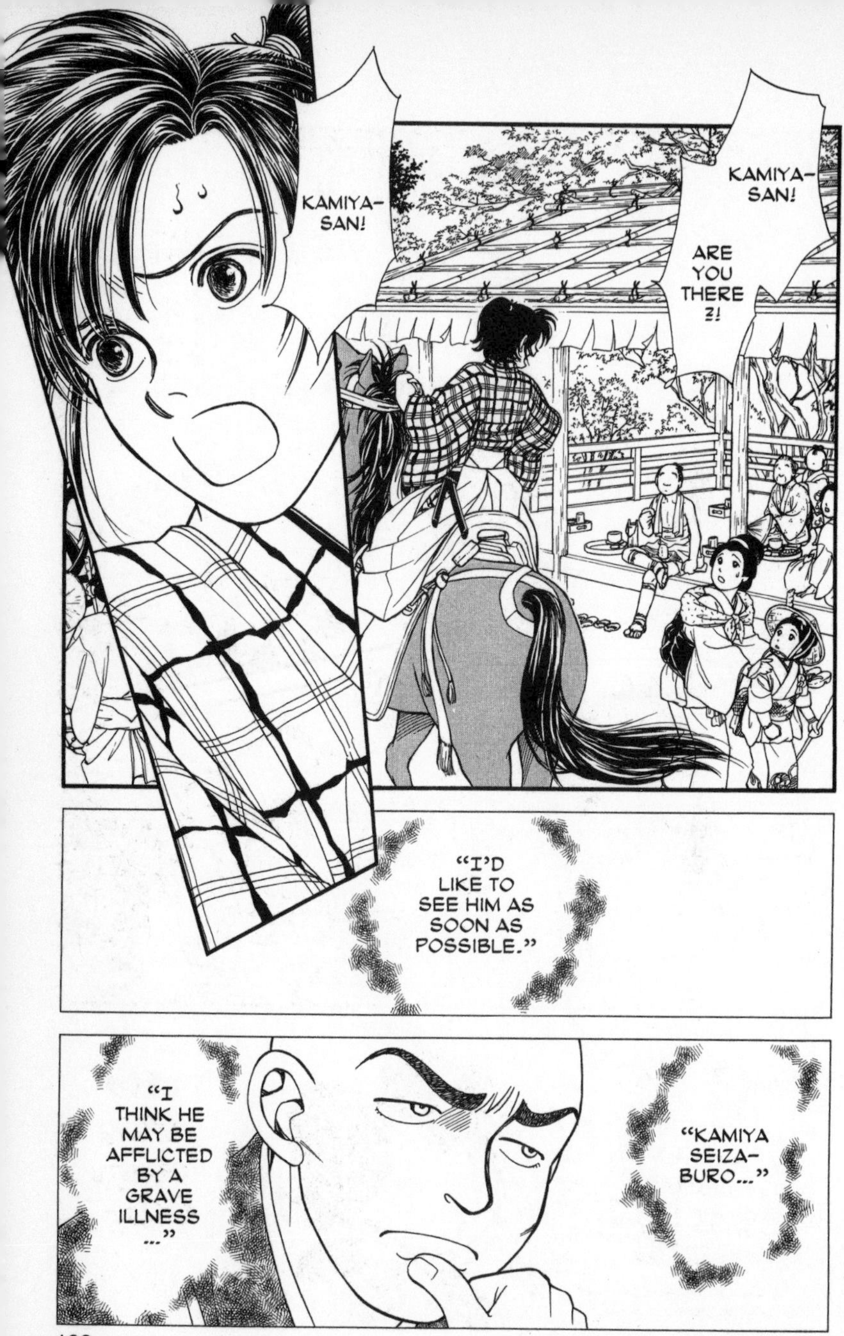
KAMIYA-SAN!
ARE YOU THERE ?!
KAMIYA-SAN!
"I'D LIKE TO SEE HIM AS SOON AS POSSIBLE."
"KAMIYA SEIZA-BURO..."
"I THINK HE MAY BE AFFLICTED BY A GRAVE ILLNESS ..."

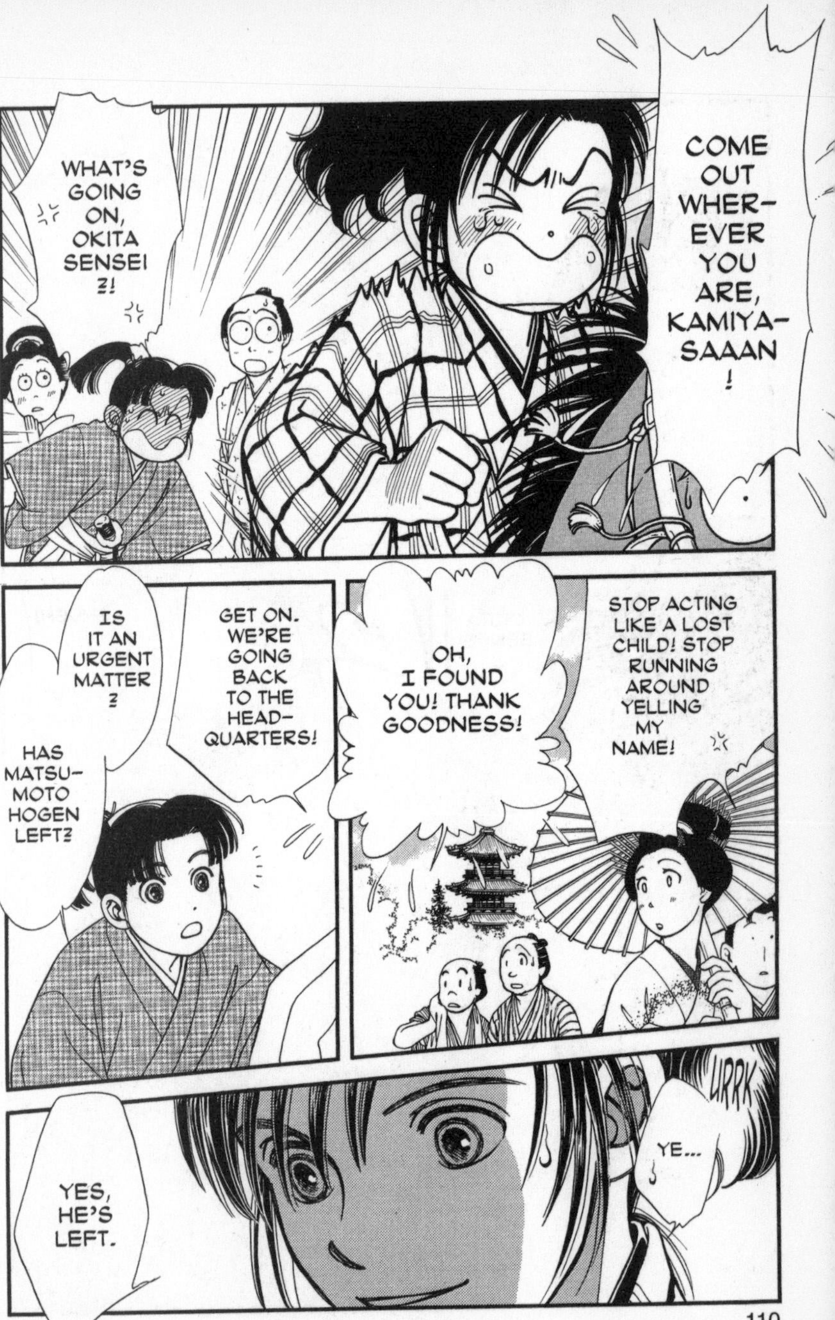
COME OUT WHEREVER YOU ARE, KAMIYA-SAAAN!
WHAT'S GOING ON, OKITA SENSEI?!
STOP ACTING LIKE A LOST CHILD! STOP RUNNING AROUND YELLING MY NAME!
OH, I FOUND YOU! THANK GOODNESS!
GET ON. WE'RE GOING BACK TO THE HEADQUARTERS!
IS IT AN URGENT MATTER?
HAS MATSUMOTO HOGEN LEFT?
URRK
YE...
YES, HE'S LEFT.

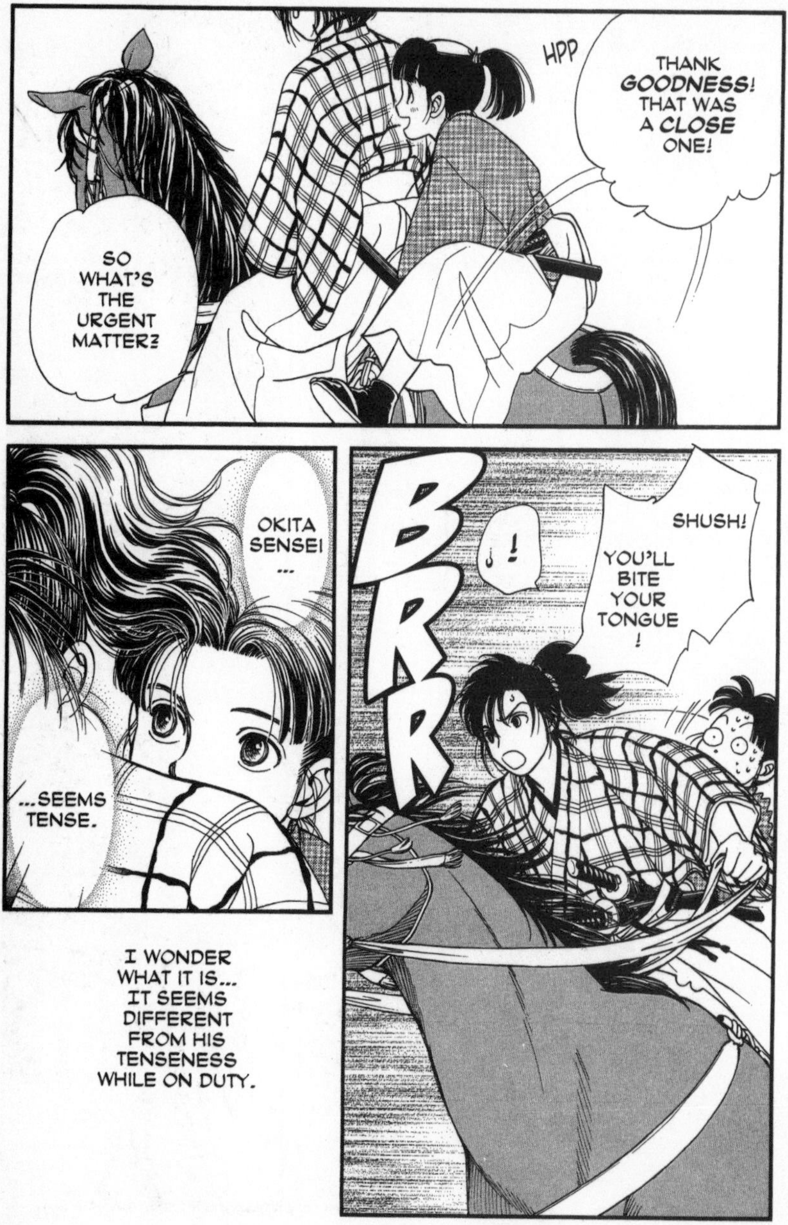
THANK GOODNESS! THAT WAS A CLOSE ONE!
HPP
SO WHAT'S THE URGENT MATTER?
BRR
!
SHUSH!
YOU'LL BITE YOUR TONGUE!
OKITA SENSEI ...
...SEEMS TENSE.
I WONDER WHAT IT IS... IT SEEMS DIFFERENT FROM HIS TENSENESS WHILE ON DUTY.

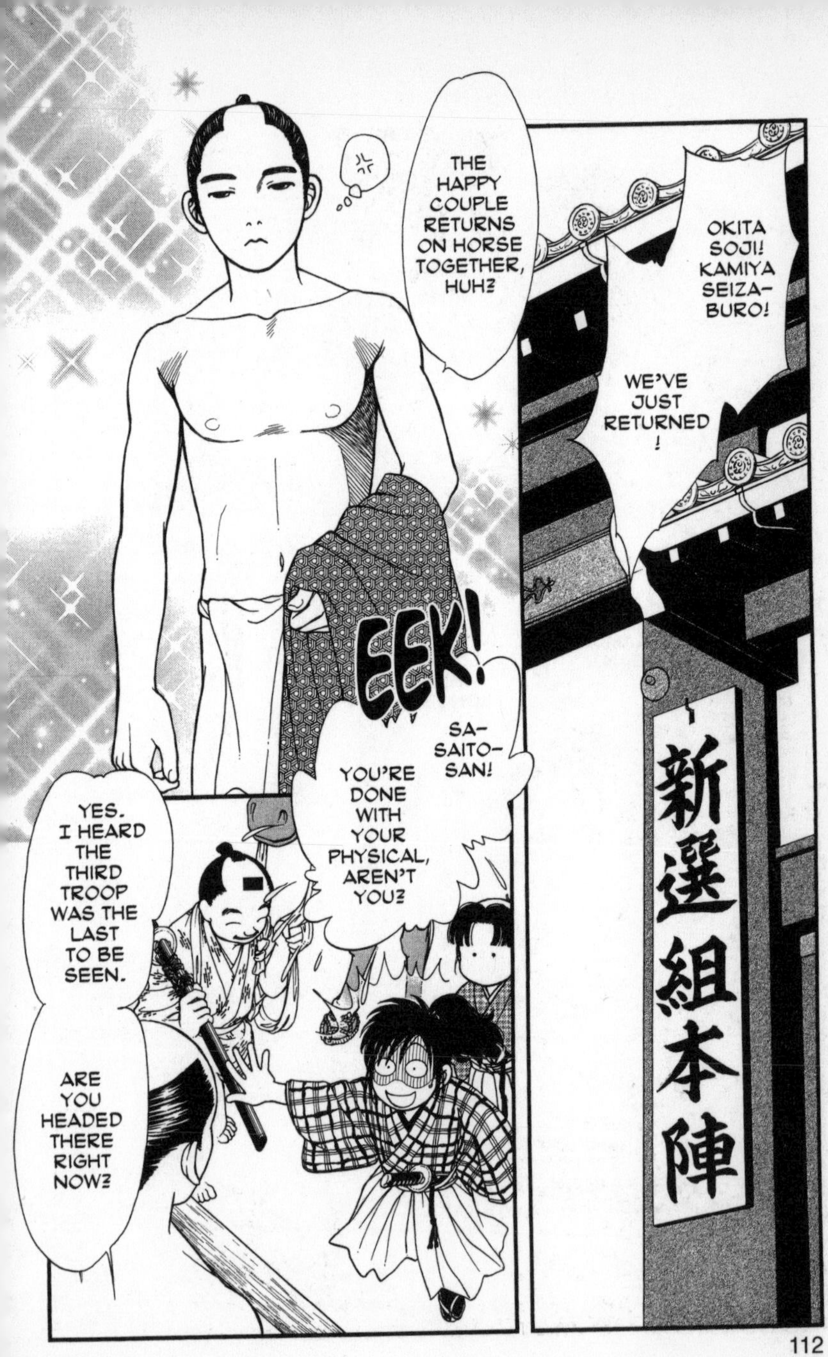
OKITA SOJI! KAMIYA SEIZABURO!
WE'VE JUST RETURNED!
新選組本陣
THE HAPPY COUPLE RETURNS ON HORSE TOGETHER, HUH?
EEK!
SA-SAITO-SAN!
YOU'RE DONE WITH YOUR PHYSICAL, AREN'T YOU?
YES. I HEARD THE THIRD TROOP WAS THE LAST TO BE SEEN.
ARE YOU HEADED THERE RIGHT NOW?

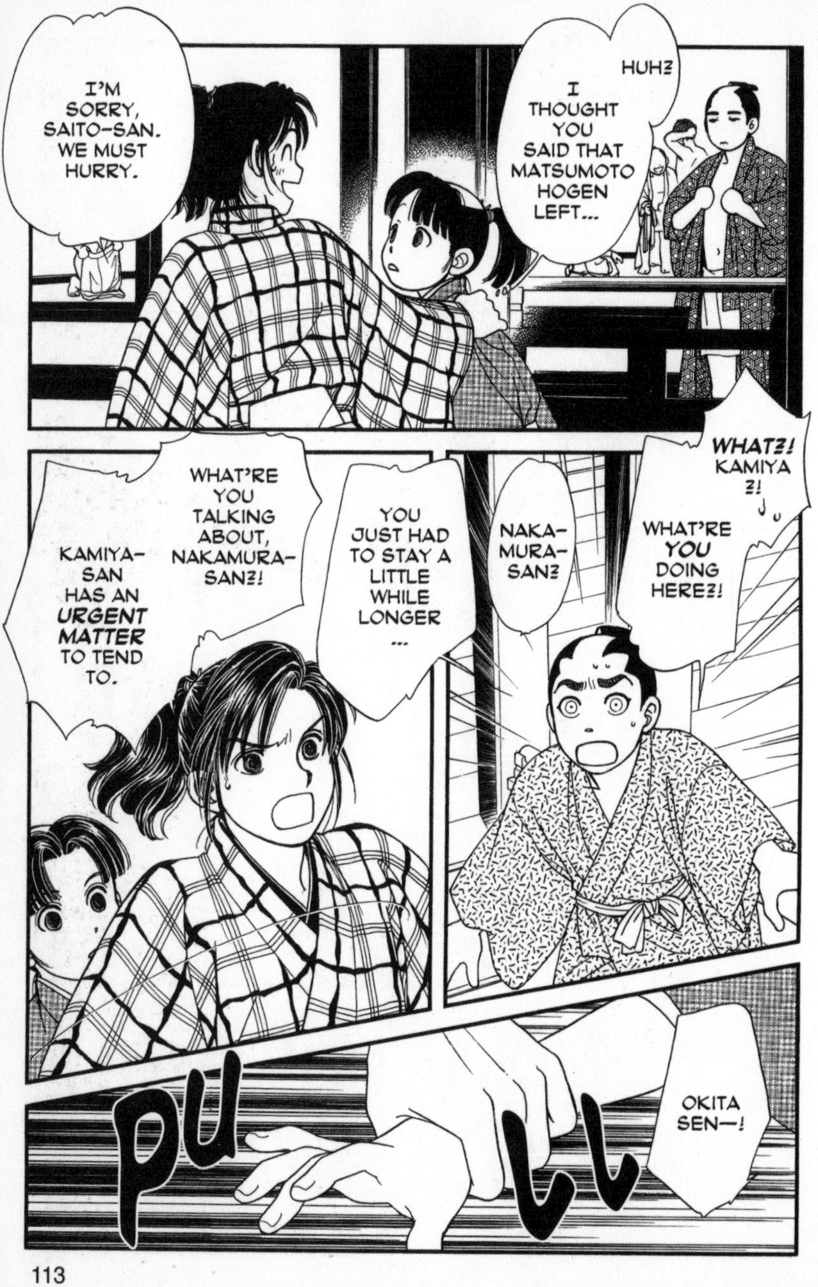
HUH?
I THOUGHT YOU SAID THAT MATSUMOTO HOGEN LEFT...
I'M SORRY, SAITO-SAN. WE MUST HURRY.
WHAT?! KAMIYA?!
WHAT'RE **YOU** DOING HERE?!
NAKA-MURA-SAN?
YOU JUST HAD TO STAY A LITTLE WHILE LONGER ...
WHAT'RE YOU TALKING ABOUT, NAKAMURA-SAN?!
KAMIYA-SAN HAS AN **URGENT MATTER** TO TEND TO.
OKITA SEN—!
PULL

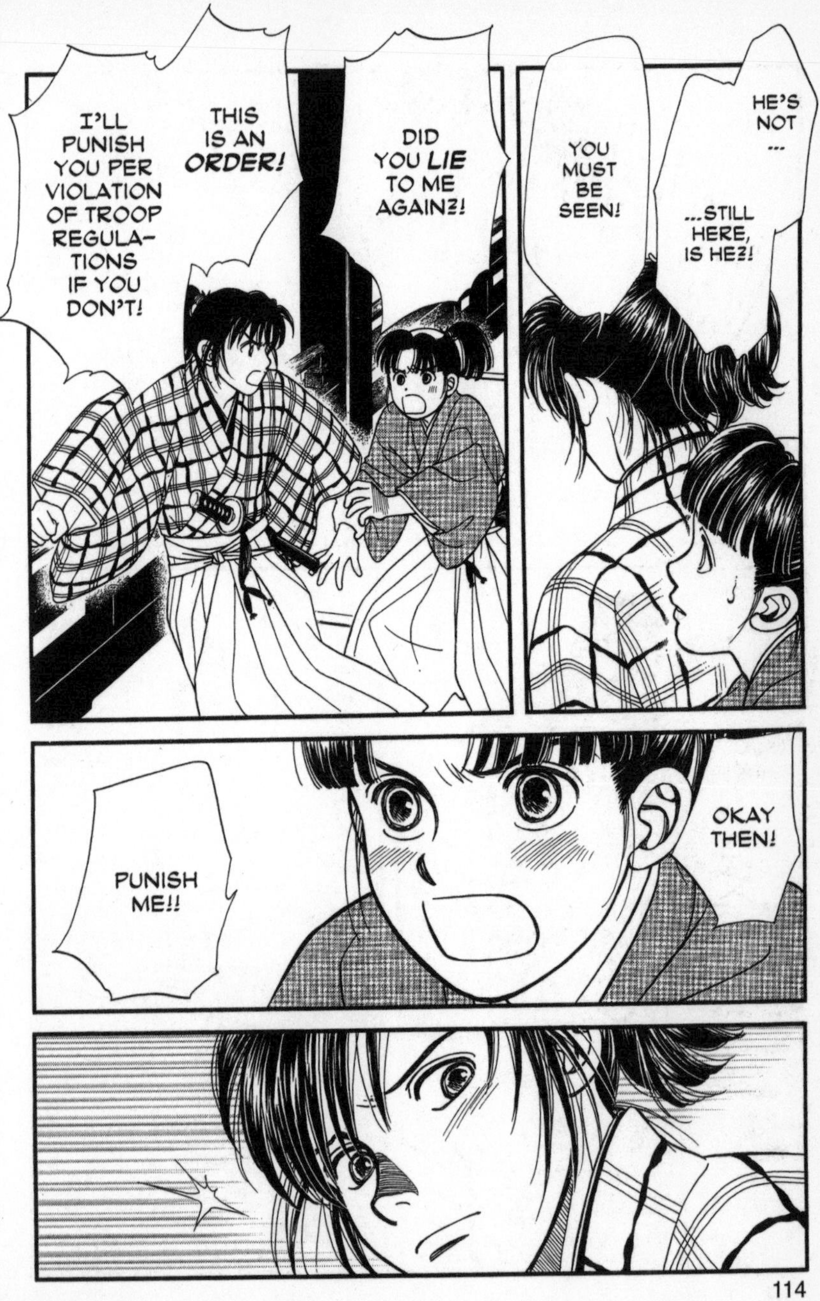
HE'S NOT ...
...STILL HERE, IS HE?!
YOU MUST BE SEEN!
DID YOU LIE TO ME AGAIN?!
THIS IS AN ORDER!
I'LL PUNISH YOU PER VIOLATION OF TROOP REGULATIONS IF YOU DON'T!
OKAY THEN!
PUNISH ME!!

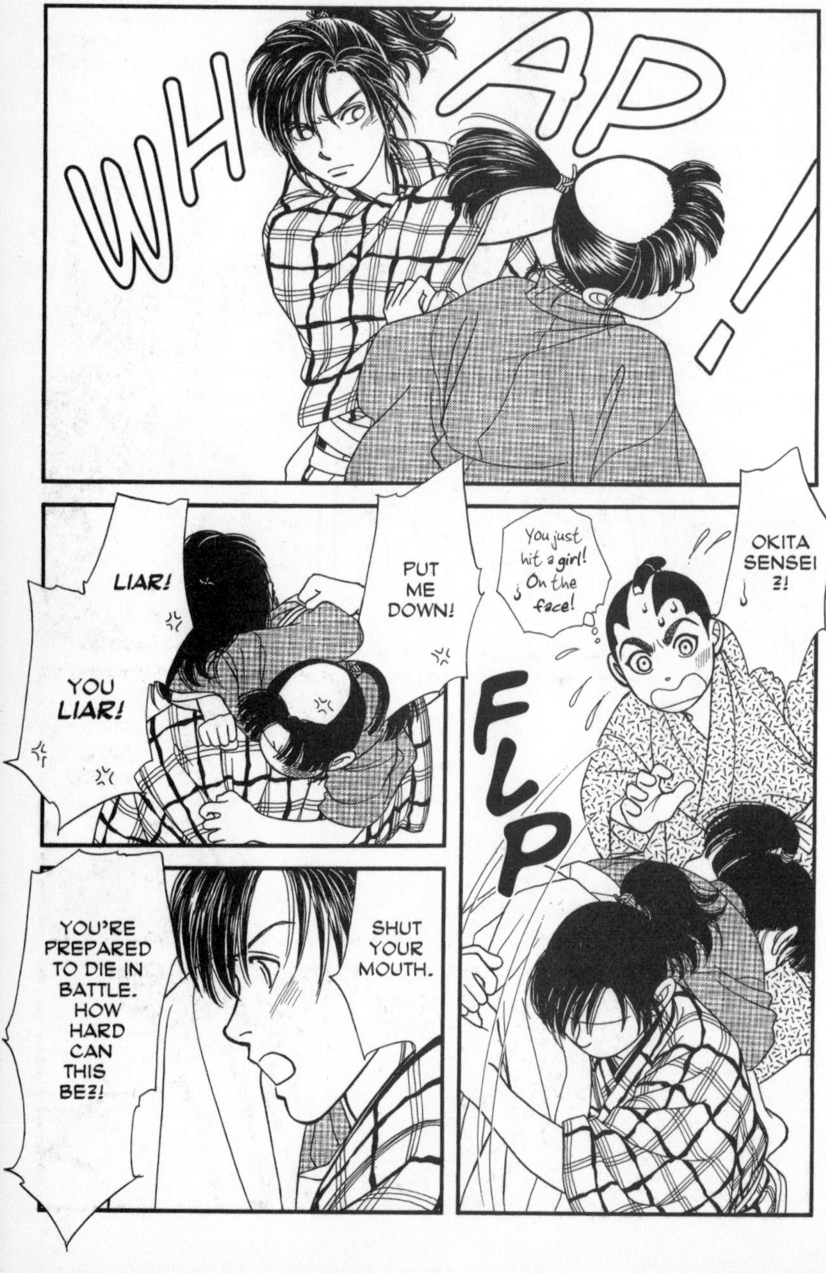
WHAP!!
OKITA SENSEI?!
You just hit a girl! On the face!
FLP
PUT ME DOWN!
LIAR!
YOU LIAR!
SHUT YOUR MOUTH.
YOU'RE PREPARED TO DIE IN BATTLE. HOW HARD CAN THIS BE?!

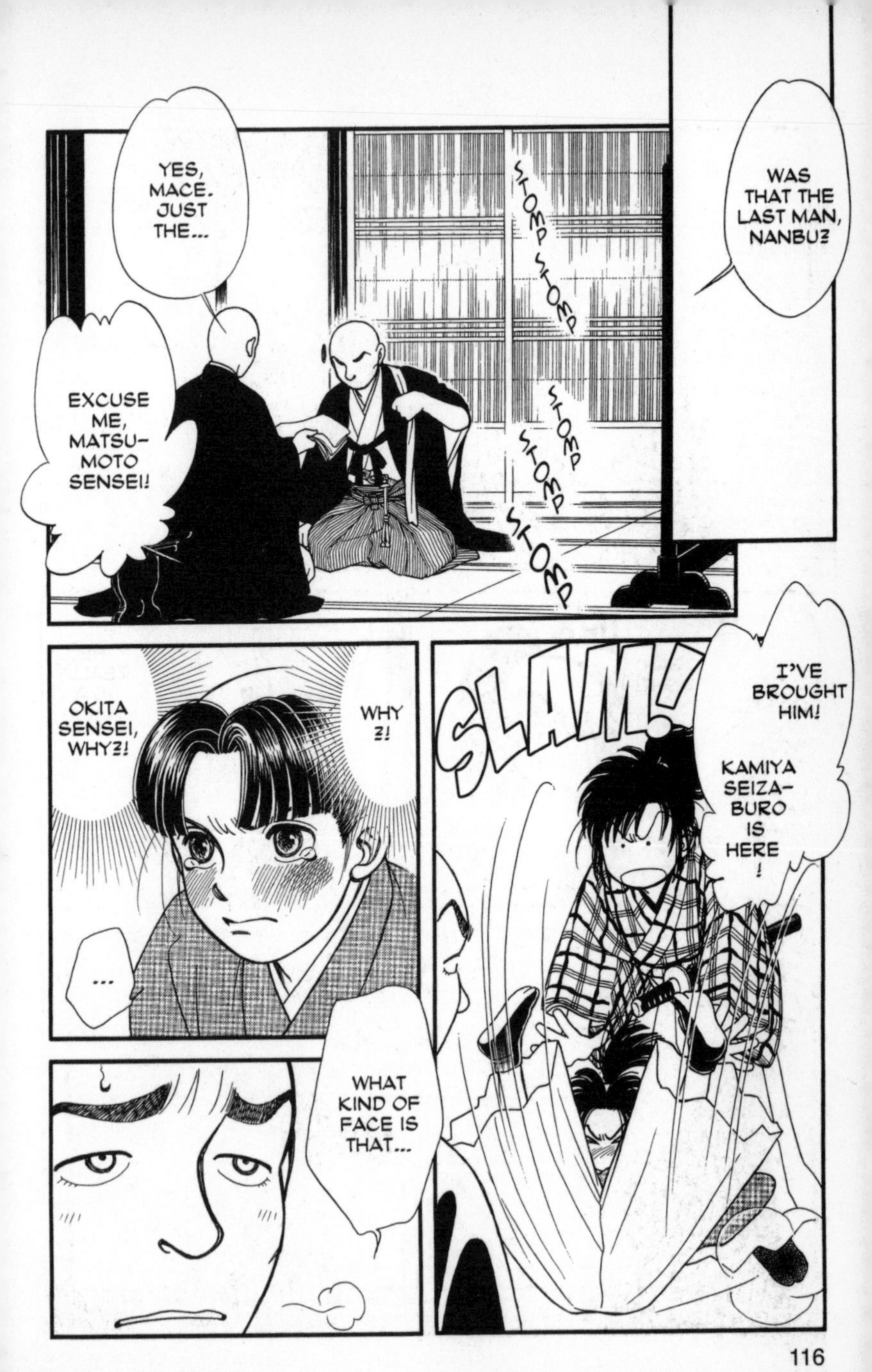
WAS THAT THE LAST MAN, NANBU?
YES, MACE. JUST THE...
STOMP STOMP STOMP
STOMP STOMP STOMP
EXCUSE ME, MATSUMOTO SENSEI!
SLAM!
I'VE BROUGHT HIM!
KAMIYA SEIZABURO IS HERE!
WHY?!
OKITA SENSEI, WHY?!
...
WHAT KIND OF FACE IS THAT...

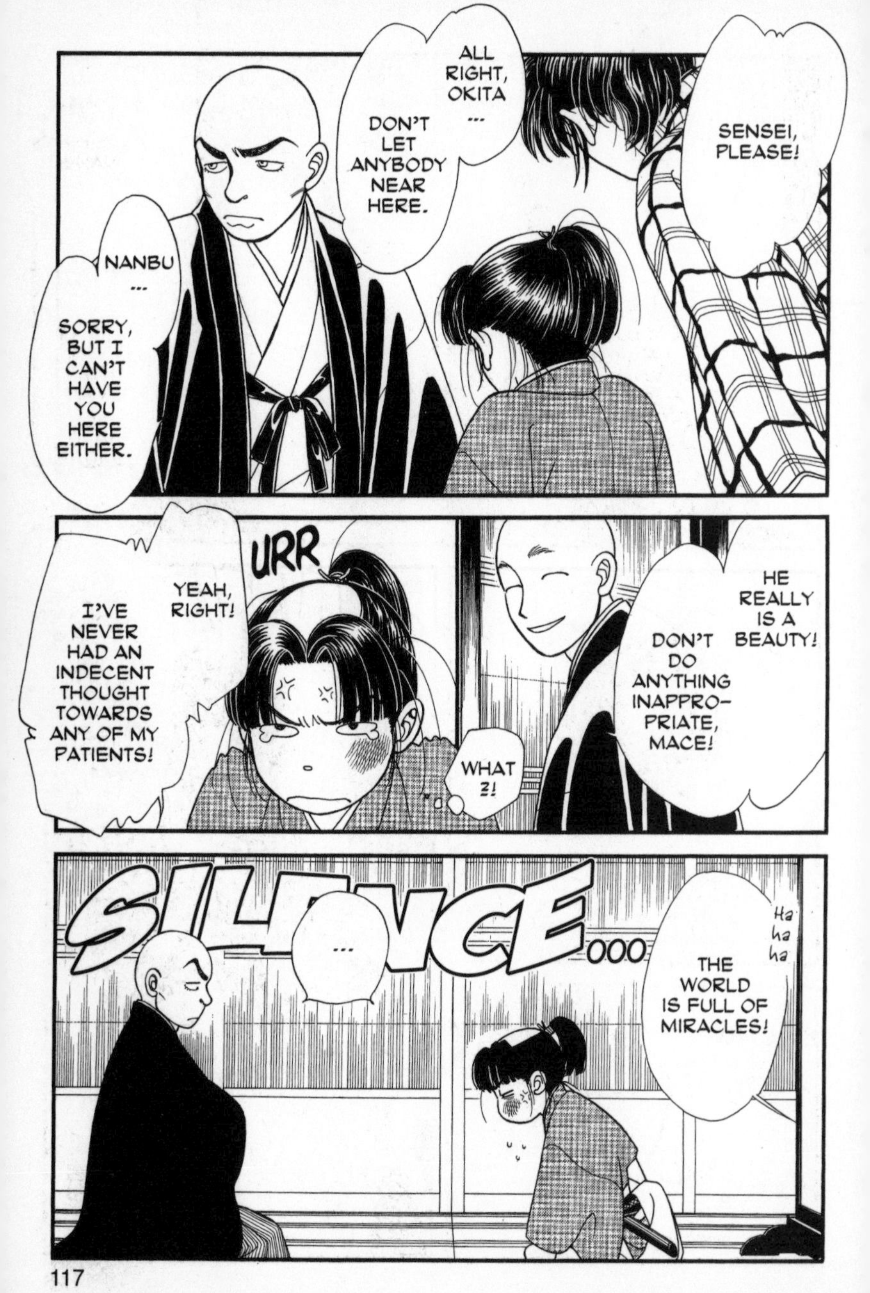
SENSEI, PLEASE!
ALL RIGHT, OKITA ...
DON'T LET ANYBODY NEAR HERE.
NANBU ...
SORRY, BUT I CAN'T HAVE YOU HERE EITHER.
HE REALLY IS A BEAUTY!
DON'T DO ANYTHING INAPPROPRIATE, MACE!
WHAT?!
URR
YEAH, RIGHT!
I'VE NEVER HAD AN INDECENT THOUGHT TOWARDS ANY OF MY PATIENTS!
Ha ha ha
THE WORLD IS FULL OF MIRACLES!
SILENCE...
...

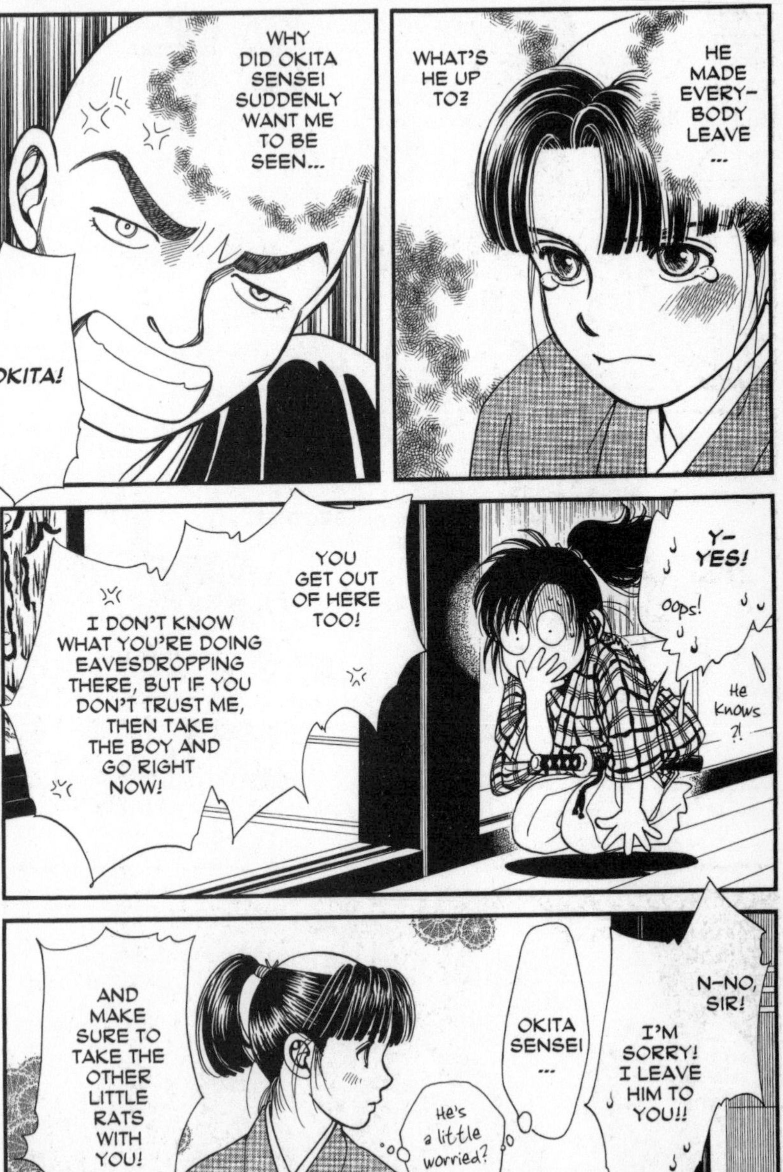
HE MADE EVERY-BODY LEAVE ...
WHAT'S HE UP TO?
WHY DID OKITA SENSEI SUDDENLY WANT ME TO BE SEEN...
OKITA!
Y-YES!
Oops!
He knows ?!
YOU GET OUT OF HERE TOO!
I DON'T KNOW WHAT YOU'RE DOING EAVESDROPPING THERE, BUT IF YOU DON'T TRUST ME, THEN TAKE THE BOY AND GO RIGHT NOW!
N-NO, SIR!
I'M SORRY! I LEAVE HIM TO YOU!!
OKITA SENSEI ...
He's a little worried?
AND MAKE SURE TO TAKE THE OTHER LITTLE RATS WITH YOU!

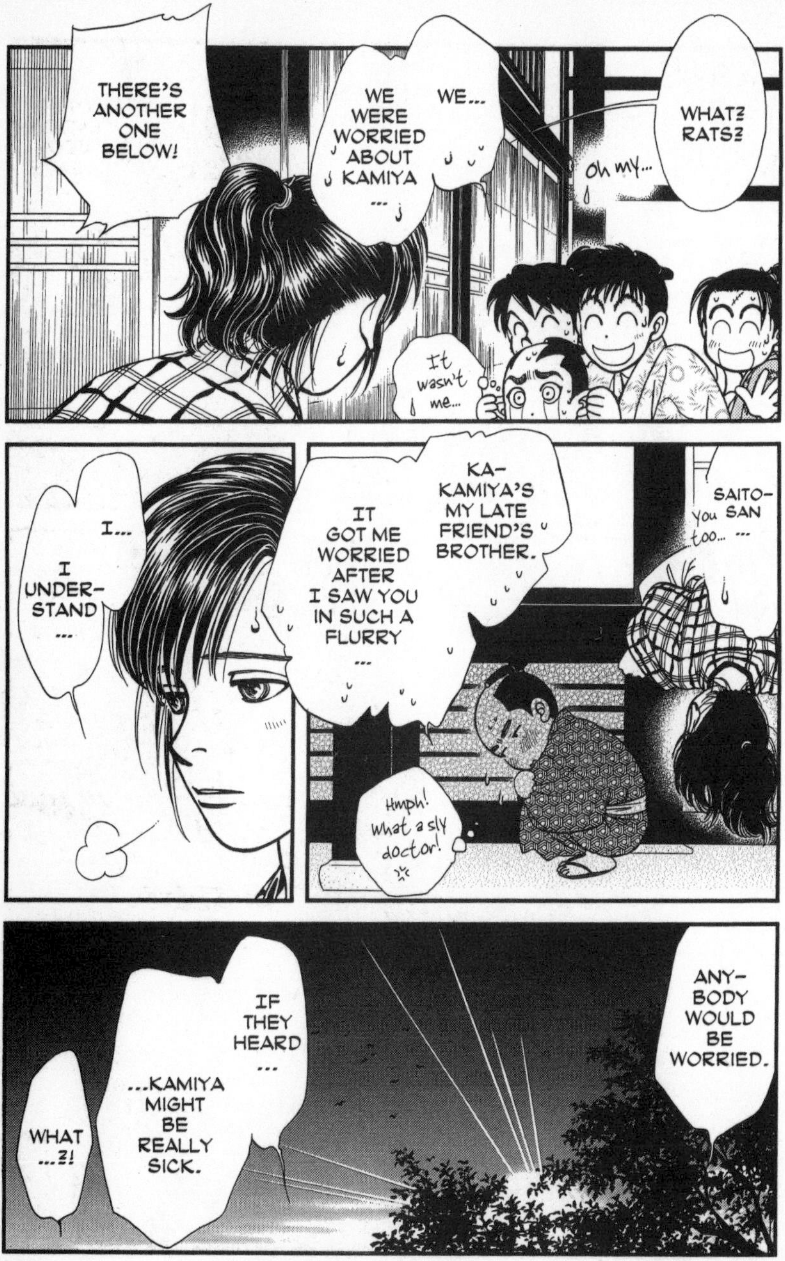
WHAT? RATS?
Oh my...
WE... WE WERE WORRIED ABOUT KAMIYA...
It wasn't me...
THERE'S ANOTHER ONE BELOW!
SAITO-SAN...
You too...
KA-KAMIYA'S MY LATE FRIEND'S BROTHER.
IT GOT ME WORRIED AFTER I SAW YOU IN SUCH A FLURRY...
Hmph! What a sly doctor!
I...
I UNDERSTAND...
ANYBODY WOULD BE WORRIED.
IF THEY HEARD...
...KAMIYA MIGHT BE REALLY SICK.
WHAT...?!

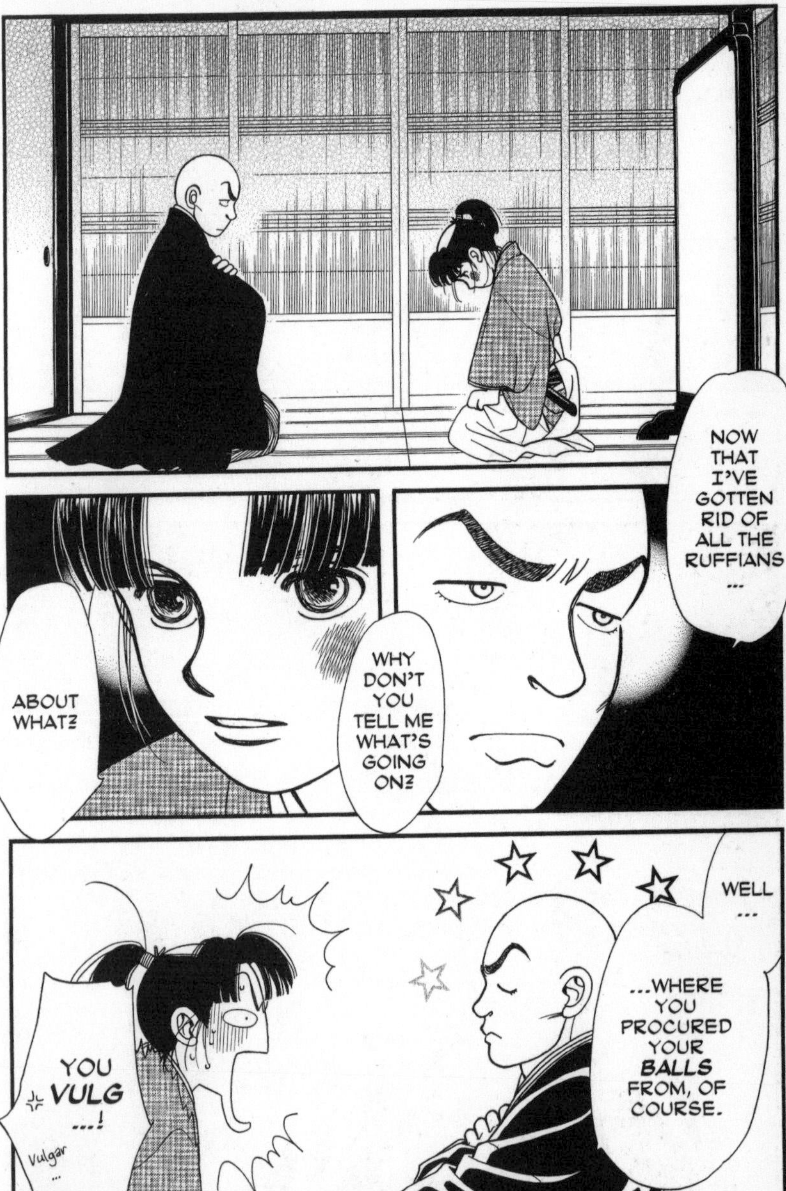
NOW THAT I'VE GOTTEN RID OF ALL THE RUFFIANS...
WHY DON'T YOU TELL ME WHAT'S GOING ON?
ABOUT WHAT?
WELL...
...WHERE YOU PROCURED YOUR BALLS FROM, OF COURSE.
YOU VULG...!
Vulgar...

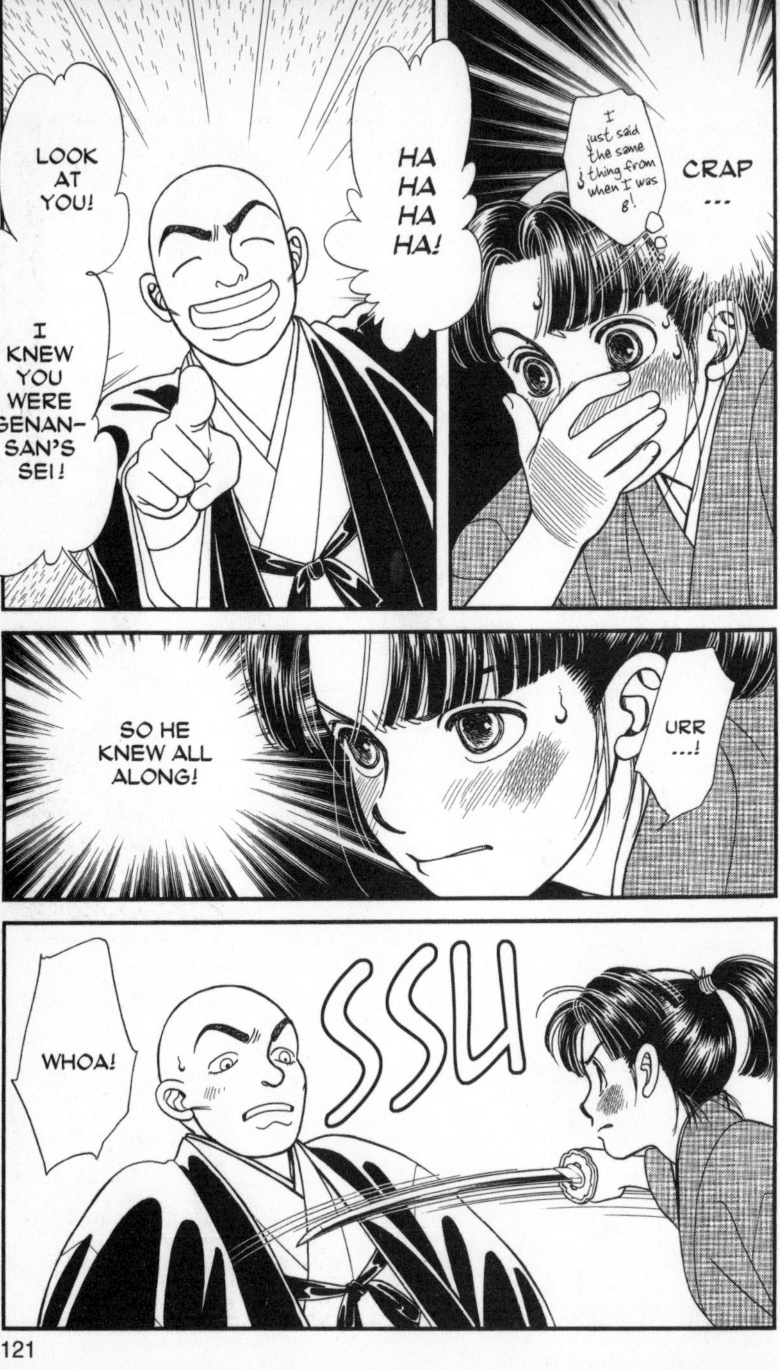
CRAP ...
I just said the same thing from when I was 8!
HA HA HA HA!
LOOK AT YOU!
I KNEW YOU WERE GENAN-SAN'S SEI!
URR ...!
SO HE KNEW ALL ALONG!
SSU
WHOA!

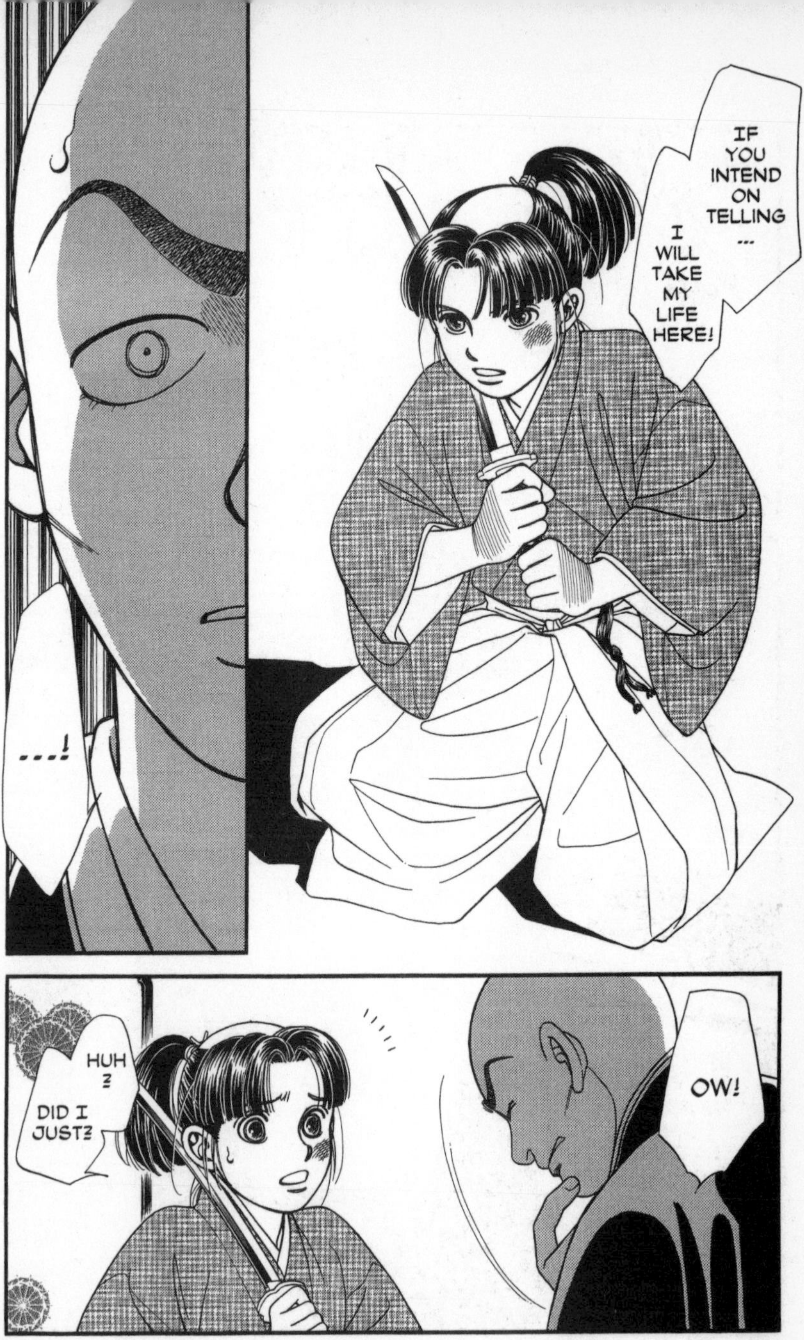
IF YOU INTEND ON TELLING...
I WILL TAKE MY LIFE HERE!
...!
OW!
HUH?
DID I JUST?

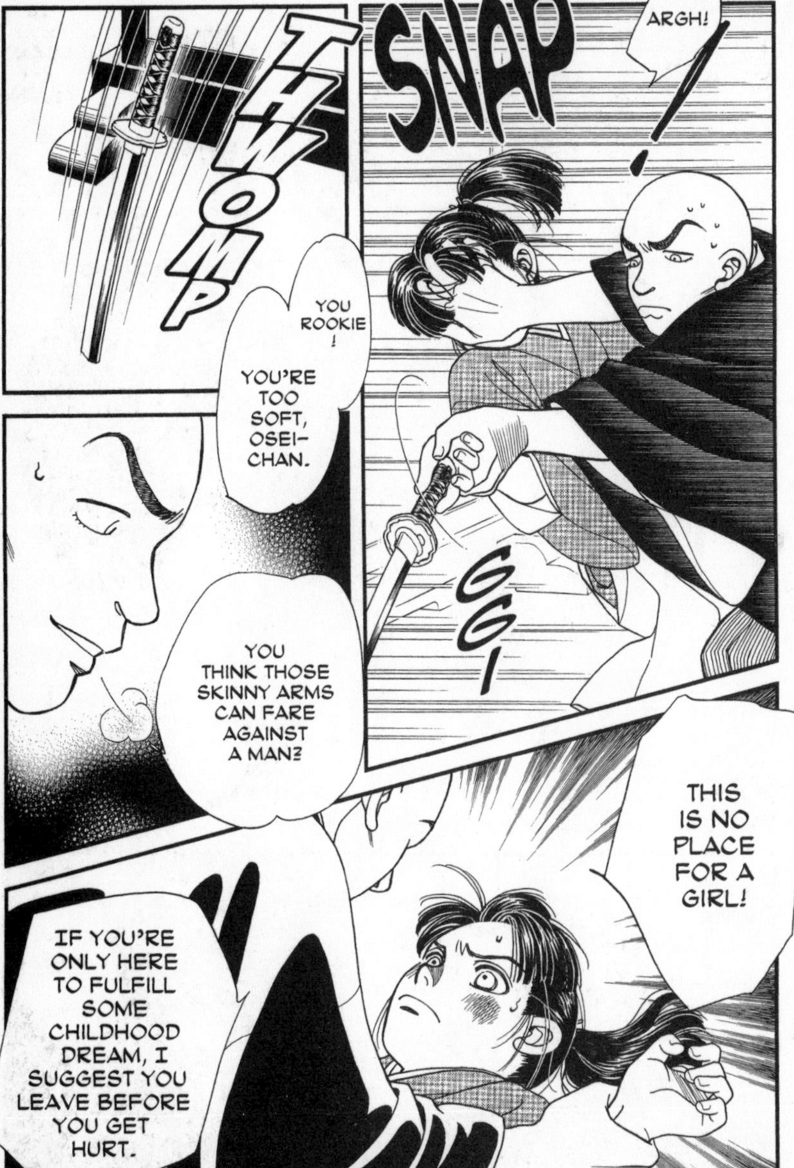
SNAP
ARGH!
GGI
THWOMP
YOU ROOKIE!
YOU'RE TOO SOFT, OSEI-CHAN.
YOU THINK THOSE SKINNY ARMS CAN FARE AGAINST A MAN?
THIS IS NO PLACE FOR A GIRL!
IF YOU'RE ONLY HERE TO FULFILL SOME CHILDHOOD DREAM, I SUGGEST YOU LEAVE BEFORE YOU GET HURT.

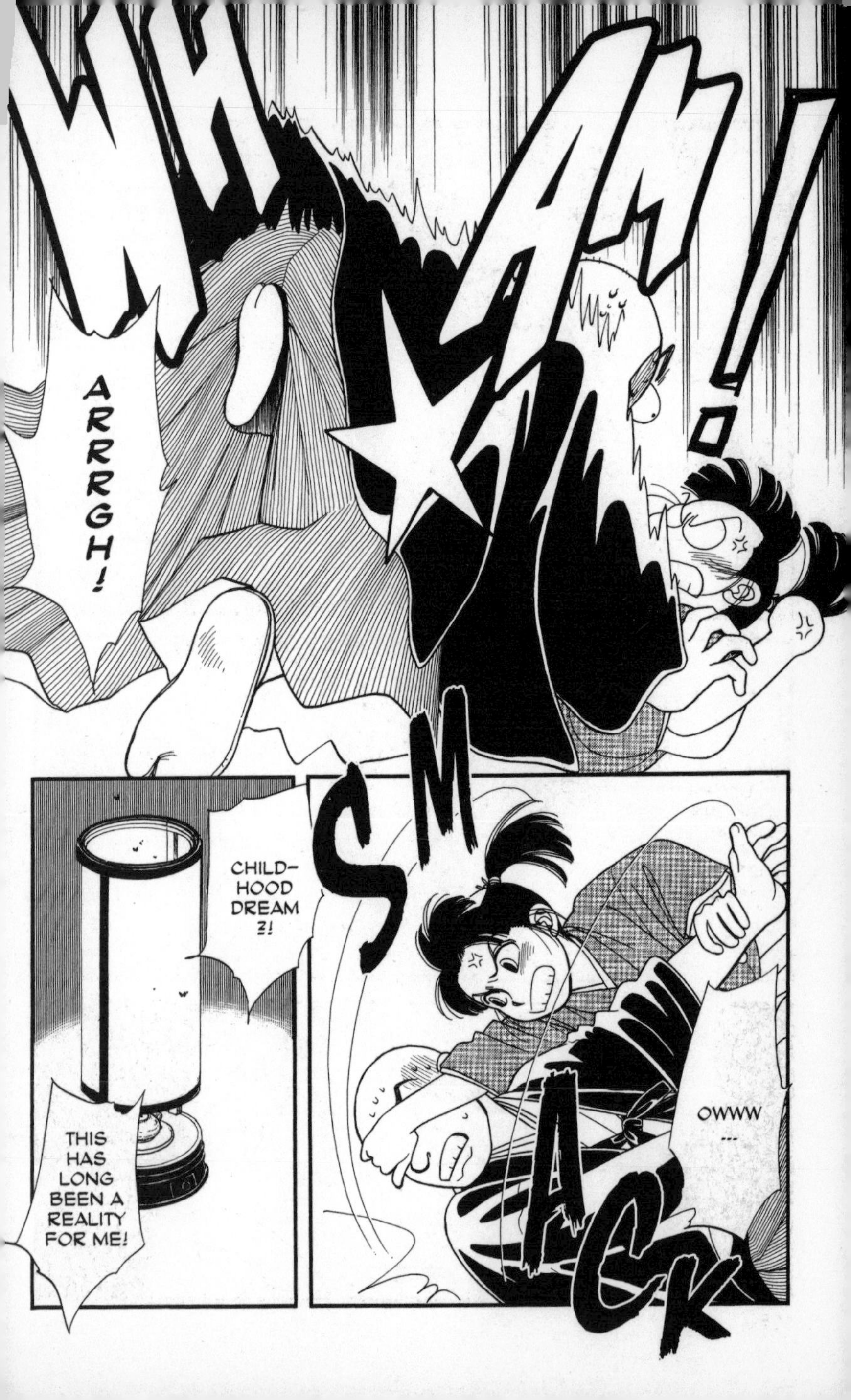
WHAM!
ARRRGH!
SMACK
OWWW...
CHILD-HOOD DREAM?!
THIS HAS LONG BEEN A REALITY FOR ME!

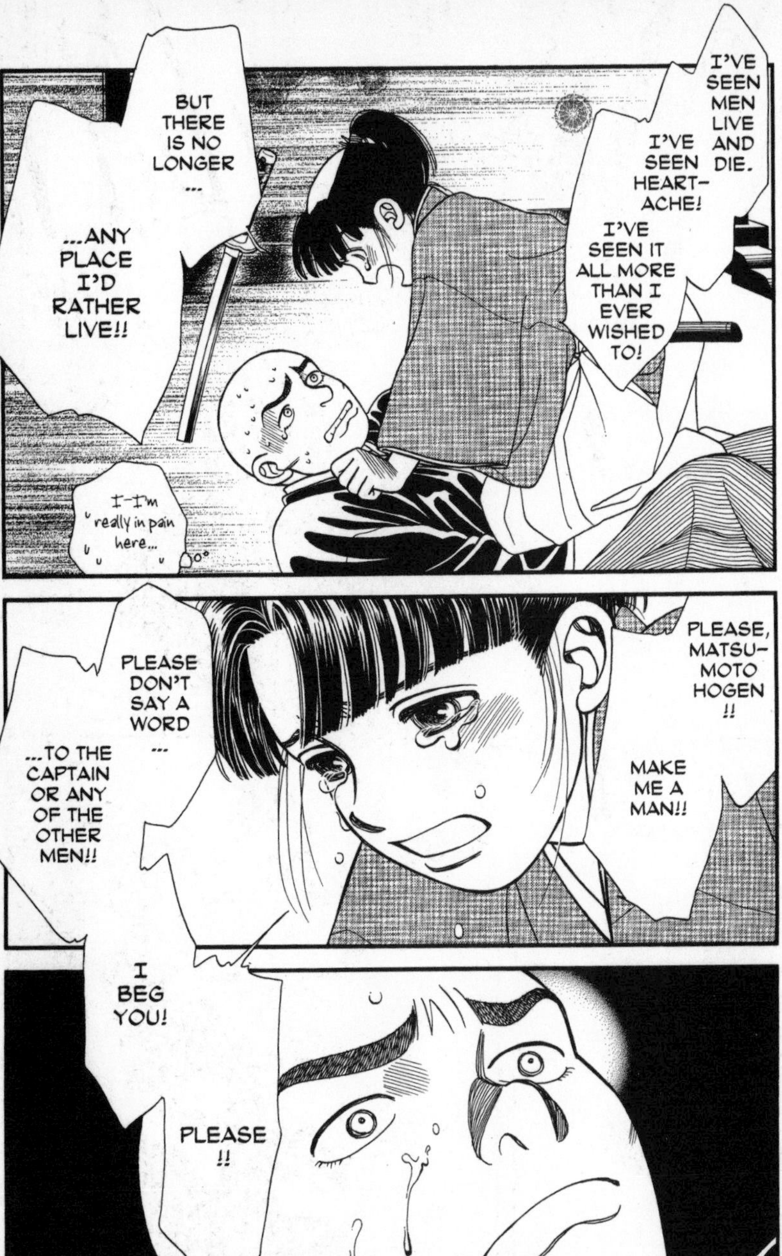
I'VE SEEN MEN LIVE AND DIE.
I'VE SEEN HEART-ACHE!
I'VE SEEN IT ALL MORE THAN I EVER WISHED TO!
BUT THERE IS NO LONGER...
...ANY PLACE I'D RATHER LIVE!!
I-I'm really in pain here...
PLEASE, MATSU-MOTO HOGEN!!
MAKE ME A MAN!!
PLEASE DON'T SAY A WORD...
...TO THE CAPTAIN OR ANY OF THE OTHER MEN!!
I BEG YOU!
PLEASE!!

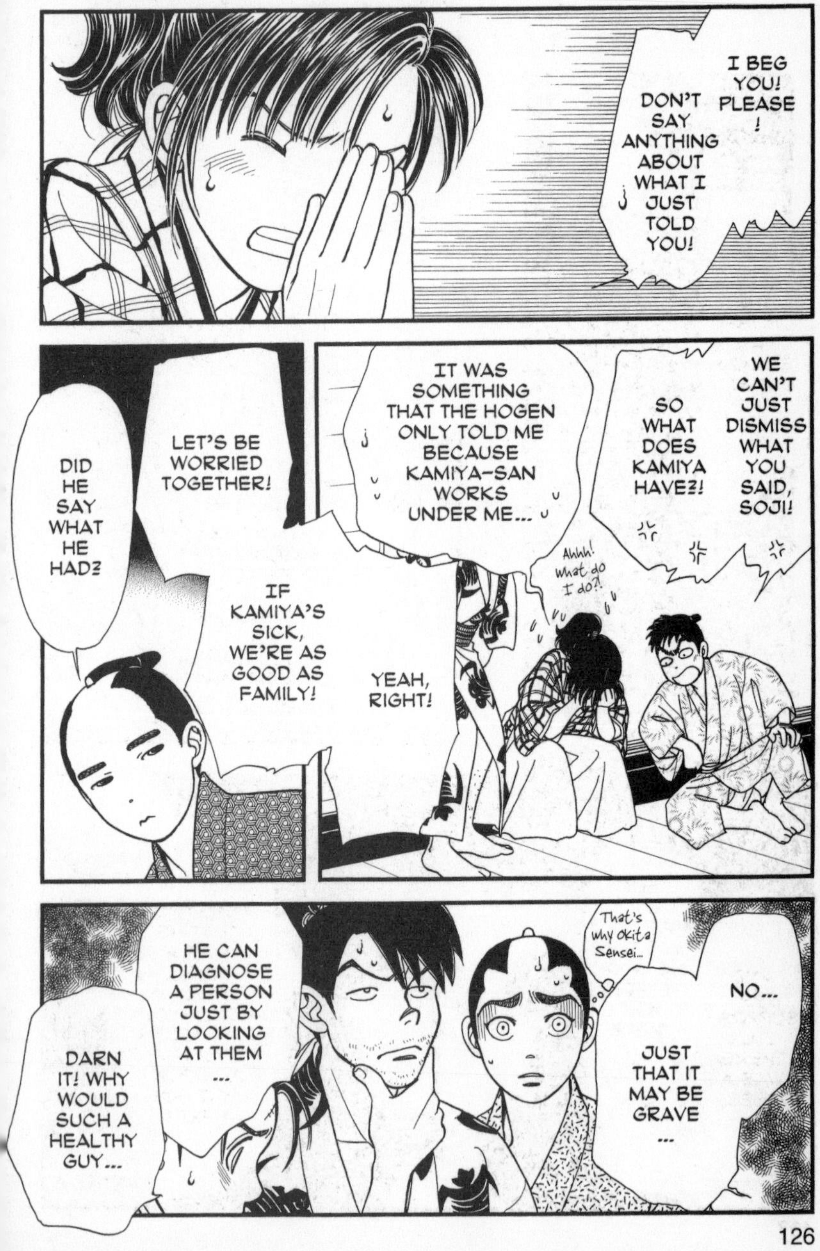
I BEG YOU! PLEASE!
DON'T SAY ANYTHING ABOUT WHAT I JUST TOLD YOU!
WE CAN'T JUST DISMISS WHAT YOU SAID, SOJI!
SO WHAT DOES KAMIYA HAVE?!
IT WAS SOMETHING THAT THE HOGEN ONLY TOLD ME BECAUSE KAMIYA-SAN WORKS UNDER ME...
Ahhh! What do I do?!
IF KAMIYA'S SICK, WE'RE AS GOOD AS FAMILY!
YEAH, RIGHT!
LET'S BE WORRIED TOGETHER!
DID HE SAY WHAT HE HAD?
NO...
JUST THAT IT MAY BE GRAVE...
That's why Okita Sensei...
HE CAN DIAGNOSE A PERSON JUST BY LOOKING AT THEM...
DARN IT! WHY WOULD SUCH A HEALTHY GUY...

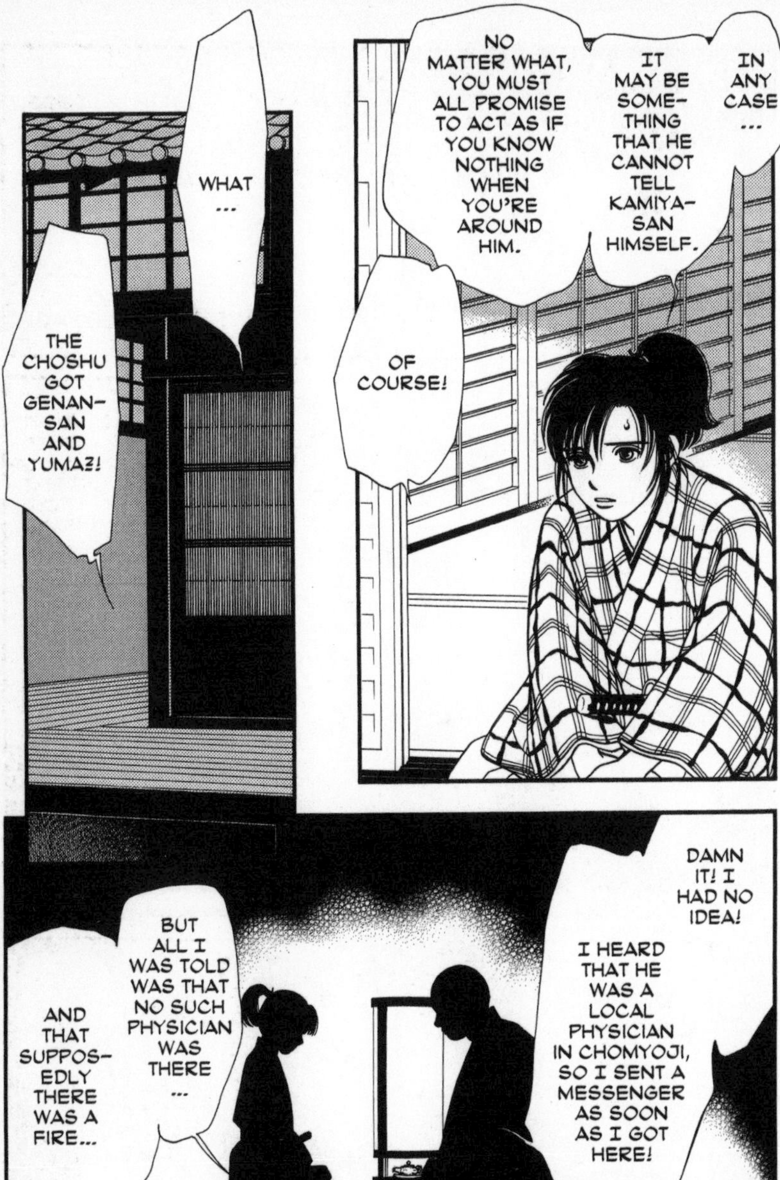
IN ANY CASE ...
IT MAY BE SOME-THING THAT HE CANNOT TELL KAMIYA-SAN HIMSELF.
NO MATTER WHAT, YOU MUST ALL PROMISE TO ACT AS IF YOU KNOW NOTHING WHEN YOU'RE AROUND HIM.
OF COURSE!
WHAT ...
THE CHOSHU GOT GENAN-SAN AND YUMA?!
DAMN IT! I HAD NO IDEA!
I HEARD THAT HE WAS A LOCAL PHYSICIAN IN CHOMYOJI, SO I SENT A MESSENGER AS SOON AS I GOT HERE!
BUT ALL I WAS TOLD WAS THAT NO SUCH PHYSICIAN WAS THERE ...
AND THAT SUPPOS-EDLY THERE WAS A FIRE...

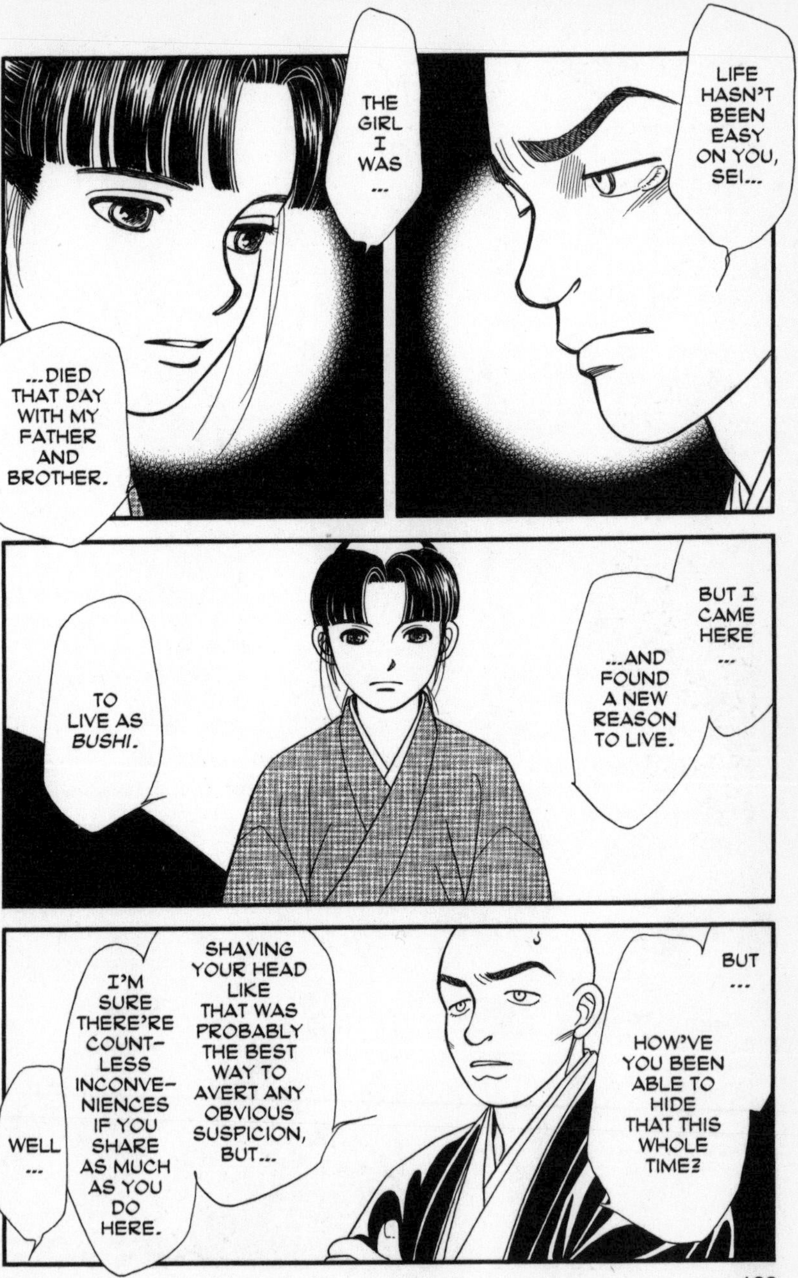
LIFE HASN'T BEEN EASY ON YOU, SEI...
THE GIRL I WAS ...
...DIED THAT DAY WITH MY FATHER AND BROTHER.
BUT I CAME HERE ...
...AND FOUND A NEW REASON TO LIVE.
TO LIVE AS *BUSHI*.
BUT ...
HOW'VE YOU BEEN ABLE TO HIDE THAT THIS WHOLE TIME?
SHAVING YOUR HEAD LIKE THAT WAS PROBABLY THE BEST WAY TO AVERT ANY OBVIOUS SUSPICION, BUT...
I'M SURE THERE'RE COUNT-LESS INCONVE-NIENCES IF YOU SHARE AS MUCH AS YOU DO HERE.
WELL ...

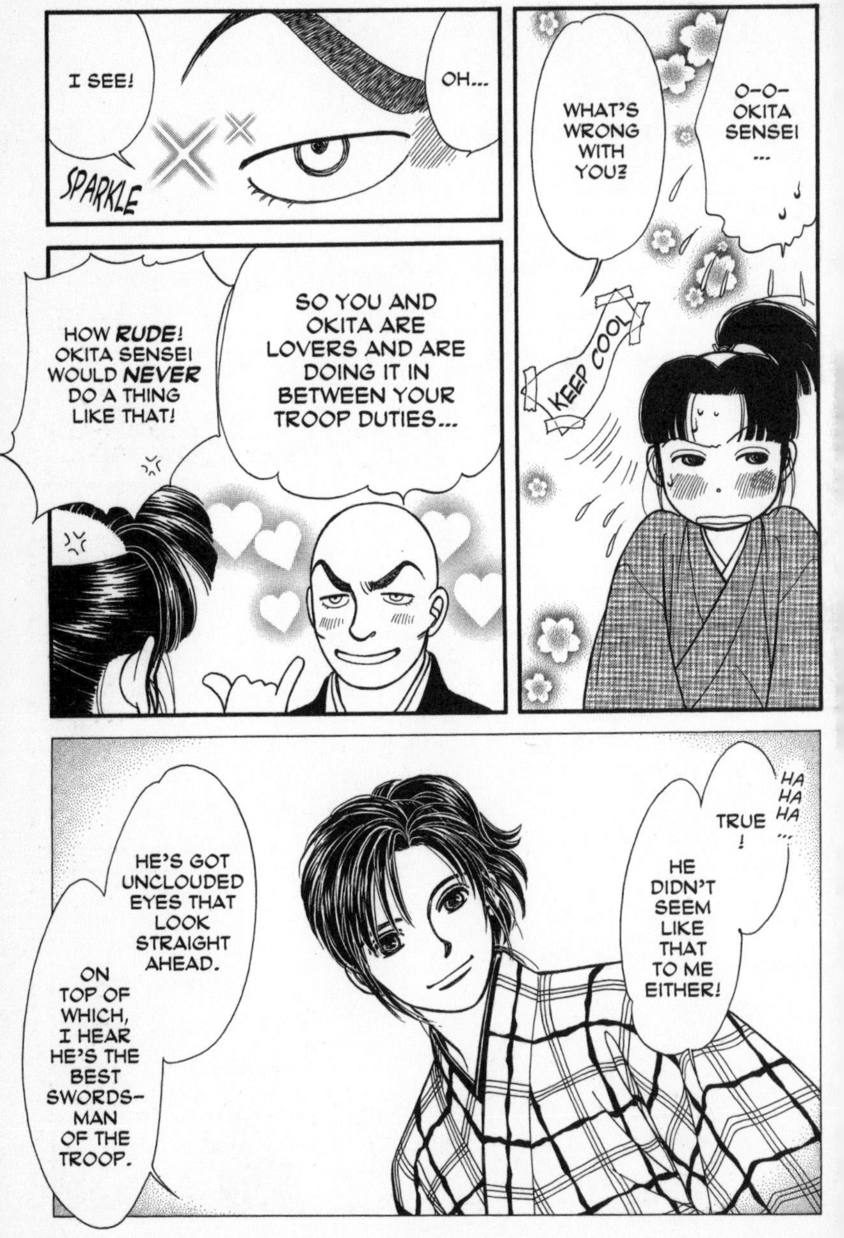
O-O-OKITA SENSEI...
WHAT'S WRONG WITH YOU?
KEEP COOL
OH...
I SEE!
SPARKLE
SO YOU AND OKITA ARE LOVERS AND ARE DOING IT IN BETWEEN YOUR TROOP DUTIES...
HOW **RUDE**! OKITA SENSEI WOULD **NEVER** DO A THING LIKE THAT!
HA HA HA...
TRUE!
HE DIDN'T SEEM LIKE THAT TO ME EITHER!
HE'S GOT UNCLOUDED EYES THAT LOOK STRAIGHT AHEAD.
ON TOP OF WHICH, I HEAR HE'S THE BEST SWORDSMAN OF THE TROOP.

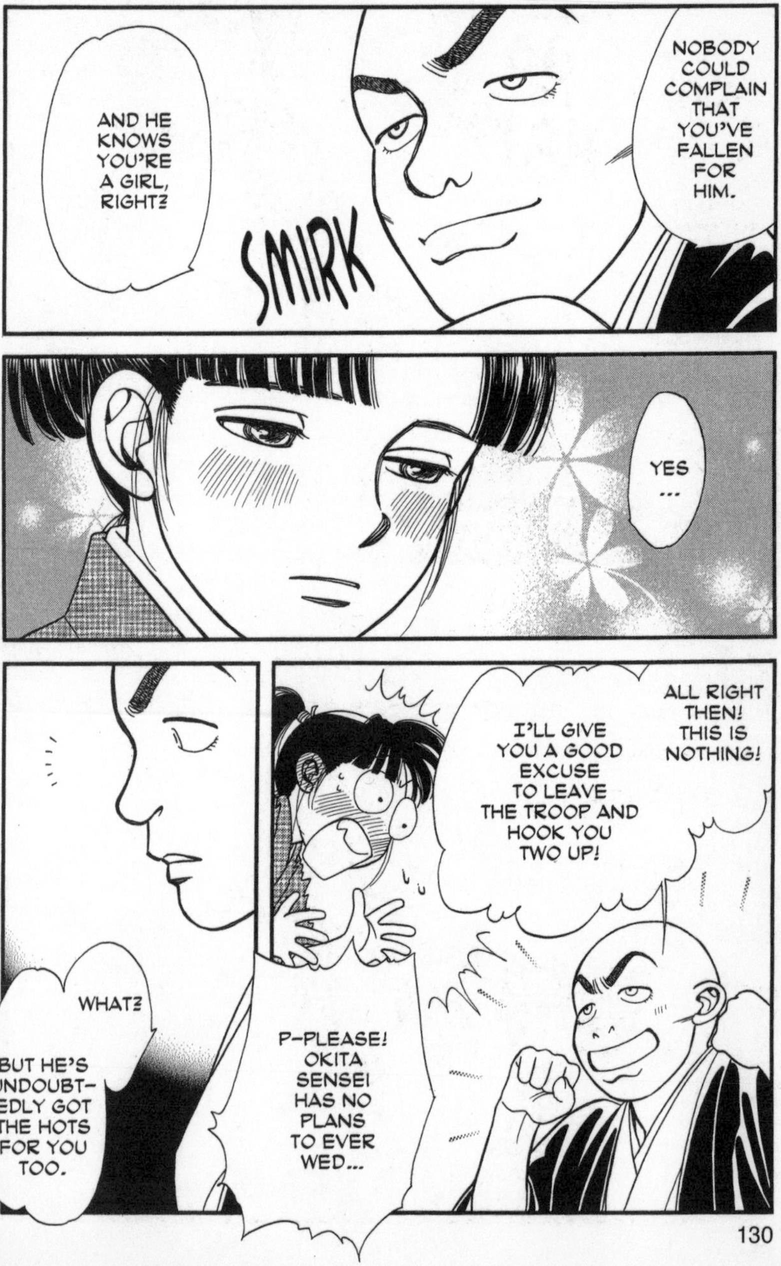
NOBODY COULD COMPLAIN THAT YOU'VE FALLEN FOR HIM.
SMIRK
AND HE KNOWS YOU'RE A GIRL, RIGHT?
YES...
ALL RIGHT THEN! THIS IS NOTHING!
I'LL GIVE YOU A GOOD EXCUSE TO LEAVE THE TROOP AND HOOK YOU TWO UP!
P-PLEASE! OKITA SENSEI HAS NO PLANS TO EVER WED...
WHAT?
BUT HE'S UNDOUBT-EDLY GOT THE HOTS FOR YOU TOO.

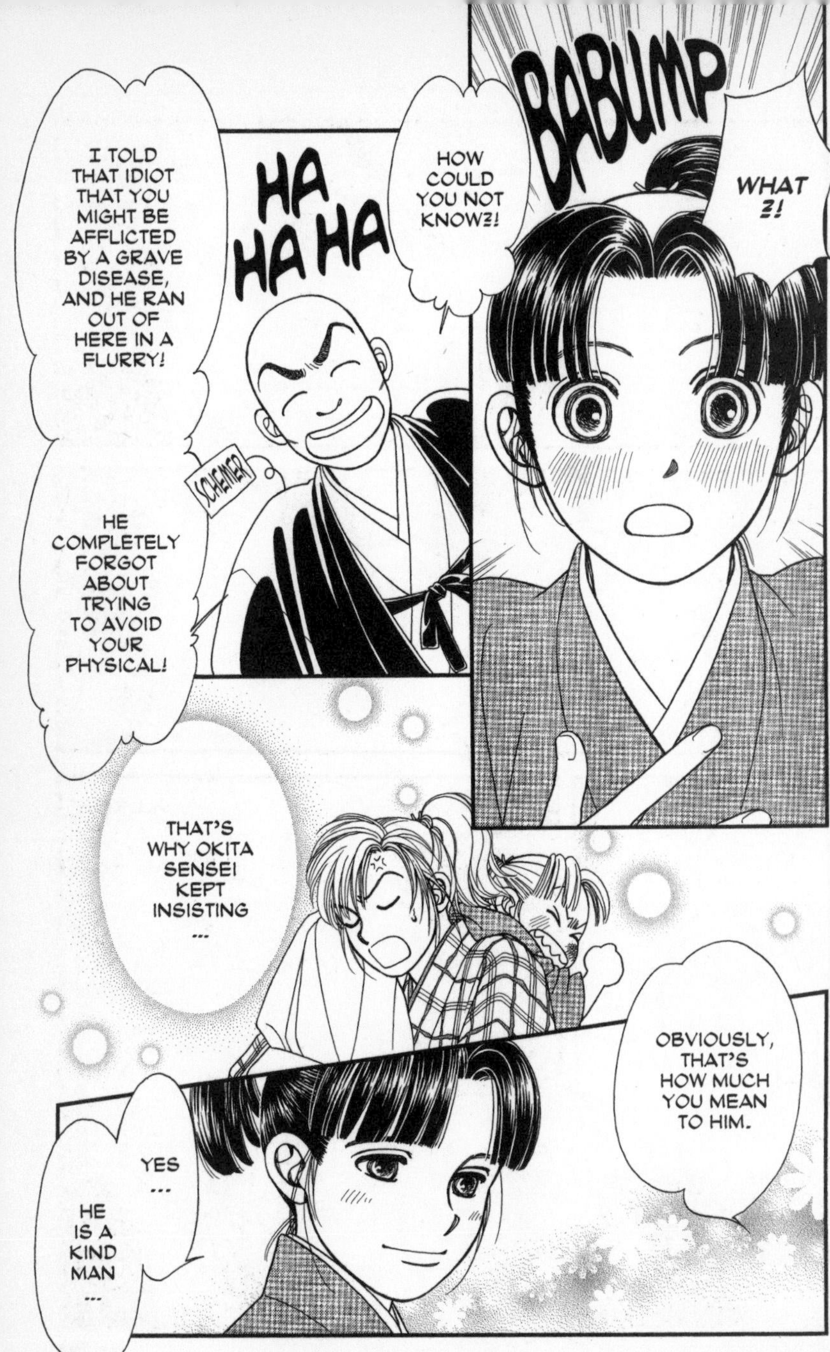

WHAT ?!
BABUMP
HOW COULD YOU NOT KNOW?!
HA HA HA
I TOLD THAT IDIOT THAT YOU MIGHT BE AFFLICTED BY A GRAVE DISEASE, AND HE RAN OUT OF HERE IN A FLURRY!
SCHEMER
HE COMPLETELY FORGOT ABOUT TRYING TO AVOID YOUR PHYSICAL!
THAT'S WHY OKITA SENSEI KEPT INSISTING ...
OBVIOUSLY, THAT'S HOW MUCH YOU MEAN TO HIM.
YES ...
HE IS A KIND MAN ...

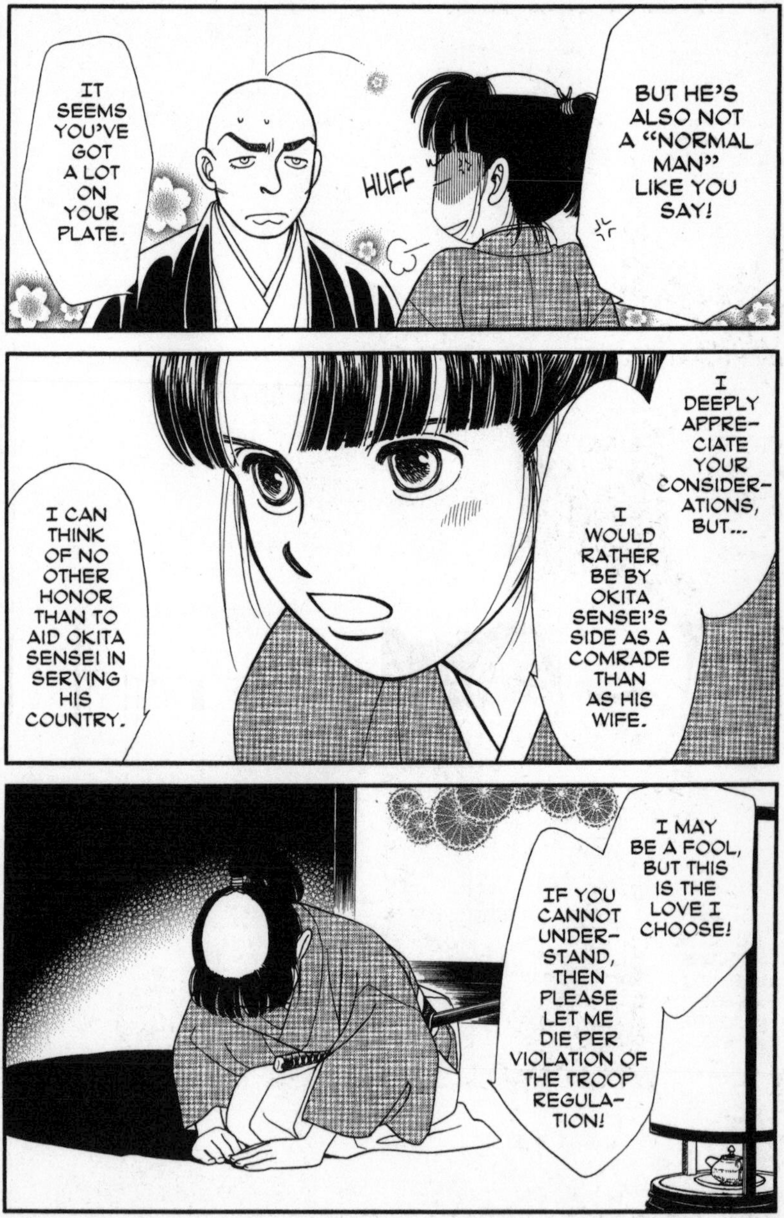
BUT HE'S ALSO NOT A "NORMAL MAN" LIKE YOU SAY!
HUFF
IT SEEMS YOU'VE GOT A LOT ON YOUR PLATE.
I DEEPLY APPRECIATE YOUR CONSIDERATIONS, BUT...
I WOULD RATHER BE BY OKITA SENSEI'S SIDE AS A COMRADE THAN AS HIS WIFE.
I CAN THINK OF NO OTHER HONOR THAN TO AID OKITA SENSEI IN SERVING HIS COUNTRY.
I MAY BE A FOOL, BUT THIS IS THE LOVE I CHOOSE!
IF YOU CANNOT UNDERSTAND, THEN PLEASE LET ME DIE PER VIOLATION OF THE TROOP REGULATION!

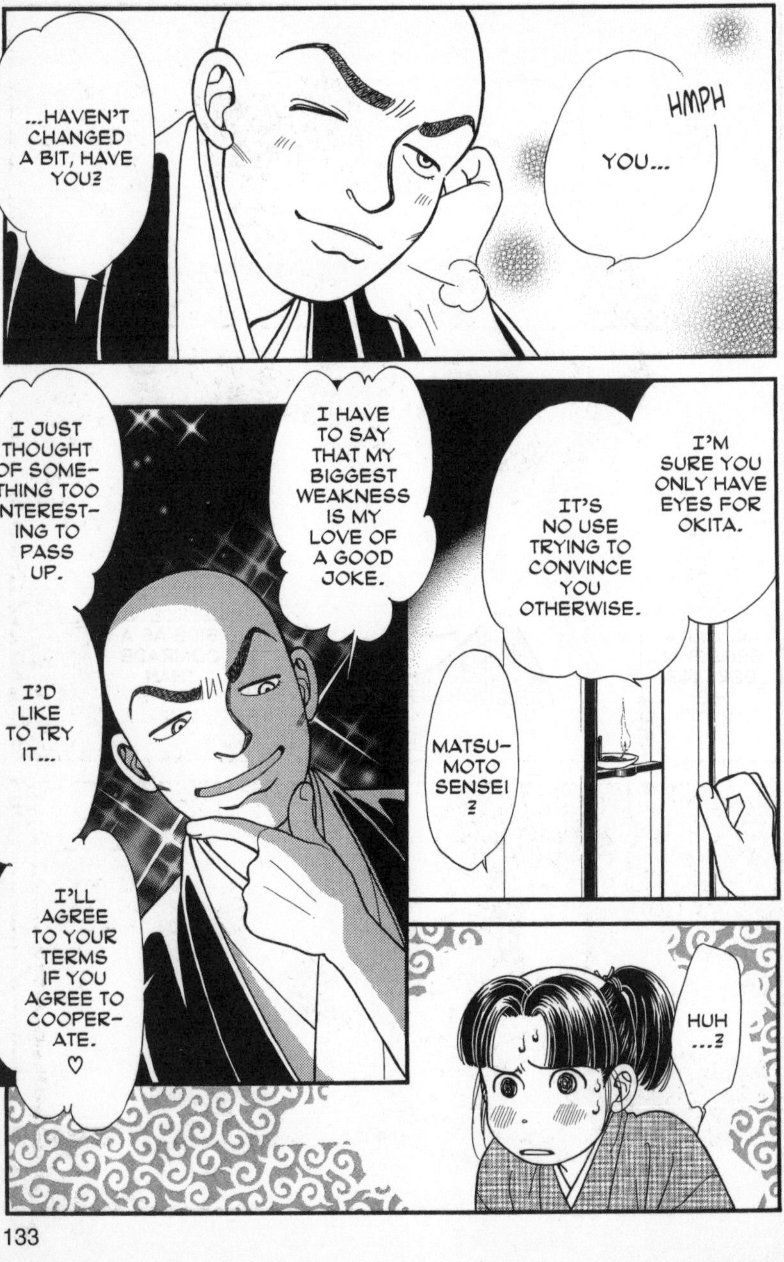
HMPH
YOU...
...HAVEN'T CHANGED A BIT, HAVE YOU?
I'M SURE YOU ONLY HAVE EYES FOR OKITA.
IT'S NO USE TRYING TO CONVINCE YOU OTHERWISE.
MATSU-MOTO SENSEI?
I HAVE TO SAY THAT MY BIGGEST WEAKNESS IS MY LOVE OF A GOOD JOKE.
I JUST THOUGHT OF SOME-THING TOO INTEREST-ING TO PASS UP.
I'D LIKE TO TRY IT...
I'LL AGREE TO YOUR TERMS IF YOU AGREE TO COOPER-ATE. ♡
HUH...?

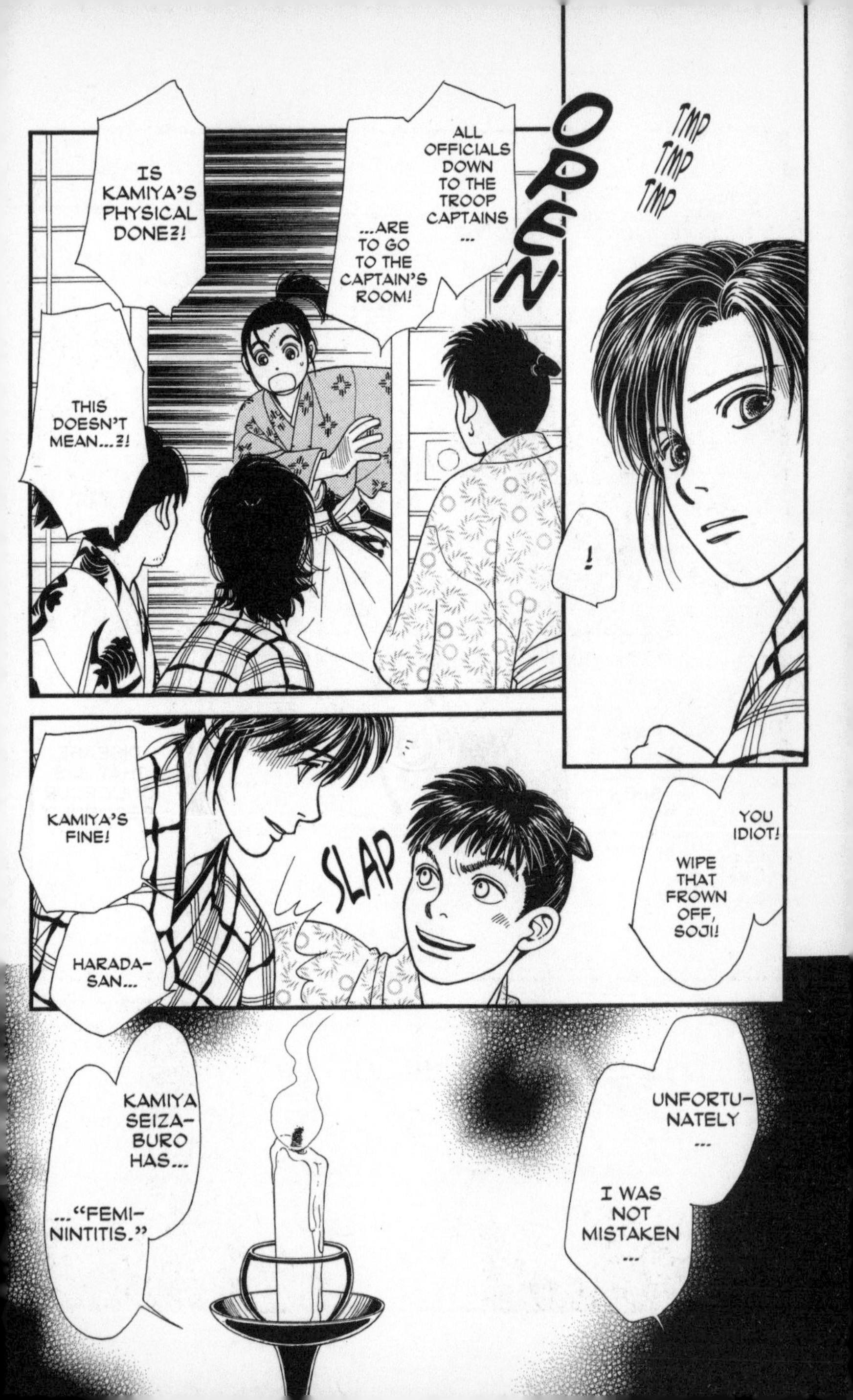
TMP TMP TMP
!
OPEN
ALL OFFICIALS DOWN TO THE TROOP CAPTAINS ...
...ARE TO GO TO THE CAPTAIN'S ROOM!
IS KAMIYA'S PHYSICAL DONE?!
THIS DOESN'T MEAN...?!
YOU IDIOT!
WIPE THAT FROWN OFF, SOJI!
SLAP
KAMIYA'S FINE!
HARADA-SAN...
UNFORTUNATELY ...
I WAS NOT MISTAKEN ...
KAMIYA SEIZABURO HAS...
..."FEMININTITIS."

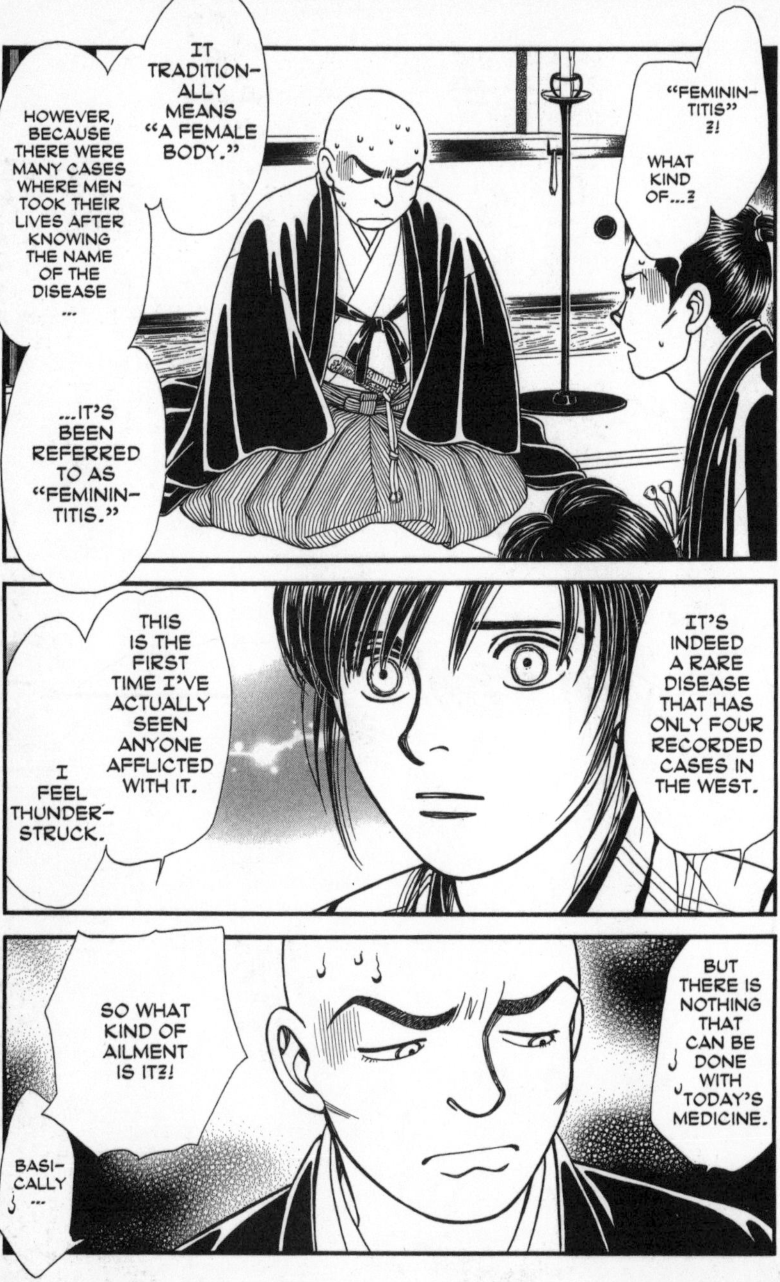
"FEMININ-TITIS" ?! WHAT KIND OF...?
IT TRADITION-ALLY MEANS "A FEMALE BODY."
HOWEVER, BECAUSE THERE WERE MANY CASES WHERE MEN TOOK THEIR LIVES AFTER KNOWING THE NAME OF THE DISEASE ...
...IT'S BEEN REFERRED TO AS "FEMININ-TITIS."
IT'S INDEED A RARE DISEASE THAT HAS ONLY FOUR RECORDED CASES IN THE WEST.
THIS IS THE FIRST TIME I'VE ACTUALLY SEEN ANYONE AFFLICTED WITH IT.
I FEEL THUNDER-STRUCK.
BUT THERE IS NOTHING THAT CAN BE DONE WITH TODAY'S MEDICINE.
SO WHAT KIND OF AILMENT IS IT?!
BASI-CALLY ...

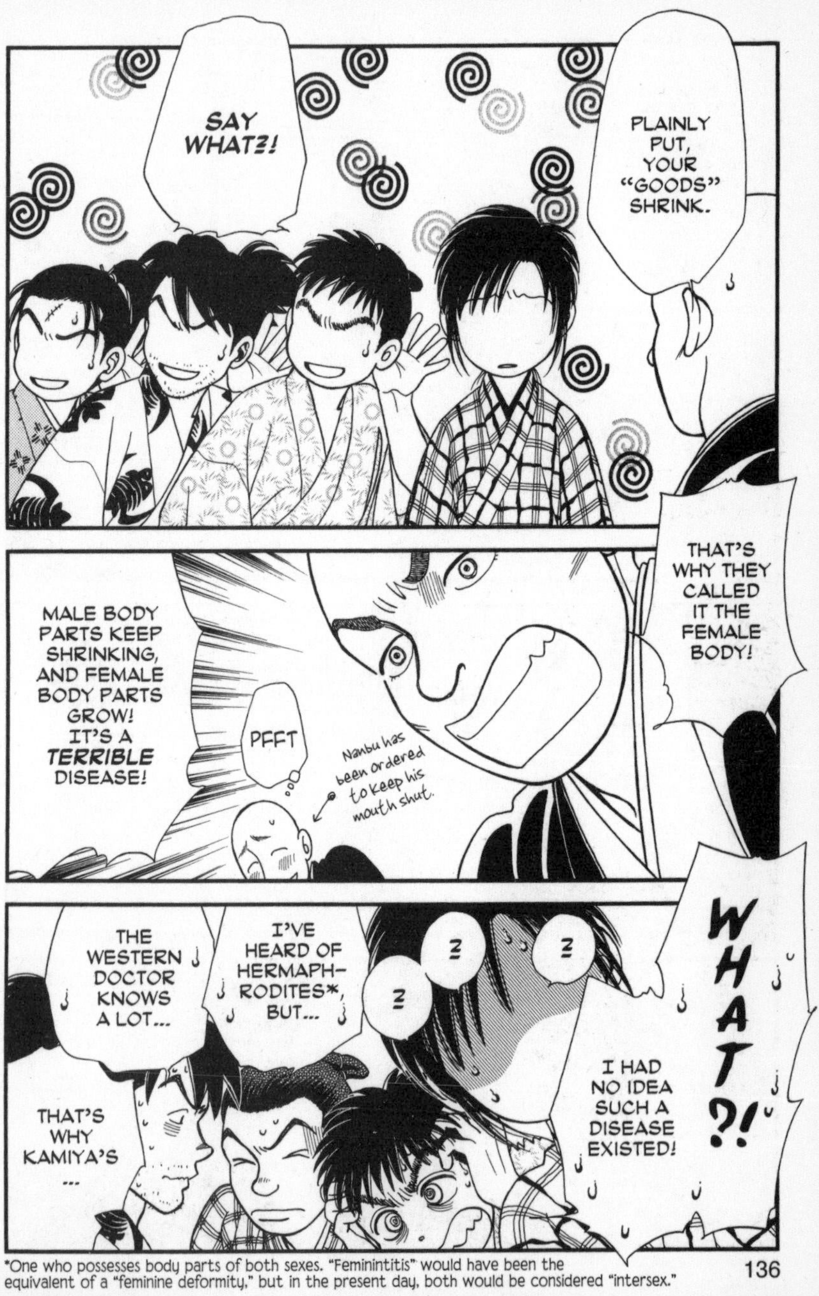
PLAINLY PUT, YOUR "GOODS" SHRINK.
SAY WHAT?!
THAT'S WHY THEY CALLED IT THE FEMALE BODY!
MALE BODY PARTS KEEP SHRINKING, AND FEMALE BODY PARTS GROW! IT'S A *TERRIBLE* DISEASE!
PFFT
Nanbu has been ordered to keep his mouth shut.
WHAT?!
I HAD NO IDEA SUCH A DISEASE EXISTED!
I'VE HEARD OF HERMAPH-RODITES*, BUT...
THE WESTERN DOCTOR KNOWS A LOT...
THAT'S WHY KAMIYA'S ...

*One who possesses body parts of both sexes. "Feminintitis" would have been the equivalent of a "feminine deformity," but in the present day, both would be considered "intersex."

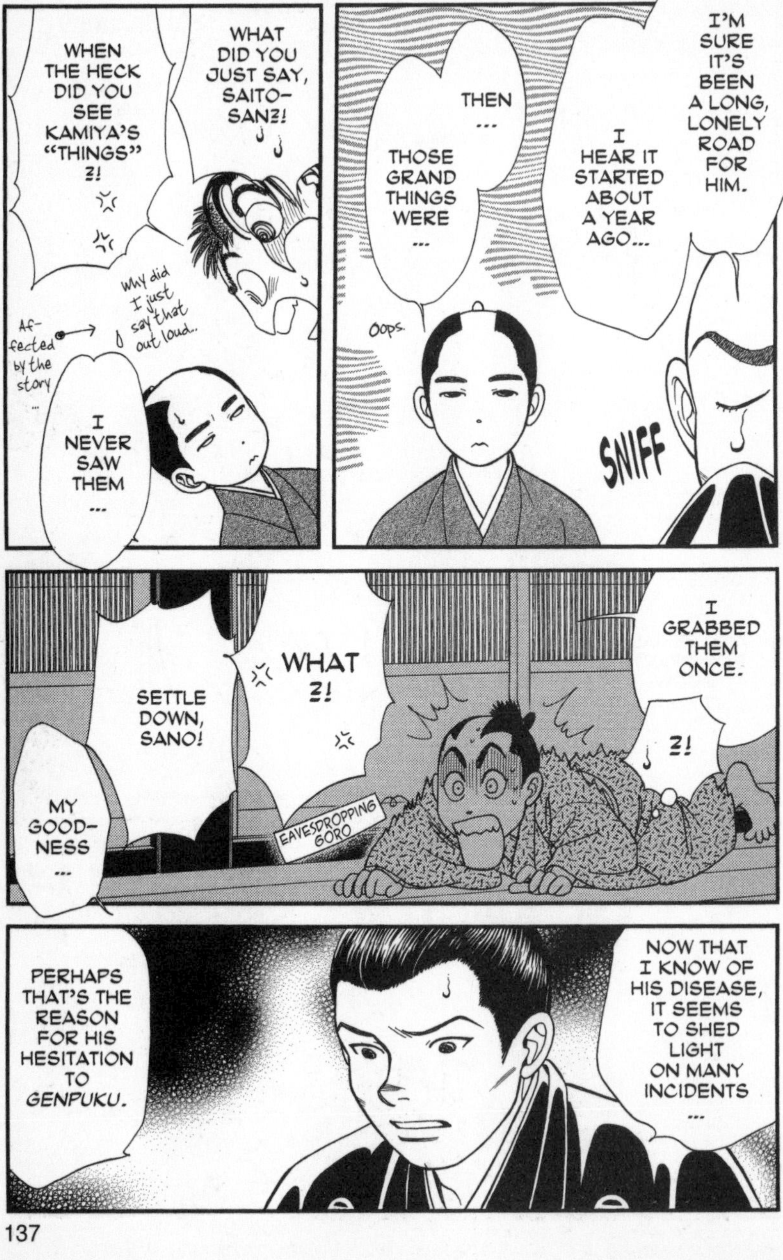
I'M SURE IT'S BEEN A LONG, LONELY ROAD FOR HIM.
I HEAR IT STARTED ABOUT A YEAR AGO...
THEN...
THOSE GRAND THINGS WERE...
Oops.
SNIFF
WHAT DID YOU JUST SAY, SAITO-SAN?!
WHEN THE HECK DID YOU SEE KAMIYA'S "THINGS"?!
Why did I just say that out loud..
Affected by the story...
I NEVER SAW THEM...
I GRABBED THEM ONCE.
?!
WHAT?!
SETTLE DOWN, SANO!
EAVESDROPPING GORO
MY GOODNESS...
NOW THAT I KNOW OF HIS DISEASE, IT SEEMS TO SHED LIGHT ON MANY INCIDENTS...
PERHAPS THAT'S THE REASON FOR HIS HESITATION TO GENPUKU.

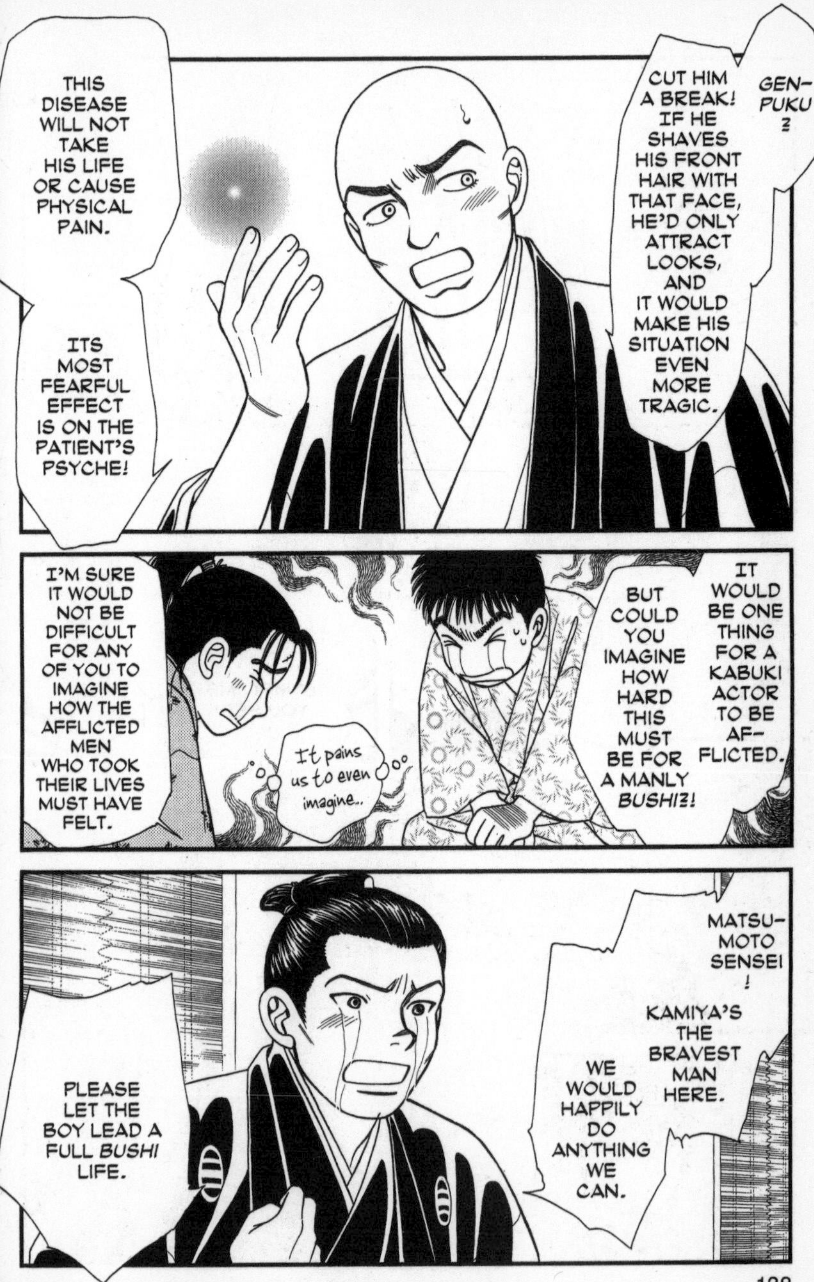
GEN-PUKU?
CUT HIM A BREAK! IF HE SHAVES HIS FRONT HAIR WITH THAT FACE, HE'D ONLY ATTRACT LOOKS, AND IT WOULD MAKE HIS SITUATION EVEN MORE TRAGIC.
THIS DISEASE WILL NOT TAKE HIS LIFE OR CAUSE PHYSICAL PAIN.
ITS MOST FEARFUL EFFECT IS ON THE PATIENT'S PSYCHE!
IT WOULD BE ONE THING FOR A KABUKI ACTOR TO BE AF-FLICTED.
BUT COULD YOU IMAGINE HOW HARD THIS MUST BE FOR A MANLY *BUSHI*?!
It pains us to even imagine..
I'M SURE IT WOULD NOT BE DIFFICULT FOR ANY OF YOU TO IMAGINE HOW THE AFFLICTED MEN WHO TOOK THEIR LIVES MUST HAVE FELT.
MATSU-MOTO SENSEI!
KAMIYA'S THE BRAVEST MAN HERE.
WE WOULD HAPPILY DO ANYTHING WE CAN.
PLEASE LET THE BOY LEAD A FULL *BUSHI* LIFE.

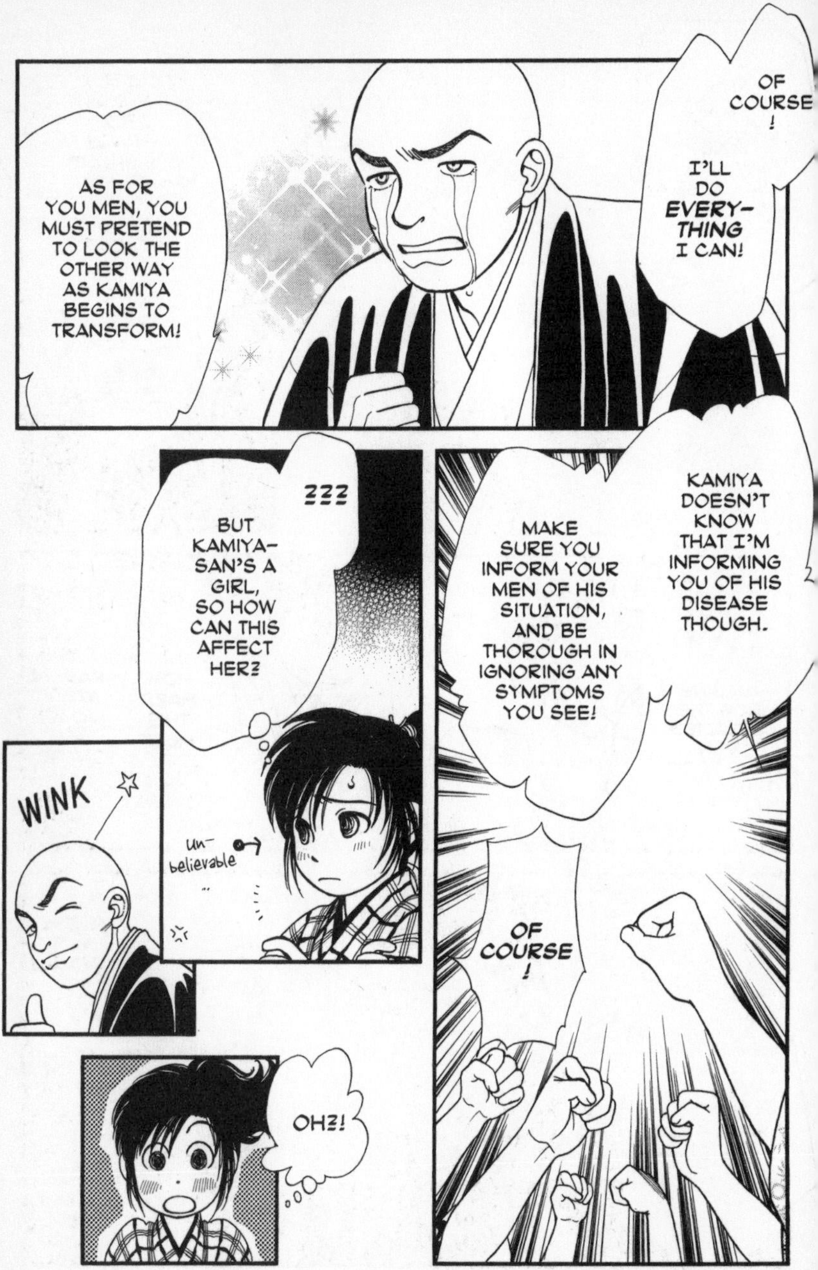
OF COURSE! I'LL DO EVERYTHING I CAN!
AS FOR YOU MEN, YOU MUST PRETEND TO LOOK THE OTHER WAY AS KAMIYA BEGINS TO TRANSFORM!
KAMIYA DOESN'T KNOW THAT I'M INFORMING YOU OF HIS DISEASE THOUGH.
MAKE SURE YOU INFORM YOUR MEN OF HIS SITUATION, AND BE THOROUGH IN IGNORING ANY SYMPTOMS YOU SEE!
OF COURSE!
BUT KAMIYA-SAN'S A GIRL, SO HOW CAN THIS AFFECT HER?
Un-believable
WINK
OH?!

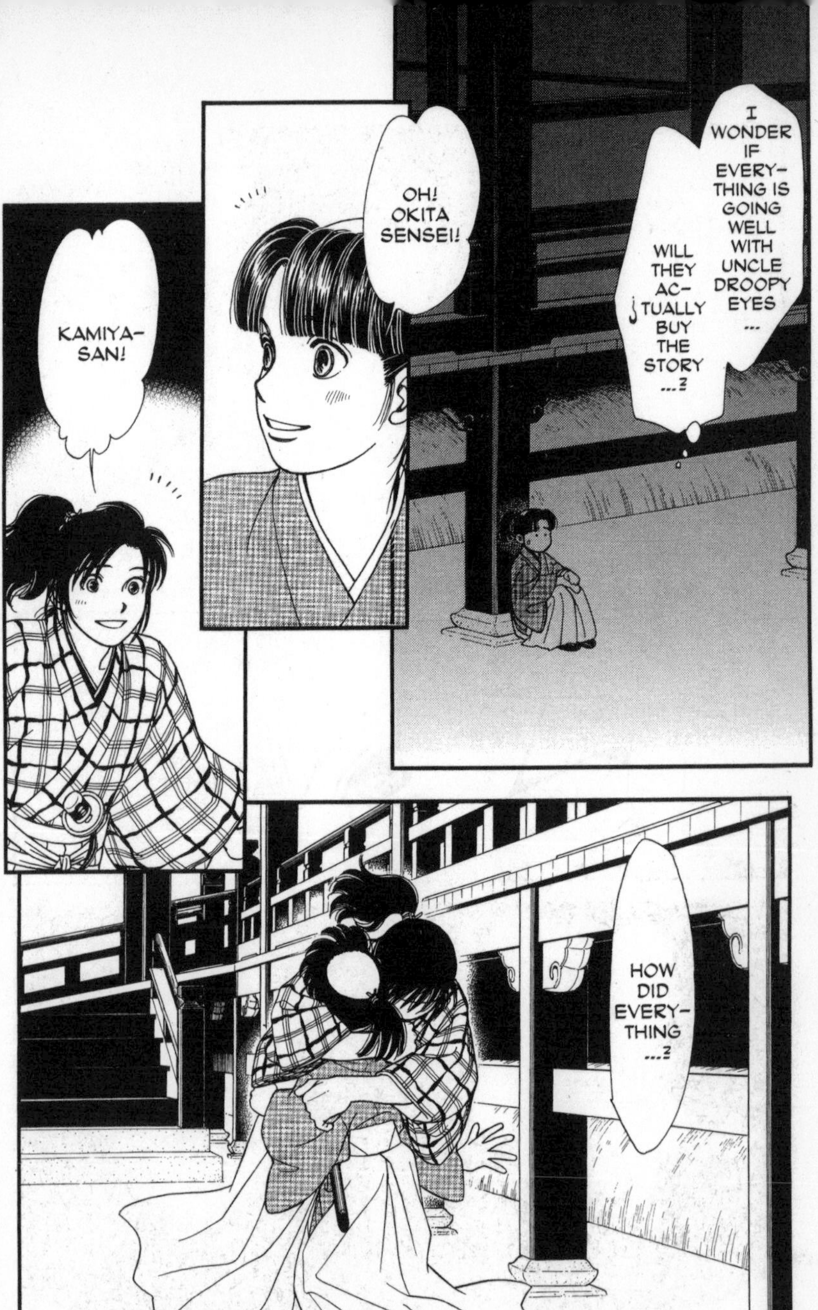
I WONDER IF EVERYTHING IS GOING WELL WITH UNCLE DROOPY EYES...
WILL THEY ACTUALLY BUY THE STORY...?
OH! OKITA SENSEI!
KAMIYA-SAN!
HOW DID EVERYTHING...?

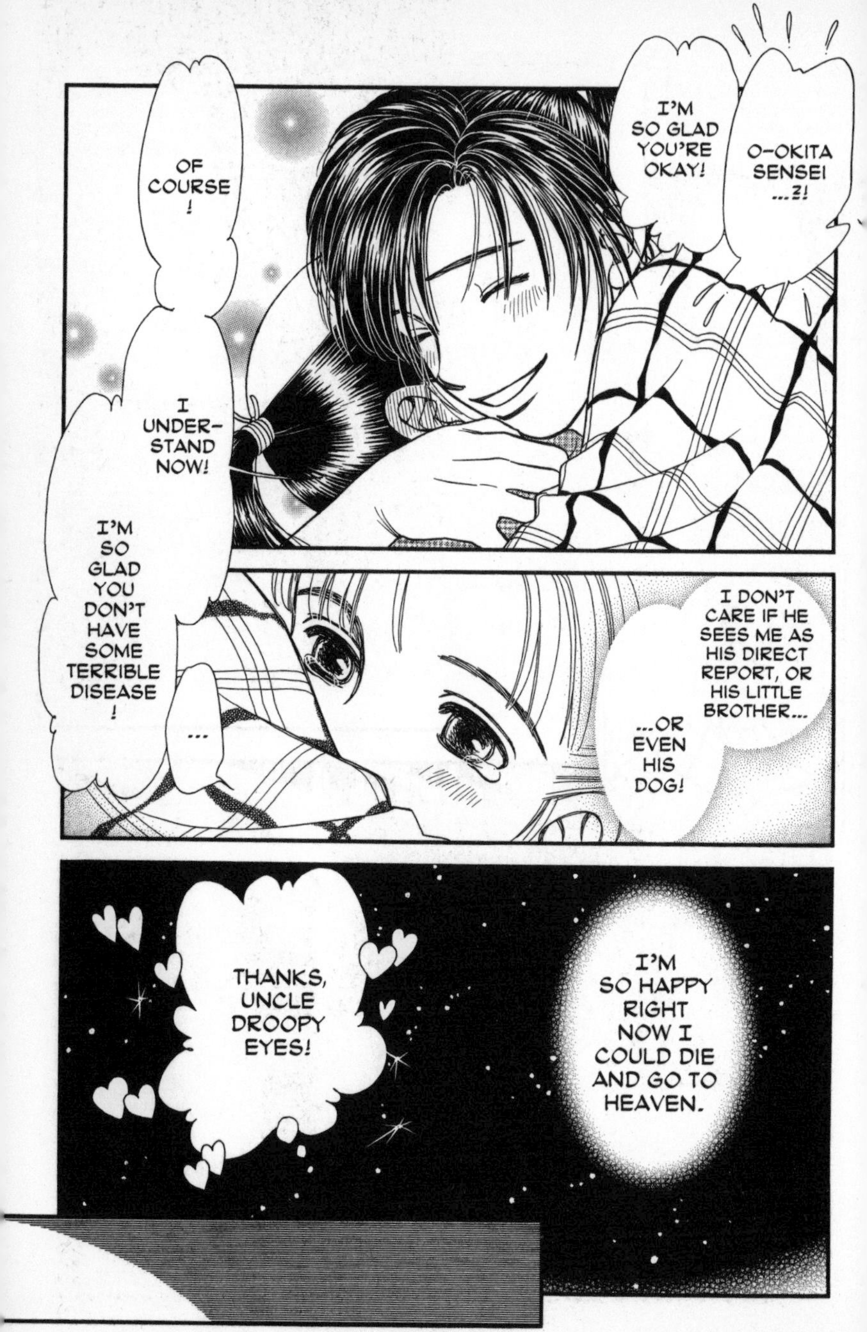
O-OKITA SENSEI ...?!
I'M SO GLAD YOU'RE OKAY!
OF COURSE!
I UNDERSTAND NOW!
I'M SO GLAD YOU DON'T HAVE SOME TERRIBLE DISEASE!
I DON'T CARE IF HE SEES ME AS HIS DIRECT REPORT, OR HIS LITTLE BROTHER...
...OR EVEN HIS DOG!
...
I'M SO HAPPY RIGHT NOW I COULD DIE AND GO TO HEAVEN.
THANKS, UNCLE DROOPY EYES!

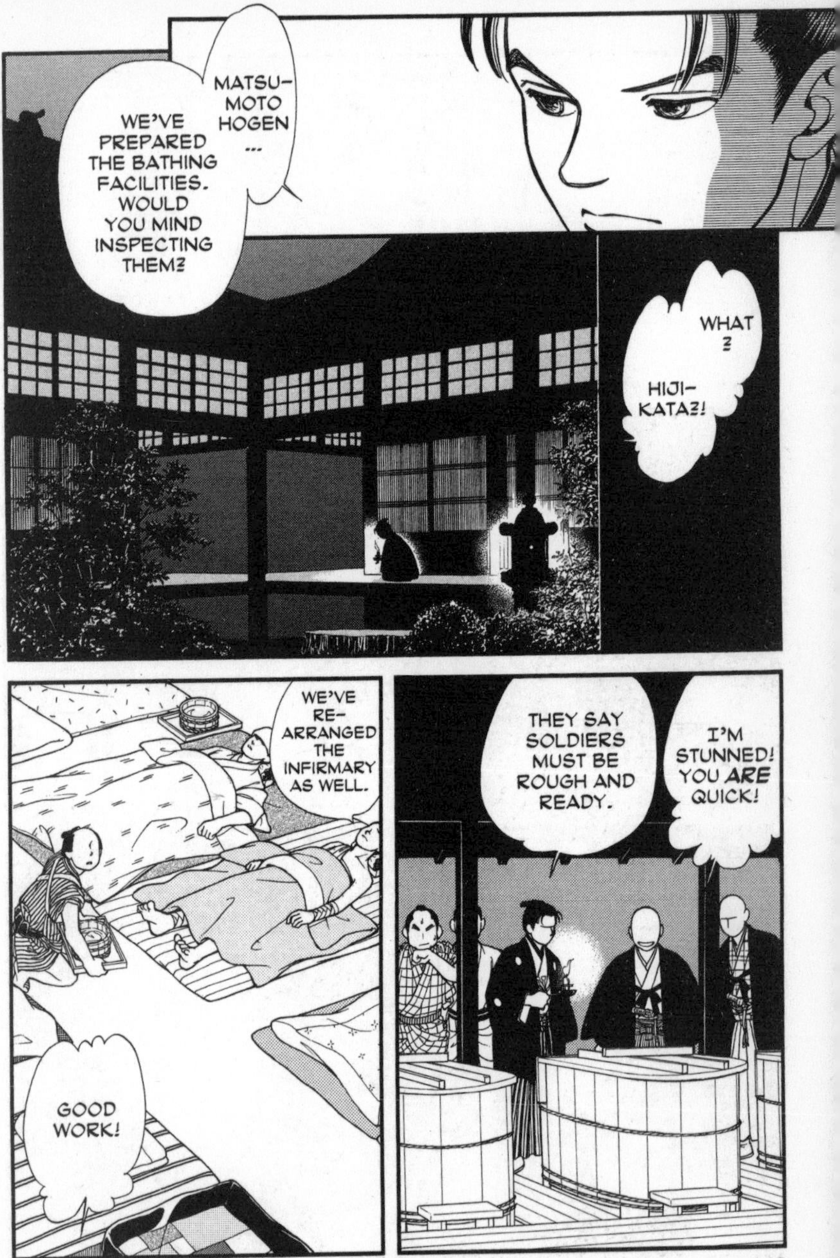
MATSU-MOTO HOGEN ...
WE'VE PREPARED THE BATHING FACILITIES. WOULD YOU MIND INSPECTING THEM?
WHAT? HIJI-KATA?!
I'M STUNNED! YOU *ARE* QUICK!
THEY SAY SOLDIERS MUST BE ROUGH AND READY.
WE'VE RE-ARRANGED THE INFIRMARY AS WELL.
GOOD WORK!

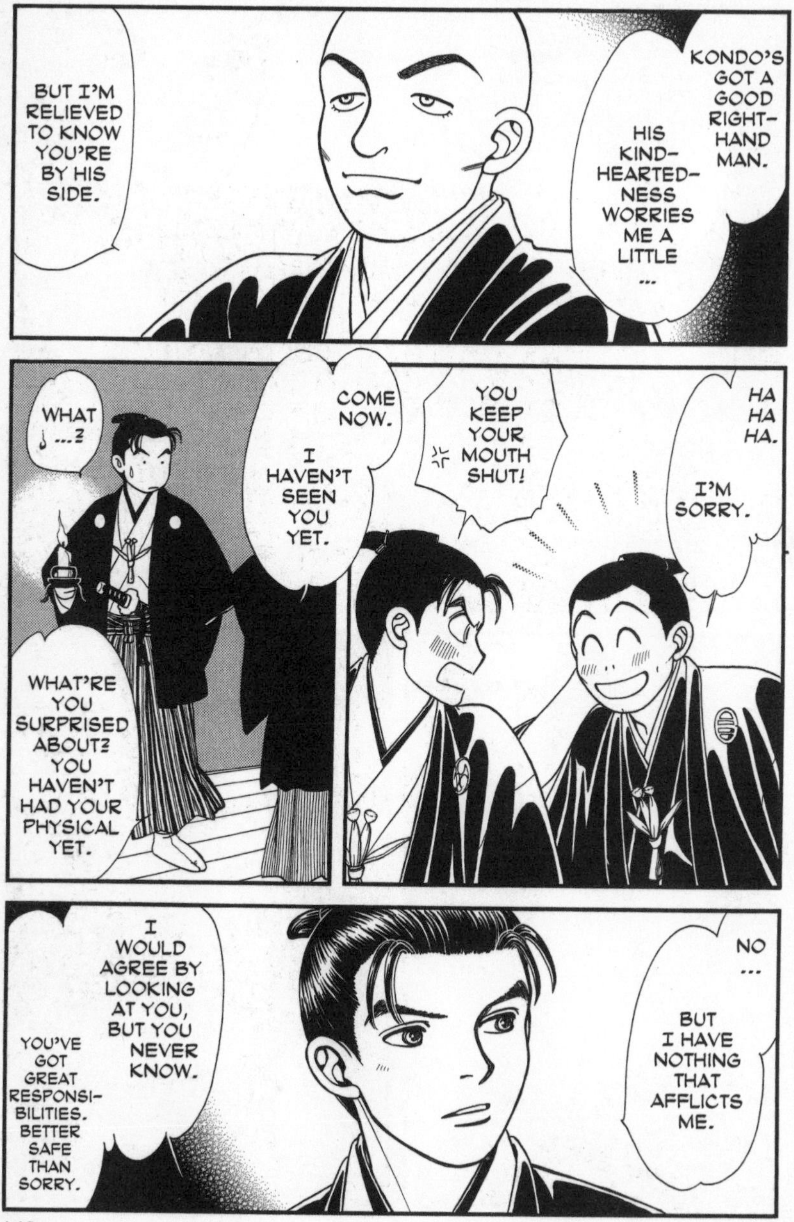
KONDO'S GOT A GOOD RIGHT-HAND MAN.
HIS KIND-HEARTED-NESS WORRIES ME A LITTLE ...
BUT I'M RELIEVED TO KNOW YOU'RE BY HIS SIDE.
HA HA HA.
I'M SORRY.
YOU KEEP YOUR MOUTH SHUT!
COME NOW.
I HAVEN'T SEEN YOU YET.
WHAT ...?
WHAT'RE YOU SURPRISED ABOUT? YOU HAVEN'T HAD YOUR PHYSICAL YET.
NO ...
BUT I HAVE NOTHING THAT AFFLICTS ME.
I WOULD AGREE BY LOOKING AT YOU, BUT YOU NEVER KNOW.
YOU'VE GOT GREAT RESPONSI-BILITIES. BETTER SAFE THAN SORRY.

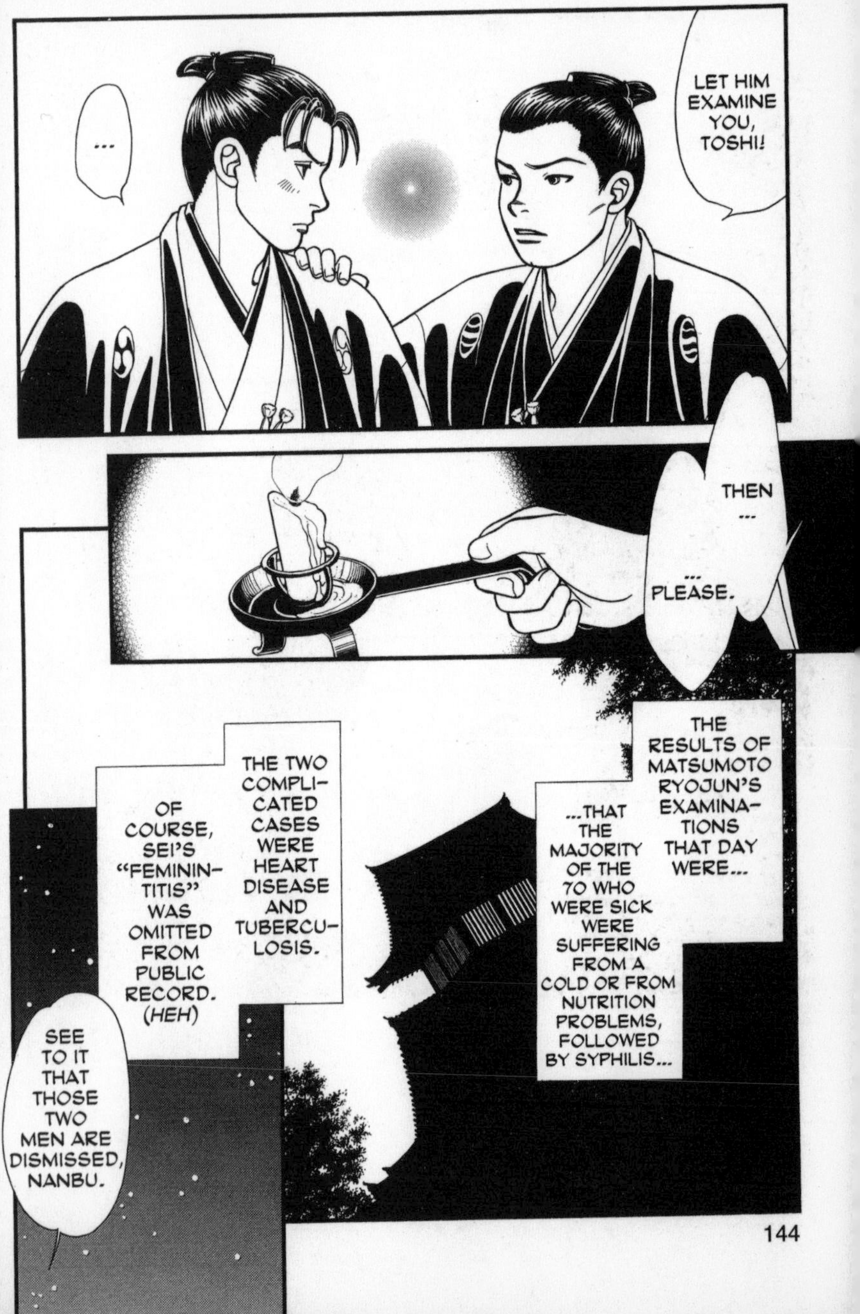
LET HIM EXAMINE YOU, TOSHI!
...
THEN ...
... PLEASE.
THE RESULTS OF MATSUMOTO RYOJUN'S EXAMINATIONS THAT DAY WERE...
...THAT THE MAJORITY OF THE 70 WHO WERE SICK WERE SUFFERING FROM A COLD OR FROM NUTRITION PROBLEMS, FOLLOWED BY SYPHILIS...
THE TWO COMPLICATED CASES WERE HEART DISEASE AND TUBERCULOSIS.
OF COURSE, SEI'S "FEMININTITIS" WAS OMITTED FROM PUBLIC RECORD. (*HEH*)
SEE TO IT THAT THOSE TWO MEN ARE DISMISSED, NANBU.

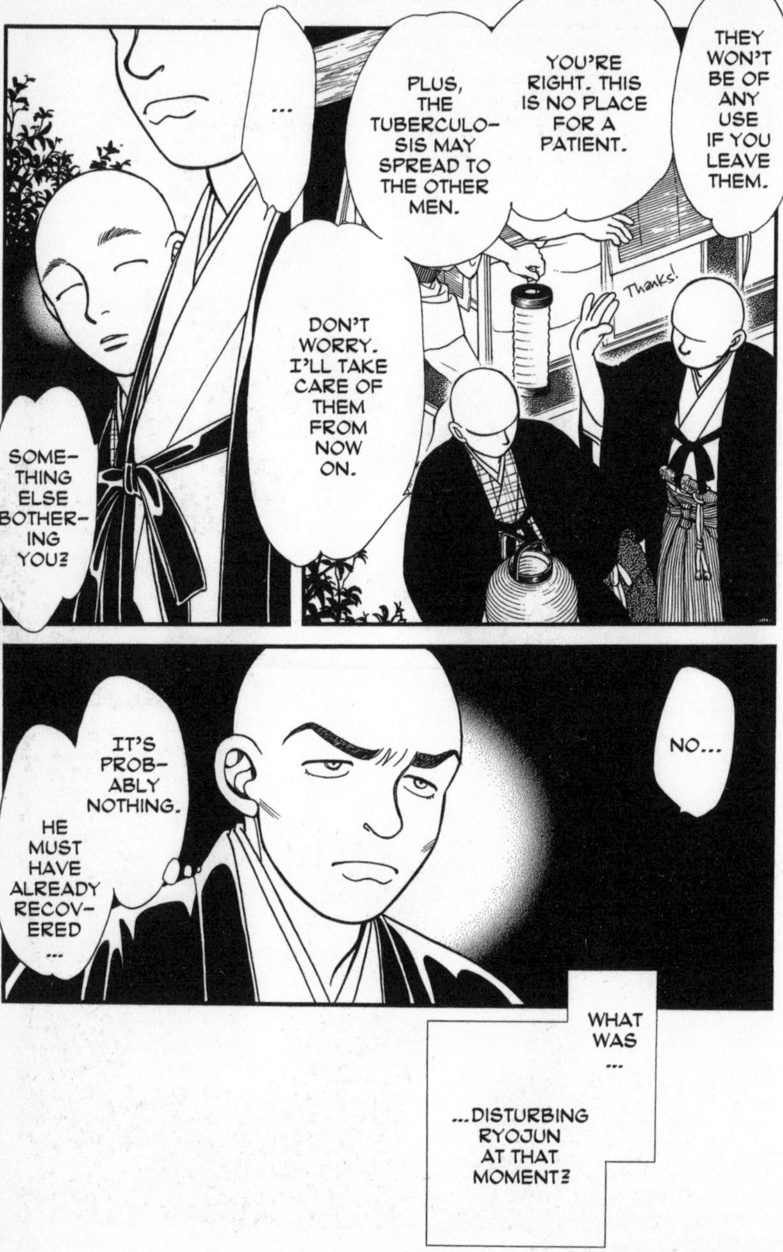
THEY WON'T BE OF ANY USE IF YOU LEAVE THEM.
YOU'RE RIGHT. THIS IS NO PLACE FOR A PATIENT.
PLUS, THE TUBERCULOSIS MAY SPREAD TO THE OTHER MEN.
Thanks!
...
DON'T WORRY. I'LL TAKE CARE OF THEM FROM NOW ON.
SOMETHING ELSE BOTHERING YOU?
NO...
IT'S PROBABLY NOTHING.
HE MUST HAVE ALREADY RECOVERED...
WHAT WAS...
...DISTURBING RYOJUN AT THAT MOMENT?

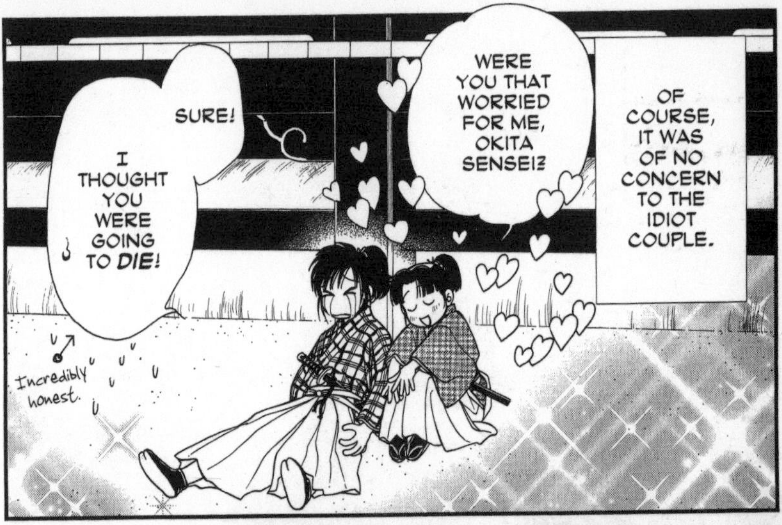
OF COURSE, IT WAS OF NO CONCERN TO THE IDIOT COUPLE.
WERE YOU THAT WORRIED FOR ME, OKITA SENSEI!?
SURE!
I THOUGHT YOU WERE GOING TO DIE!
Incredibly honest.

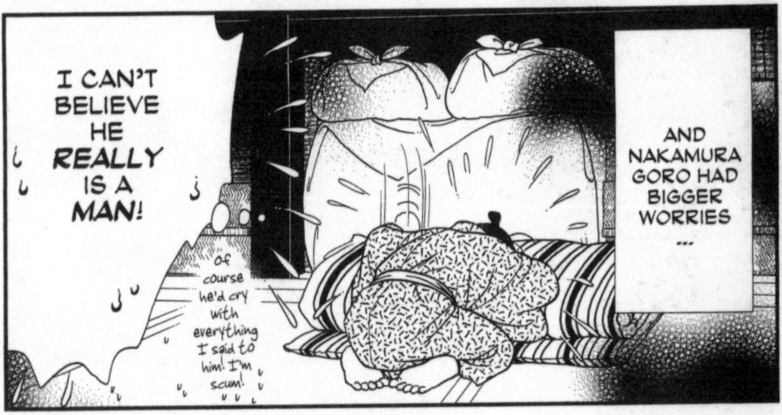
AND NAKAMURA GORO HAD BIGGER WORRIES...
I CAN'T BELIEVE HE REALLY IS A MAN!
Of course he'd cry with everything I said to him! I'm scum!

BUT THE INCIDENT SETTLED BOTH THE *GENPUKU* AND GORO MATTERS.

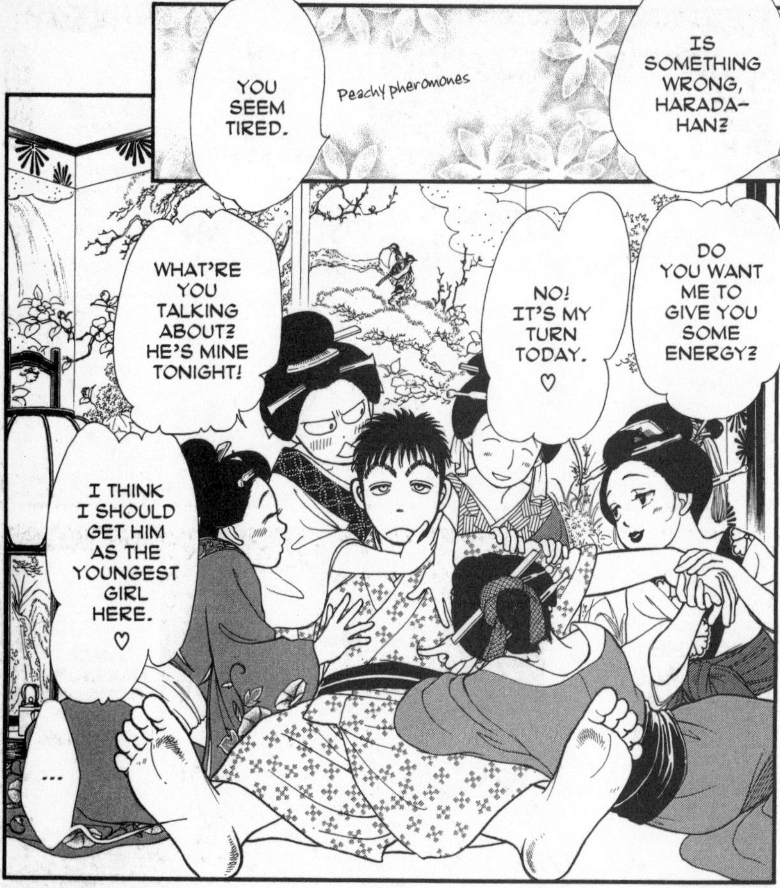
IS SOMETHING WRONG, HARADA-HAN?
Peachy pheromones
YOU SEEM TIRED.
DO YOU WANT ME TO GIVE YOU SOME ENERGY?
NO! IT'S MY TURN TODAY. ♡
WHAT'RE YOU TALKING ABOUT? HE'S MINE TONIGHT!
I THINK I SHOULD GET HIM AS THE YOUNGEST GIRL HERE. ♡
...

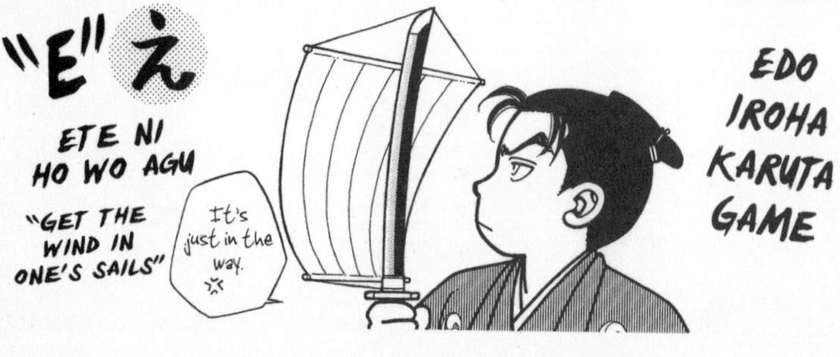
EDO IROHA KARUTA GAME
"E" え
ETE NI HO WO AGU
"GET THE WIND IN ONE'S SAILS"
It's just in the way.

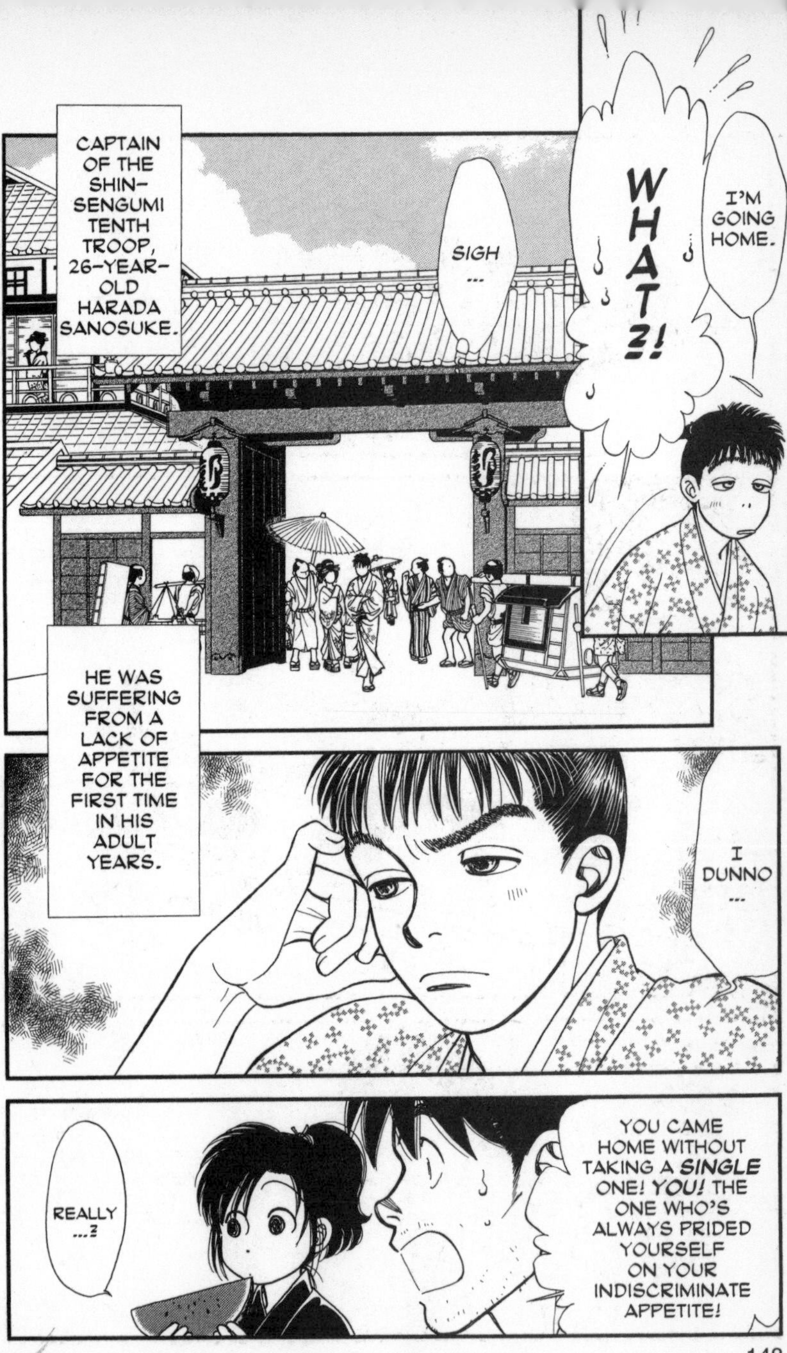
I'M GOING HOME.
WHAT?!
CAPTAIN OF THE SHIN-SENGUMI TENTH TROOP, 26-YEAR-OLD HARADA SANOSUKE.
SIGH ...
HE WAS SUFFERING FROM A LACK OF APPETITE FOR THE FIRST TIME IN HIS ADULT YEARS.
I DUNNO ...
YOU CAME HOME WITHOUT TAKING A *SINGLE* ONE! *YOU!* THE ONE WHO'S ALWAYS PRIDED YOURSELF ON YOUR INDISCRIMINATE APPETITE!
REALLY ...?

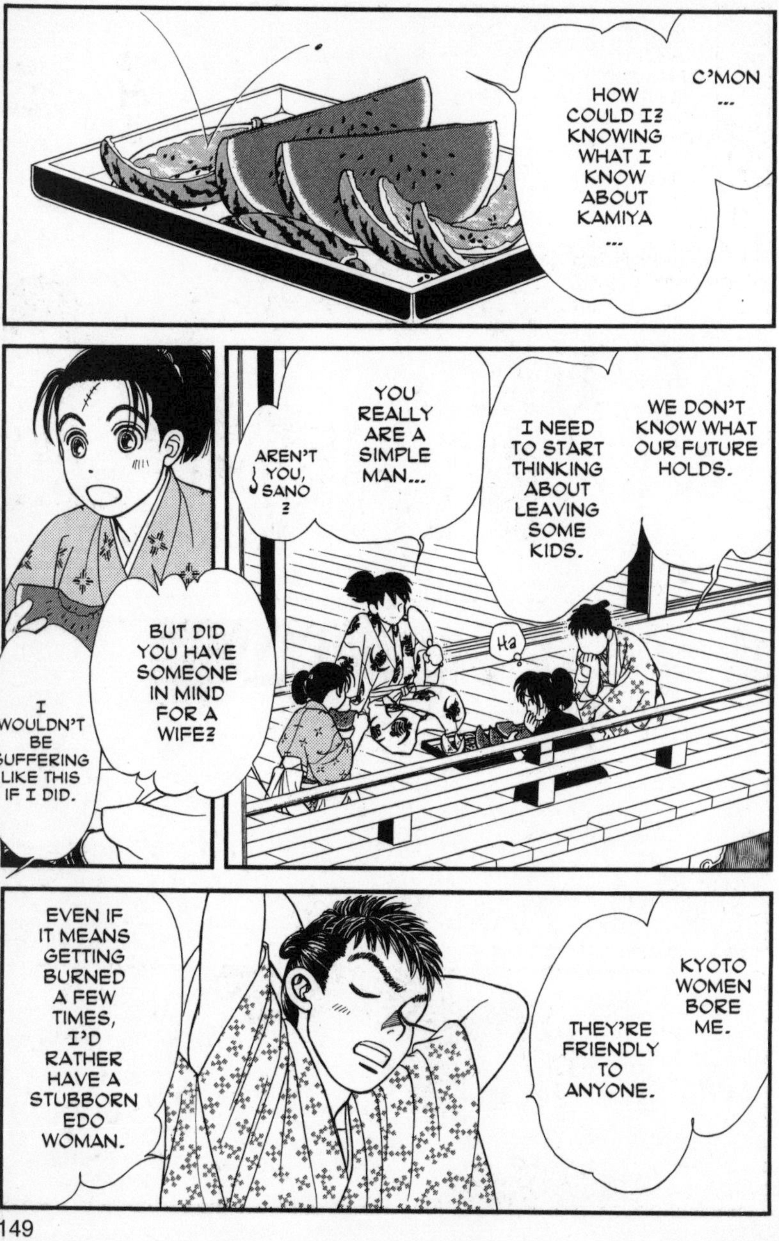
C'MON ...
HOW COULD I? KNOWING WHAT I KNOW ABOUT KAMIYA ...
WE DON'T KNOW WHAT OUR FUTURE HOLDS.
I NEED TO START THINKING ABOUT LEAVING SOME KIDS.
YOU REALLY ARE A SIMPLE MAN...
AREN'T YOU, SANO?
Ha
BUT DID YOU HAVE SOMEONE IN MIND FOR A WIFE?
I WOULDN'T BE SUFFERING LIKE THIS IF I DID.
KYOTO WOMEN BORE ME.
THEY'RE FRIENDLY TO ANYONE.
EVEN IF IT MEANS GETTING BURNED A FEW TIMES, I'D RATHER HAVE A STUBBORN EDO WOMAN.

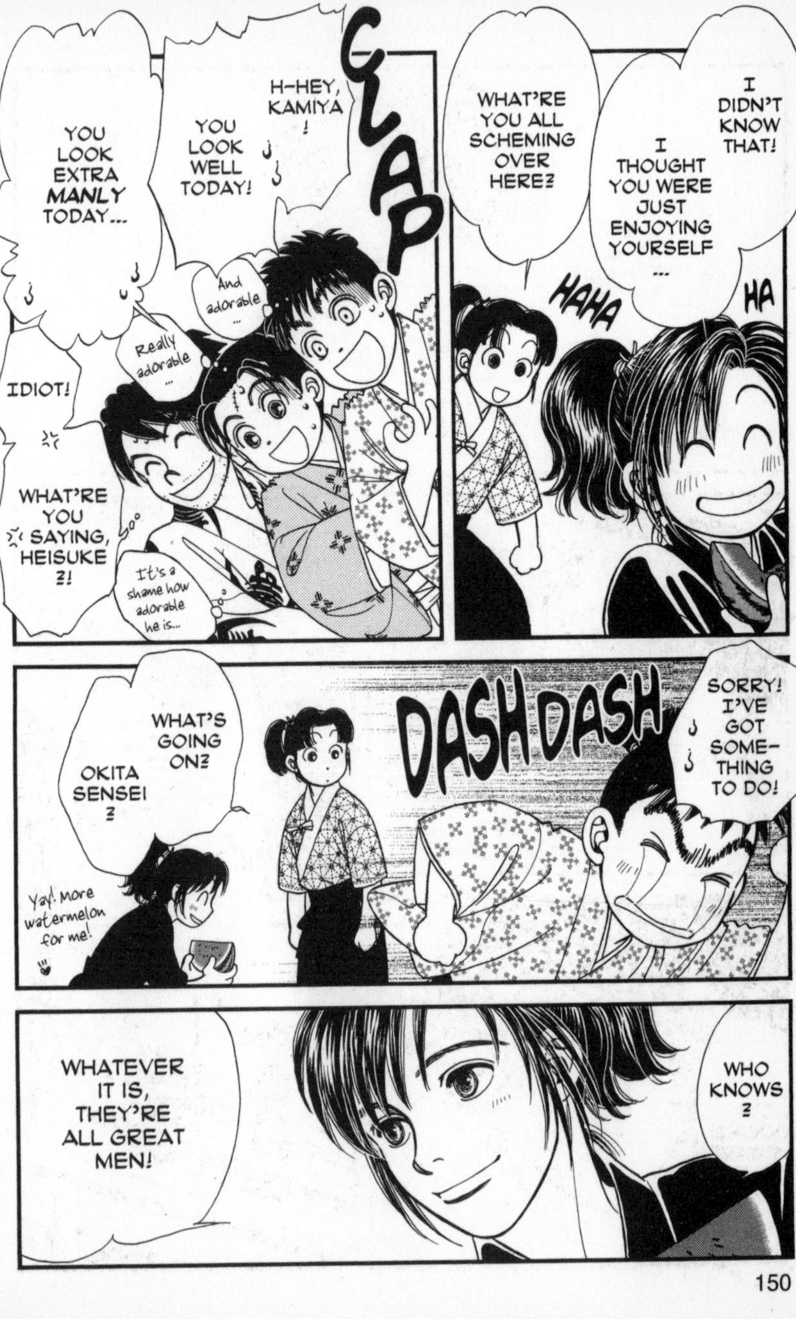

I DIDN'T KNOW THAT!
I THOUGHT YOU WERE JUST ENJOYING YOURSELF ...
HA
HAHA
WHAT'RE YOU ALL SCHEMING OVER HERE?
CLAP
H-HEY, KAMIYA!
YOU LOOK WELL TODAY!
And adorable...
YOU LOOK EXTRA MANLY TODAY...
Really adorable...
IDIOT!
WHAT'RE YOU SAYING, HEISUKE?!
It's a shame how adorable he is...
SORRY! I'VE GOT SOME-THING TO DO!
DASH DASH
WHAT'S GOING ON?
OKITA SENSEI?
Yay! More watermelon for me!
WHO KNOWS?
WHATEVER IT IS, THEY'RE ALL GREAT MEN!

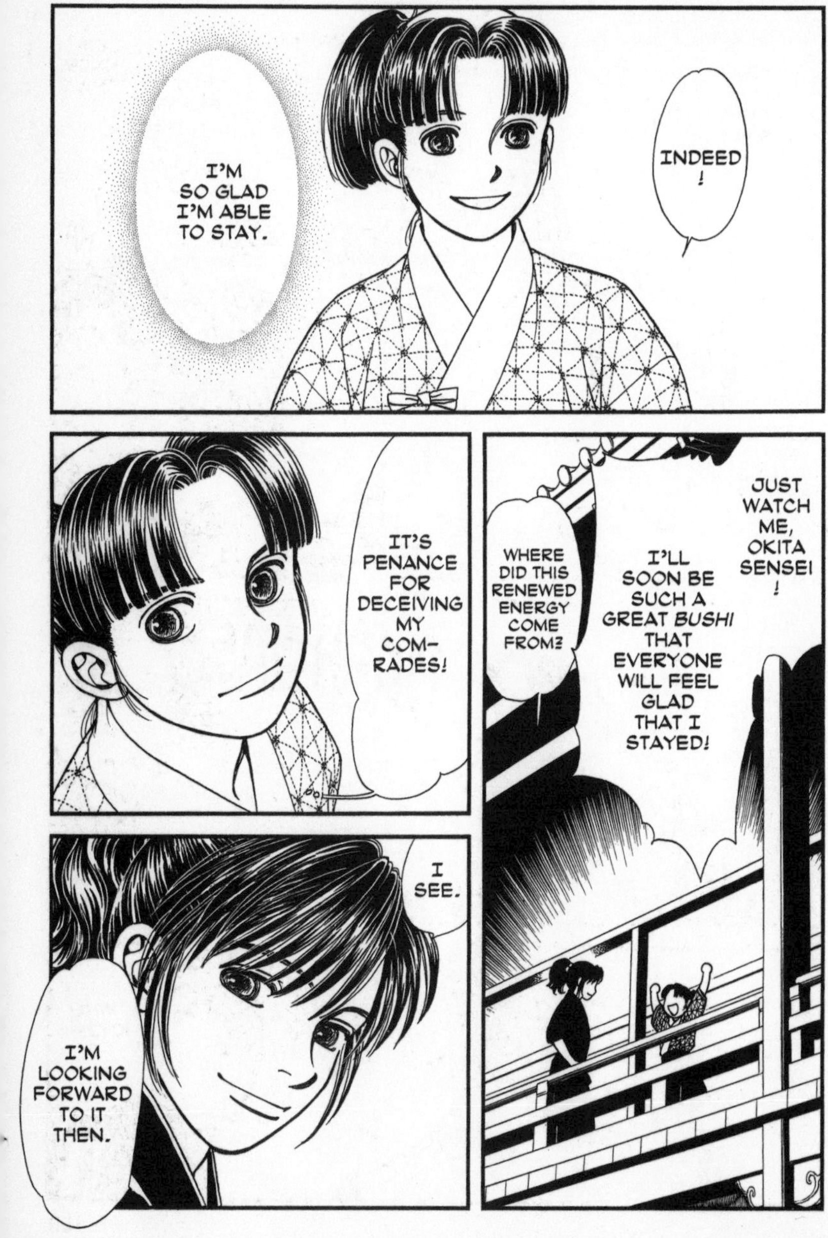
INDEED!
I'M SO GLAD I'M ABLE TO STAY.
JUST WATCH ME, OKITA SENSEI!
I'LL SOON BE SUCH A GREAT *BUSHI* THAT EVERYONE WILL FEEL GLAD THAT I STAYED!
WHERE DID THIS RENEWED ENERGY COME FROM?
IT'S PENANCE FOR DECEIVING MY COM-RADES!
I SEE.
I'M LOOKING FORWARD TO IT THEN.

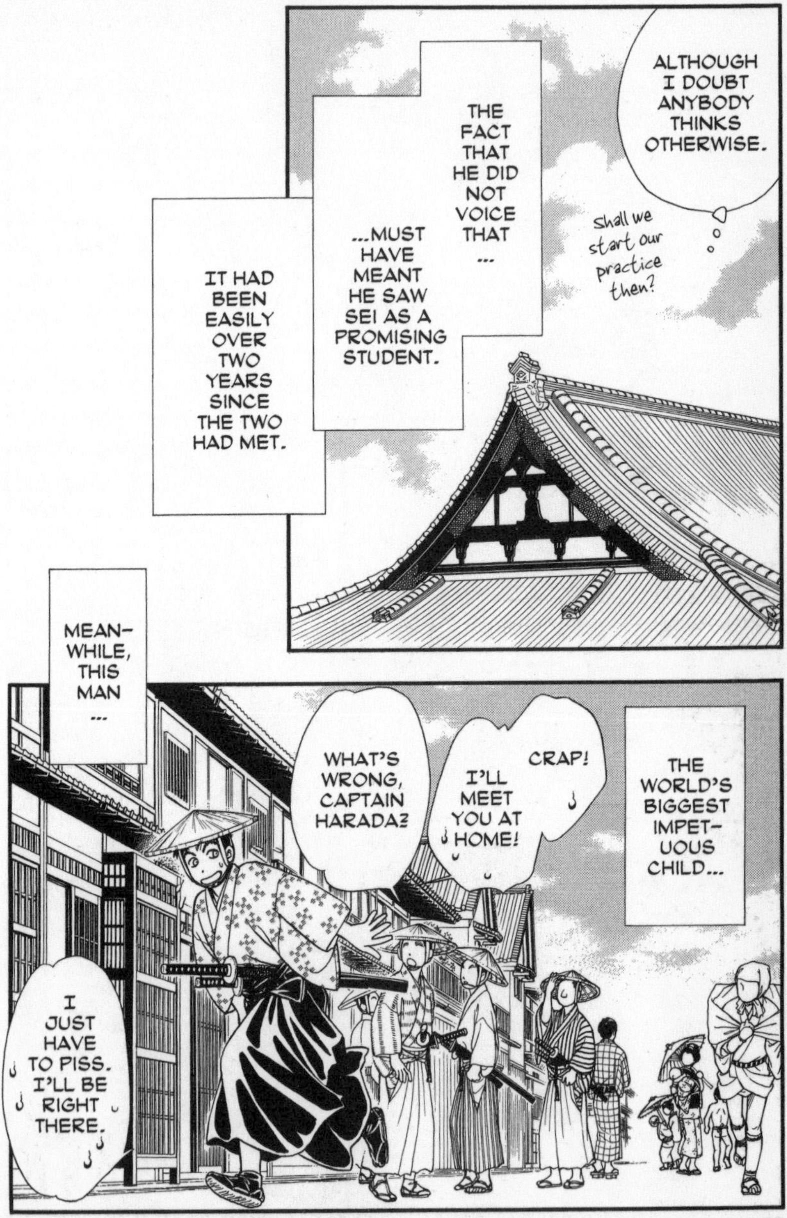
ALTHOUGH I DOUBT ANYBODY THINKS OTHERWISE.
Shall we start our practice then?
THE FACT THAT HE DID NOT VOICE THAT...
...MUST HAVE MEANT HE SAW SEI AS A PROMISING STUDENT.
IT HAD BEEN EASILY OVER TWO YEARS SINCE THE TWO HAD MET.
MEAN-WHILE, THIS MAN...
THE WORLD'S BIGGEST IMPET-UOUS CHILD...
CRAP! I'LL MEET YOU AT HOME!
WHAT'S WRONG, CAPTAIN HARADA?
I JUST HAVE TO PISS. I'LL BE RIGHT THERE.

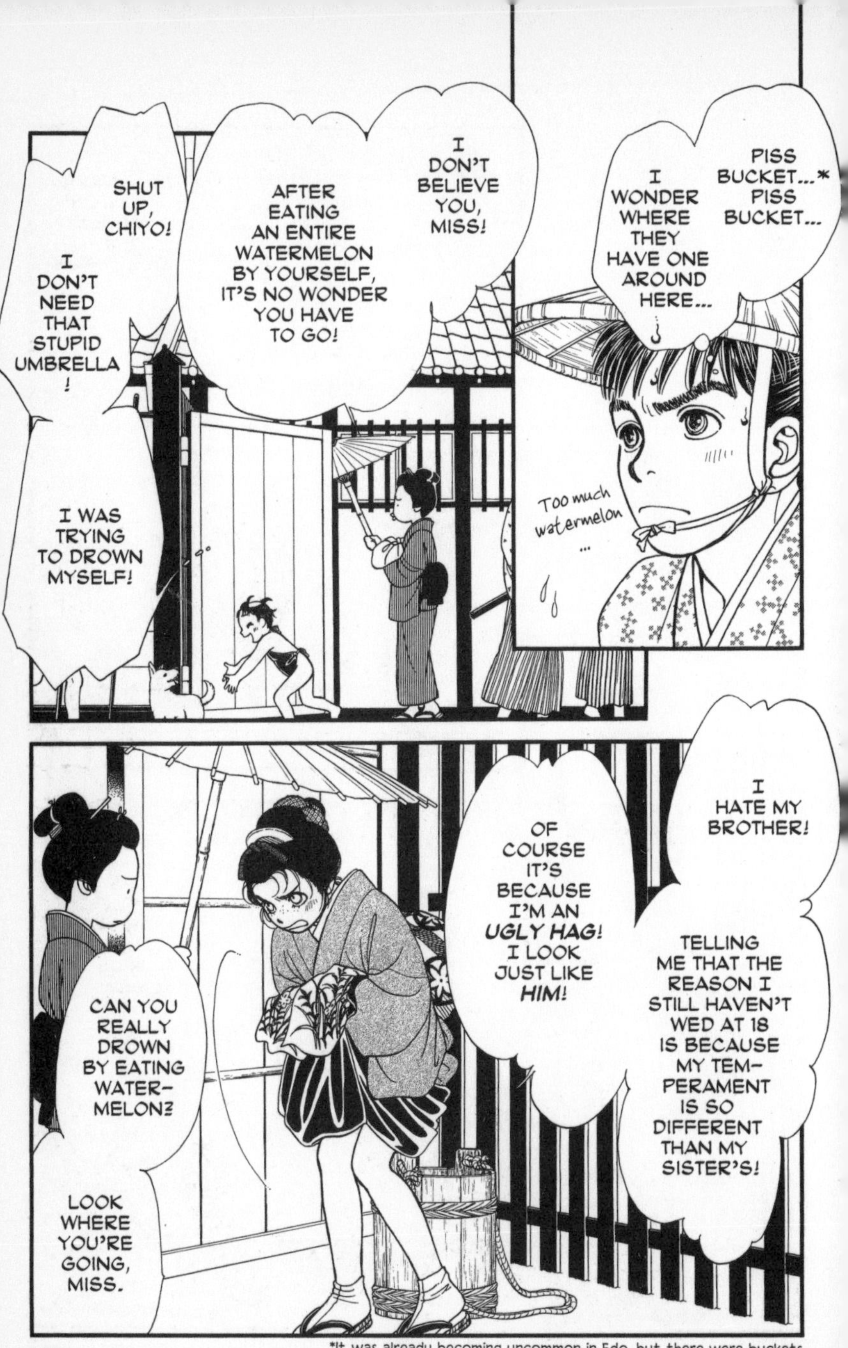
PISS BUCKET...* PISS BUCKET...
I WONDER WHERE THEY HAVE ONE AROUND HERE...
Too much watermelon ...
I DON'T BELIEVE YOU, MISS!
AFTER EATING AN ENTIRE WATERMELON BY YOURSELF, IT'S NO WONDER YOU HAVE TO GO!
SHUT UP, CHIYO!
I DON'T NEED THAT STUPID UMBRELLA!
I WAS TRYING TO DROWN MYSELF!
I HATE MY BROTHER!
TELLING ME THAT THE REASON I STILL HAVEN'T WED AT 18 IS BECAUSE MY TEM-PERAMENT IS SO DIFFERENT THAN MY SISTER'S!
OF COURSE IT'S BECAUSE I'M AN UGLY HAG! I LOOK JUST LIKE HIM!
CAN YOU REALLY DROWN BY EATING WATER-MELON?
LOOK WHERE YOU'RE GOING, MISS.

*It was already becoming uncommon in Edo, but there were buckets placed in various parts of town in Kyoto as public restrooms.

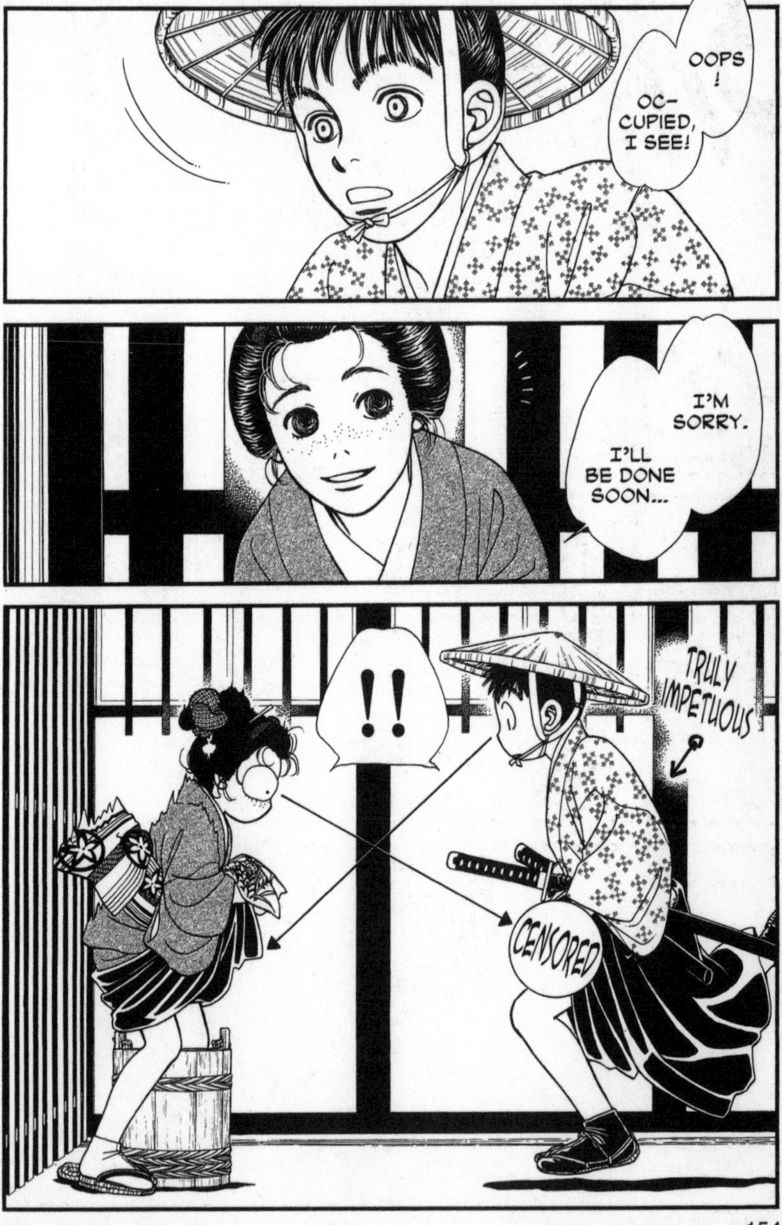

OOPS!
OC-CUPIED, I SEE!
I'M SORRY.
I'LL BE DONE SOON...
TRULY IMPETUOUS
!!
CENSORED

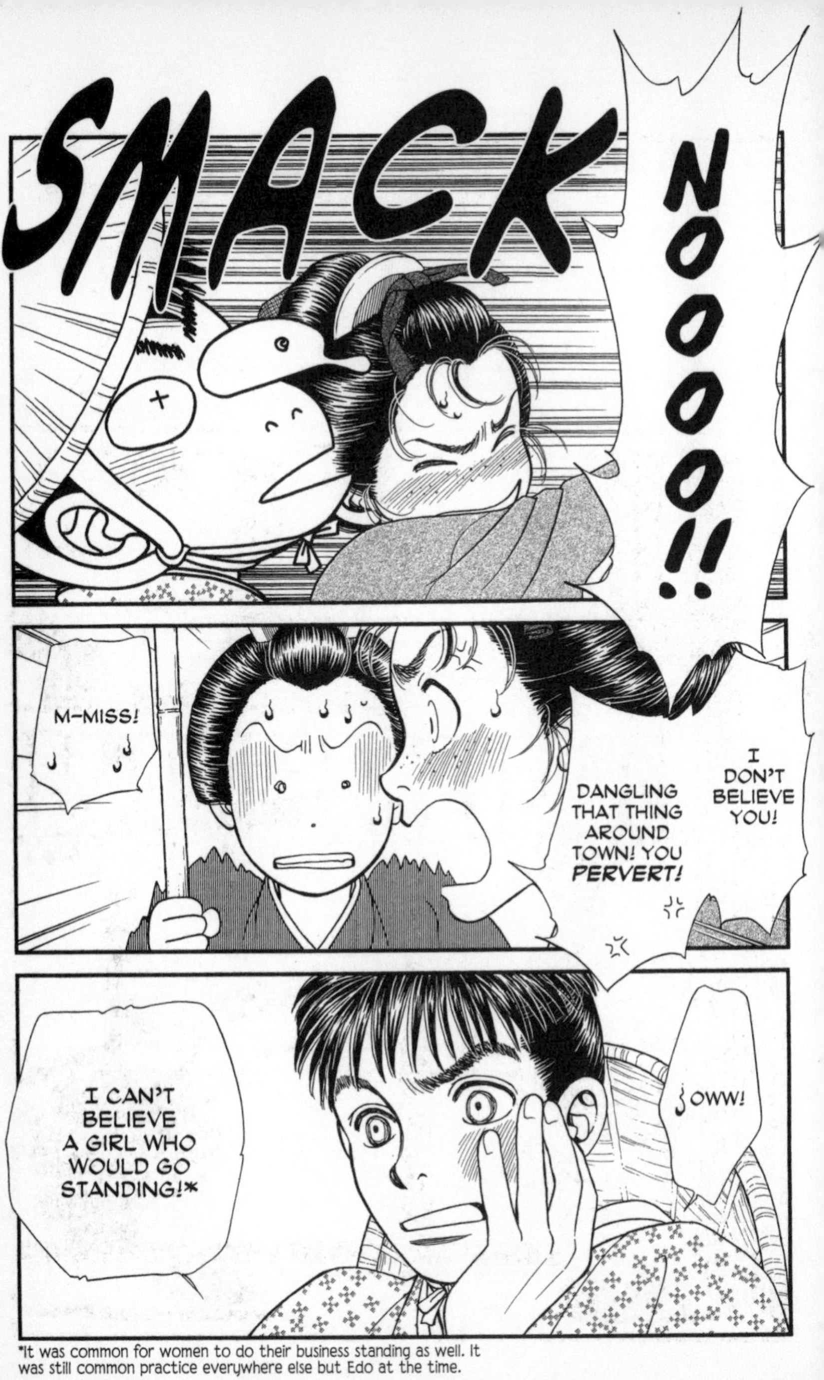
NOOOOO!!
SMACK
I DON'T BELIEVE YOU!
DANGLING THAT THING AROUND TOWN! YOU PERVERT!
M-MISS!
OWW!
I CAN'T BELIEVE A GIRL WHO WOULD GO STANDING!*

*It was common for women to do their business standing as well. It was still common practice everywhere else but Edo at the time.

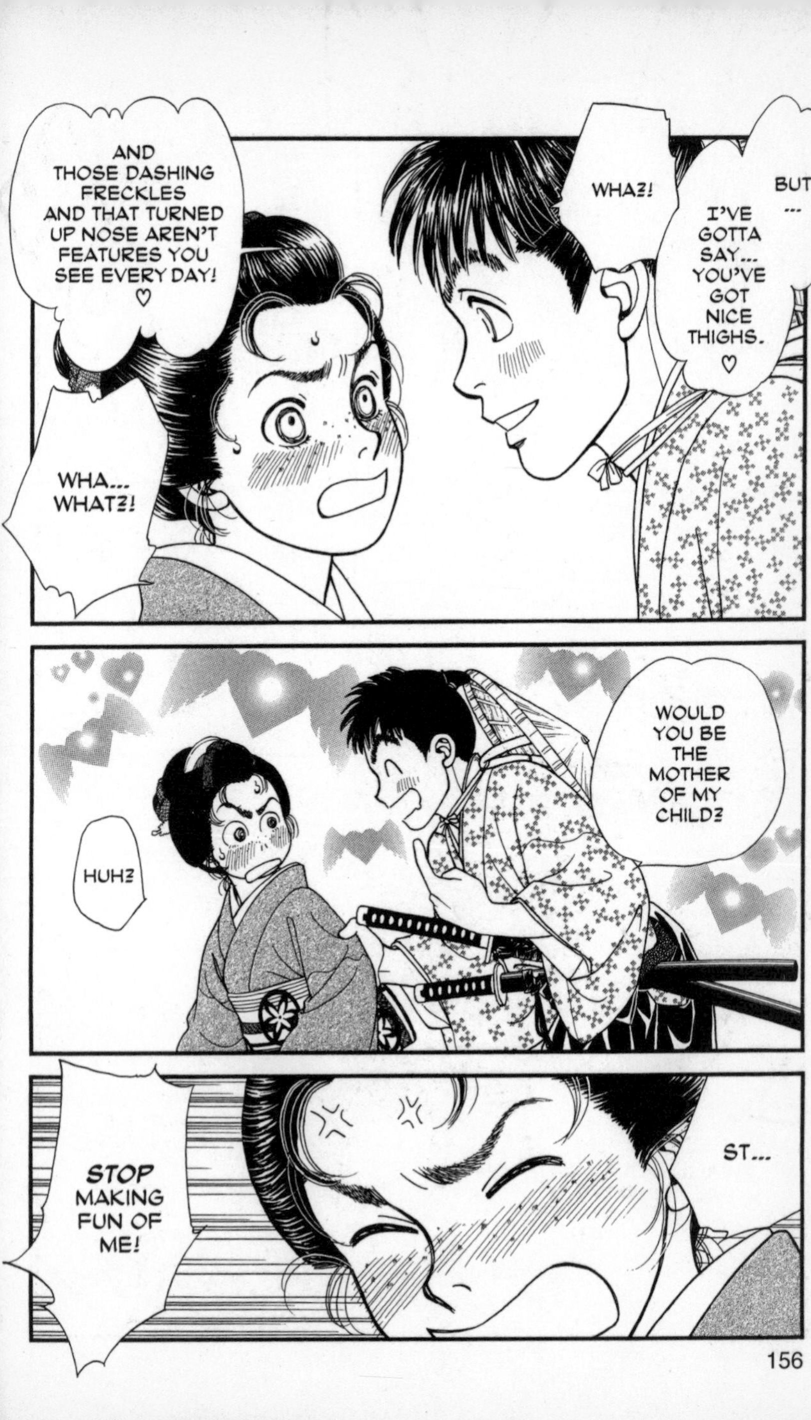
BUT... I'VE GOTTA SAY... YOU'VE GOT NICE THIGHS. ♡
WHA?!
AND THOSE DASHING FRECKLES AND THAT TURNED UP NOSE AREN'T FEATURES YOU SEE EVERY DAY! ♡
WHA... WHAT?!
WOULD YOU BE THE MOTHER OF MY CHILD?
HUH?
ST...
STOP MAKING FUN OF ME!

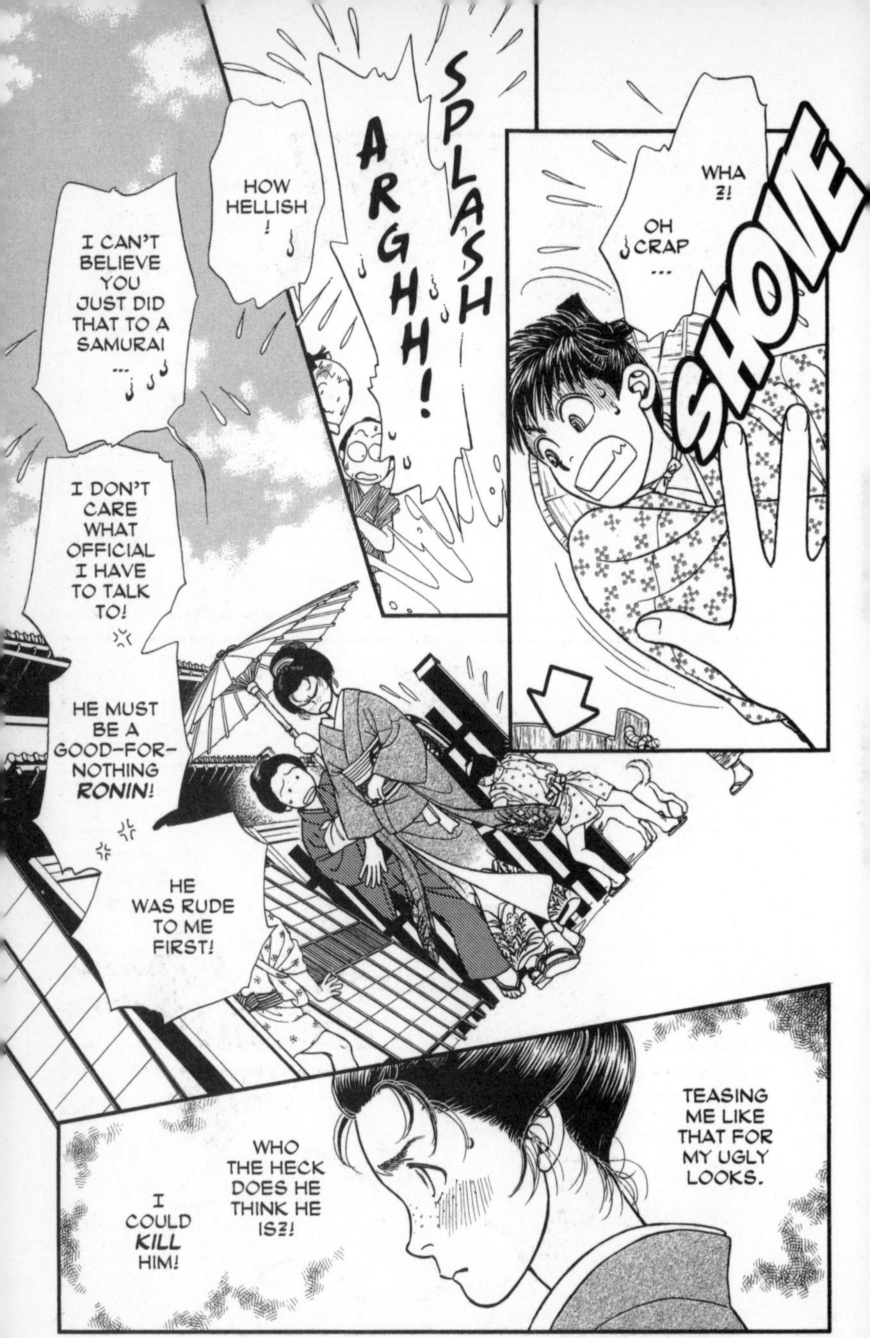
WHA?!
OH CRAP...
SHOVE
SPLASH
ARGHH!
HOW HELLISH!
I CAN'T BELIEVE YOU JUST DID THAT TO A SAMURAI...
I DON'T CARE WHAT OFFICIAL I HAVE TO TALK TO!
HE MUST BE A GOOD-FOR-NOTHING ***RONIN***!
HE WAS RUDE TO ME FIRST!
TEASING ME LIKE THAT FOR MY UGLY LOOKS.
WHO THE HECK DOES HE THINK HE IS?!
I COULD ***KILL*** HIM!

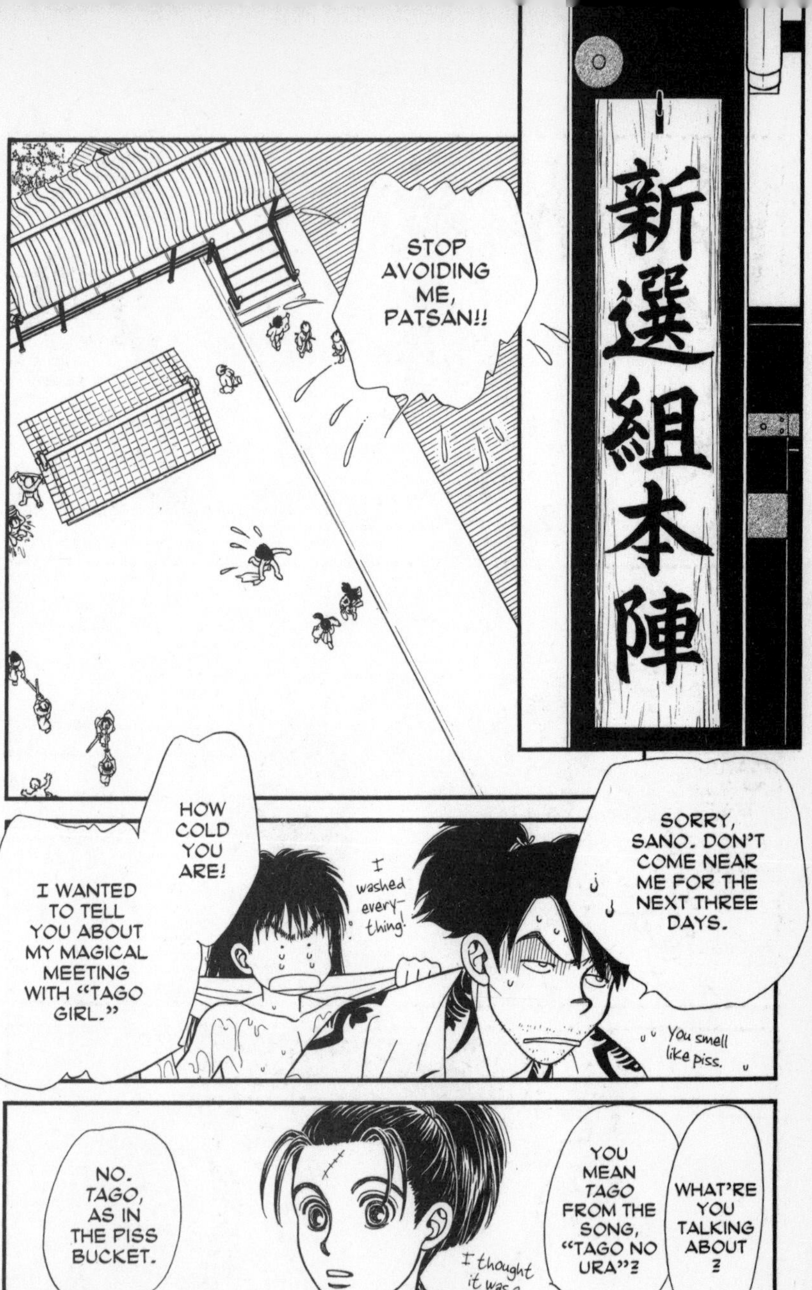
新選組本陣
STOP AVOIDING ME, PATSAN!!
SORRY, SANO. DON'T COME NEAR ME FOR THE NEXT THREE DAYS.
You smell like piss.
I washed every-thing!
HOW COLD YOU ARE!
I WANTED TO TELL YOU ABOUT MY MAGICAL MEETING WITH "TAGO GIRL."
WHAT'RE YOU TALKING ABOUT?
YOU MEAN *TAGO* FROM THE SONG, "TAGO NO URA"?
I thought it was a pseudonym.
NO. *TAGO*, AS IN THE PISS BUCKET.

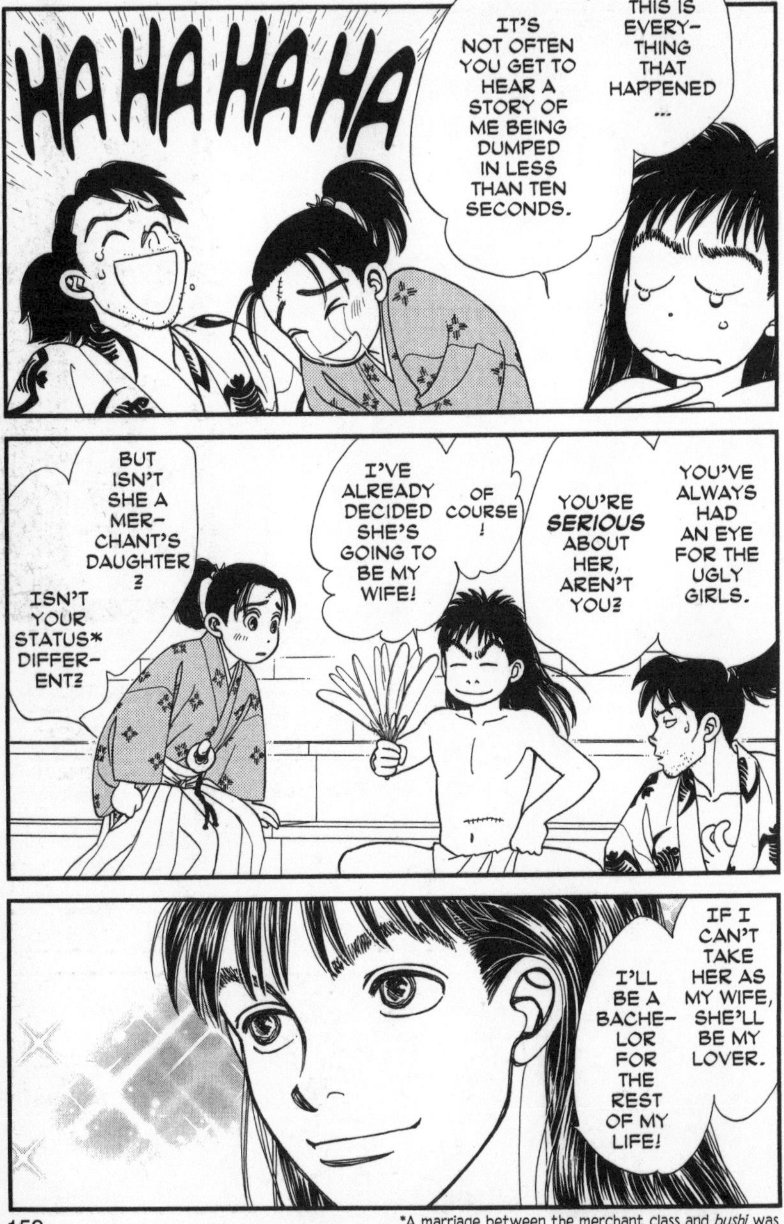
THIS IS EVERYTHING THAT HAPPENED ...
IT'S NOT OFTEN YOU GET TO HEAR A STORY OF ME BEING DUMPED IN LESS THAN TEN SECONDS.
HA HA HA HA HA
YOU'VE ALWAYS HAD AN EYE FOR THE UGLY GIRLS.
YOU'RE *SERIOUS* ABOUT HER, AREN'T YOU?
OF COURSE!
I'VE ALREADY DECIDED SHE'S GOING TO BE MY WIFE!
BUT ISN'T SHE A MERCHANT'S DAUGHTER?
ISN'T YOUR STATUS* DIFFERENT?
IF I CAN'T TAKE HER AS MY WIFE, SHE'LL BE MY LOVER.
I'LL BE A BACHELOR FOR THE REST OF MY LIFE!

*A marriage between the merchant class and *bushi* was generally not permitted at the time.

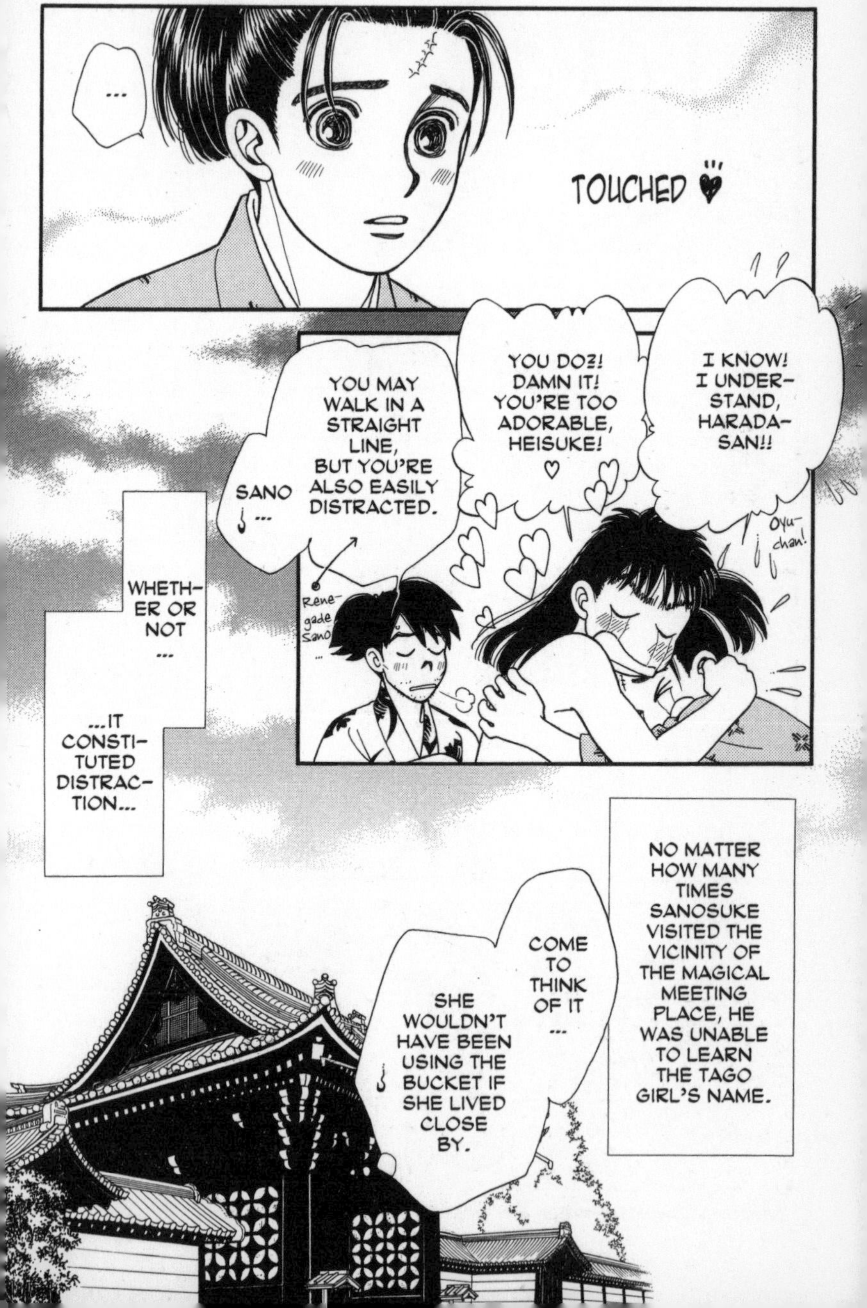
...
TOUCHED
I KNOW! I UNDER-STAND, HARADA-SAN!!
Oyu-chan!
YOU DO?! DAMN IT! YOU'RE TOO ADORABLE, HEISUKE!
YOU MAY WALK IN A STRAIGHT LINE, BUT YOU'RE ALSO EASILY DISTRACTED.
SANO ...
Rene-gade Sano ...
WHETH-ER OR NOT ...
...IT CONSTI-TUTED DISTRAC-TION...
NO MATTER HOW MANY TIMES SANOSUKE VISITED THE VICINITY OF THE MAGICAL MEETING PLACE, HE WAS UNABLE TO LEARN THE TAGO GIRL'S NAME.
COME TO THINK OF IT ...
SHE WOULDN'T HAVE BEEN USING THE BUCKET IF SHE LIVED CLOSE BY.

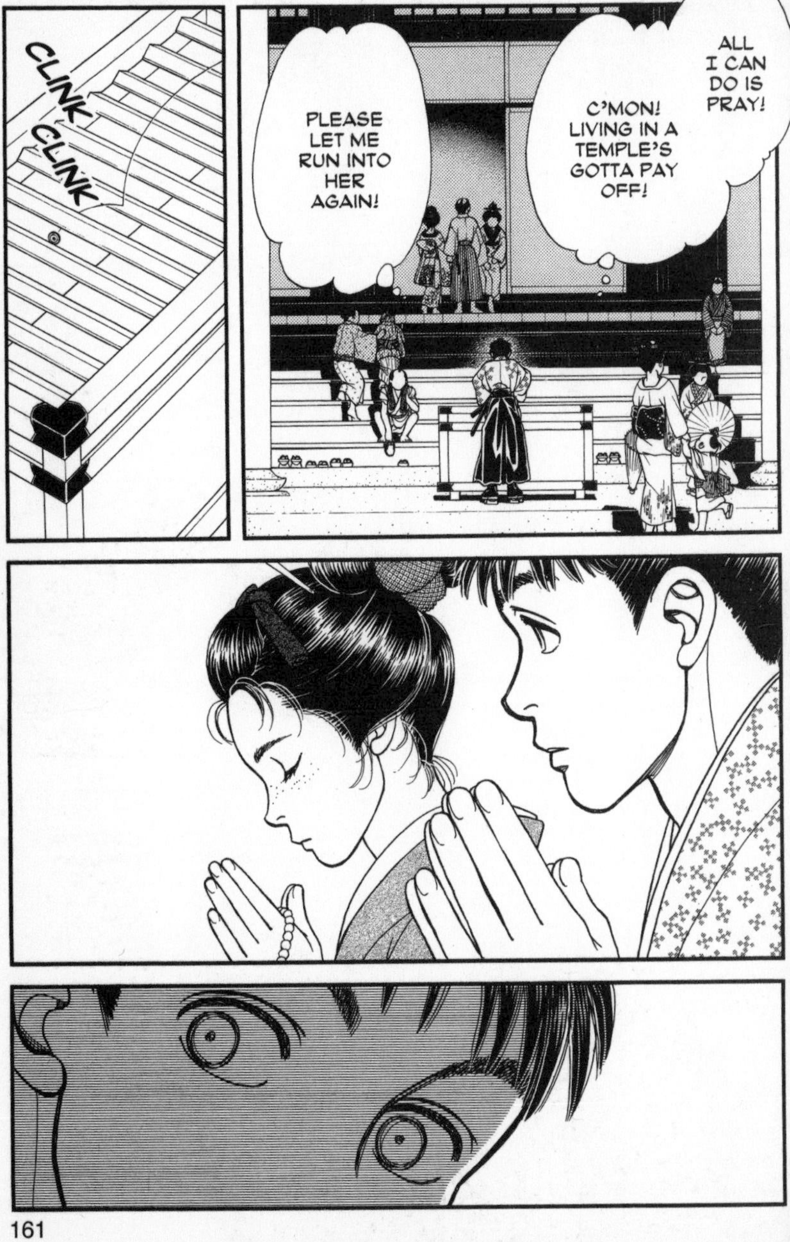
ALL I CAN DO IS PRAY!
C'MON! LIVING IN A TEMPLE'S GOTTA PAY OFF!
PLEASE LET ME RUN INTO HER AGAIN!
CLINK CLINK

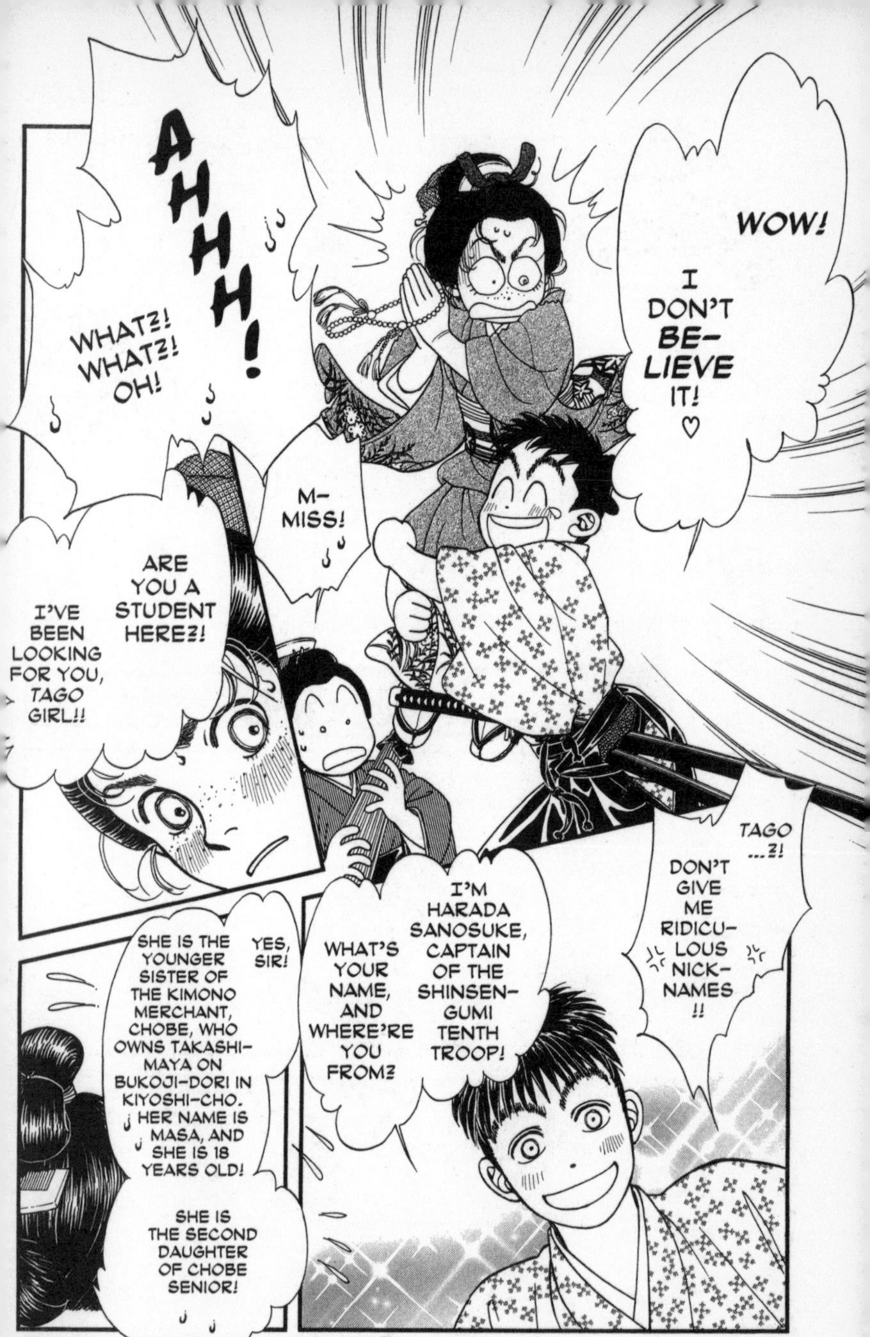
WOW!
I DON'T BE-LIEVE IT! ♡
AHHH!
WHAT?! WHAT?! OH!
M-MISS!
ARE YOU A STUDENT HERE?!
I'VE BEEN LOOKING FOR YOU, *TAGO* GIRL!!
TAGO ...?!
DON'T GIVE ME RIDICU-LOUS NICK-NAMES!!
I'M HARADA SANOSUKE, CAPTAIN OF THE SHINSEN-GUMI TENTH TROOP!
WHAT'S YOUR NAME, AND WHERE'RE YOU FROM?
YES, SIR!
SHE IS THE YOUNGER SISTER OF THE KIMONO MERCHANT, CHOBE, WHO OWNS TAKASHI-MAYA ON BUKOJI-DORI IN KIYOSHI-CHO. HER NAME IS MASA, AND SHE IS 18 YEARS OLD!
SHE IS THE SECOND DAUGHTER OF CHOBE SENIOR!

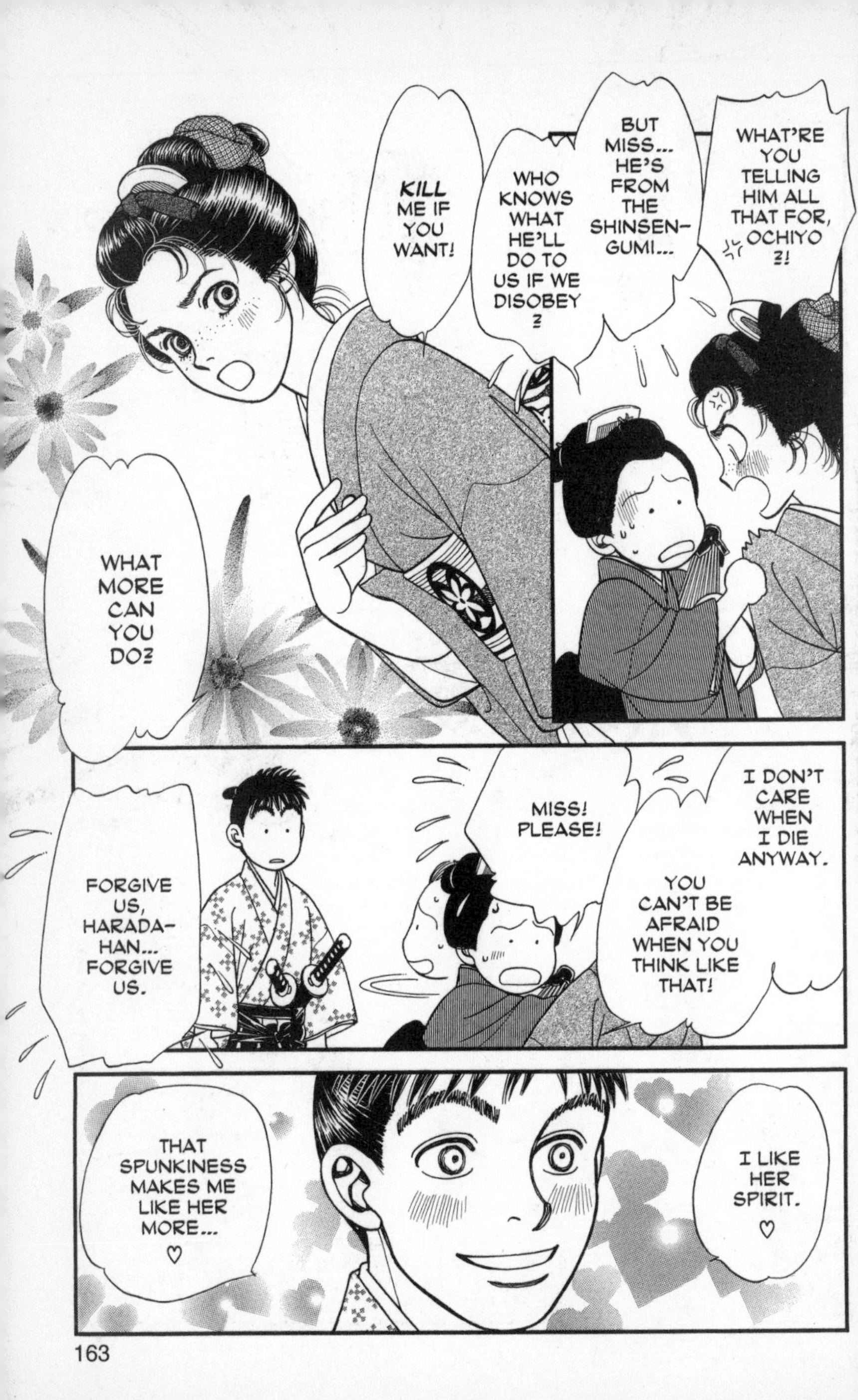
WHAT'RE YOU TELLING HIM ALL THAT FOR, OCHIYO?!
BUT MISS... HE'S FROM THE SHINSEN-GUMI...
WHO KNOWS WHAT HE'LL DO TO US IF WE DISOBEY?
KILL ME IF YOU WANT!
WHAT MORE CAN YOU DO?
I DON'T CARE WHEN I DIE ANYWAY.
YOU CAN'T BE AFRAID WHEN YOU THINK LIKE THAT!
MISS! PLEASE!
FORGIVE US, HARADA-HAN... FORGIVE US.
I LIKE HER SPIRIT. ♡
THAT SPUNKINESS MAKES ME LIKE HER MORE... ♡

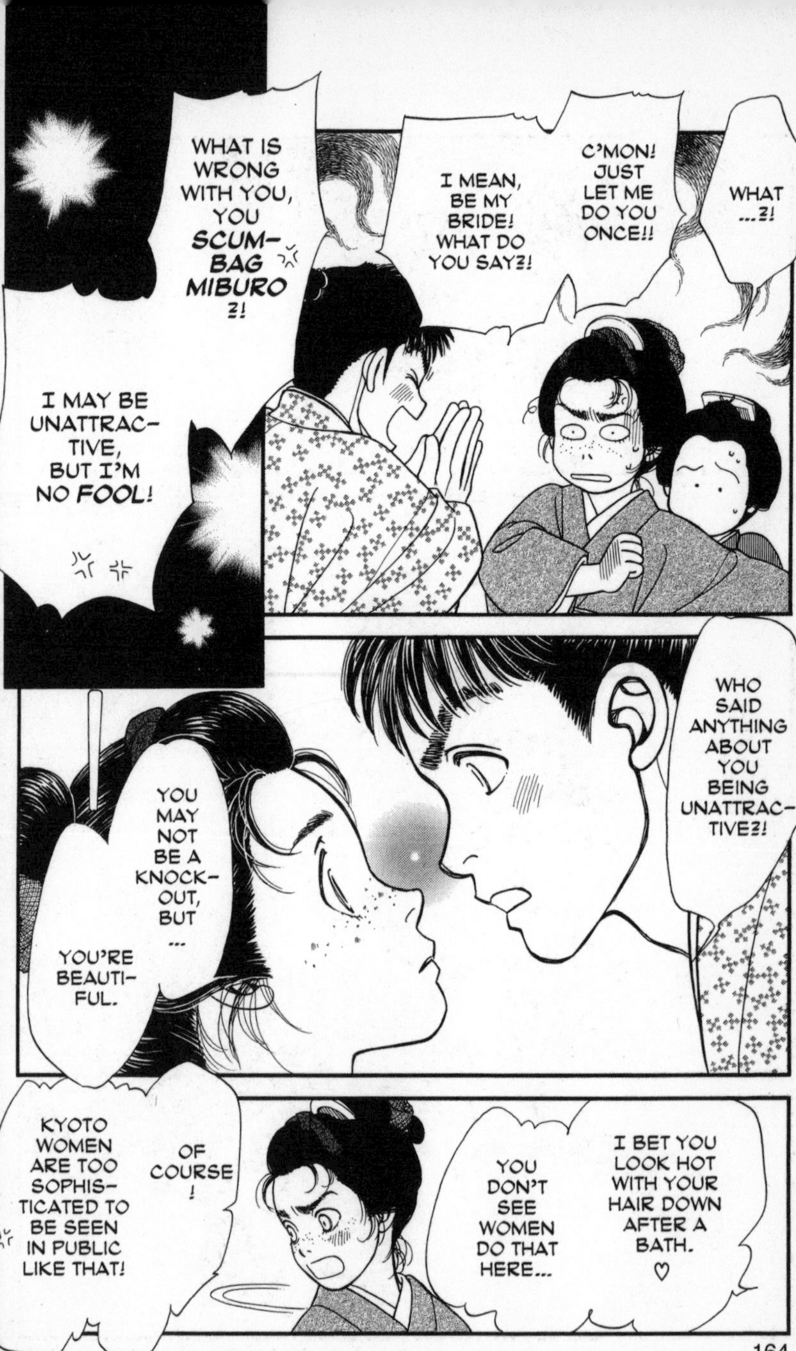
WHAT ...?!
C'MON! JUST LET ME DO YOU ONCE!!
I MEAN, BE MY BRIDE! WHAT DO YOU SAY?!
WHAT IS WRONG WITH YOU, YOU **SCUMBAG MIBURO**?!
I MAY BE UNATTRACTIVE, BUT I'M NO **FOOL**!
WHO SAID ANYTHING ABOUT YOU BEING UNATTRACTIVE?!
YOU MAY NOT BE A KNOCKOUT, BUT ...
YOU'RE BEAUTIFUL.
I BET YOU LOOK HOT WITH YOUR HAIR DOWN AFTER A BATH. ♡
YOU DON'T SEE WOMEN DO THAT HERE...
OF COURSE!
KYOTO WOMEN ARE TOO SOPHISTICATED TO BE SEEN IN PUBLIC LIKE THAT!

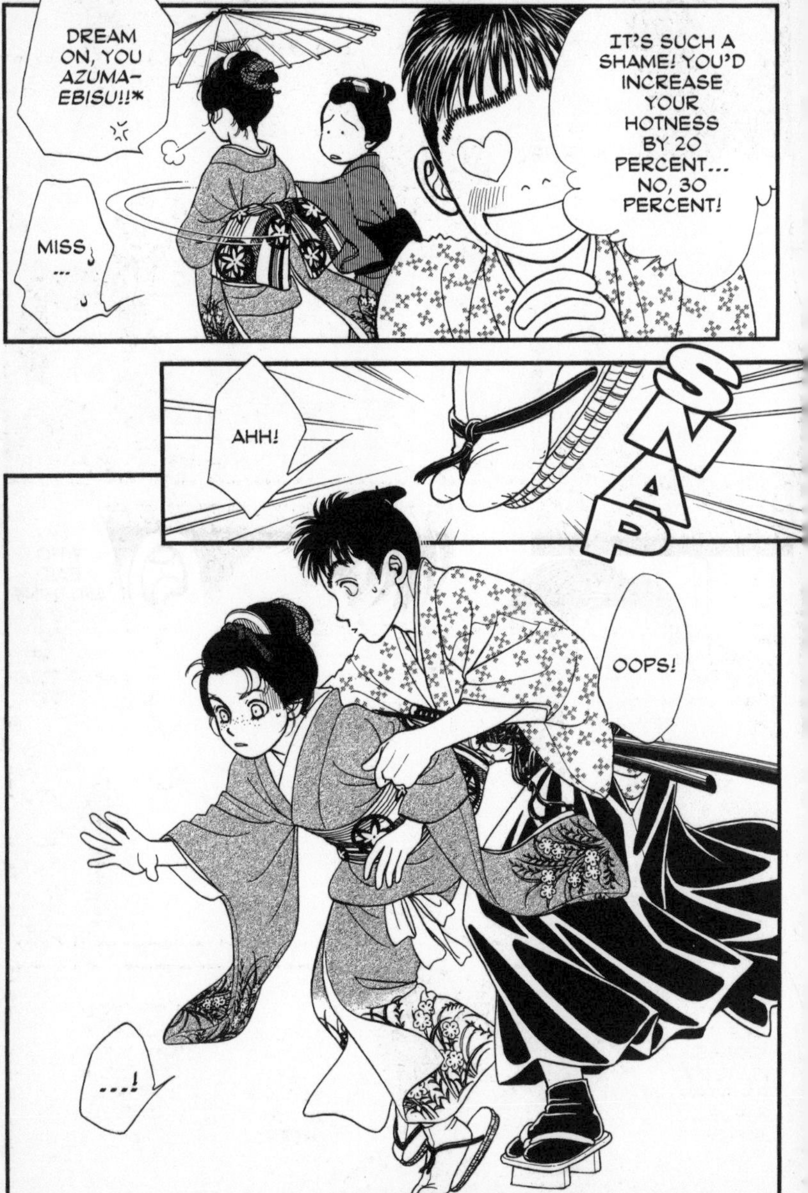
IT'S SUCH A SHAME! YOU'D INCREASE YOUR HOTNESS BY 20 PERCENT... NO, 30 PERCENT!
DREAM ON, YOU AZUMA-EBISU!!*
MISS ...
SNAP
AHH!
OOPS!
...!

*A name that the people of Kyoto used to taunt *bushi* from the East that meant "barbarians of the East."

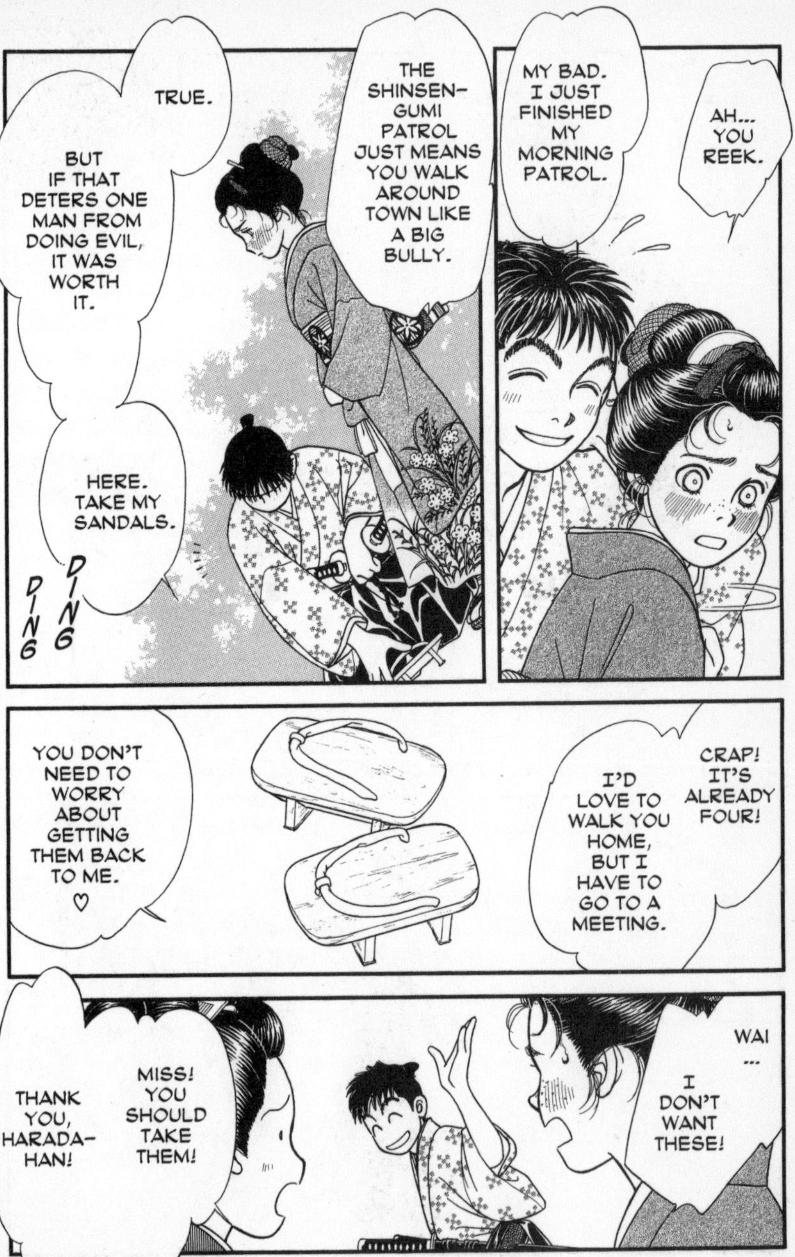
AH... YOU REEK.
MY BAD. I JUST FINISHED MY MORNING PATROL.
THE SHINSEN-GUMI PATROL JUST MEANS YOU WALK AROUND TOWN LIKE A BIG BULLY.
TRUE.
BUT IF THAT DETERS ONE MAN FROM DOING EVIL, IT WAS WORTH IT.
HERE. TAKE MY SANDALS.
DING DING
CRAP! IT'S ALREADY FOUR!
I'D LOVE TO WALK YOU HOME, BUT I HAVE TO GO TO A MEETING.
YOU DON'T NEED TO WORRY ABOUT GETTING THEM BACK TO ME. ♡
WAI...
I DON'T WANT THESE!
MISS! YOU SHOULD TAKE THEM!
THANK YOU, HARADA-HAN!

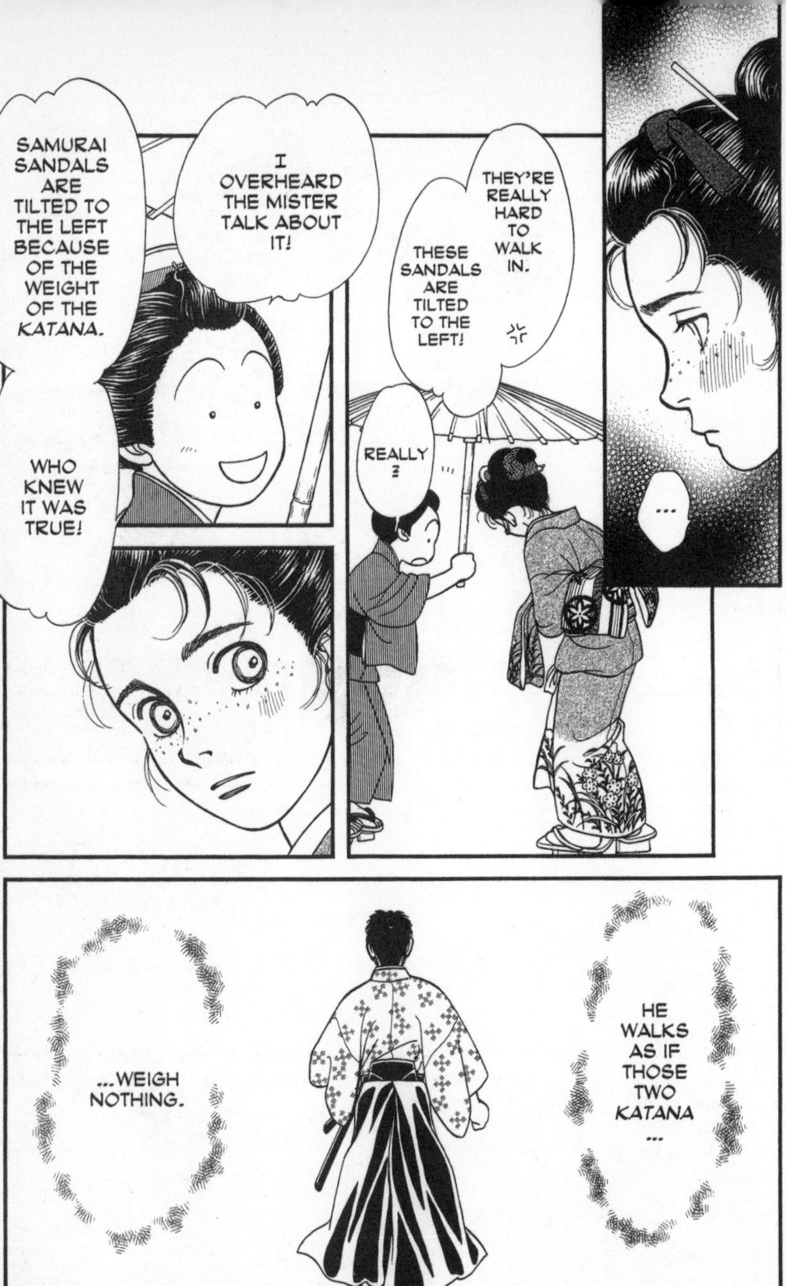
...
THEY'RE REALLY HARD TO WALK IN.
THESE SANDALS ARE TILTED TO THE LEFT!
REALLY?
I OVERHEARD THE MISTER TALK ABOUT IT!
SAMURAI SANDALS ARE TILTED TO THE LEFT BECAUSE OF THE WEIGHT OF THE *KATANA*.
WHO KNEW IT WAS TRUE!
HE WALKS AS IF THOSE TWO *KATANA*...
...WEIGH NOTHING.

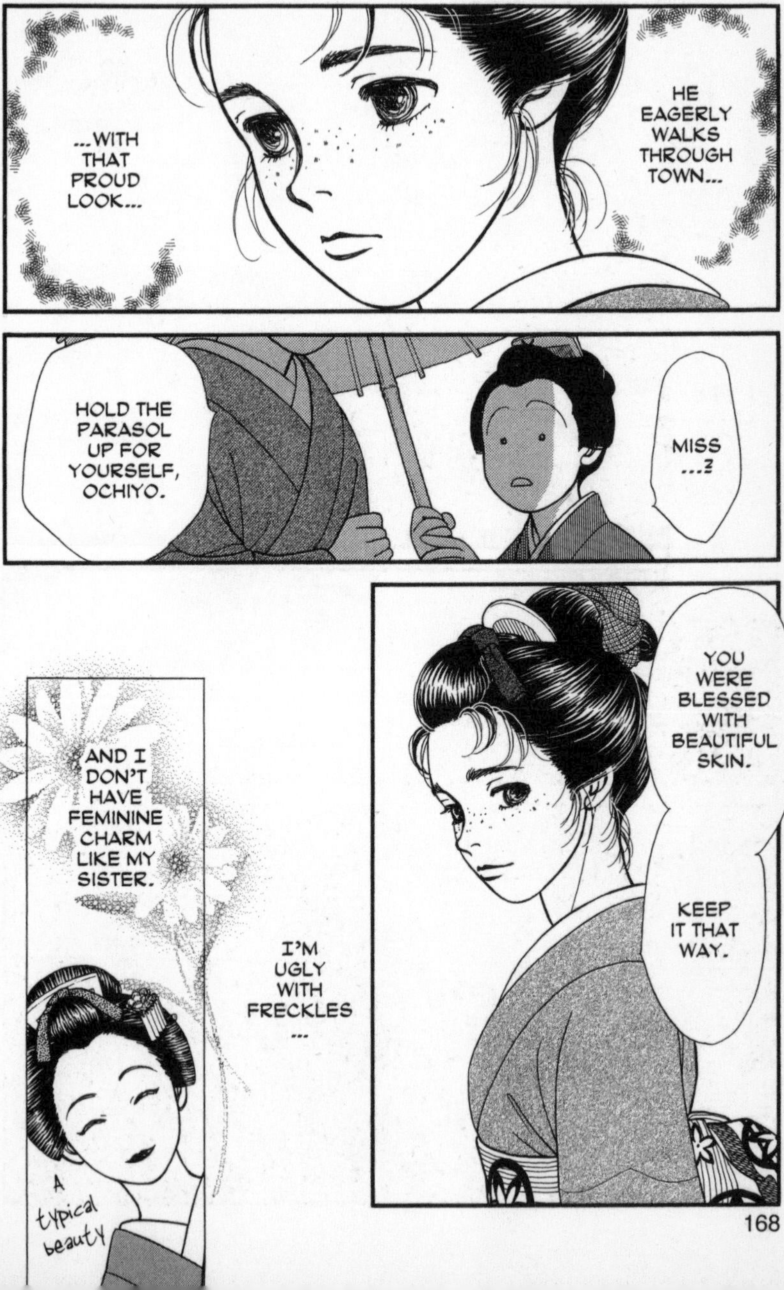
HE EAGERLY WALKS THROUGH TOWN...
...WITH THAT PROUD LOOK...
MISS ...?
HOLD THE PARASOL UP FOR YOURSELF, OCHIYO.
YOU WERE BLESSED WITH BEAUTIFUL SKIN.
KEEP IT THAT WAY.
I'M UGLY WITH FRECKLES ...
AND I DON'T HAVE FEMININE CHARM LIKE MY SISTER.
A typical beauty

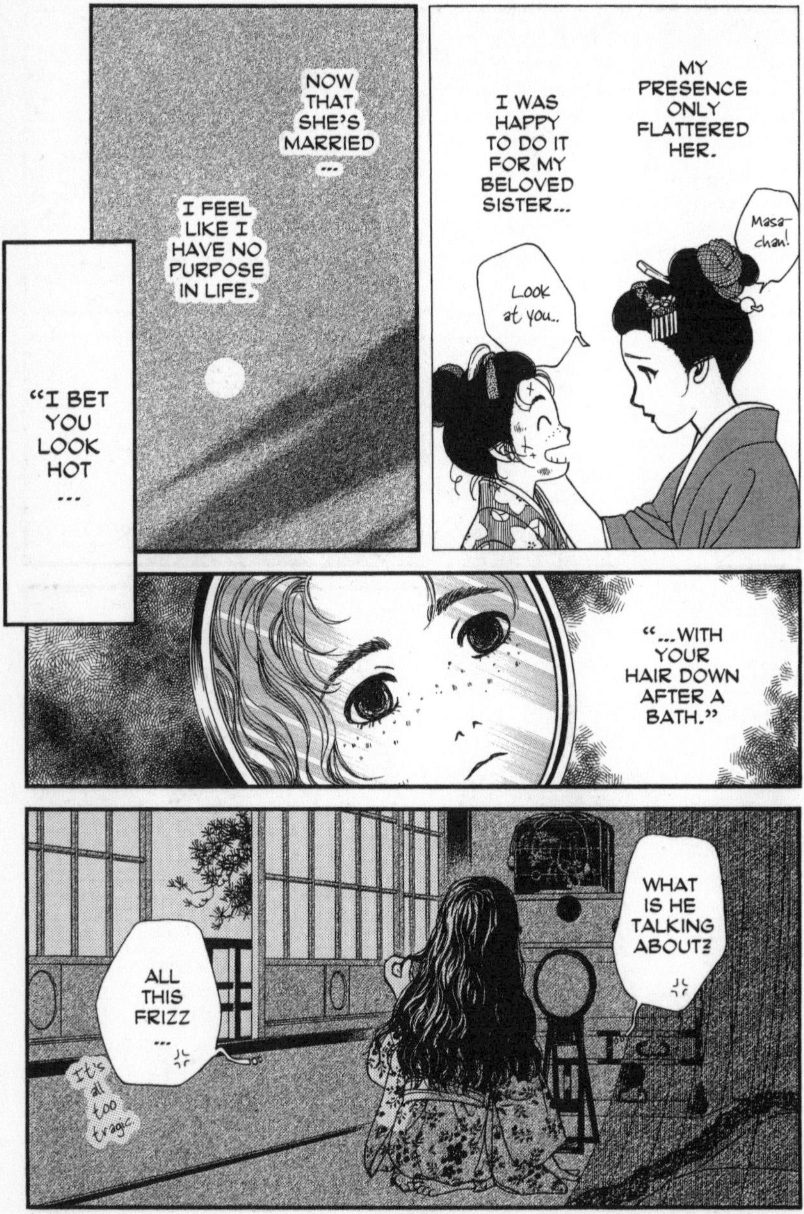
MY PRESENCE ONLY FLATTERED HER.
I WAS HAPPY TO DO IT FOR MY BELOVED SISTER...
Masa-chan!
Look at you..
NOW THAT SHE'S MARRIED...
I FEEL LIKE I HAVE NO PURPOSE IN LIFE.
"I BET YOU LOOK HOT...
"...WITH YOUR HAIR DOWN AFTER A BATH."
WHAT IS HE TALKING ABOUT?
ALL THIS FRIZZ...
It's all too tragic

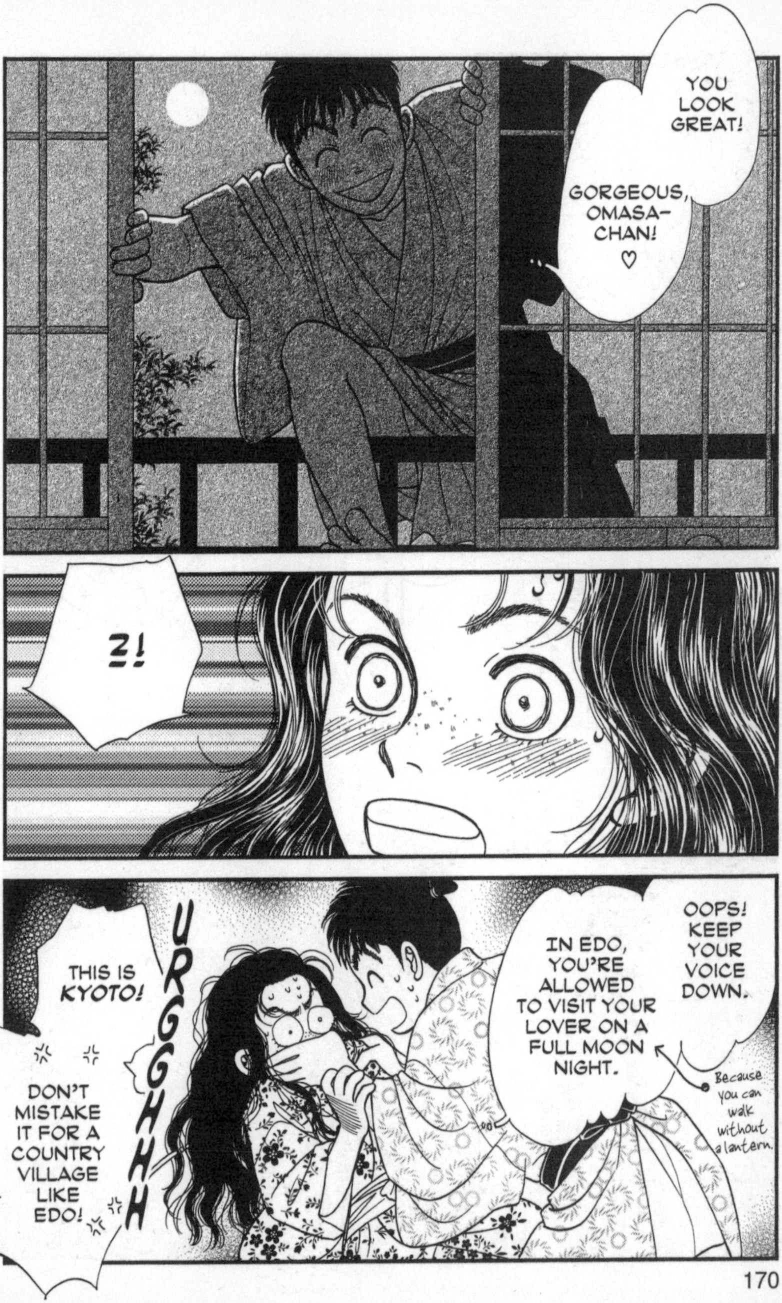
YOU LOOK GREAT!
GORGEOUS, OMASA-CHAN! ♡
?!
OOPS! KEEP YOUR VOICE DOWN.
IN EDO, YOU'RE ALLOWED TO VISIT YOUR LOVER ON A FULL MOON NIGHT.
Because you can walk without a lantern.
URGGHHHH
THIS IS KYOTO!
DON'T MISTAKE IT FOR A COUNTRY VILLAGE LIKE EDO!

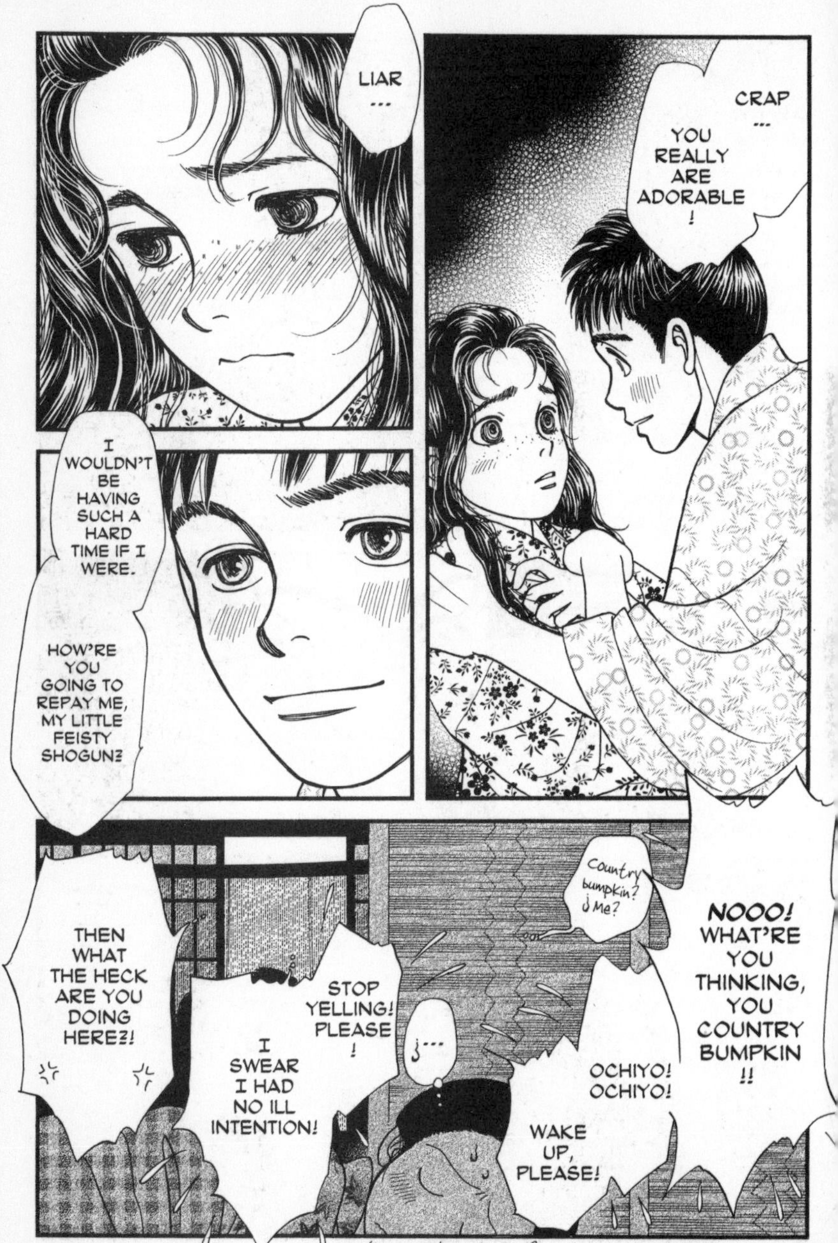
CRAP ... YOU REALLY ARE ADORABLE!
LIAR ...
I WOULDN'T BE HAVING SUCH A HARD TIME IF I WERE.
HOW'RE YOU GOING TO REPAY ME, MY LITTLE FEISTY SHOGUN?
NOOO! WHAT'RE YOU THINKING, YOU COUNTRY BUMPKIN!!
Country bumpkin? ¿Me?
OCHIYO! OCHIYO!
WAKE UP, PLEASE!
¿...
STOP YELLING! PLEASE!
I SWEAR I HAD NO ILL INTENTION!
THEN WHAT THE HECK ARE YOU DOING HERE?!

("Urr... What should I do?" Chiyo's internal monologue)

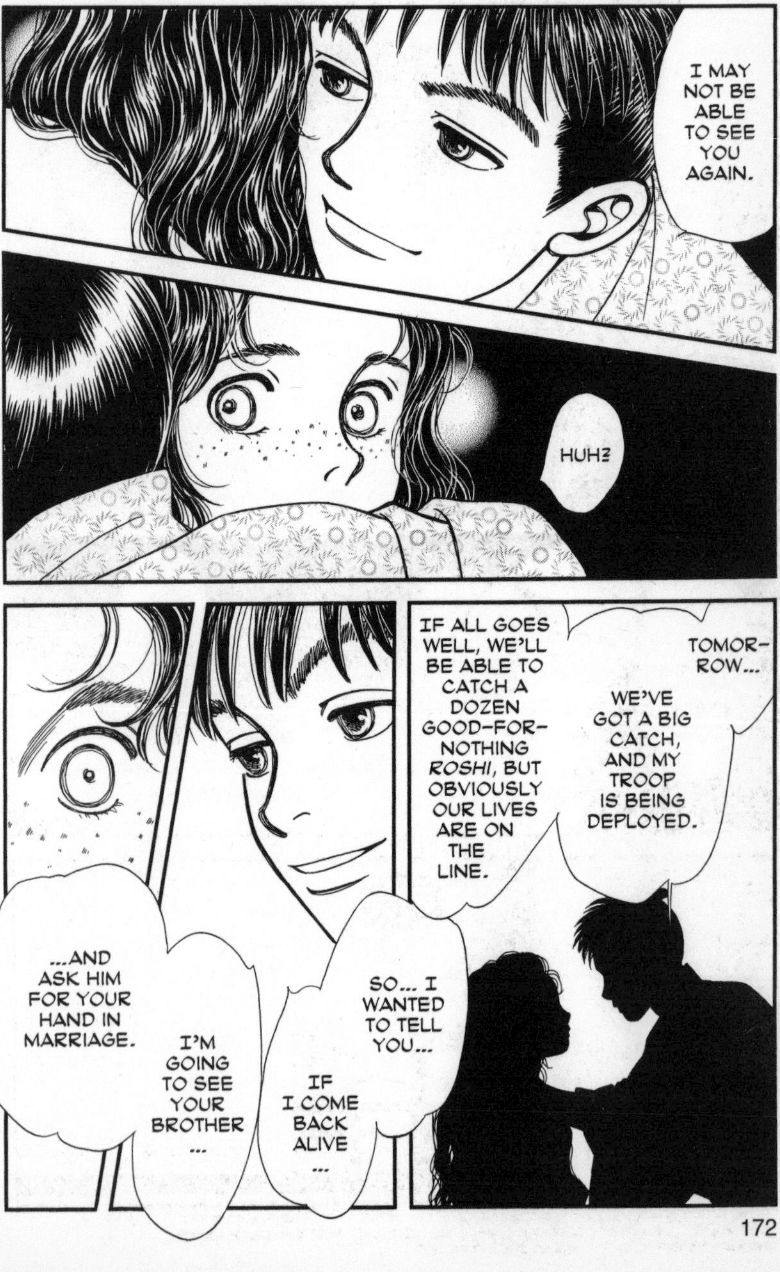
I MAY NOT BE ABLE TO SEE YOU AGAIN.
HUH?
TOMORROW...
WE'VE GOT A BIG CATCH, AND MY TROOP IS BEING DEPLOYED.
IF ALL GOES WELL, WE'LL BE ABLE TO CATCH A DOZEN GOOD-FOR-NOTHING *ROSHI*, BUT OBVIOUSLY OUR LIVES ARE ON THE LINE.
SO... I WANTED TO TELL YOU...
IF I COME BACK ALIVE...
I'M GOING TO SEE YOUR BROTHER...
...AND ASK HIM FOR YOUR HAND IN MARRIAGE.

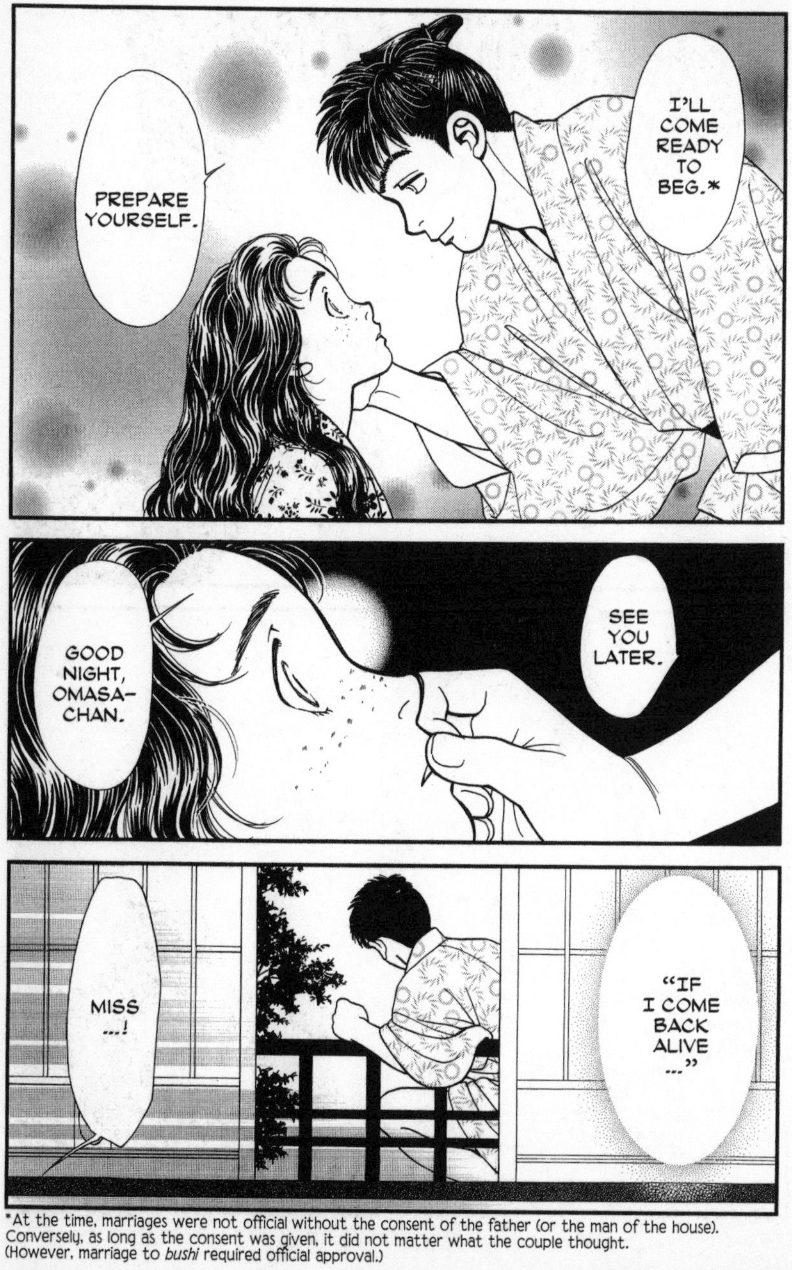
I'LL COME READY TO BEG.*
PREPARE YOURSELF.
SEE YOU LATER.
GOOD NIGHT, OMASA-CHAN.
"IF I COME BACK ALIVE ..."
MISS ...!

*At the time, marriages were not official without the consent of the father (or the man of the house). Conversely, as long as the consent was given, it did not matter what the couple thought. (However, marriage to *bushi* required official approval.)

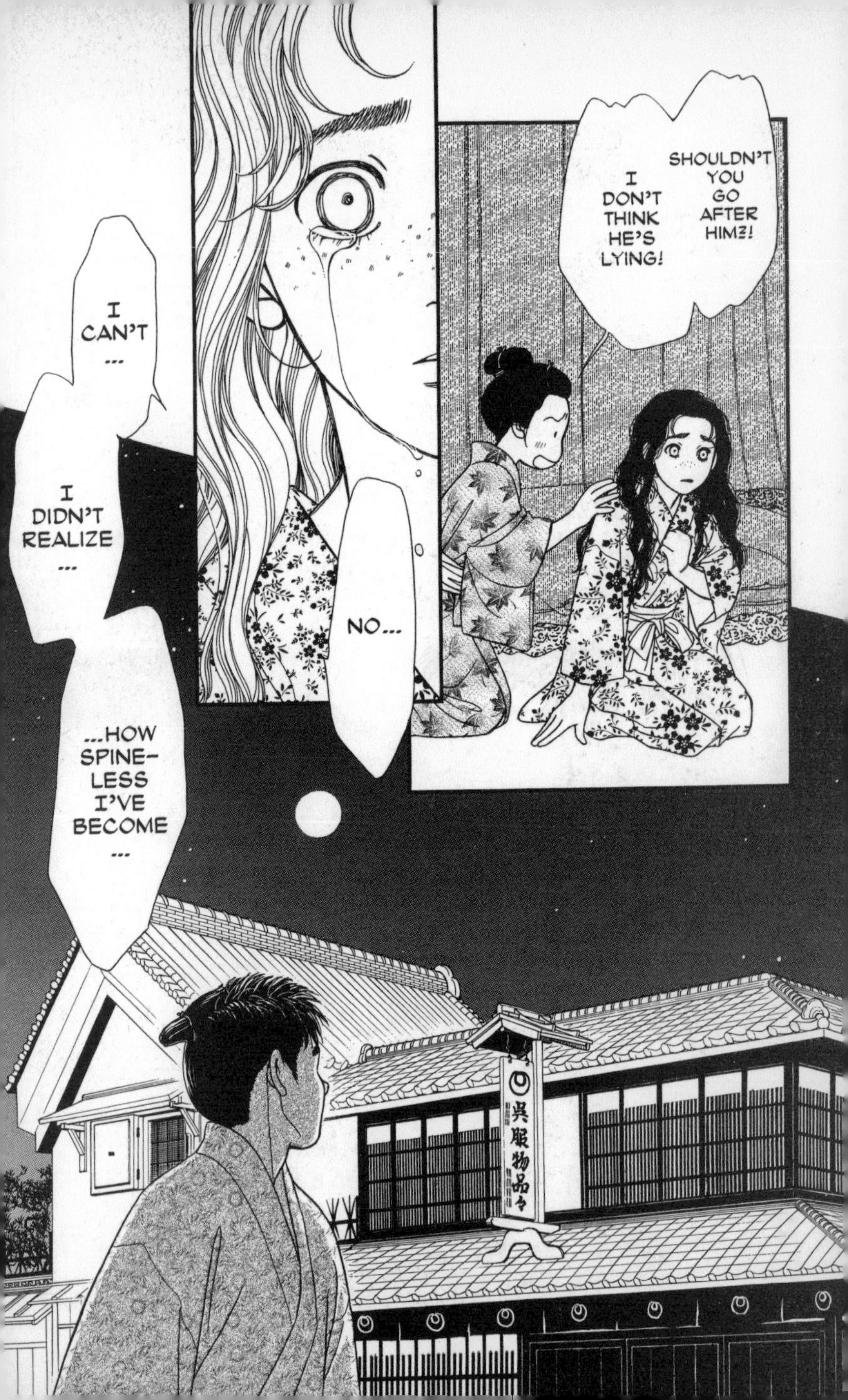
SHOULDN'T YOU GO AFTER HIM?!
I DON'T THINK HE'S LYING!
NO...
I CAN'T...
I DIDN'T REALIZE...
...HOW SPINE-LESS I'VE BECOME...

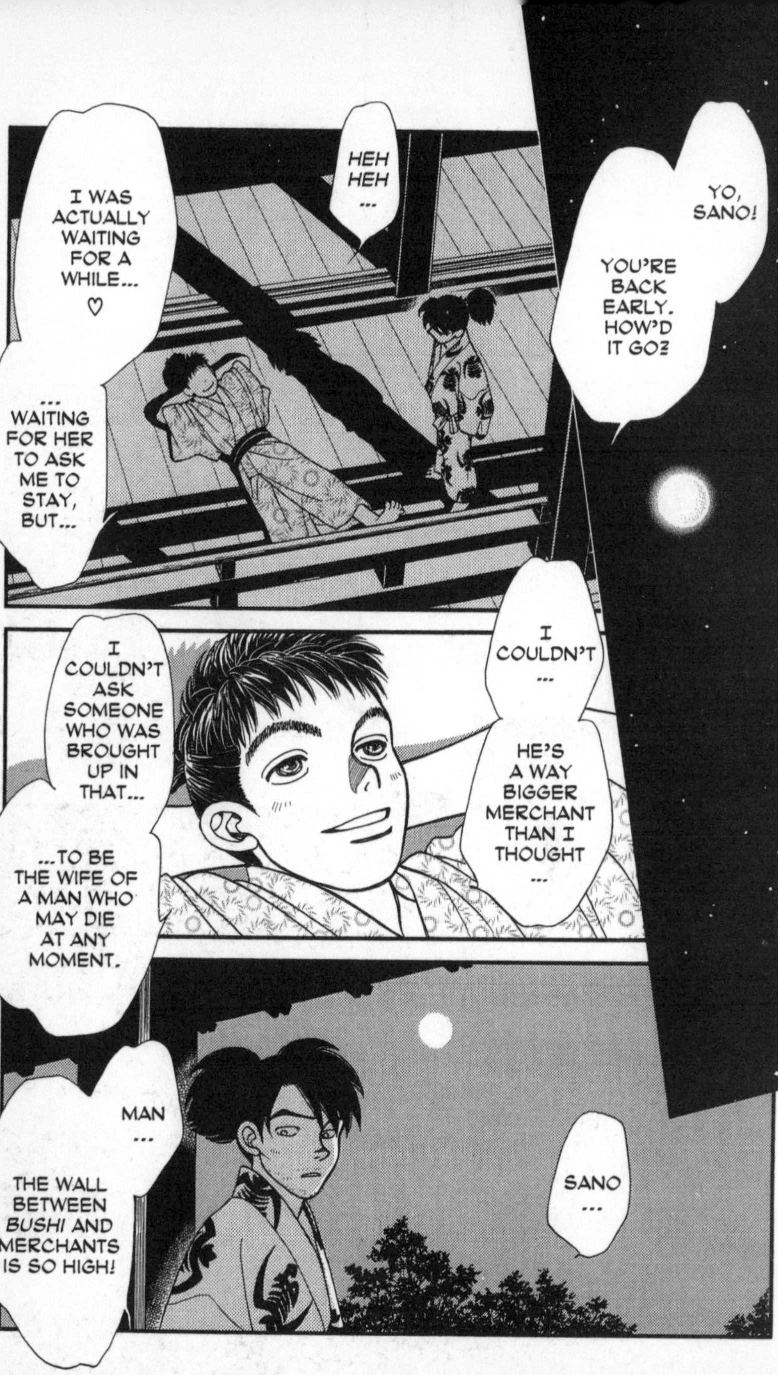
YO, SANO!
YOU'RE BACK EARLY. HOW'D IT GO?
HEH HEH ...
I WAS ACTUALLY WAITING FOR A WHILE... ♡
... WAITING FOR HER TO ASK ME TO STAY, BUT...
I COULDN'T ...
HE'S A WAY BIGGER MERCHANT THAN I THOUGHT ...
I COULDN'T ASK SOMEONE WHO WAS BROUGHT UP IN THAT...
...TO BE THE WIFE OF A MAN WHO MAY DIE AT ANY MOMENT.
SANO ...
MAN ...
THE WALL BETWEEN *BUSHI* AND MERCHANTS IS SO HIGH!

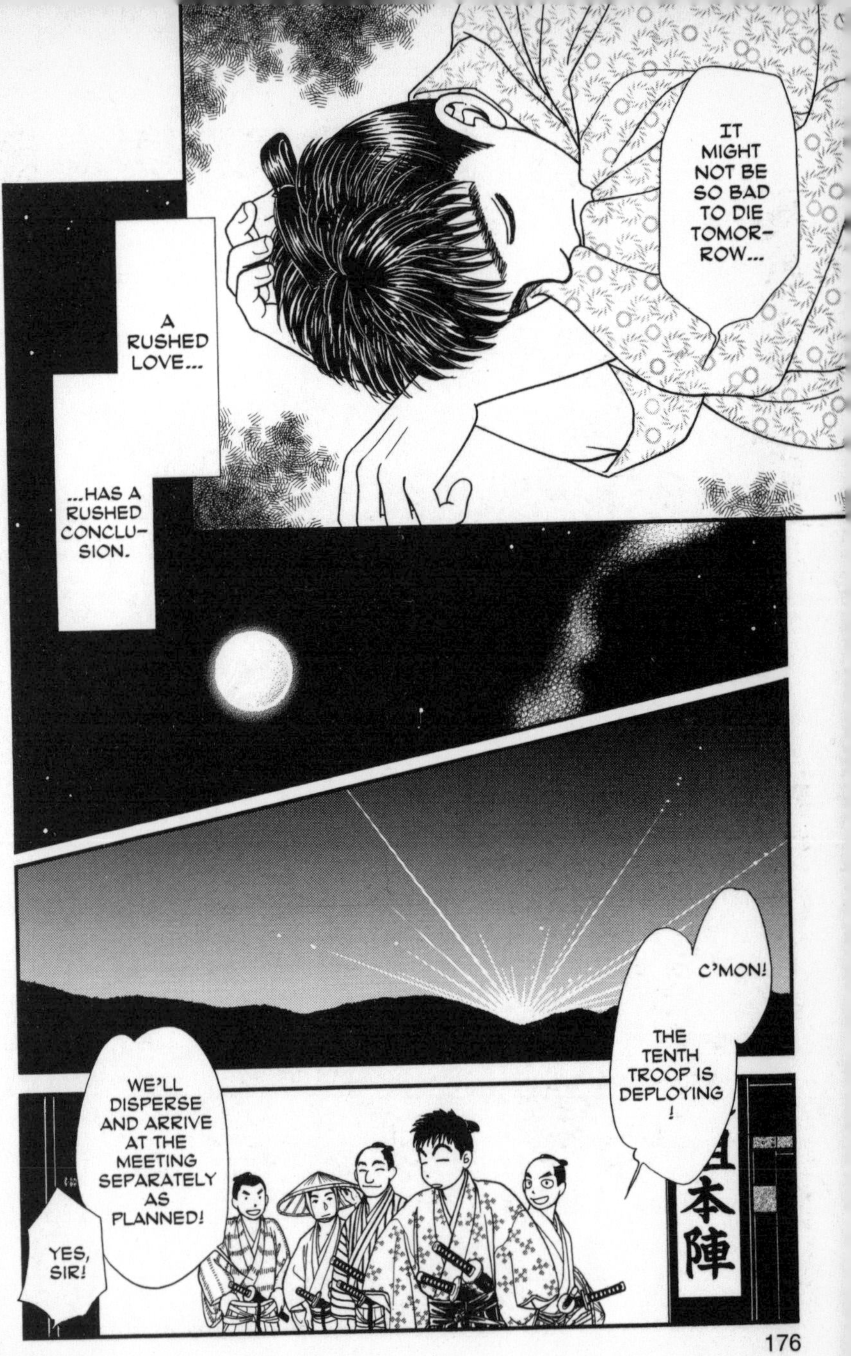
IT MIGHT NOT BE SO BAD TO DIE TOMOR-ROW...
A RUSHED LOVE...
...HAS A RUSHED CONCLU-SION.
C'MON!
THE TENTH TROOP IS DEPLOYING!
本陣
WE'LL DISPERSE AND ARRIVE AT THE MEETING SEPARATELY AS PLANNED!
YES, SIR!

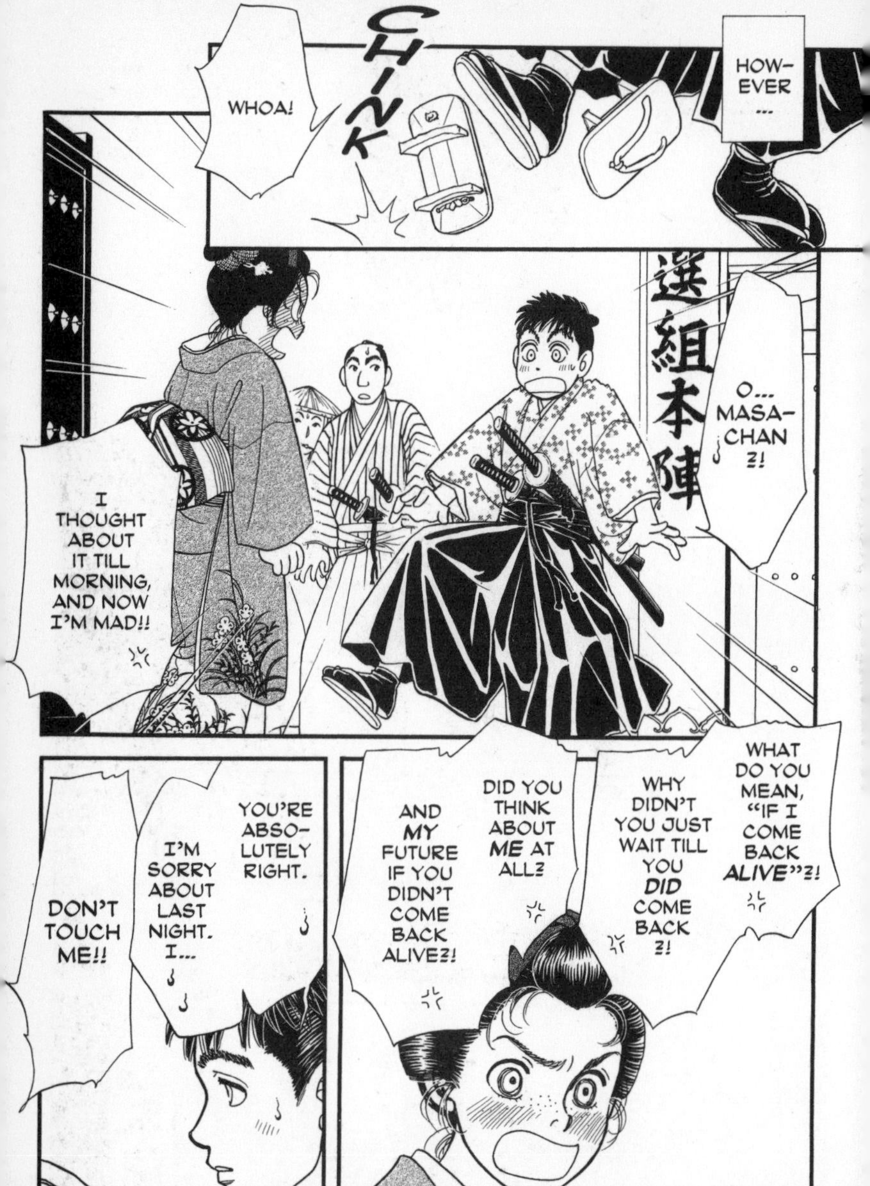

HOWEVER ...
CHINK
WHOA!
O... MASA-CHAN?!
選組本陣
I THOUGHT ABOUT IT TILL MORNING, AND NOW I'M MAD!!
WHAT DO YOU MEAN, "IF I COME BACK ALIVE"?!
WHY DIDN'T YOU JUST WAIT TILL YOU DID COME BACK?!
DID YOU THINK ABOUT ME AT ALL?
AND MY FUTURE IF YOU DIDN'T COME BACK ALIVE?!
YOU'RE ABSOLUTELY RIGHT.
I'M SORRY ABOUT LAST NIGHT. I...
DON'T TOUCH ME!!

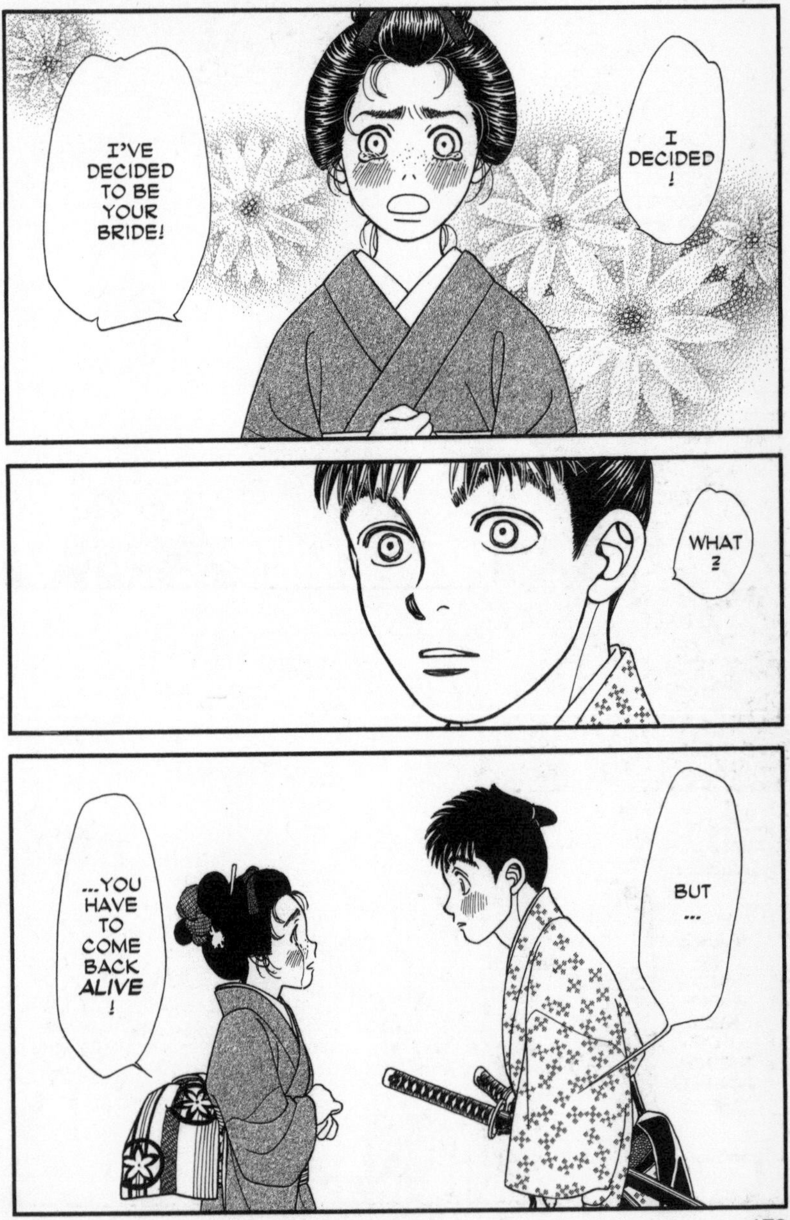
I DECIDED!
I'VE DECIDED TO BE YOUR BRIDE!
WHAT?
BUT...
...YOU HAVE TO COME BACK ALIVE!

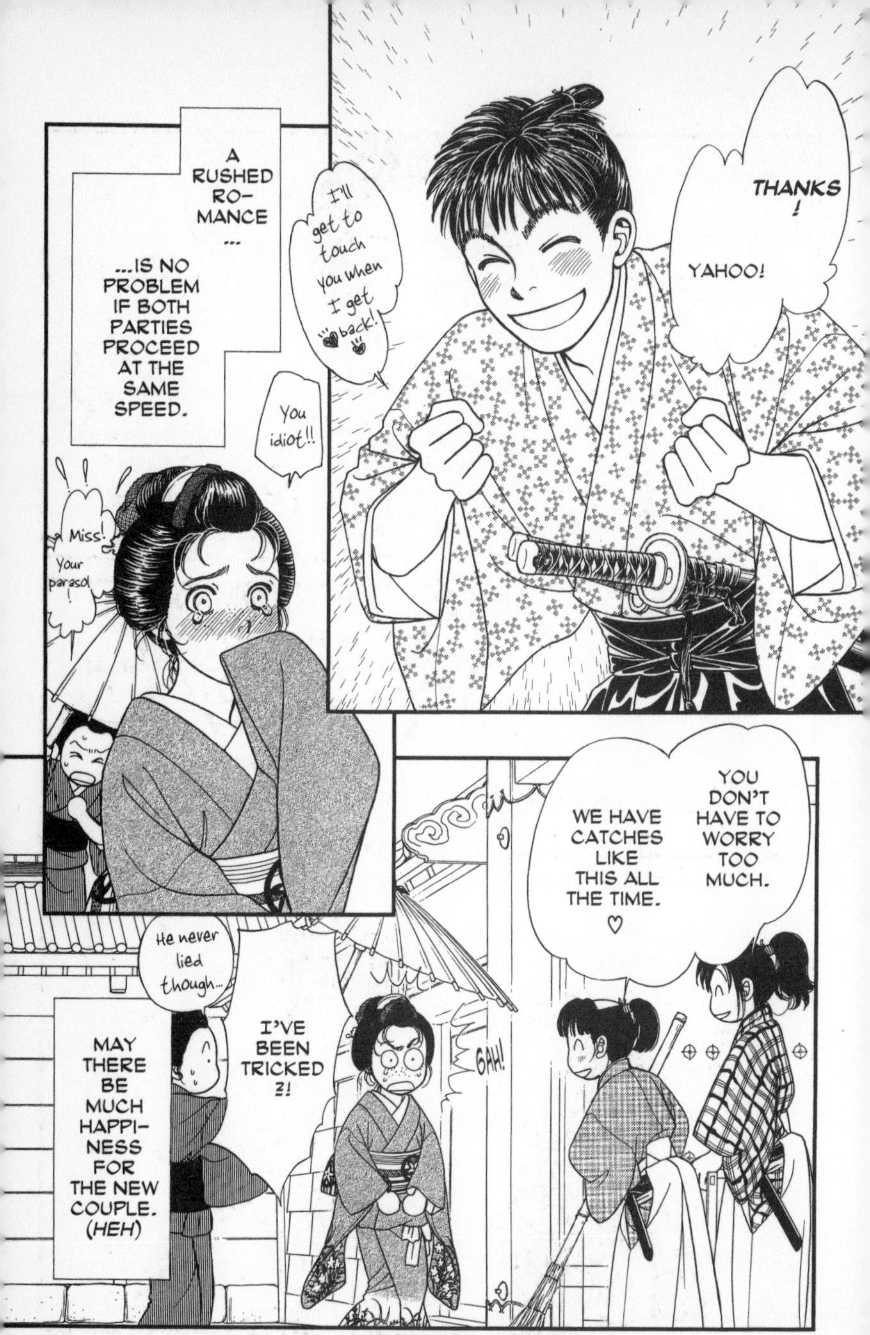
THANKS!
YAHOO!
I'll get to touch you when I get back!
A RUSHED ROMANCE...
...IS NO PROBLEM IF BOTH PARTIES PROCEED AT THE SAME SPEED.
You idiot!!
Miss! Your parasol!
YOU DON'T HAVE TO WORRY TOO MUCH.
WE HAVE CATCHES LIKE THIS ALL THE TIME. ♡
GAH!
I'VE BEEN TRICKED?!
He never lied though...
MAY THERE BE MUCH HAPPINESS FOR THE NEW COUPLE. (HEH)

 To Be Continued!

TAEKO WATANABE PRESENTS

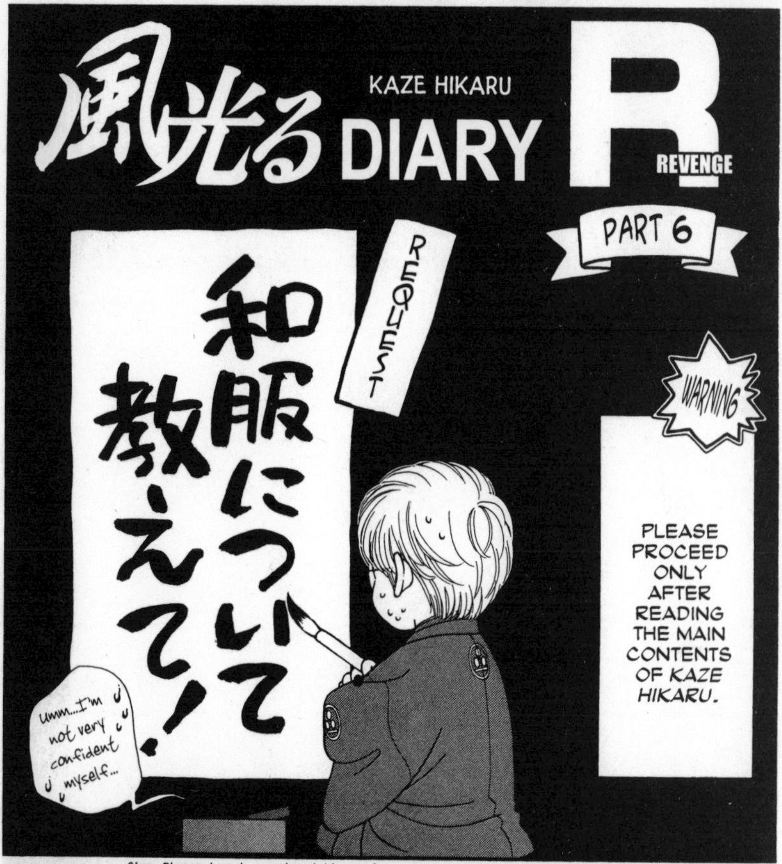
風光る
KAZE HIKARU
DIARY
R
REVENGE
PART 6
WARNING
PLEASE PROCEED ONLY AFTER READING THE MAIN CONTENTS OF KAZE HIKARU.
REQUEST
和服について教えて!
umm...I'm not very confident myself...

Sign: Please teach me about kimono!

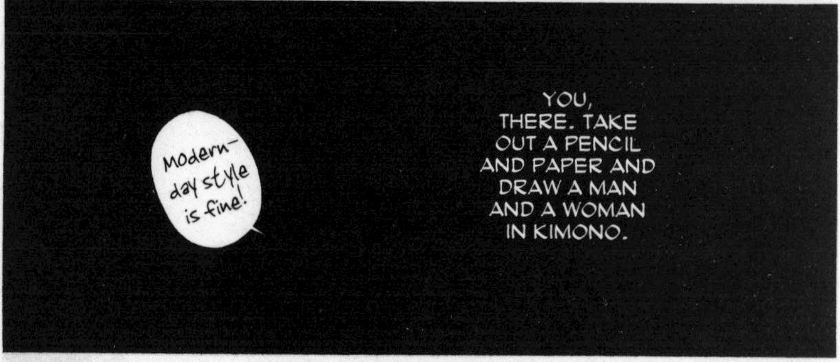
YOU, THERE. TAKE OUT A PENCIL AND PAPER AND DRAW A MAN AND A WOMAN IN KIMONO.
Modern-day style is fine!

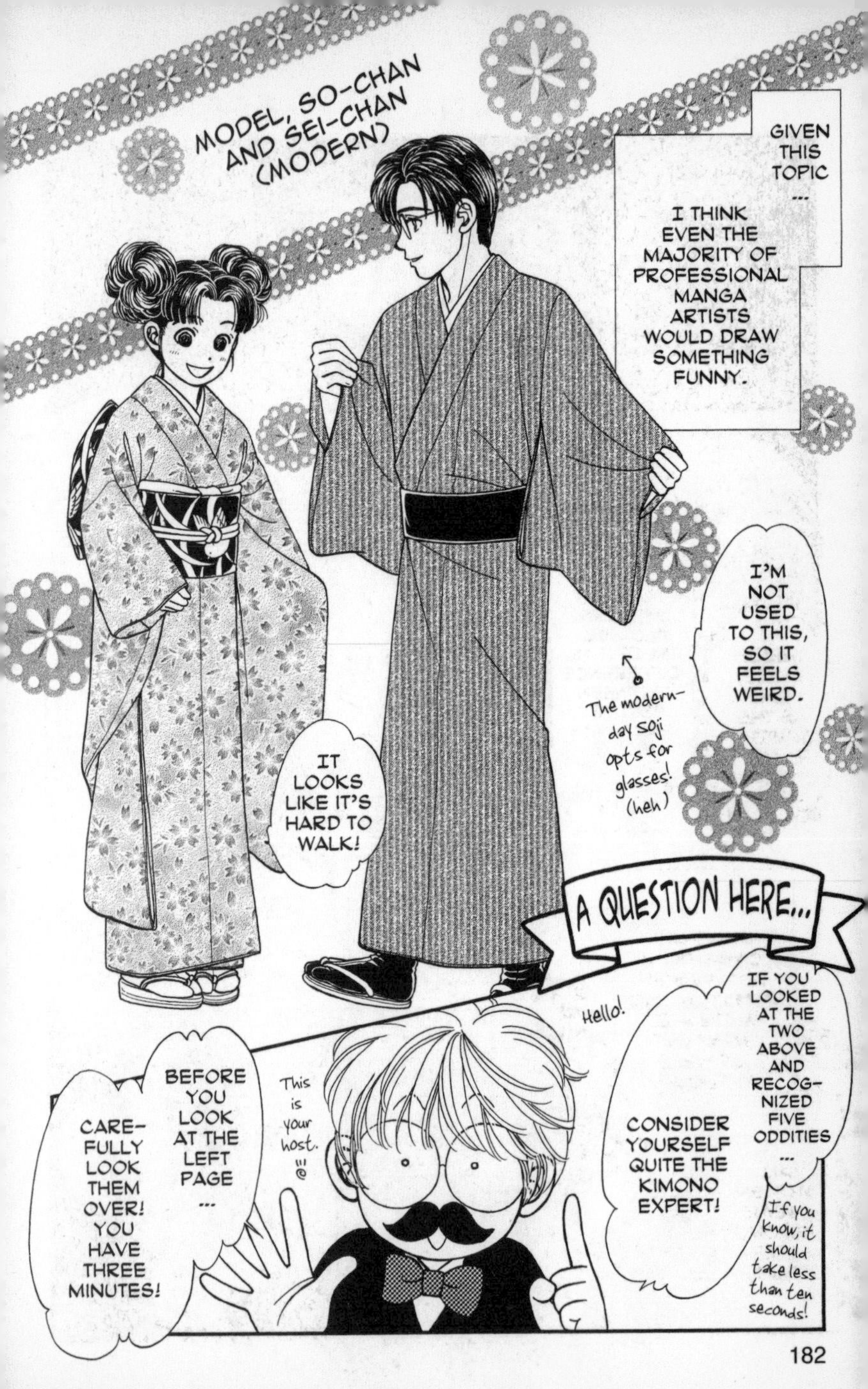
MODEL, SO-CHAN AND SEI-CHAN (MODERN)
GIVEN THIS TOPIC... I THINK EVEN THE MAJORITY OF PROFESSIONAL MANGA ARTISTS WOULD DRAW SOMETHING FUNNY.
I'M NOT USED TO THIS, SO IT FEELS WEIRD.
The modern-day Soji opts for glasses! (heh)
IT LOOKS LIKE IT'S HARD TO WALK!
A QUESTION HERE...
Hello!
IF YOU LOOKED AT THE TWO ABOVE AND RECOGNIZED FIVE ODDITIES...
If you know, it should take less than ten seconds!
CONSIDER YOURSELF QUITE THE KIMONO EXPERT!
This is your host.
BEFORE YOU LOOK AT THE LEFT PAGE...
CARE-FULLY LOOK THEM OVER! YOU HAVE THREE MINUTES!

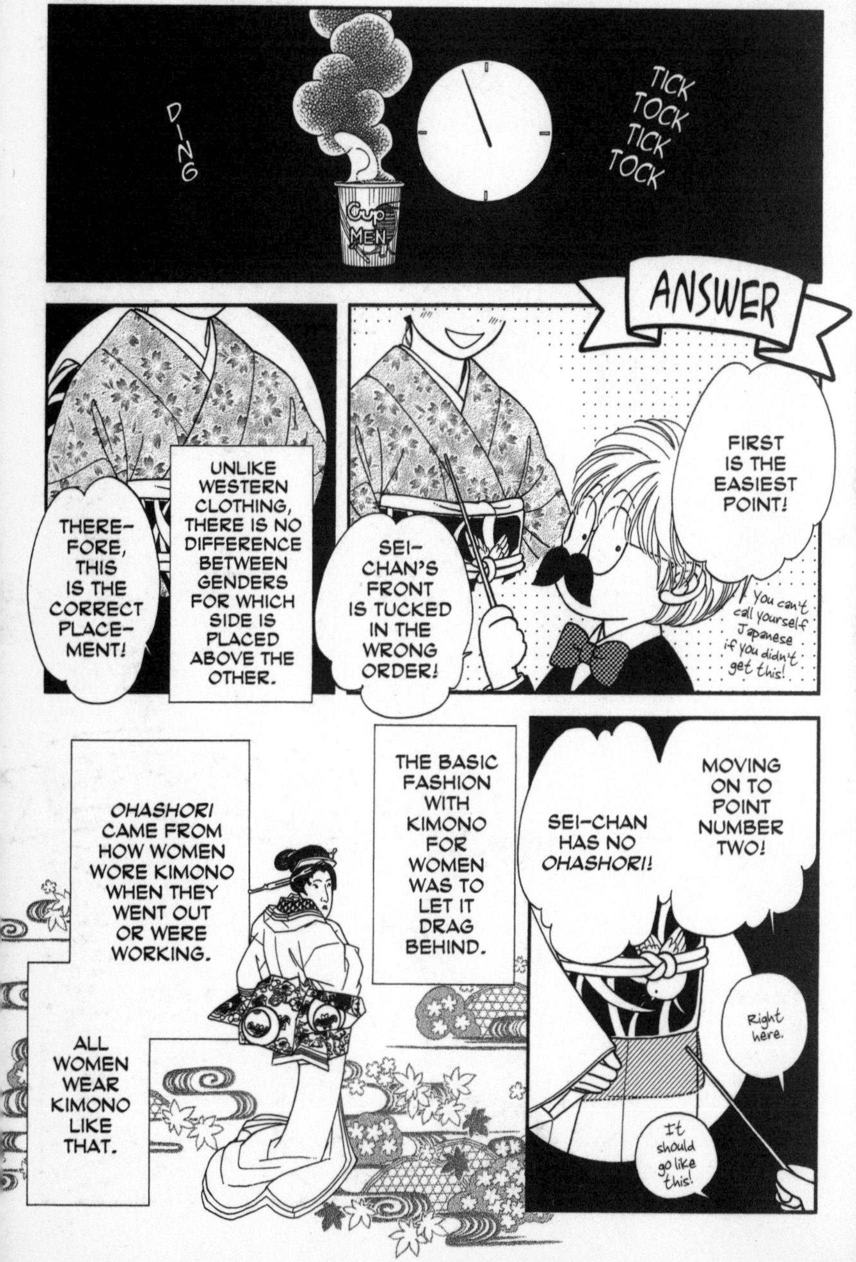
TICK TOCK TICK TOCK
Cup MEN
DING
ANSWER
FIRST IS THE EASIEST POINT!
You can't call yourself Japanese if you didn't get this!
SEI-CHAN'S FRONT IS TUCKED IN THE WRONG ORDER!
UNLIKE WESTERN CLOTHING, THERE IS NO DIFFERENCE BETWEEN GENDERS FOR WHICH SIDE IS PLACED ABOVE THE OTHER.
THEREFORE, THIS IS THE CORRECT PLACEMENT!
MOVING ON TO POINT NUMBER TWO!
SEI-CHAN HAS NO *OHASHORI*!
Right here.
It should go like this!
THE BASIC FASHION WITH KIMONO FOR WOMEN WAS TO LET IT DRAG BEHIND.
OHASHORI CAME FROM HOW WOMEN WORE KIMONO WHEN THEY WENT OUT OR WERE WORKING.
ALL WOMEN WEAR KIMONO LIKE THAT.

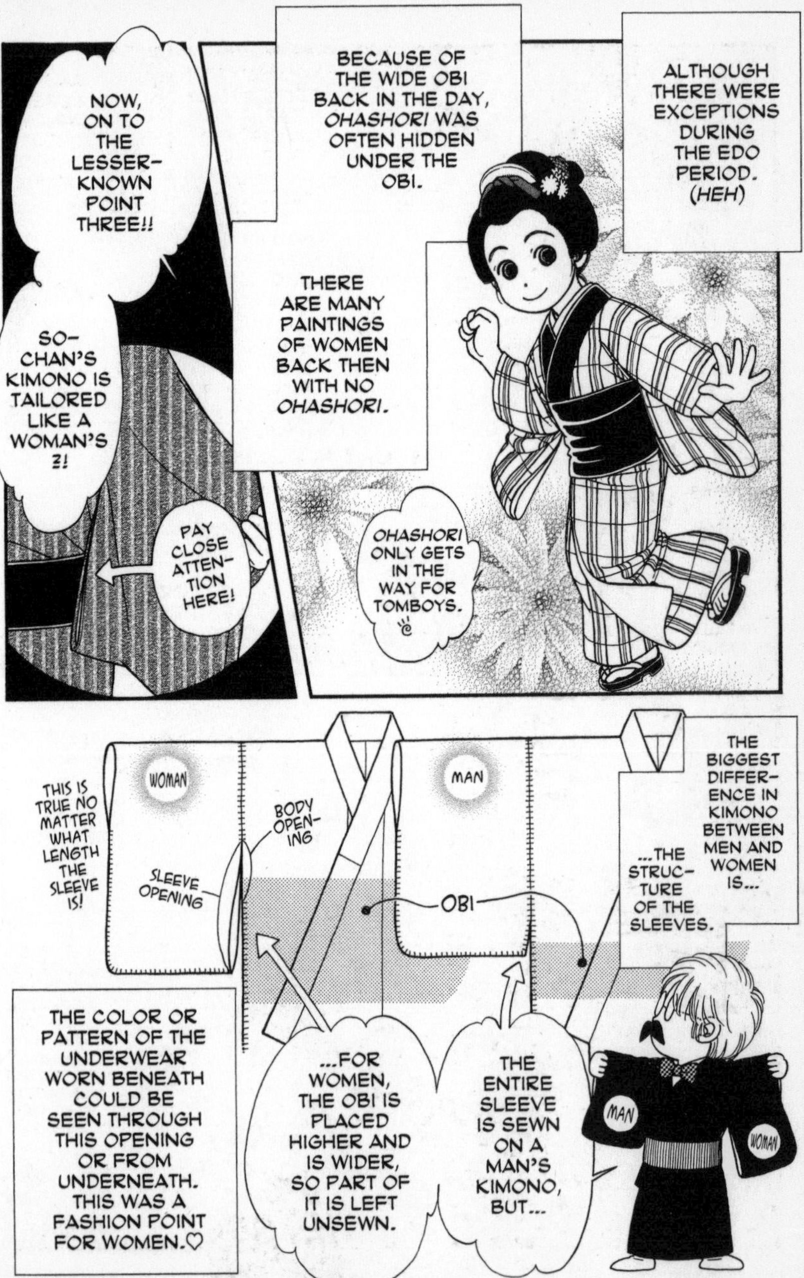
ALTHOUGH THERE WERE EXCEPTIONS DURING THE EDO PERIOD. (*HEH*)
BECAUSE OF THE WIDE OBI BACK IN THE DAY, *OHASHORI* WAS OFTEN HIDDEN UNDER THE OBI.
THERE ARE MANY PAINTINGS OF WOMEN BACK THEN WITH NO *OHASHORI*.
OHASHORI ONLY GETS IN THE WAY FOR TOMBOYS.
NOW, ON TO THE LESSER-KNOWN POINT THREE!!
SO-CHAN'S KIMONO IS TAILORED LIKE A WOMAN'S?!
PAY CLOSE ATTENTION HERE!
THE BIGGEST DIFFERENCE IN KIMONO BETWEEN MEN AND WOMEN IS...
...THE STRUCTURE OF THE SLEEVES.
MAN
WOMAN
THE ENTIRE SLEEVE IS SEWN ON A MAN'S KIMONO, BUT...
...FOR WOMEN, THE OBI IS PLACED HIGHER AND IS WIDER, SO PART OF IT IS LEFT UNSEWN.
MAN
OBI
WOMAN
BODY OPENING
SLEEVE OPENING
THIS IS TRUE NO MATTER WHAT LENGTH THE SLEEVE IS!
THE COLOR OR PATTERN OF THE UNDERWEAR WORN BENEATH COULD BE SEEN THROUGH THIS OPENING OR FROM UNDERNEATH. THIS WAS A FASHION POINT FOR WOMEN.♡

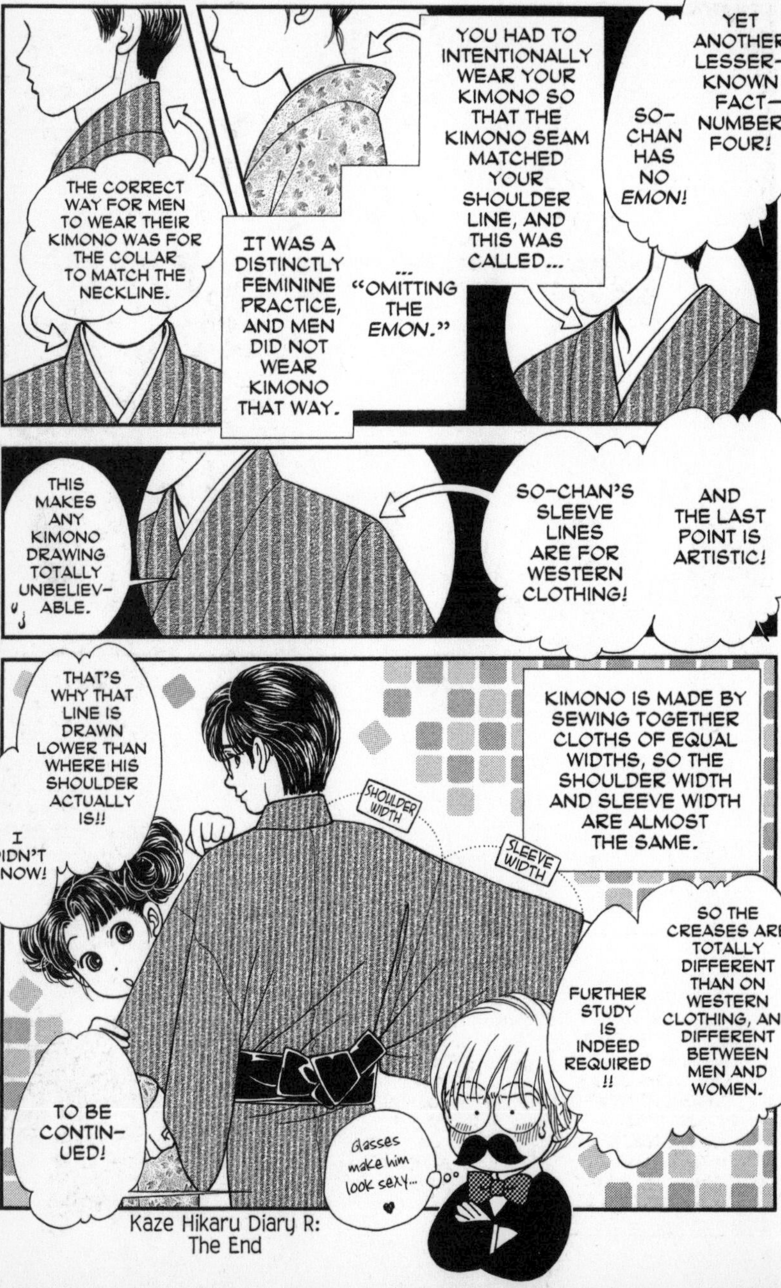
YET ANOTHER LESSER-KNOWN FACT—NUMBER FOUR!
SO-CHAN HAS NO *EMON*!
YOU HAD TO INTENTIONALLY WEAR YOUR KIMONO SO THAT THE KIMONO SEAM MATCHED YOUR SHOULDER LINE, AND THIS WAS CALLED...
..."OMITTING THE *EMON*."
IT WAS A DISTINCTLY FEMININE PRACTICE, AND MEN DID NOT WEAR KIMONO THAT WAY.
THE CORRECT WAY FOR MEN TO WEAR THEIR KIMONO WAS FOR THE COLLAR TO MATCH THE NECKLINE.
AND THE LAST POINT IS ARTISTIC!
SO-CHAN'S SLEEVE LINES ARE FOR WESTERN CLOTHING!
THIS MAKES ANY KIMONO DRAWING TOTALLY UNBELIEV-ABLE.
KIMONO IS MADE BY SEWING TOGETHER CLOTHS OF EQUAL WIDTHS, SO THE SHOULDER WIDTH AND SLEEVE WIDTH ARE ALMOST THE SAME.
SHOULDER WIDTH
SLEEVE WIDTH
SO THE CREASES ARE TOTALLY DIFFERENT THAN ON WESTERN CLOTHING, AND DIFFERENT BETWEEN MEN AND WOMEN.
FURTHER STUDY IS INDEED REQUIRED !!
THAT'S WHY THAT LINE IS DRAWN LOWER THAN WHERE HIS SHOULDER ACTUALLY IS!!
I DIDN'T KNOW!
Glasses make him look sexy...
TO BE CONTIN-UED!

Kaze Hikaru Diary R:
The End

Decoding Kaze Hikaru

Kaze Hikaru is a historical drama based in 19th century Japan and thus contains some fairly mystifying terminology. In this glossary we'll break down archaic phrases, terms, and other linguistic curiosities for you, so that you can move through life with the smug assurance that you are indeed a know-it-all.

First and foremost, because *Kaze Hikaru* is a period story, we kept all character names in their traditional Japanese form—that is, family name followed by first name. For example, the character Okita Soji's family name is Okita and his personal name is Soji.

AKO-ROSHI:
The *ronin* (samurai) of Ako; featured in the immortal Kabuki play *Chushingura* (Loyalty), aka *47 Samurai*.

ANI-UE:
Literally, "brother above"; an honorific for an elder male sibling.

BAKUFU:
Literally, "tent government." Shogunate; the feudal, military government that dominated Japan for more than 200 years.

BUSHI:
A samurai or warrior (part of the compound word *bushido*, which means "way of the warrior").

CHICHI-UE:
An honorific suffix meaning "father above."

DO:
In kendo (a Japanese fencing sport that uses bamboo swords), a short way of describing the offensive single-hit strike *shikake waza ippon uchi*.

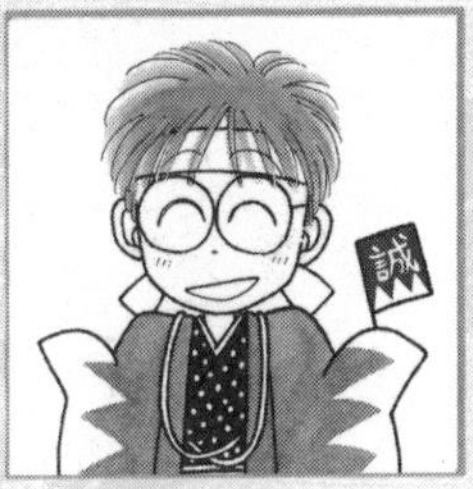
誠

While challenging myself to draw my dreaded close-ups during this series, I did a strange expression this time. I'm not sure whether Sei-chan is sad, wistful, lonely or just...sleepy?

In any case, the season is autumn, but the spider lily meant to reflect it looks ominous... For those of you feeling slightly depressed, try bringing volume 14 over and place it to the left of this volume. What do you see? Doesn't Sei look pretty happy? (heh)

It's moments like these when I think of things like this that I appreciate my happy-go-lucky nature.

Taeko Watanabe debuted as a manga artist in 1979 with her story *Waka-chan no Netsuai Jidai* (Love Struck Days of Waka). *Kaze Hikaru* is her longest-running series, but she has created a number of other popular series. Watanabe is a two-time winner of the prestigious Shogakukan Manga Award in the girls category—her manga *Hajime-chan ga Ichiban!* (Hajime-chan Is Number One!) claimed the award in 1991 and *Kaze Hikaru* took it in 2003.

Watanabe read hundreds of historical sources to create *Kaze Hikaru.* She is from Tokyo.

KAZE HIKARU VOL. 15
Shojo Beat Manga Edition

STORY AND ART BY
TAEKO WATANABE

Translation & English Adaptation/Mai Ihara
Touch-up Art & Lettering/Rina Mapa
Cover Design/Izumi Evers
Interior Design/Julie Behn
Editor/Jonathan Tarbox

VP, Production/Alvin Lu
VP, Publishing Licensing/Rika Inouye
VP, Sales & Product Marketing/Gonzalo Ferreyra
VP, Creative/Linda Espinosa
Publisher/Hyoe Narita

Printed in Canada

Published by VIZ Media, LLC
P.O. Box 77010
San Francisco, CA 94107

10 9 8 7 6 5 4 3 2 1
First printing, November 2009

www.viz.com

RATED T+ FOR OLDER TEEN

PARENTAL ADVISORY
KAZE HIKARU is rated T+ for Older Teen and is recommended for ages 16 and up. This volume contains realistic violence, alcohol use, and sexual themes.

ratings.viz.com

www.shojobeat.com